HOSHIN ENGI VOL. 12
The SHONEN JUMP Manga Edition

STORY AND ART BY RYU FUJISAKI

Based on the novel *Hoshin Engi*, translated by Tsutomu Ano,
published by Kodansha Bunko

Translation & Adaptation/Tomo Kimura
Touch-up Art & Lettering/HudsonYards
Design/Matt Hinrichs
Editor/Jonathan Tarbox

Editor in Chief, Books/Alvin Lu
Editor in Chief, Magazines/Marc Weidenbaum
VP, Publishing Licensing/Rika Inouye
VP, Sales & Product Marketing/Gonzalo Ferreyra
VP, Creative/Linda Espinosa
Publisher/Hyoe Narita

Published by VIZ Media, LLC
P.O. Box 77010
San Francisco, CA 94107

SHONEN JUMP Manga Edition
10 9 8 7 6 5 4 3 2 1
First printing, April 2009

THE WORLD'S
MOST POPULAR MANGA

www.viz.com

www.shonenjump.com

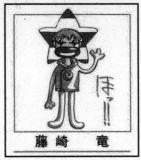

藤崎　竜 (Sigh!!)

There's something I think about a lot: when a manga is a series, I get the feeling that portions of it will come out that I regret as the series progresses. That's the bad part and the good part, I suppose.

Ryu Fujisaki

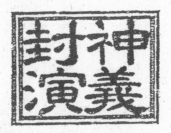

Ryu Fujisaki's *Worlds* came in second place for the prestigious 40th Tezuka Award. His *Psycho +, Wāqwāq* and *Hoshin Engi* have all run in *Weekly Shonen Jump* magazine, and *Hoshin Engi* anime is available on DVD in Japan and North America. A lover of science fiction, literature and history, Fujisaki has made *Hoshin Engi* a mix of genres that truly showcases his amazing art and imagination.

HOSHIN ENGI VOL. 12
The SHONEN JUMP Manga Edition

STORY AND ART BY RYU FUJISAKI
Based on the novel *Hoshin Engi*, translated by Tsutomu Ano,
published by Kodansha Bunko

Translation & Adaptation/Tomo Kimura
Touch-up Art & Lettering/HudsonYards
Design/Matt Hinrichs
Editor/Jonathan Tarbox

Editor in Chief, Books/Alvin Lu
Editor in Chief, Magazines/Marc Weidenbaum
VP, Publishing Licensing/Rika Inouye
VP, Sales & Product Marketing/Gonzalo Ferreyra
VP, Creative/Linda Espinosa
Publisher/Hyoe Narita

Printed in the U.S.A.

Published by VIZ Media, LLC
P.O. Box 77010
San Francisco, CA 94107

SHONEN JUMP Manga Edition
10 9 8 7 6 5 4 3 2 1
First printing, April 2009

www.viz.com

THE WORLD'S MOST POPULAR MANGA
www.shonenjump.com

RATED T FOR TEEN
PARENTAL ADVISORY
HOSHIN ENGI is rated T for Teen and is recommended for ages 13 and up. This volume contains realistic and fantasy violence.
ratings.viz.com

HOSHIN ENGI

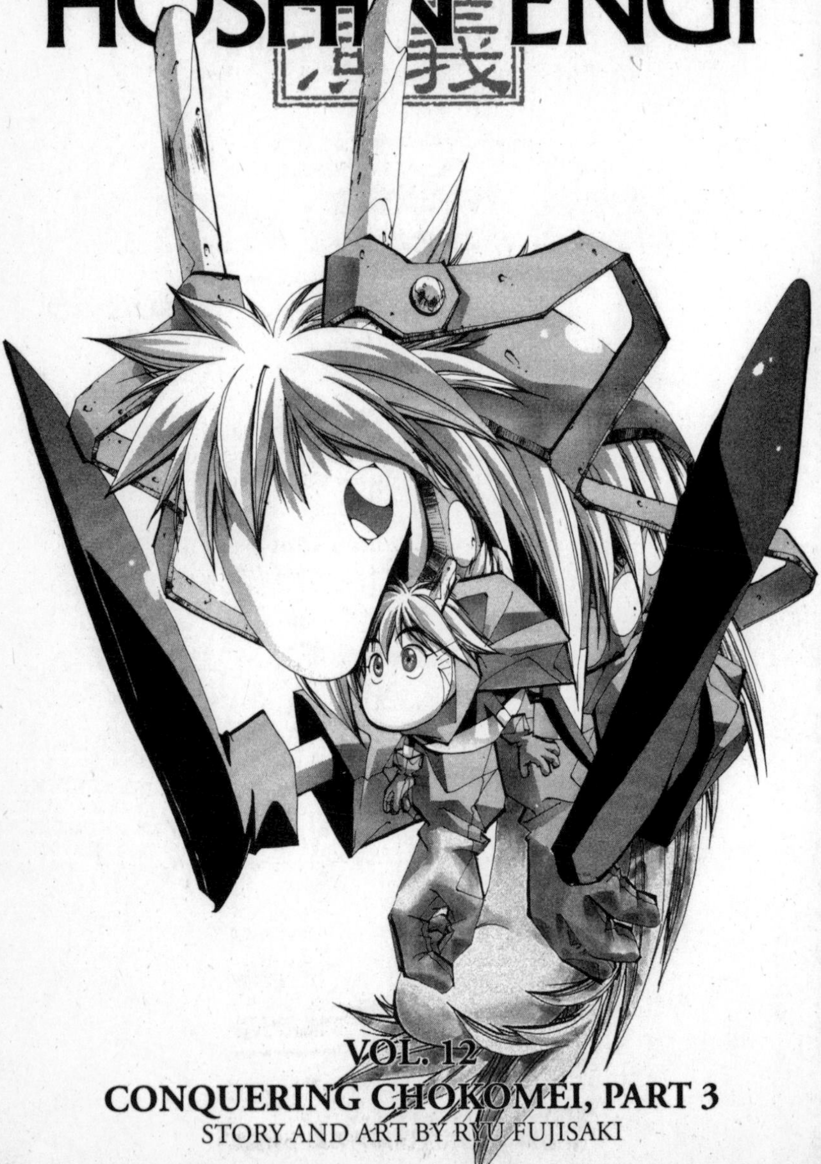

VOL. 12
CONQUERING CHOKOMEI, PART 3

STORY AND ART BY RYU FUJISAKI

THE CHARACTERS

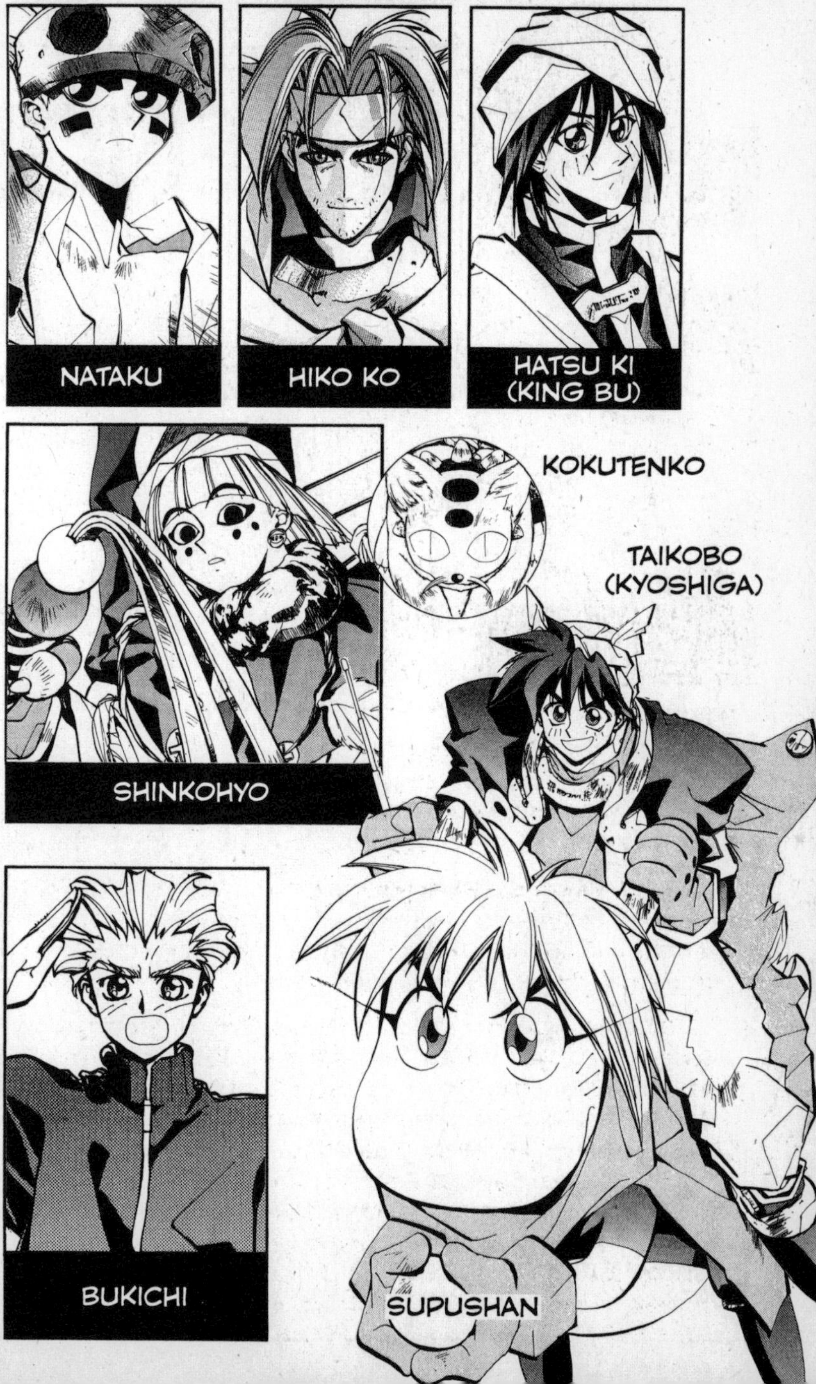
HATSU KI (KING BU)
HIKO KO
NATAKU
KOKUTENKO
TAIKOBO (KYOSHIGA)
SHINKOHYO
SUPUSHAN
BUKICHI

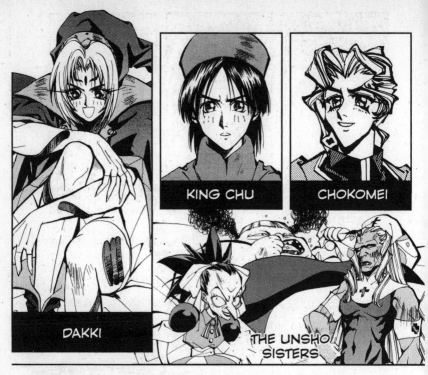

KING CHU

CHOKOMEI

DAKKI

THE UNSHO
SISTERS

The Story Thus Far

Ancient China, over 3,000 years ago. It is the era of the Yin Dynasty.

After King Chu, the emperor, married the beautiful Dakki, the good king was no longer himself, and became an unmanly and foolish ruler. Dakki, a *Sennyo* with a wicked heart, took control of Yin and the country fell into chaos.

To save the human world, the Hoshin Project was put into action. The project will seal evil Sennin and Doshi into the Shinkai, and cause Seihakuko Sho Ki to set up a new dynasty to replace Yin. Taikobo, who was chosen to execute this project, acts to install Sho Ki's heir Hatsu Ki as the next king. Hatsu Ki takes the title King Bu and declares Seiki is now the Kingdom of Zhou. He appoints Taikibo as gunshi to advance against Yin. But on the way to the royal capital of Choka, Chokomei challenges them to fight. Taikobo and his comrades defeat Chokomei's disciples one after another, then face the hideous Unsho Sisters!!

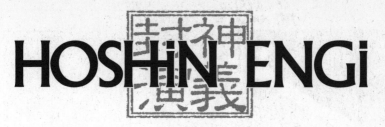

HOSHIN ENGI

VOL. 12
CONQUERING CHOKOMEI, PART 3

CONTENTS

CHAPTER 98
CONQUERING CHOKOMEI, PART 14
THE ANGELIC UNSHO SISTERS!

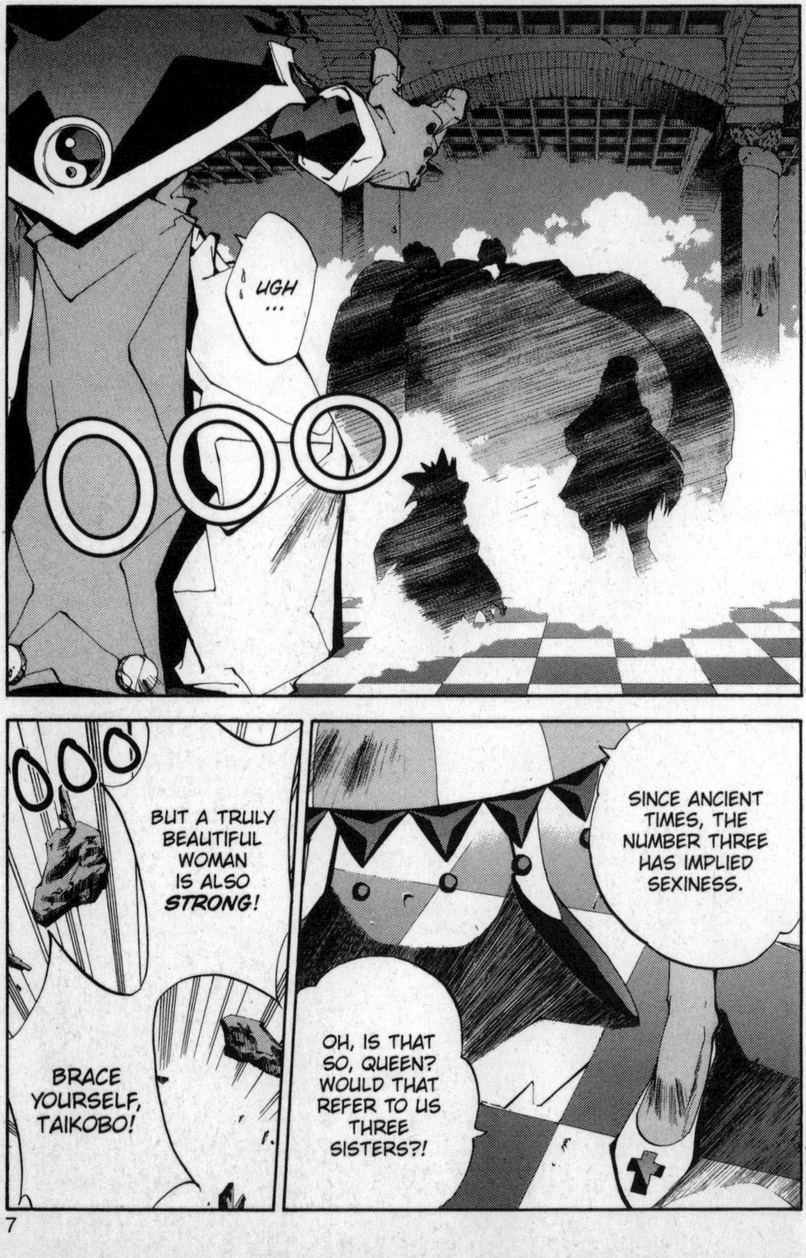
UGH ...
SINCE ANCIENT TIMES, THE NUMBER THREE HAS IMPLIED SEXINESS.
OH, IS THAT SO, QUEEN? WOULD THAT REFER TO US THREE SISTERS?!
BUT A TRULY BEAUTIFUL WOMAN IS ALSO STRONG!
BRACE YOURSELF, TAIKOBO!

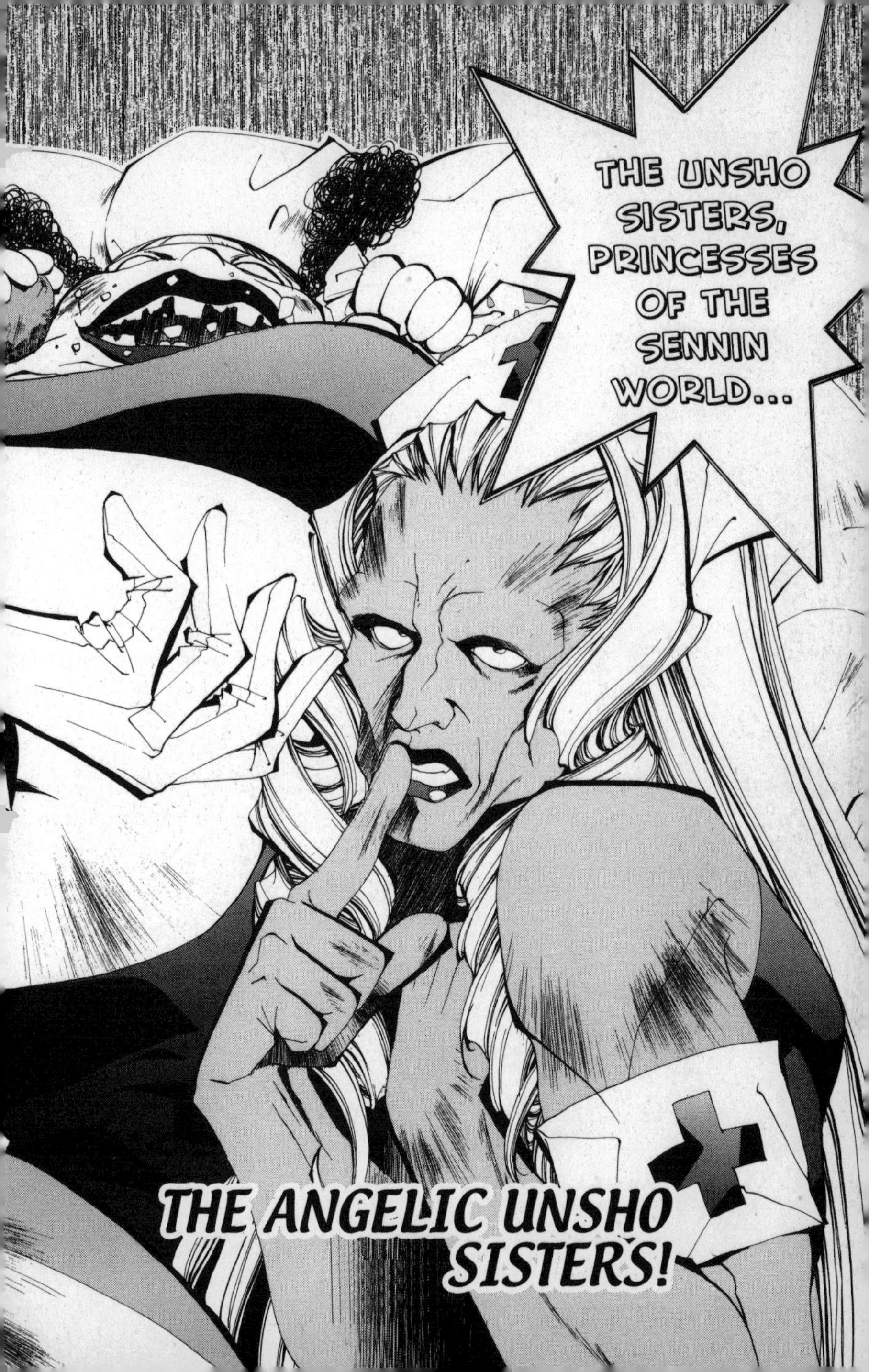
THE UNSHO SISTERS, PRINCESSES OF THE SENNIN WORLD...
THE ANGELIC UNSHO SISTERS!

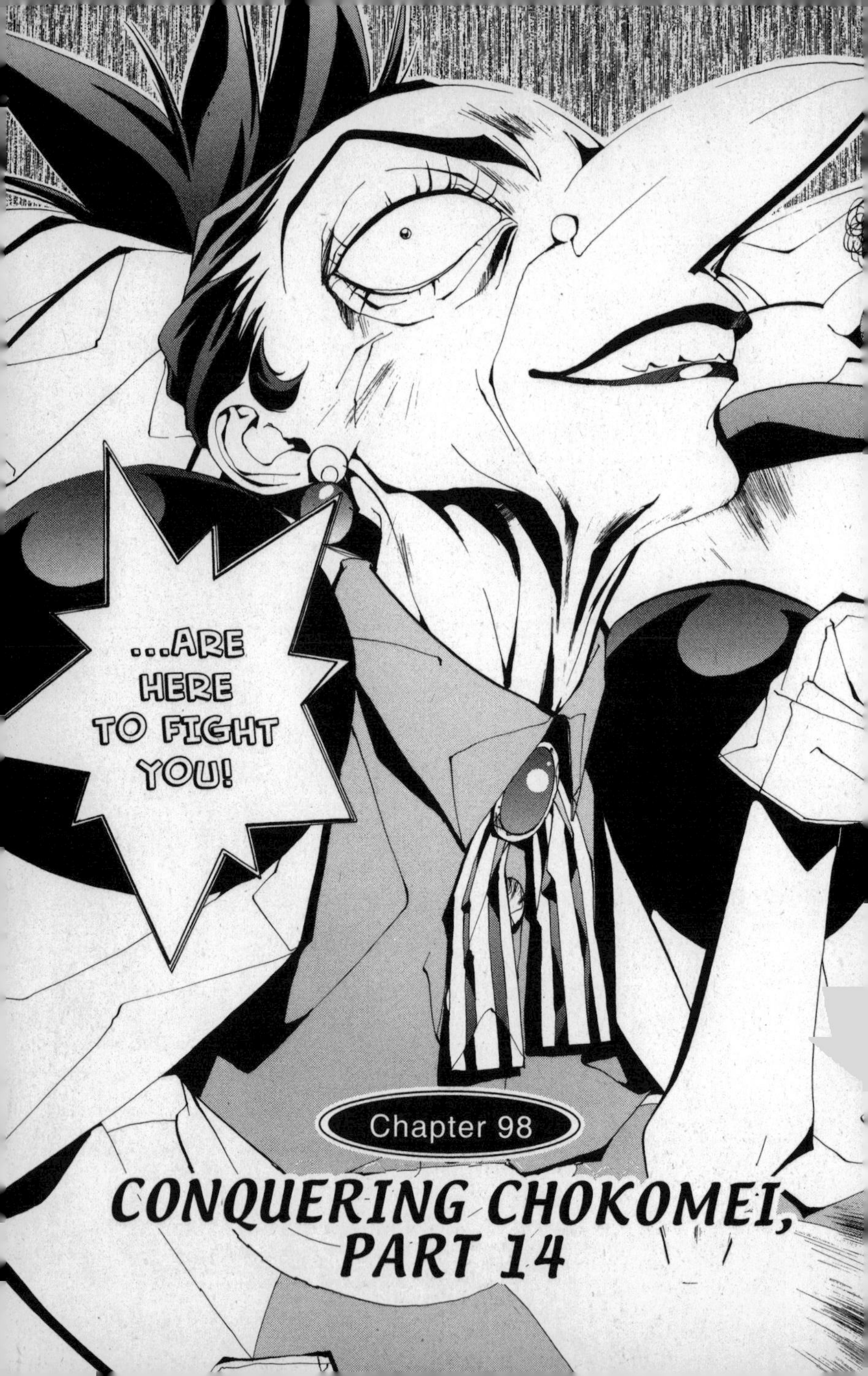
...ARE HERE TO FIGHT YOU!
Chapter 98
CONQUERING CHOKOMEI, PART 14

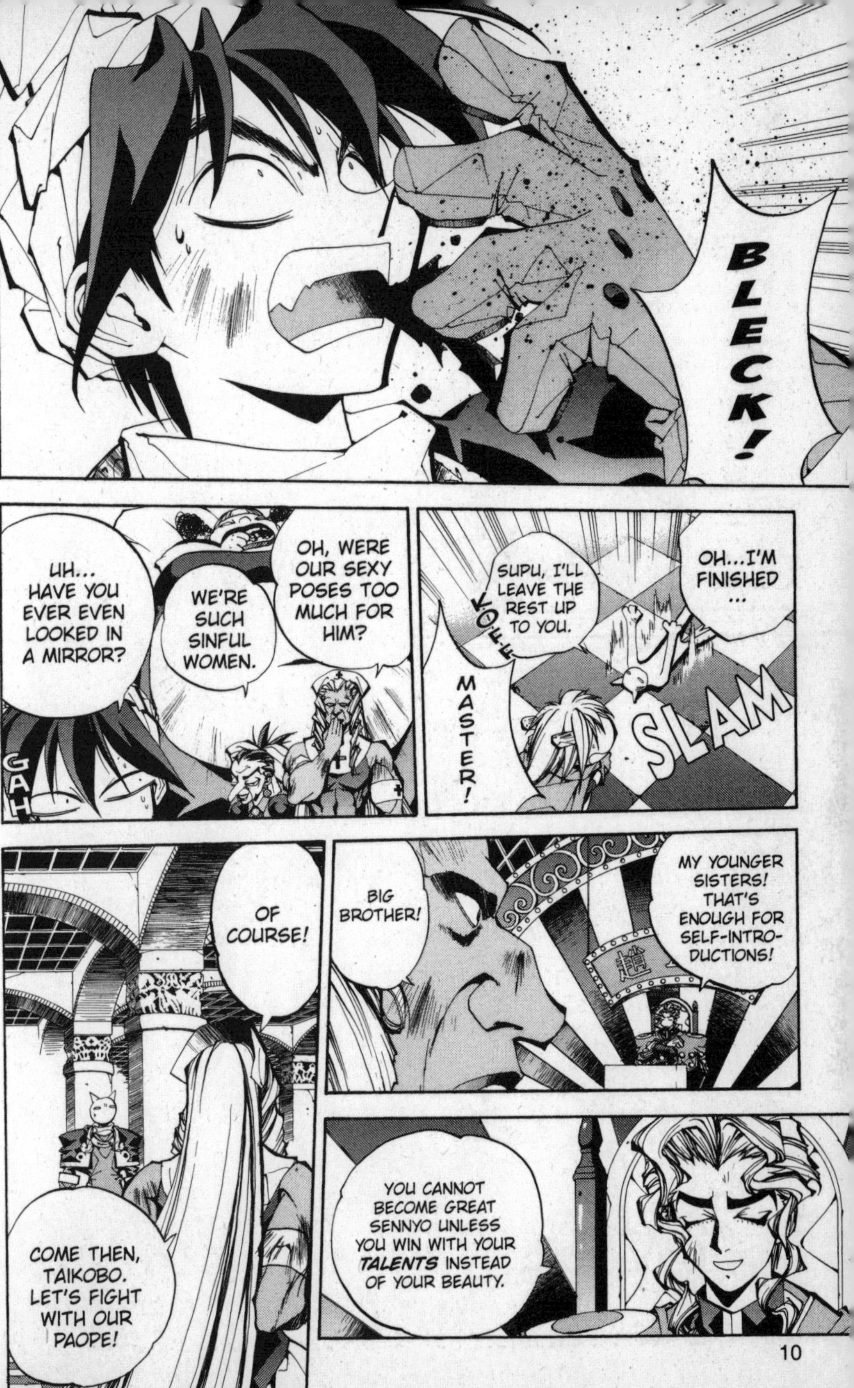
BLECK!
OH...I'M FINISHED ...
SUPU, I'LL LEAVE THE REST UP TO YOU.
KOFF
MASTER!
SLAM
OH, WERE OUR SEXY POSES TOO MUCH FOR HIM?
WE'RE SUCH SINFUL WOMEN.
UH... HAVE YOU EVER EVEN LOOKED IN A MIRROR?
GAH
MY YOUNGER SISTERS! THAT'S ENOUGH FOR SELF-INTRO-DUCTIONS!
BIG BROTHER!
YOU CANNOT BECOME GREAT SENNYO UNLESS YOU WIN WITH YOUR TALENTS INSTEAD OF YOUR BEAUTY.
OF COURSE!
COME THEN, TAIKOBO. LET'S FIGHT WITH OUR PAOPE!

READ THIS WAY

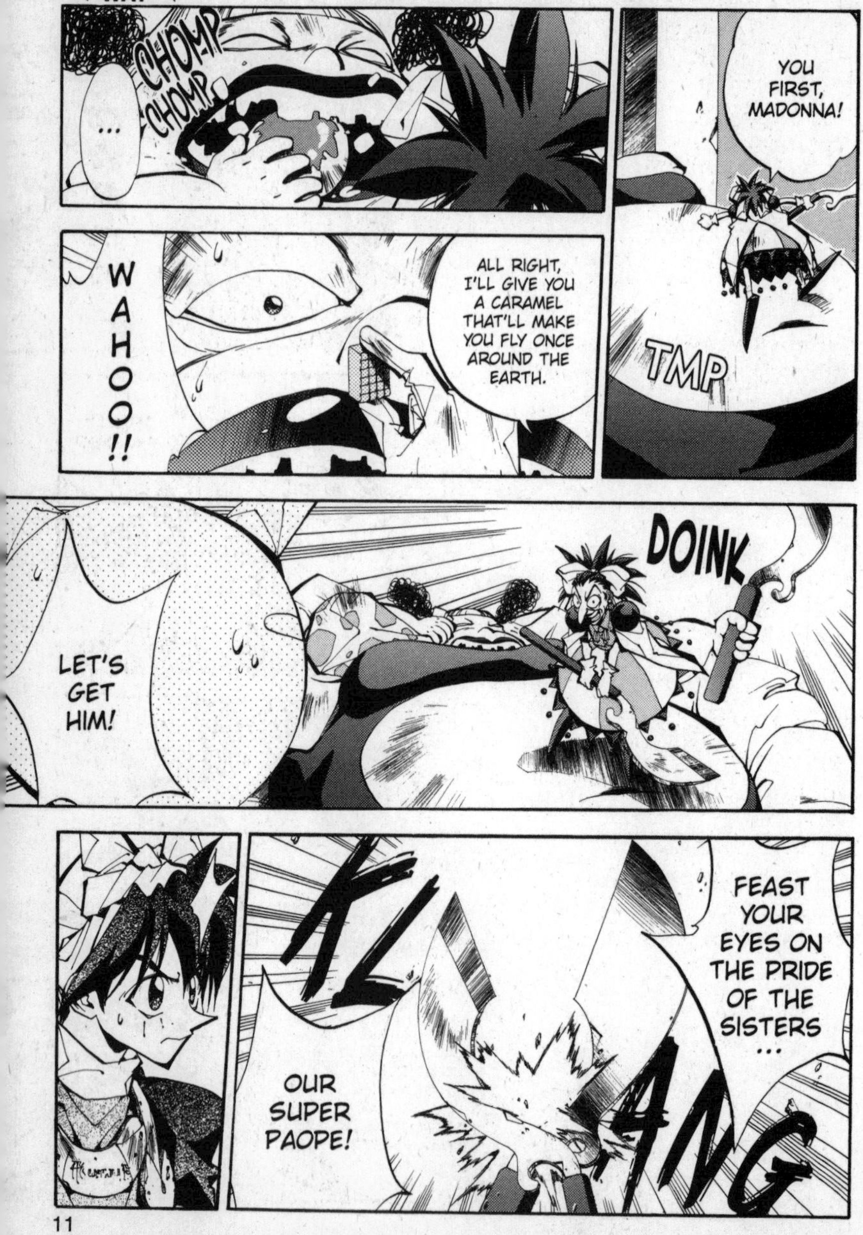
YOU FIRST, MADONNA!
TMP
CHOMP CHOMP
...
ALL RIGHT, I'LL GIVE YOU A CARAMEL THAT'LL MAKE YOU FLY ONCE AROUND THE EARTH.
WAHOO!!
DOINK
LET'S GET HIM!
FEAST YOUR EYES ON THE PRIDE OF THE SISTERS ...
KLANG
OUR SUPER PAOPE!

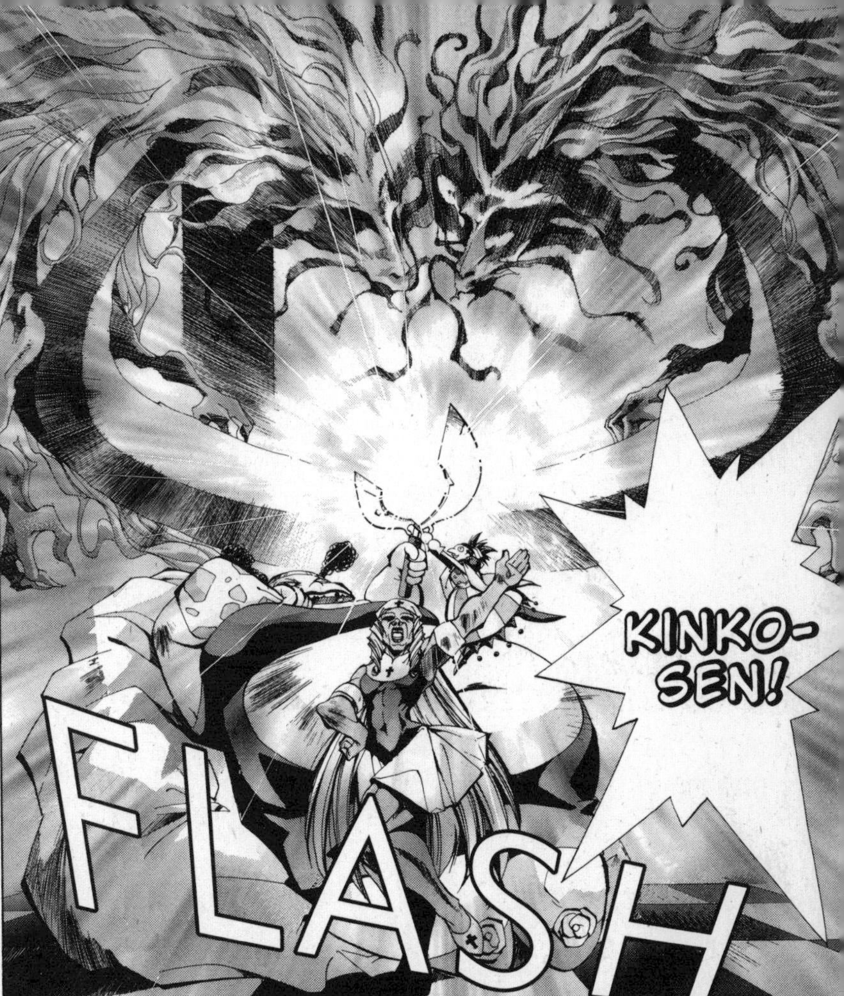
KINKO-
SEN!
FLASH

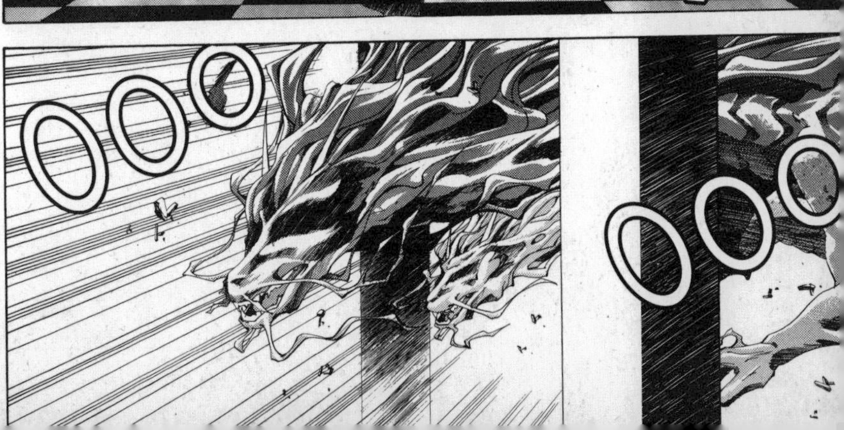
OOOO
OOOO

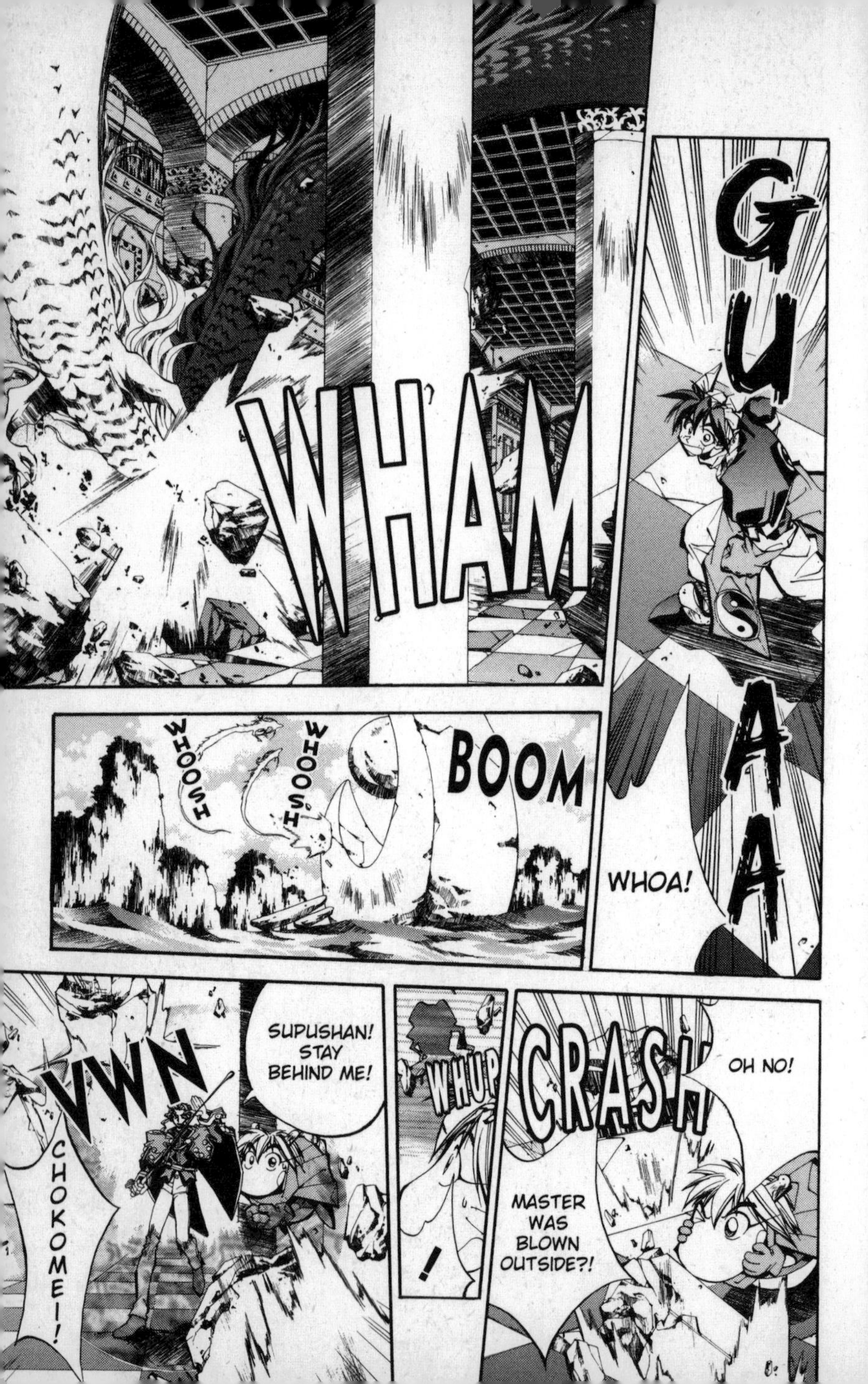
GUAA
WHOA!
WHAM
BOOM
WHOOSH
WHOOSH
OH NO!
CRASH
MASTER WAS BLOWN OUTSIDE?!
WHUP
!
SUPUSHAN! STAY BEHIND ME!
VWN
CHOKOME!!

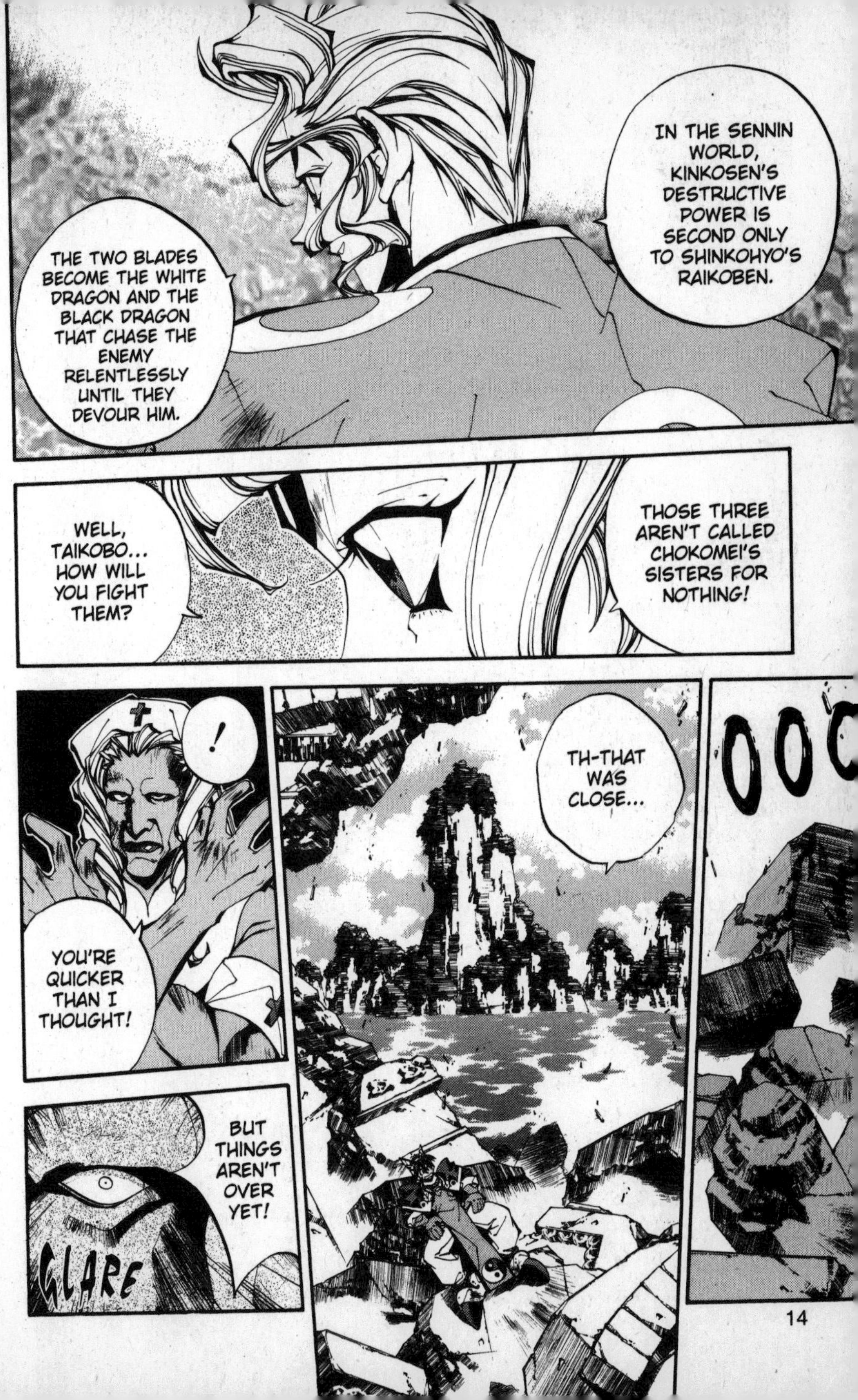
IN THE SENNIN WORLD, KINKOSEN'S DESTRUCTIVE POWER IS SECOND ONLY TO SHINKOHYO'S RAIKOBEN.
THE TWO BLADES BECOME THE WHITE DRAGON AND THE BLACK DRAGON THAT CHASE THE ENEMY RELENTLESSLY UNTIL THEY DEVOUR HIM.
THOSE THREE AREN'T CALLED CHOKOMEI'S SISTERS FOR NOTHING!
WELL, TAIKOBO... HOW WILL YOU FIGHT THEM?
TH-THAT WAS CLOSE...
!
YOU'RE QUICKER THAN I THOUGHT!
BUT THINGS AREN'T OVER YET!
GLARE

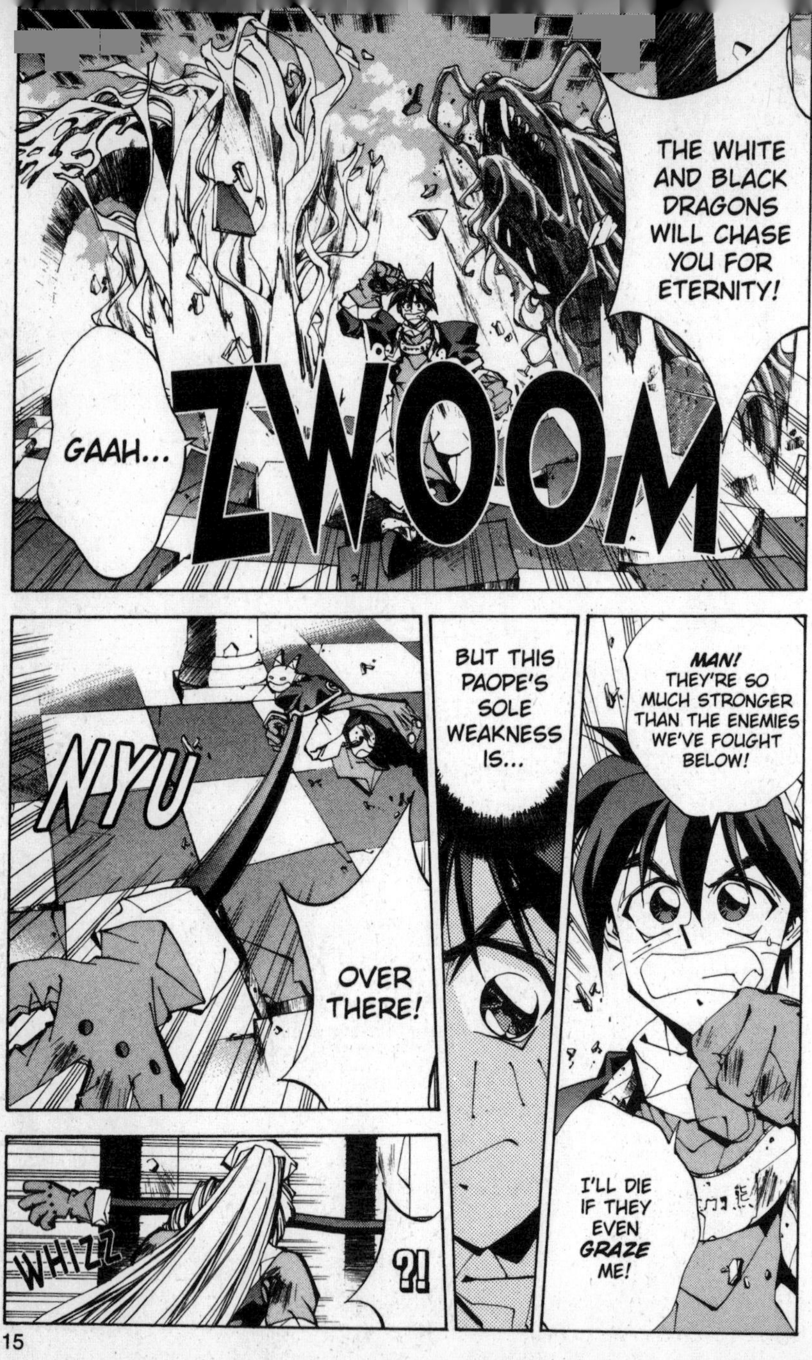
THE WHITE AND BLACK DRAGONS WILL CHASE YOU FOR ETERNITY!
ZWOOM
GAAH...
MAN! THEY'RE SO MUCH STRONGER THAN THE ENEMIES WE'VE FOUGHT BELOW!
I'LL DIE IF THEY EVEN *GRAZE* ME!
BUT THIS PAOPE'S SOLE WEAKNESS IS...
NYU
OVER THERE!
?!
WHIZZ

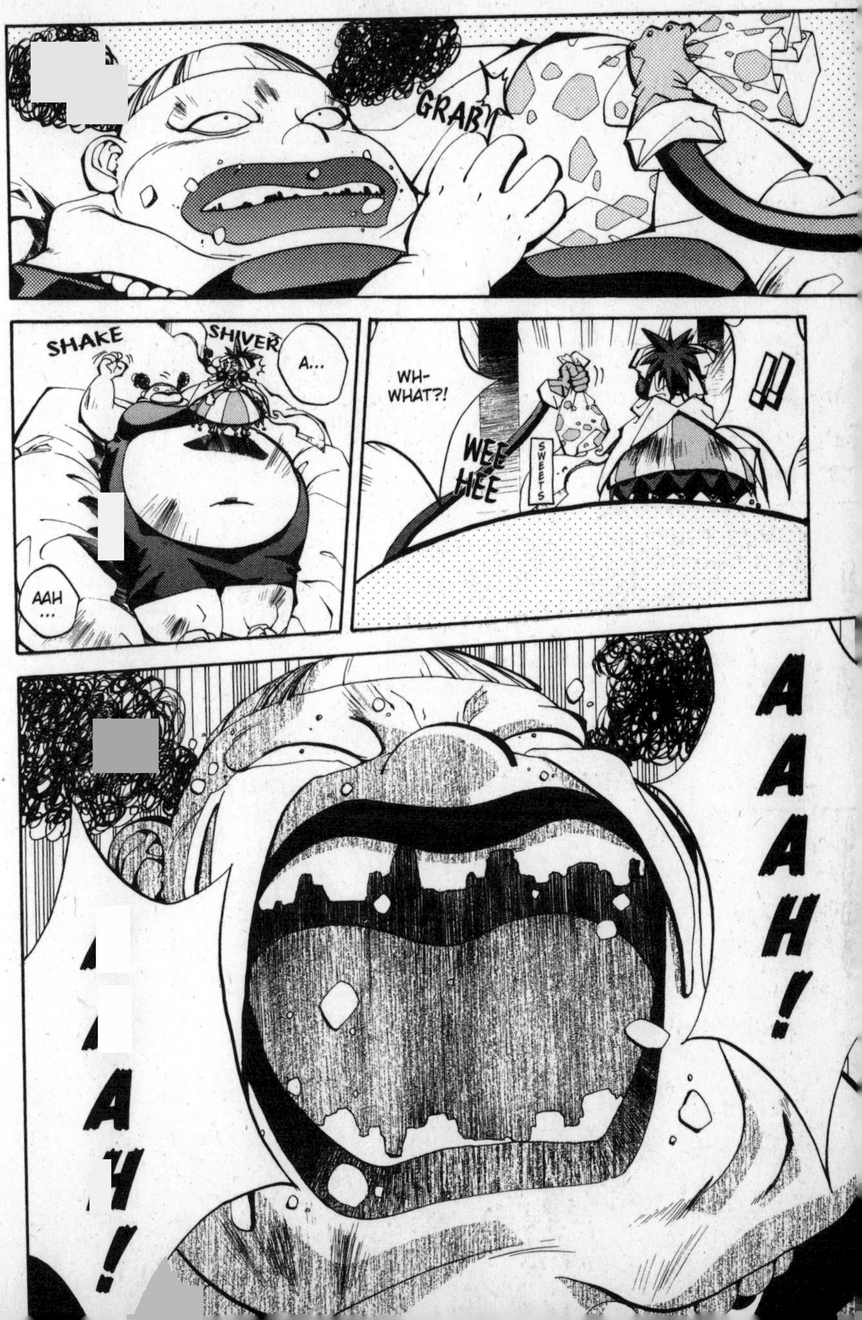
GRAB!
!!
WH- WHAT?!
WEE HEE
SWEETS
A...
SHIVER
SHAKE
AAH ...
AAAAH!

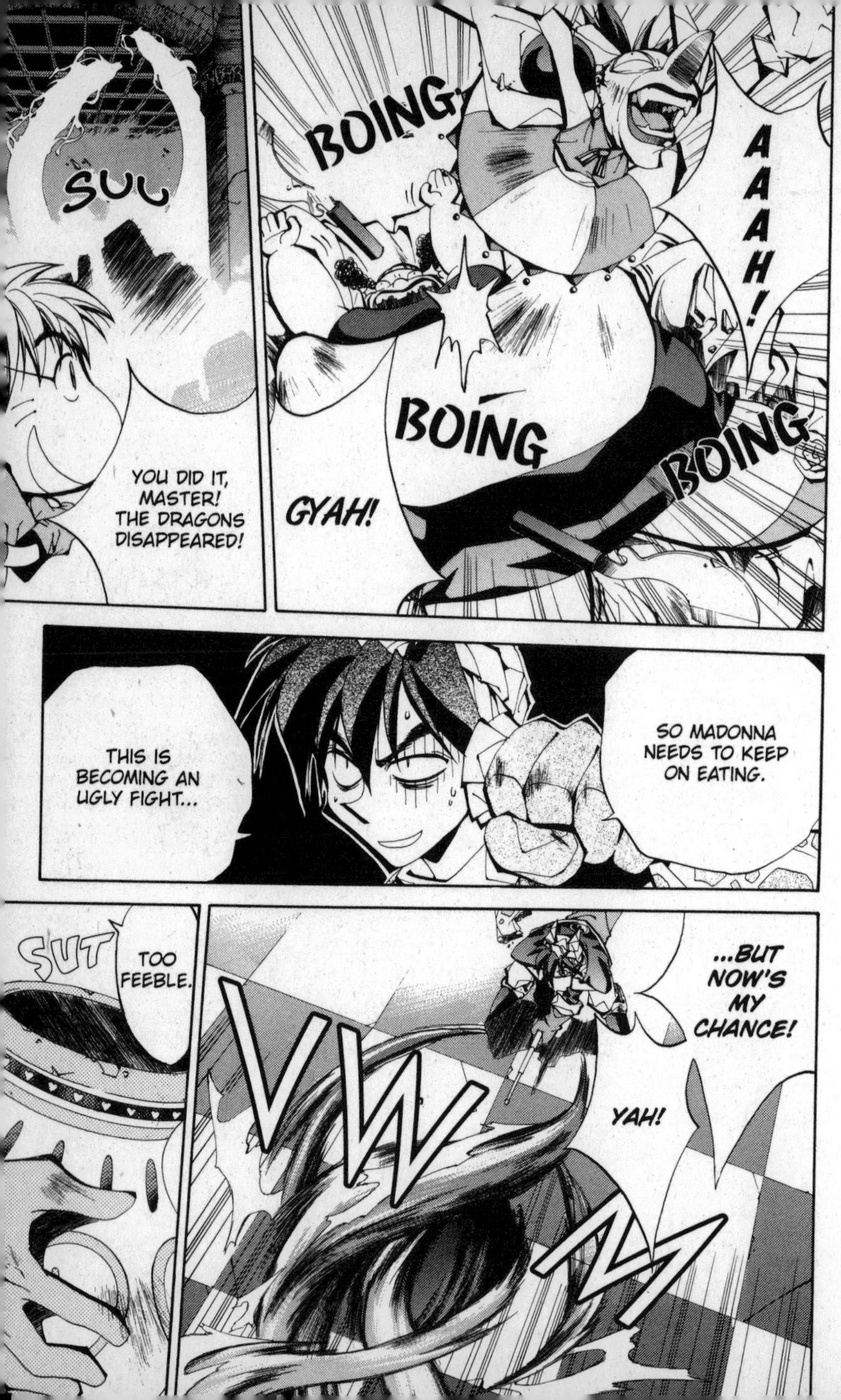
AAAAH!
BOING
BOING
BOING
GYAH!
SUU
YOU DID IT, MASTER! THE DRAGONS DISAPPEARED!
SO MADONNA NEEDS TO KEEP ON EATING.
THIS IS BECOMING AN UGLY FIGHT...
...BUT NOW'S MY CHANCE!
YAH!
VWM
SUT
TOO FEEBLE.

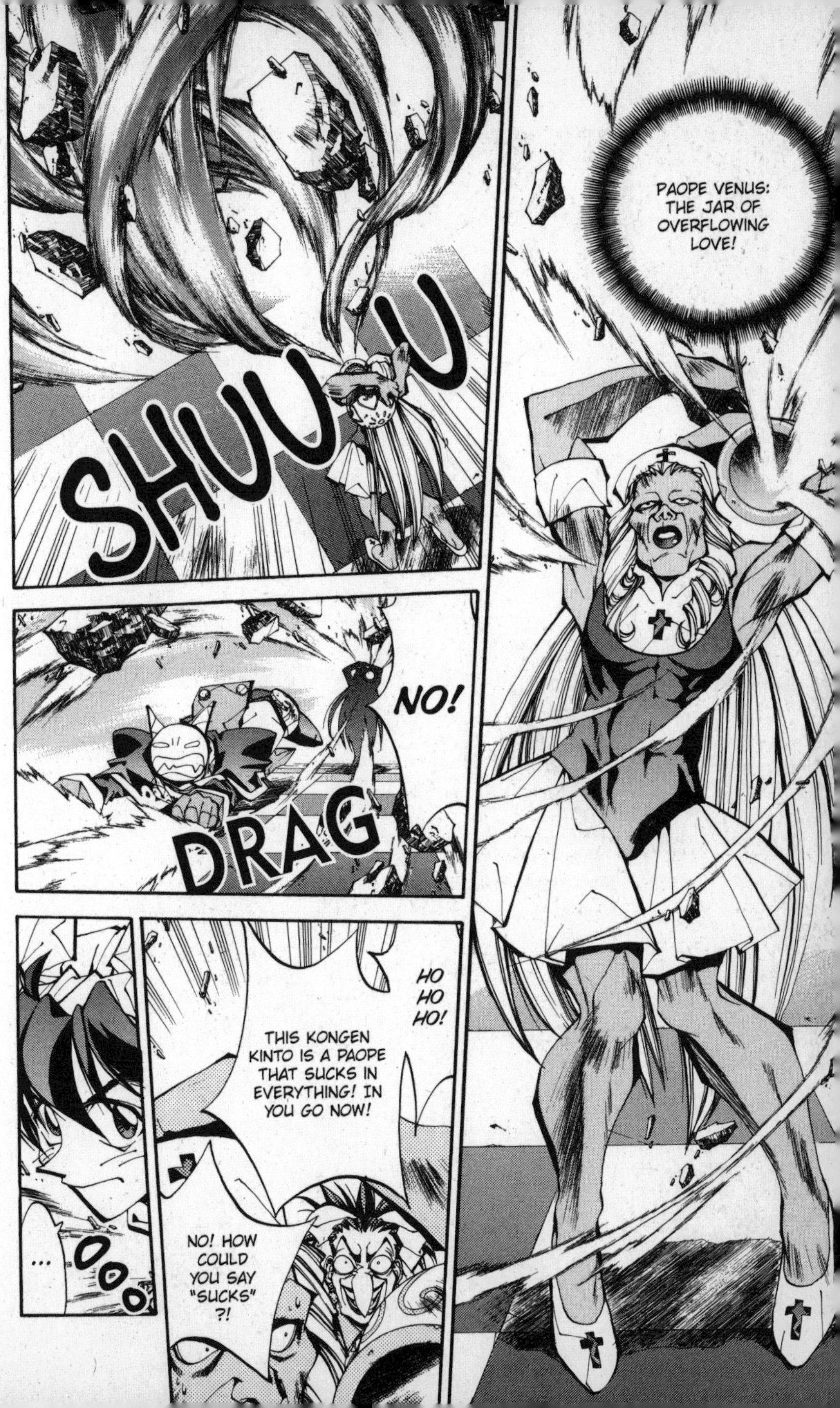
PAOPE VENUS: THE JAR OF OVERFLOWING LOVE!
SHUUU
NO!
DRAG
HO HO HO!
THIS KONGEN KINTO IS A PAOPE THAT SUCKS IN EVERYTHING! IN YOU GO NOW!
NO! HOW COULD YOU SAY "SUCKS" ?!
...
OOO

READ THIS WAY

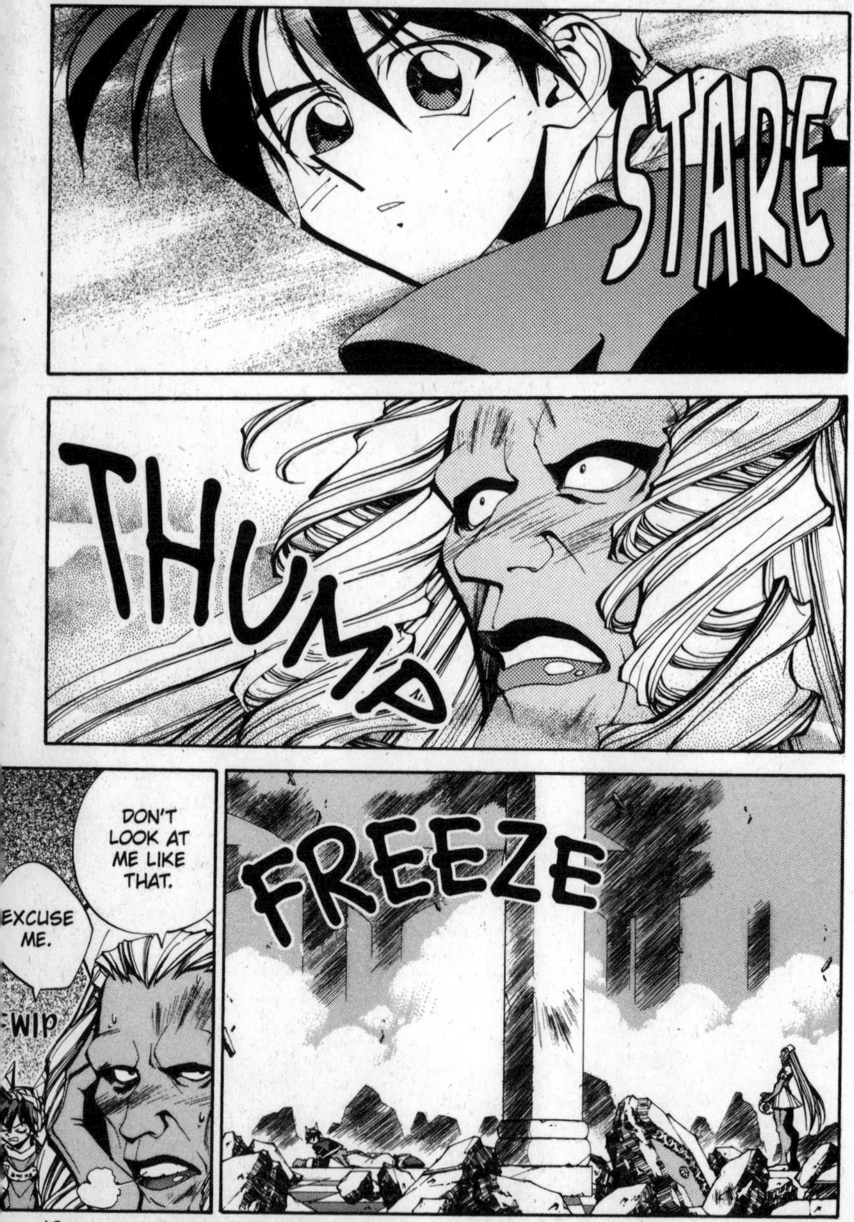

STARE
THUMP
FREEZE
DON'T LOOK AT ME LIKE THAT.
EXCUSE ME.
WIP

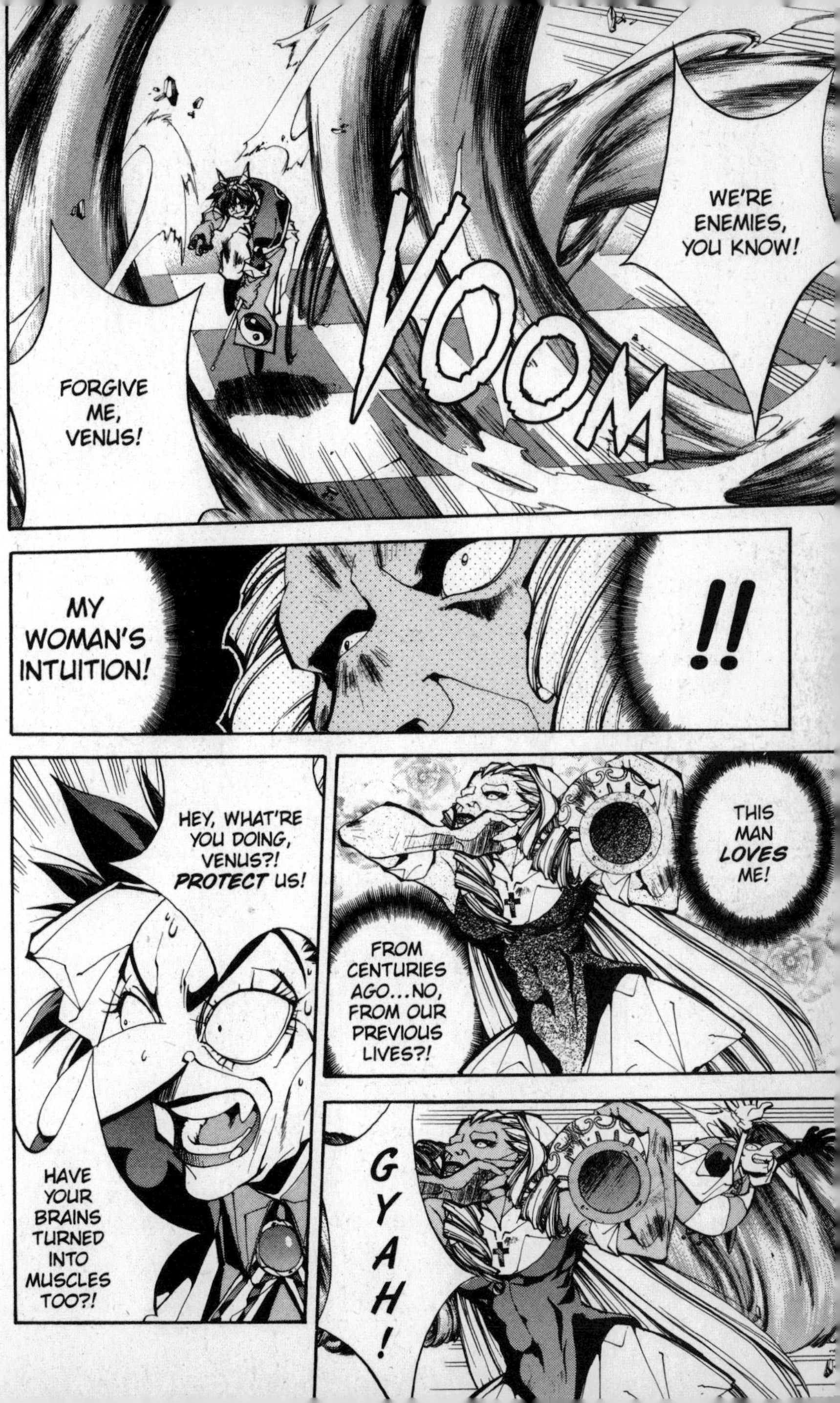
WE'RE ENEMIES, YOU KNOW!
VOOM
FORGIVE ME, VENUS!
!!
MY WOMAN'S INTUITION!
THIS MAN *LOVES* ME!
FROM CENTURIES AGO...NO, FROM OUR PREVIOUS LIVES?!
GYAH!
HEY, WHAT'RE YOU DOING, VENUS?! ***PROTECT*** US!
HAVE YOUR BRAINS TURNED INTO MUSCLES TOO?!

READ THIS WAY

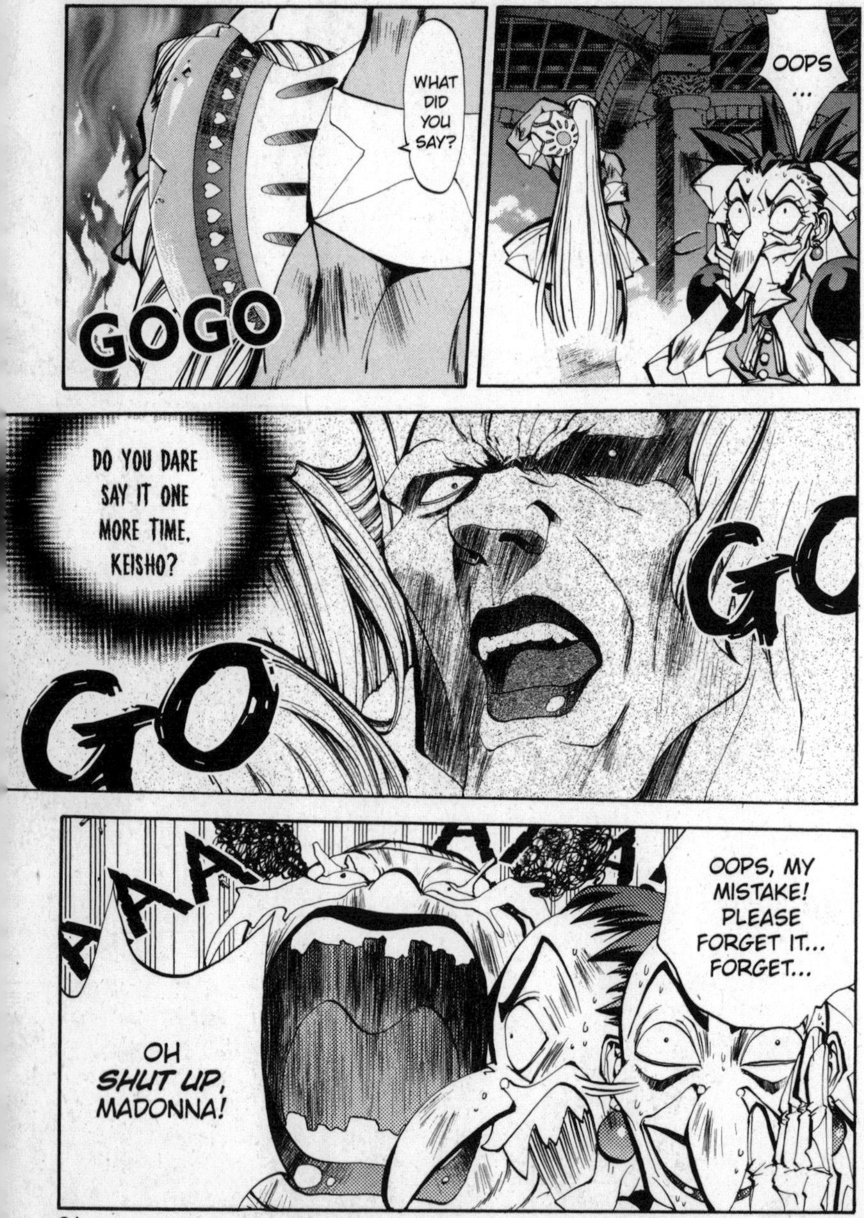

OOPS ...
WHAT DID YOU SAY?
GOGO
DO YOU DARE SAY IT ONE MORE TIME, KEISHO?
GO
GO
OOPS, MY MISTAKE! PLEASE FORGET IT... FORGET...
OH *SHUT UP*, MADONNA!

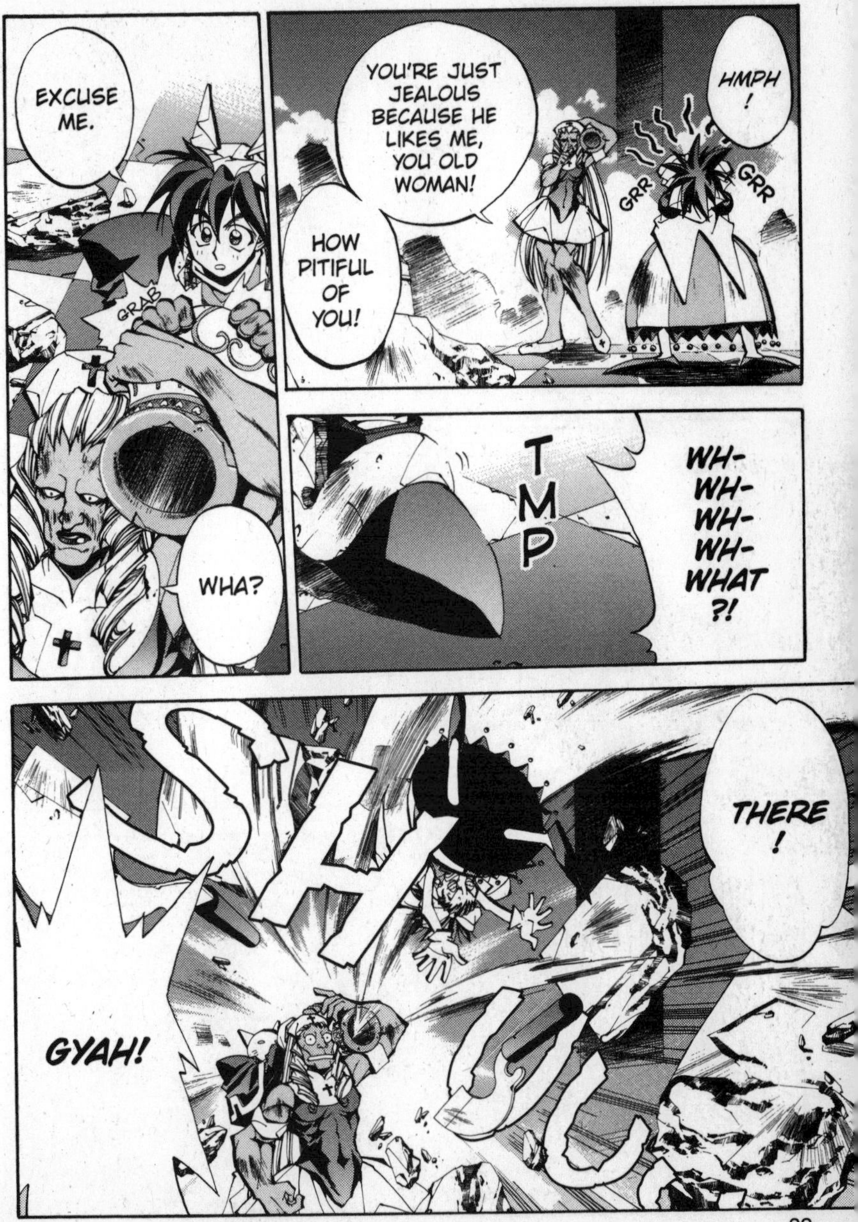
HMPH!
GRR
GRR
YOU'RE JUST JEALOUS BECAUSE HE LIKES ME, YOU OLD WOMAN!
HOW PITIFUL OF YOU!
WH-WH-WH-WH-WHAT?!
TMP
EXCUSE ME.
GRAB
WHA?
THERE!
GYAH!

READ THIS WAY

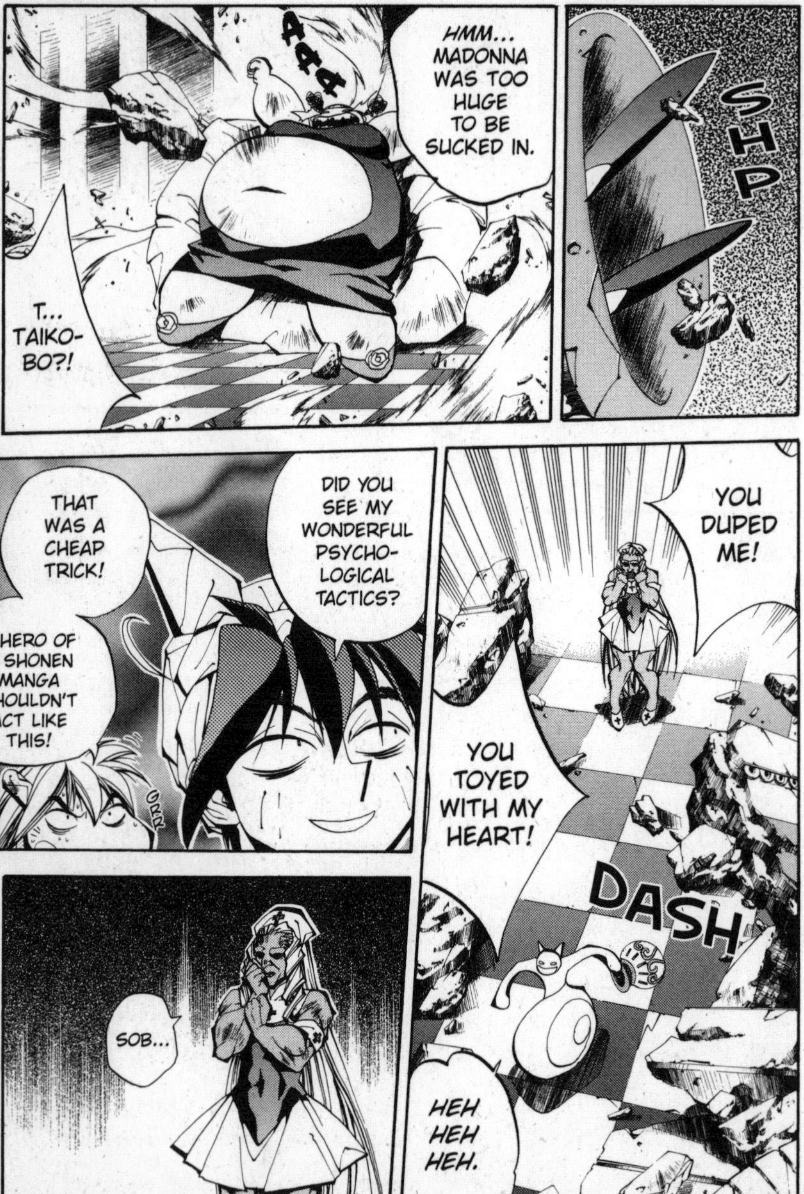
SHP
HMM... MADONNA WAS TOO HUGE TO BE SUCKED IN.
T... TAIKO-BO?!
YOU DUPED ME!
YOU TOYED WITH MY HEART!
DASH
HEH HEH HEH.
DID YOU SEE MY WONDERFUL PSYCHO-LOGICAL TACTICS?
THAT WAS A CHEAP TRICK!
A HERO OF A SHONEN MANGA SHOULDN'T ACT LIKE THIS!
GRR
SOB...

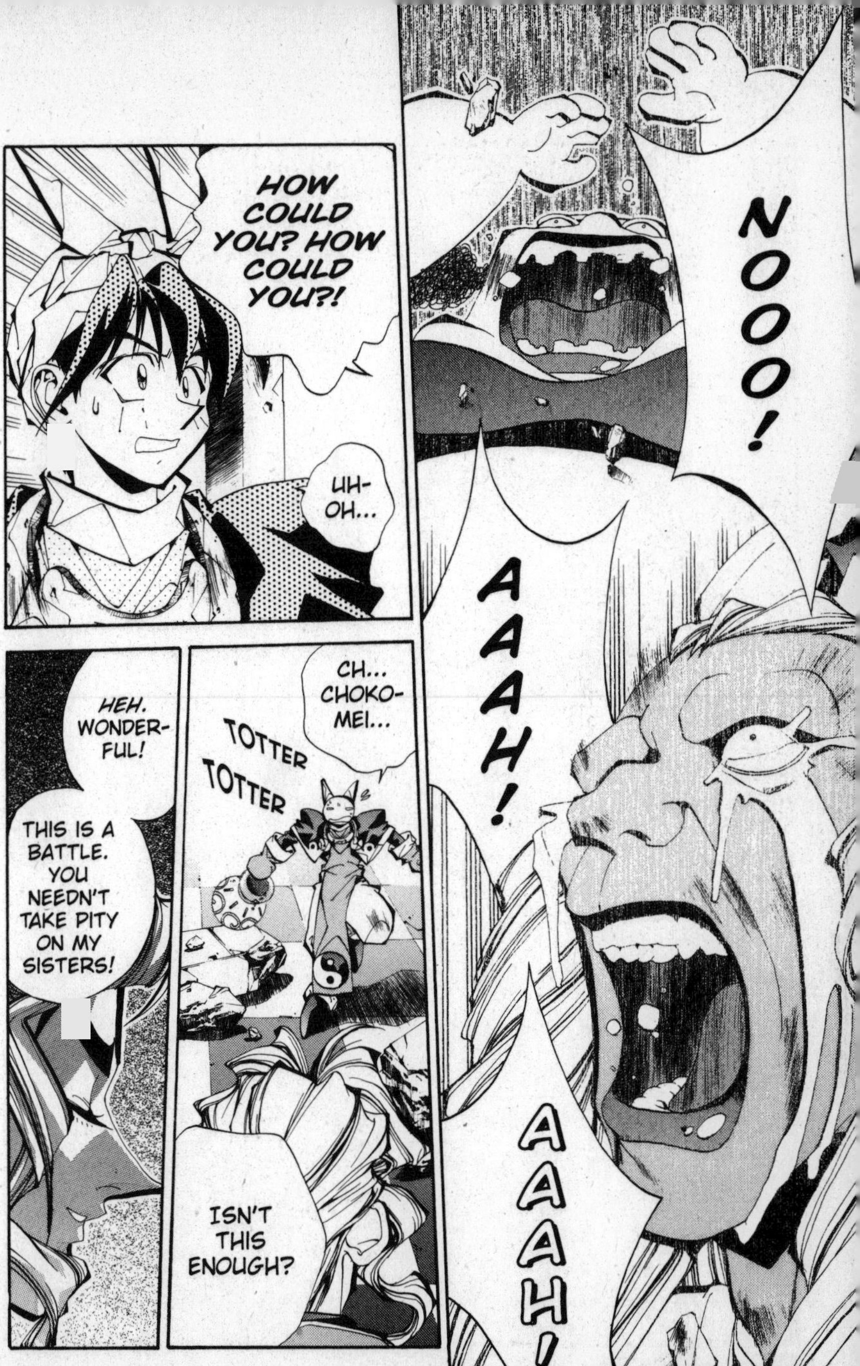
NOOOO!
AAAAH!
AAAAH!
HOW COULD YOU? HOW COULD YOU?!
UH-OH...
CH... CHOKO-MEI...
TOTTER TOTTER
ISN'T THIS ENOUGH?
HEH. WONDERFUL!
THIS IS A BATTLE. YOU NEEDN'T TAKE PITY ON MY SISTERS!

READ THIS WAY

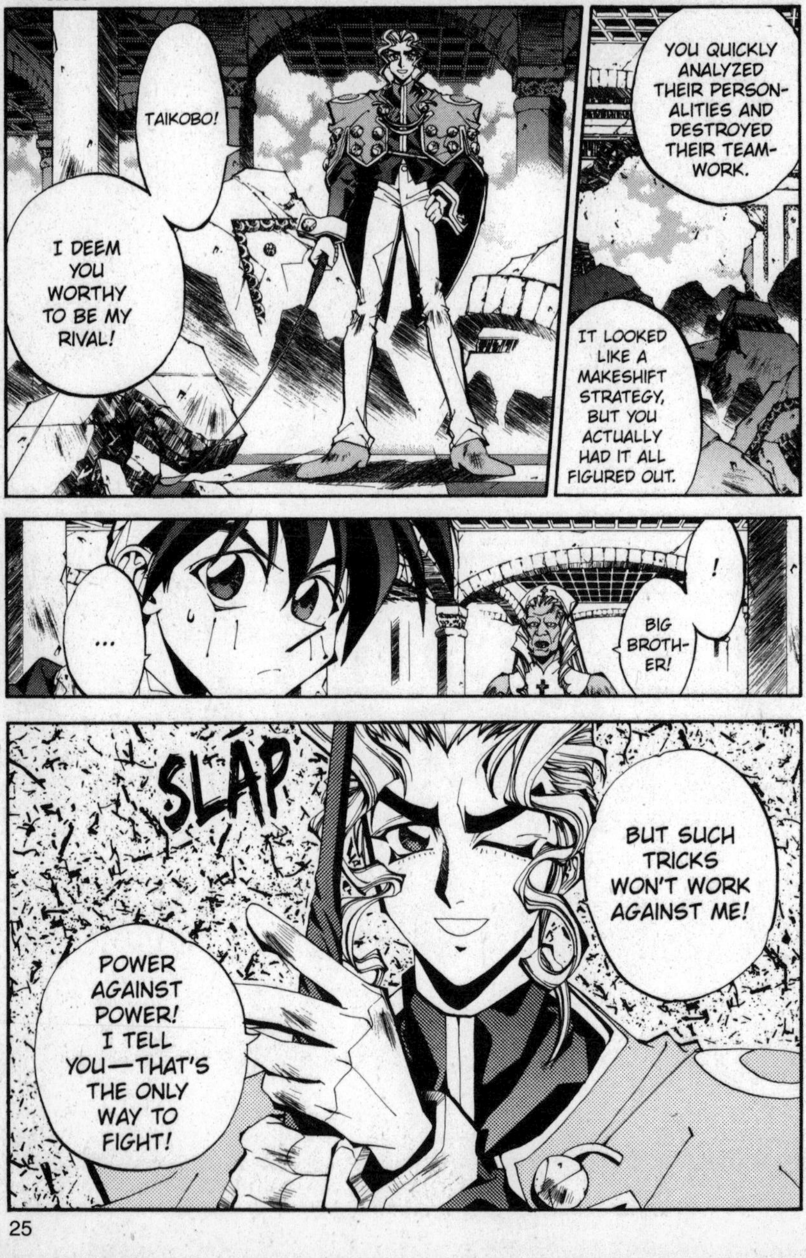
YOU QUICKLY ANALYZED THEIR PERSON-ALITIES AND DESTROYED THEIR TEAM-WORK.
IT LOOKED LIKE A MAKESHIFT STRATEGY, BUT YOU ACTUALLY HAD IT ALL FIGURED OUT.
TAIKOBO!
I DEEM YOU WORTHY TO BE MY RIVAL!
!
BIG BROTH-ER!
...
SLAP
BUT SUCH TRICKS WON'T WORK AGAINST ME!
POWER AGAINST POWER! I TELL YOU—THAT'S THE ONLY WAY TO FIGHT!

封神演義

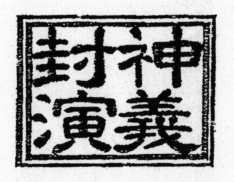

Chapter 99

MEDIUM-BOSS BATTLE, PART 1
BLACK

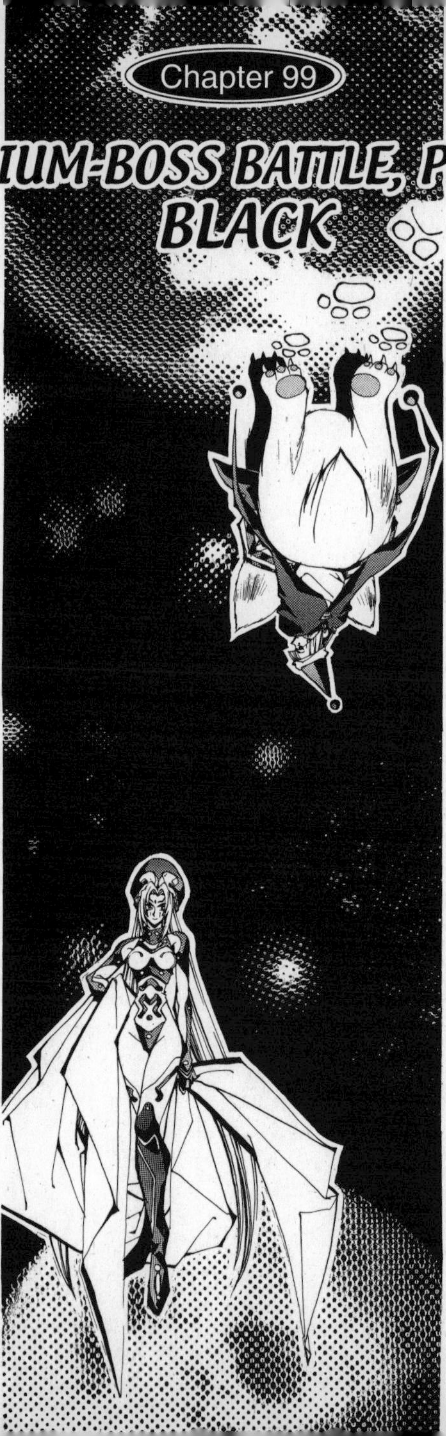

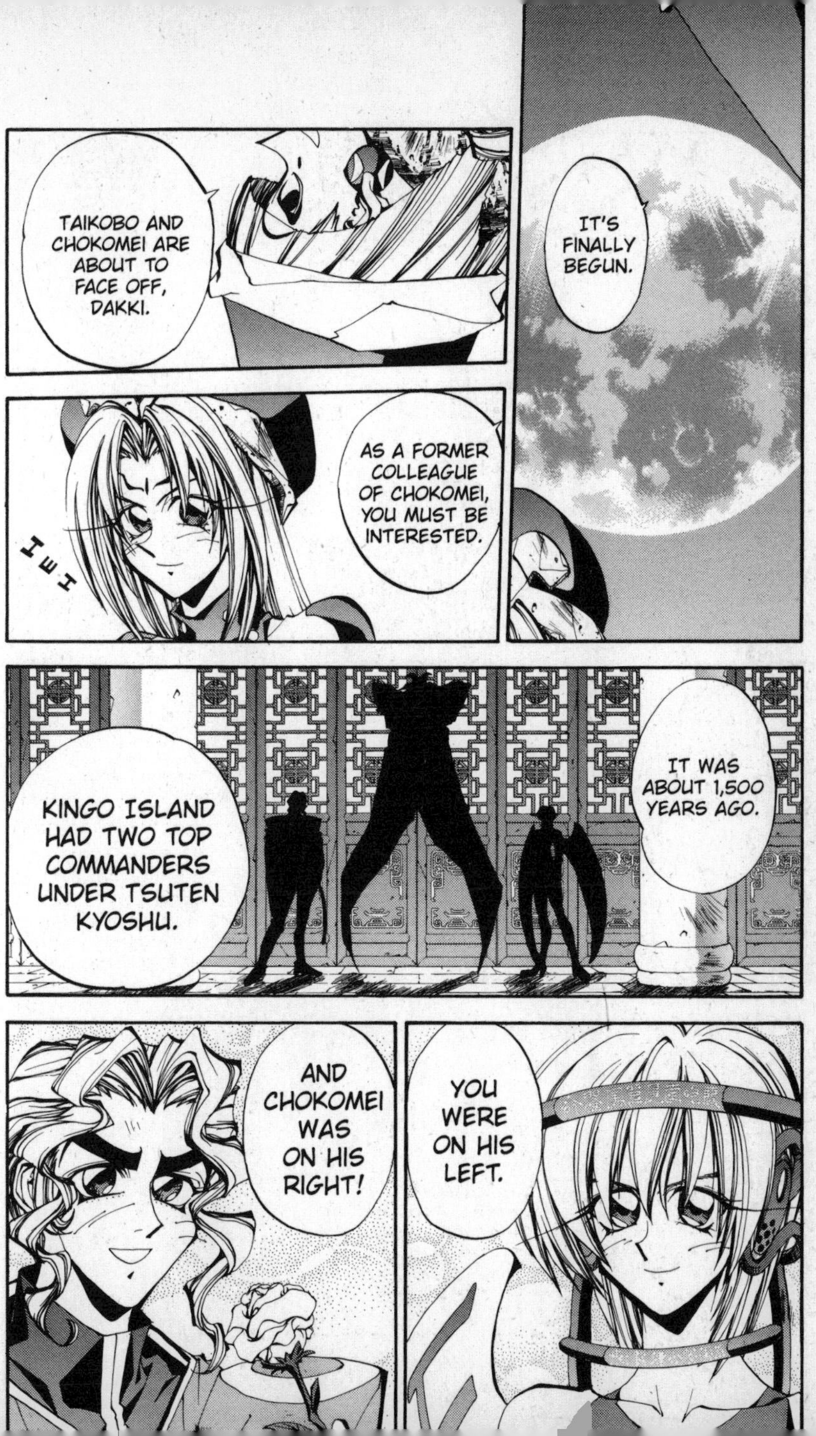
IT'S FINALLY BEGUN.
TAIKOBO AND CHOKOMEI ARE ABOUT TO FACE OFF, DAKKI.
AS A FORMER COLLEAGUE OF CHOKOMEI, YOU MUST BE INTERESTED.
HEH
IT WAS ABOUT 1,500 YEARS AGO.
KINGO ISLAND HAD TWO TOP COMMANDERS UNDER TSUTEN KYOSHU.
YOU WERE ON HIS LEFT.
AND CHOKOMEI WAS ON HIS RIGHT!

READ THIS WAY

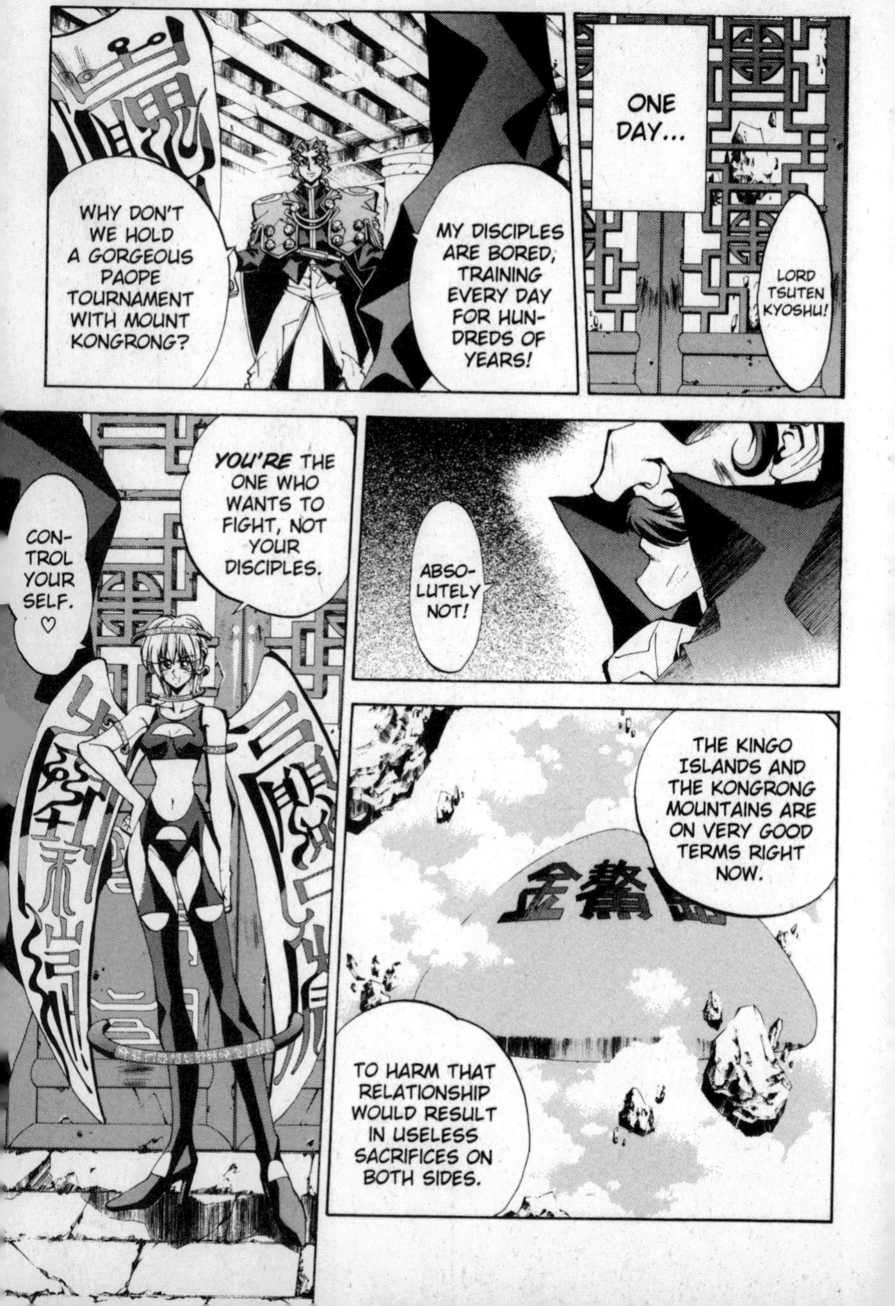
ONE DAY...
LORD TSUTEN KYOSHU!
MY DISCIPLES ARE BORED, TRAINING EVERY DAY FOR HUN-DREDS OF YEARS!
WHY DON'T WE HOLD A GORGEOUS PAOPE TOURNAMENT WITH MOUNT KONGRONG?
ABSO-LUTELY NOT!
THE KINGO ISLANDS AND THE KONGRONG MOUNTAINS ARE ON VERY GOOD TERMS RIGHT NOW.
TO HARM THAT RELATIONSHIP WOULD RESULT IN USELESS SACRIFICES ON BOTH SIDES.
YOU'RE THE ONE WHO WANTS TO FIGHT, NOT YOUR DISCIPLES.
CON-TROL YOUR SELF. ♡

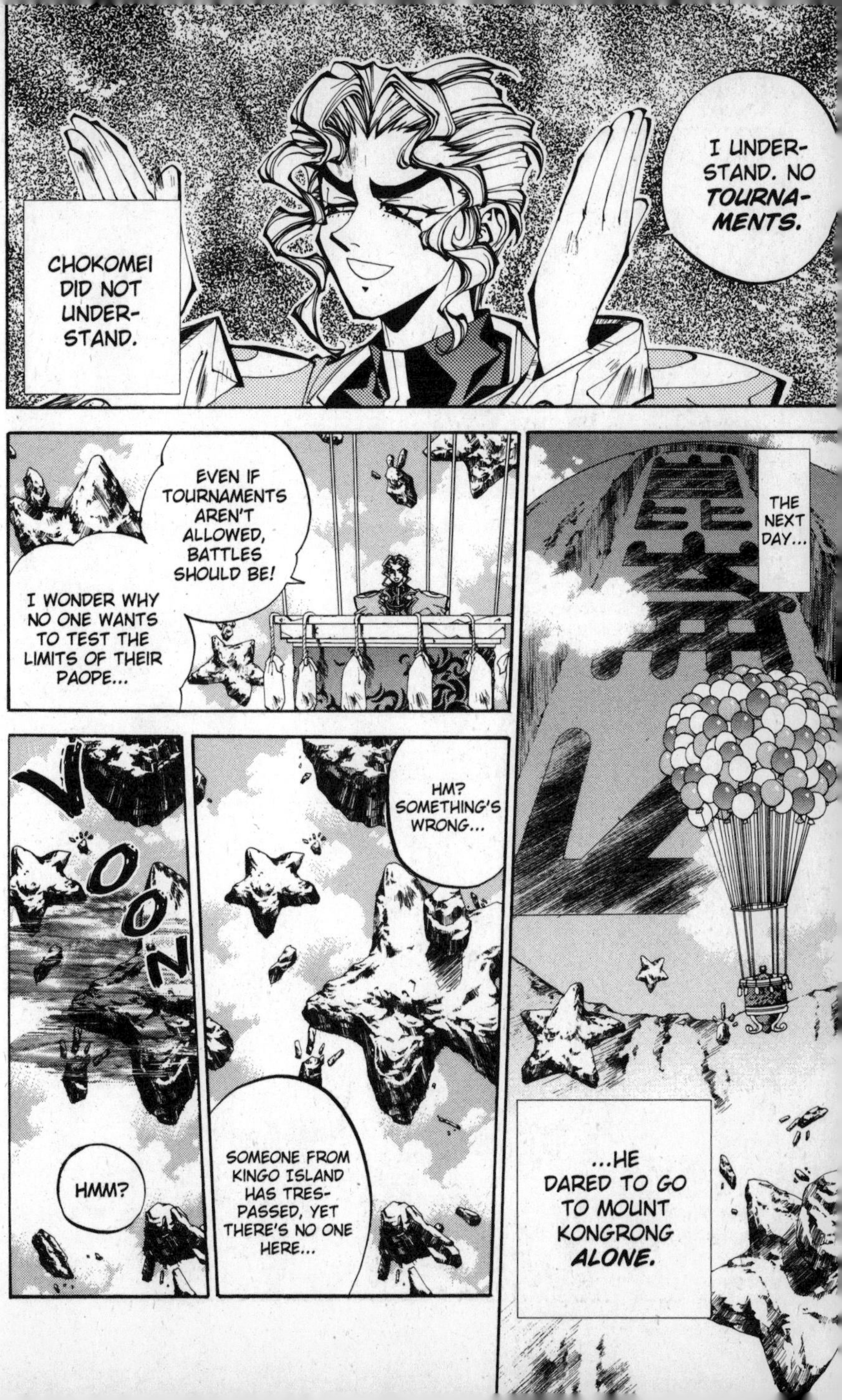
I UNDERSTAND. NO *TOURNAMENTS.*
CHOKOMEI DID NOT UNDERSTAND.
THE NEXT DAY...
...HE DARED TO GO TO MOUNT KONGRONG *ALONE.*
EVEN IF TOURNAMENTS AREN'T ALLOWED, BATTLES SHOULD BE!
I WONDER WHY NO ONE WANTS TO TEST THE LIMITS OF THEIR PAOPE...
HM? SOMETHING'S WRONG...
SOMEONE FROM KINGO ISLAND HAS TRES-PASSED, YET THERE'S NO ONE HERE...
VOON
HMM?

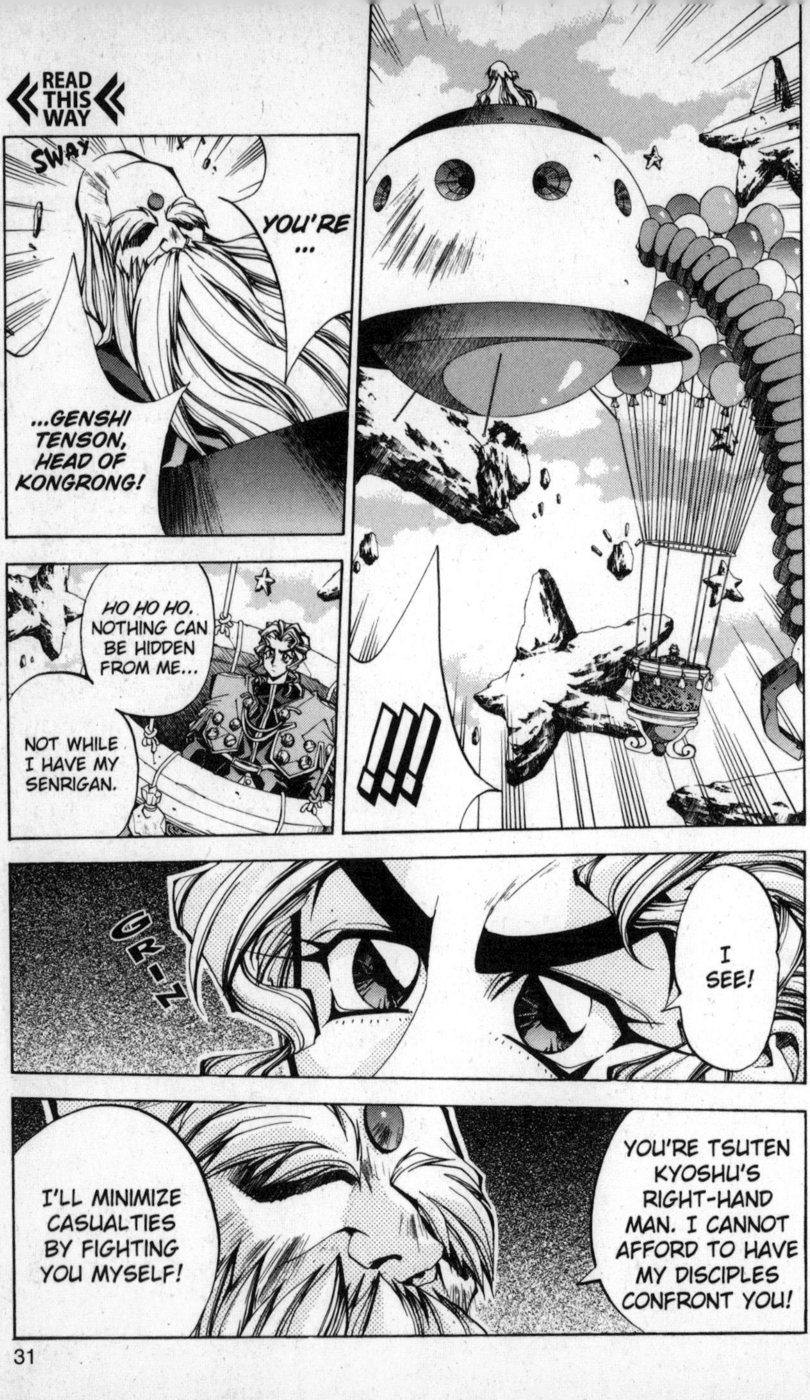
READ THIS WAY
!!!
SWAY
YOU'RE ...
...GENSHI TENSON, HEAD OF KONGRONG!
HO HO HO. NOTHING CAN BE HIDDEN FROM ME...
NOT WHILE I HAVE MY SENRIGAN.
GR-R-Z
I SEE!
YOU'RE TSUTEN KYOSHU'S RIGHT-HAND MAN. I CANNOT AFFORD TO HAVE MY DISCIPLES CONFRONT YOU!
I'LL MINIMIZE CASUALTIES BY FIGHTING YOU MYSELF!

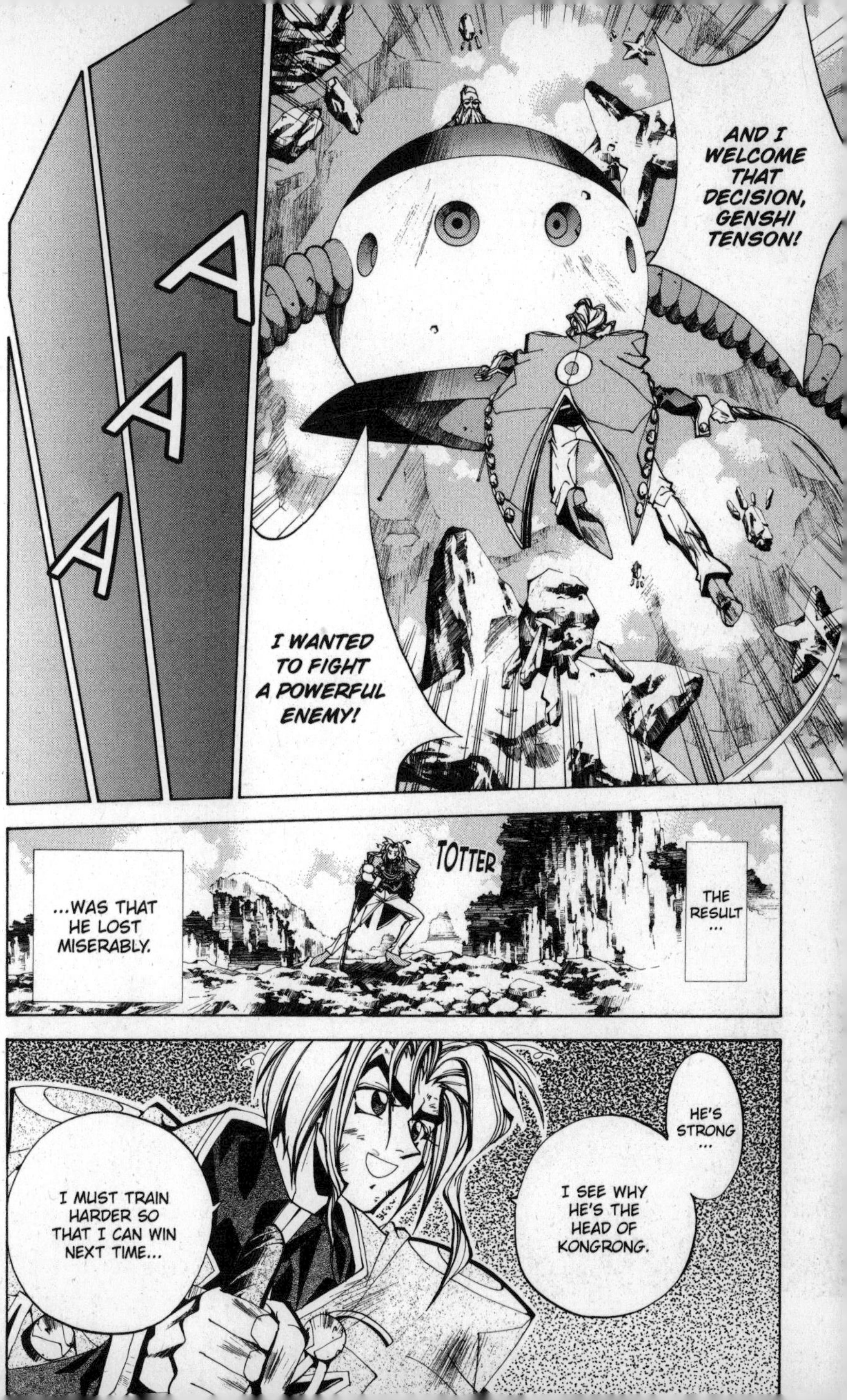
AND I WELCOME THAT DECISION, GENSHI TENSON!
I WANTED TO FIGHT A POWERFUL ENEMY!
AAA
THE RESULT...
TOTTER
...WAS THAT HE LOST MISERABLY.
HE'S STRONG...
I SEE WHY HE'S THE HEAD OF KONGRONG.
I MUST TRAIN HARDER SO THAT I CAN WIN NEXT TIME...

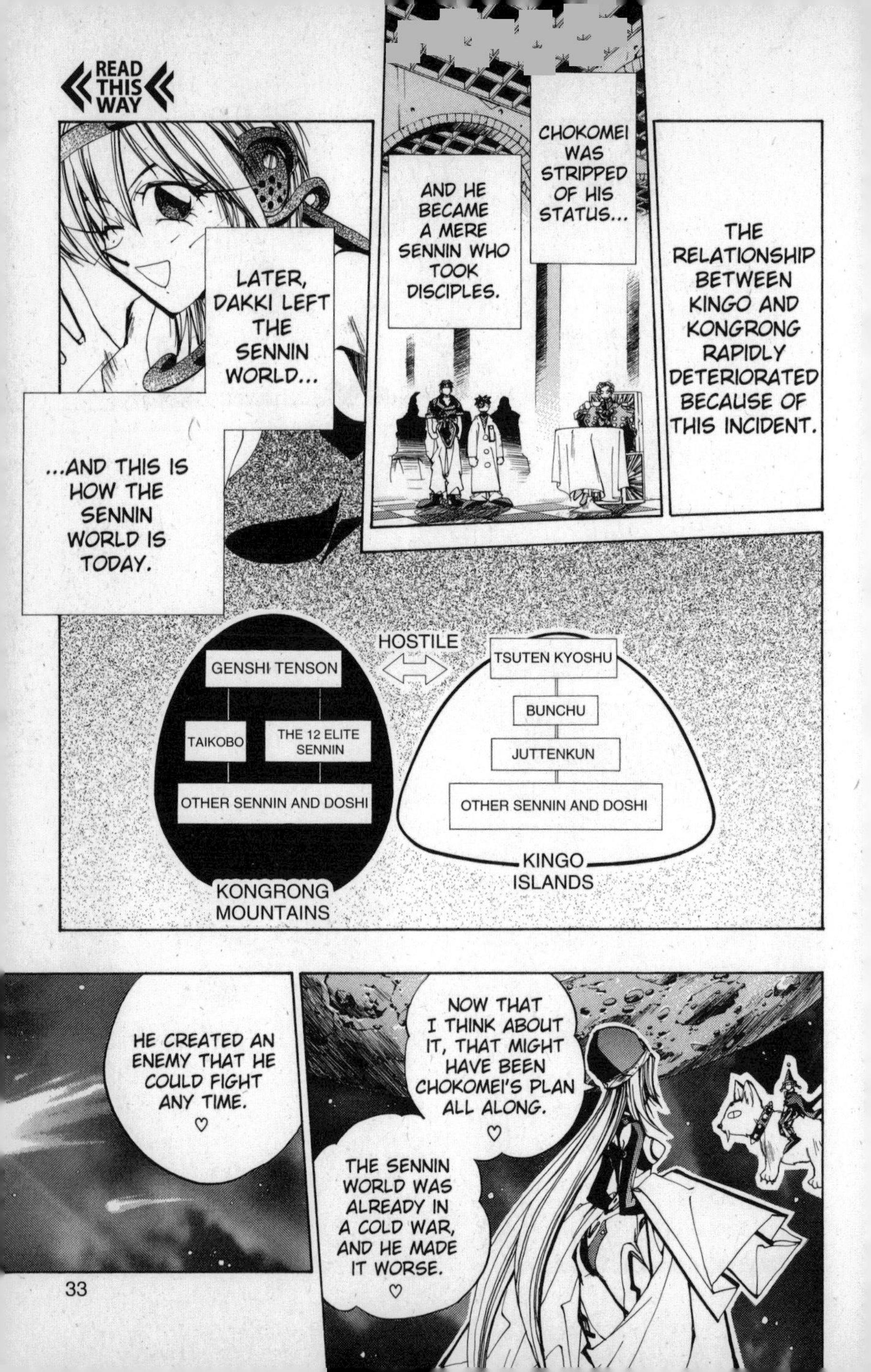
READ THIS WAY
THE RELATIONSHIP BETWEEN KINGO AND KONGRONG RAPIDLY DETERIORATED BECAUSE OF THIS INCIDENT.
CHOKOMEI WAS STRIPPED OF HIS STATUS...
AND HE BECAME A MERE SENNIN WHO TOOK DISCIPLES.
LATER, DAKKI LEFT THE SENNIN WORLD...
...AND THIS IS HOW THE SENNIN WORLD IS TODAY.
HOSTILE
TSUTEN KYOSHU
BUNCHU
JUTTENKUN
OTHER SENNIN AND DOSHI
KINGO ISLANDS
GENSHI TENSON
TAIKOBO
THE 12 ELITE SENNIN
OTHER SENNIN AND DOSHI
KONGRONG MOUNTAINS
NOW THAT I THINK ABOUT IT, THAT MIGHT HAVE BEEN CHOKOMEI'S PLAN ALL ALONG. ♡
THE SENNIN WORLD WAS ALREADY IN A COLD WAR, AND HE MADE IT WORSE. ♡
HE CREATED AN ENEMY THAT HE COULD FIGHT ANY TIME. ♡

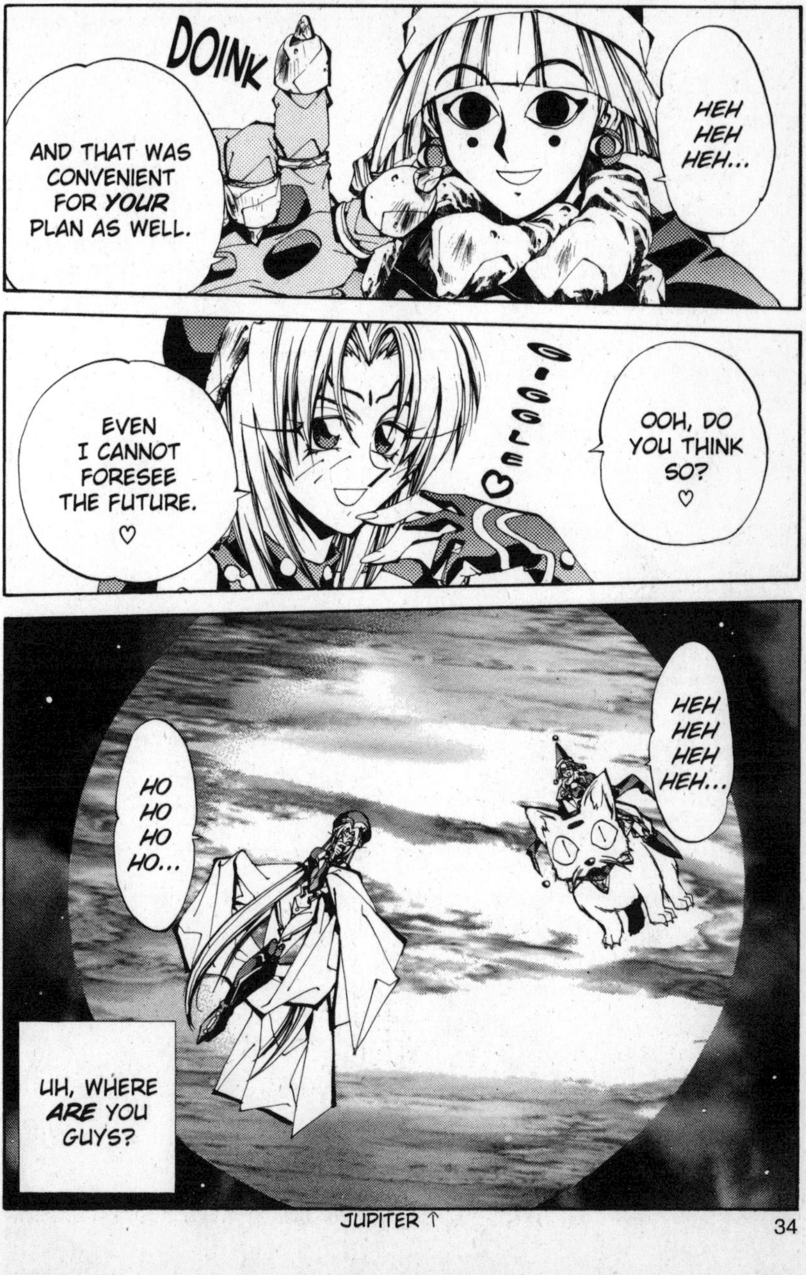
HEH HEH HEH...
DOINK
AND THAT WAS CONVENIENT FOR *YOUR* PLAN AS WELL.
OOH, DO YOU THINK SO? ♡
GIGGLE ♡
EVEN I CANNOT FORESEE THE FUTURE. ♡
HEH HEH HEH HEH...
HO HO HO HO...
UH, WHERE *ARE* YOU GUYS?

JUPITER ↑

READ THIS WAY

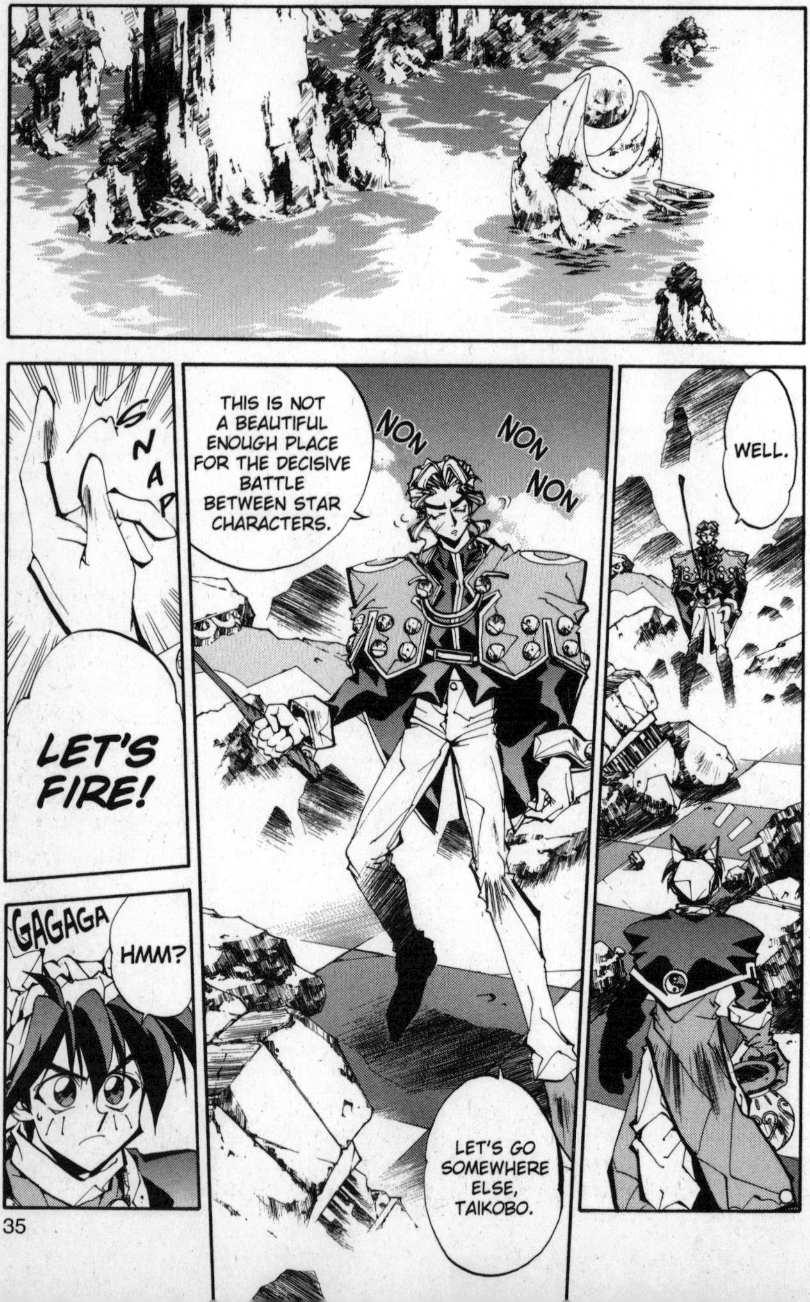
WELL.
THIS IS NOT A BEAUTIFUL ENOUGH PLACE FOR THE DECISIVE BATTLE BETWEEN STAR CHARACTERS.
NON
NON
NON
LET'S GO SOMEWHERE ELSE, TAIKOBO.
SNAP
LET'S FIRE!
GAGAGA
HMM?

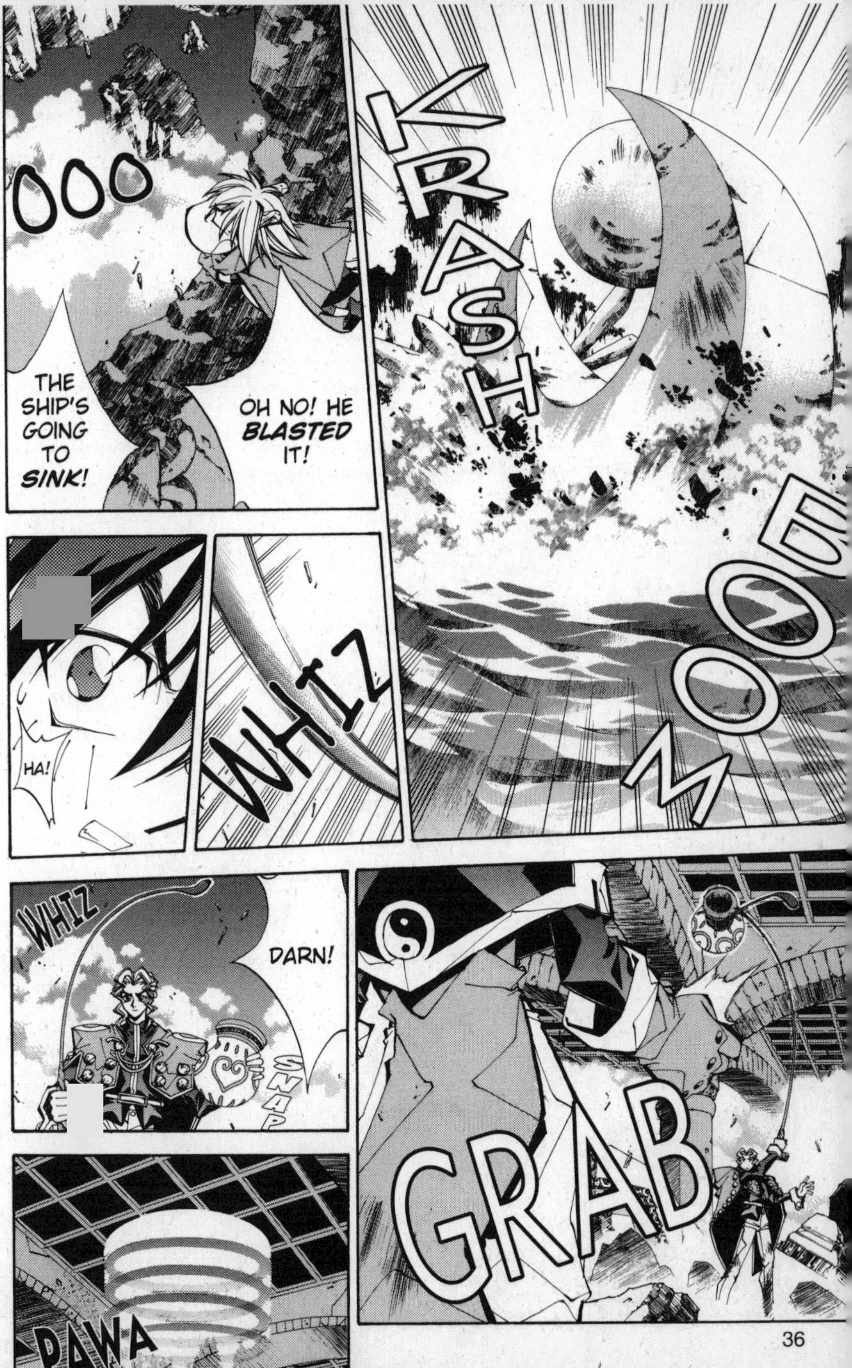
KRASH
BOOOM
OOO
OH NO! HE BLASTED IT!
THE SHIP'S GOING TO SINK!
WHIZ
HA!
GRAB
WHIZ
DARN!
SNAP
PAWA

READ THIS WAY

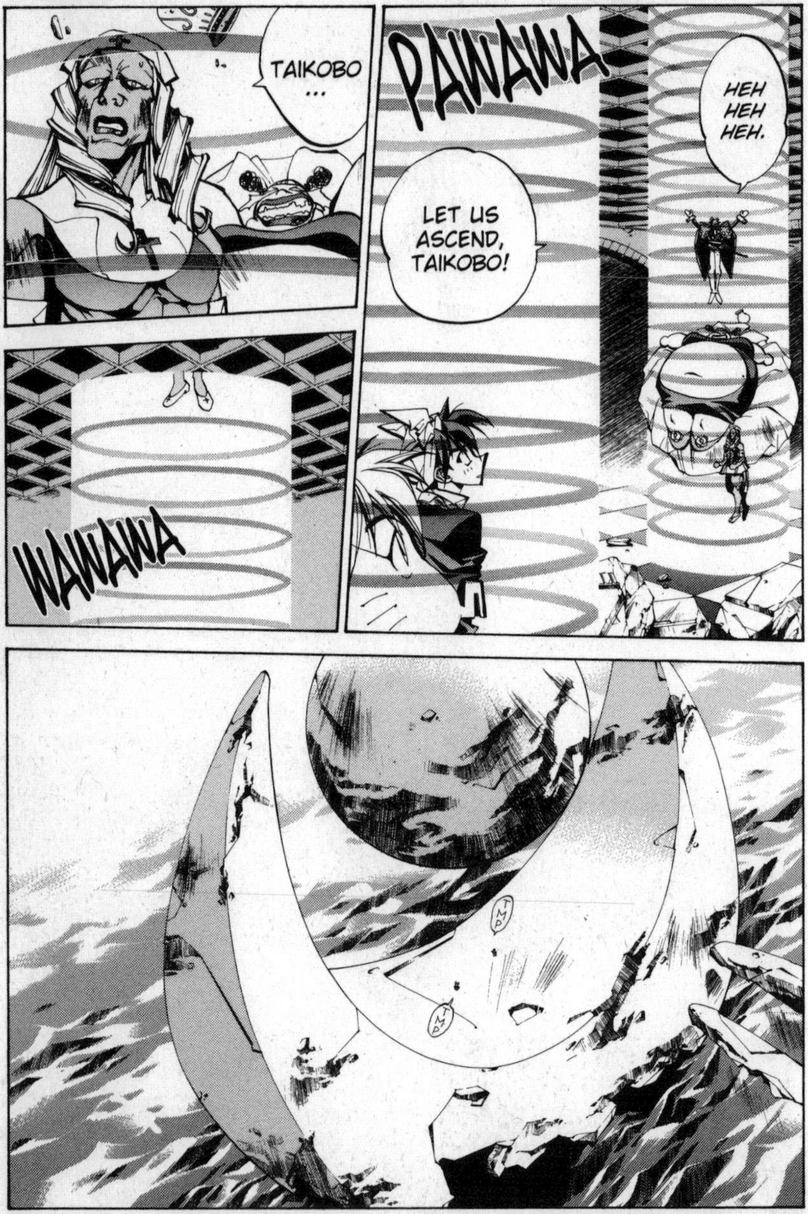
HEH HEH HEH.
PAWAWA
LET US ASCEND, TAIKOBO!
TAIKOBO ...
WAWAWA
TMP
TMP

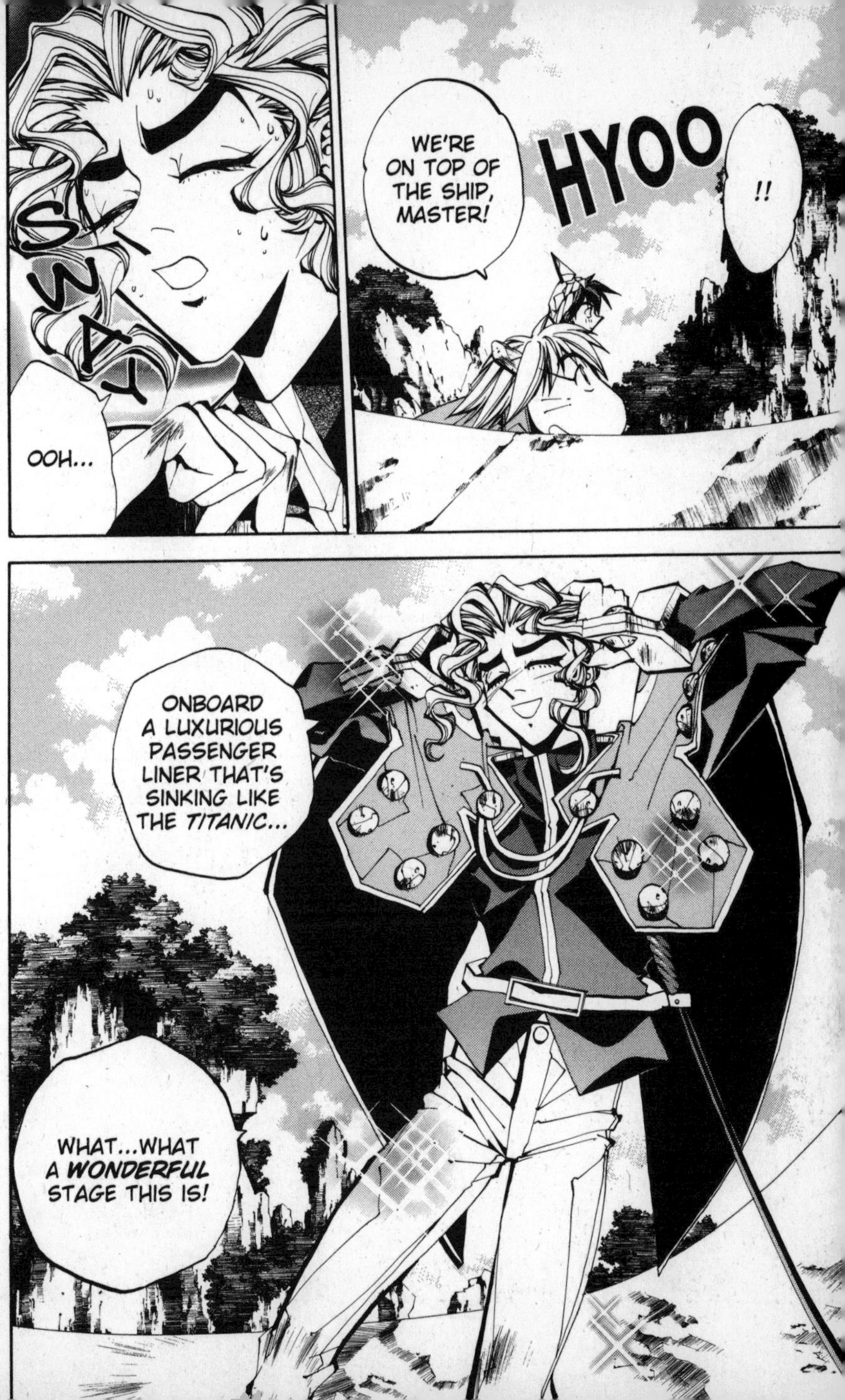
!!
HYOO
WE'RE ON TOP OF THE SHIP, MASTER!
SWAY
OOH...
ONBOARD A LUXURIOUS PASSENGER LINER THAT'S SINKING LIKE THE *TITANIC*...
WHAT...WHAT A ***WONDERFUL*** STAGE THIS IS!

READ THIS WAY

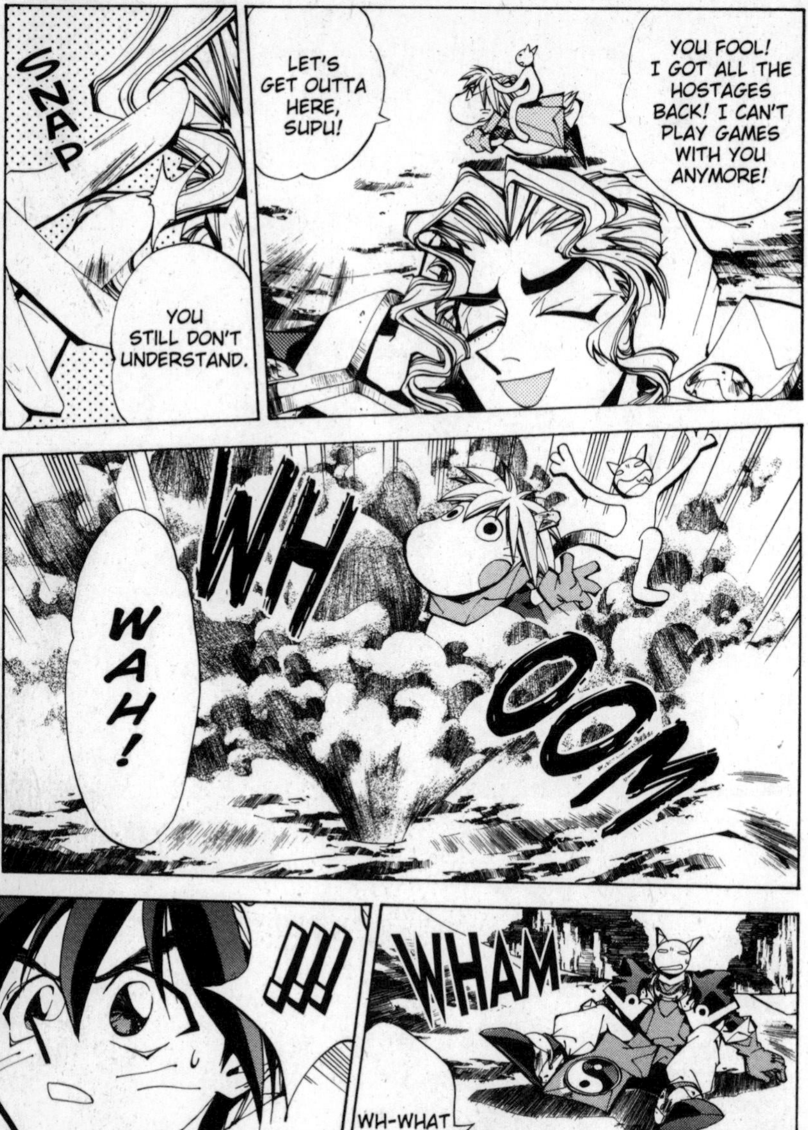
YOU FOOL! I GOT ALL THE HOSTAGES BACK! I CAN'T PLAY GAMES WITH YOU ANYMORE!
LET'S GET OUTTA HERE, SUPU!
SNAP
YOU STILL DON'T UNDERSTAND.
WHOOM
WAH!
WHAM
WH-WHAT THE...?!
!!!

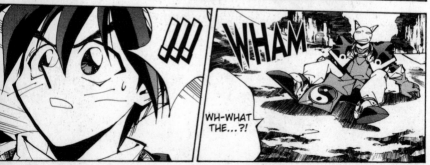

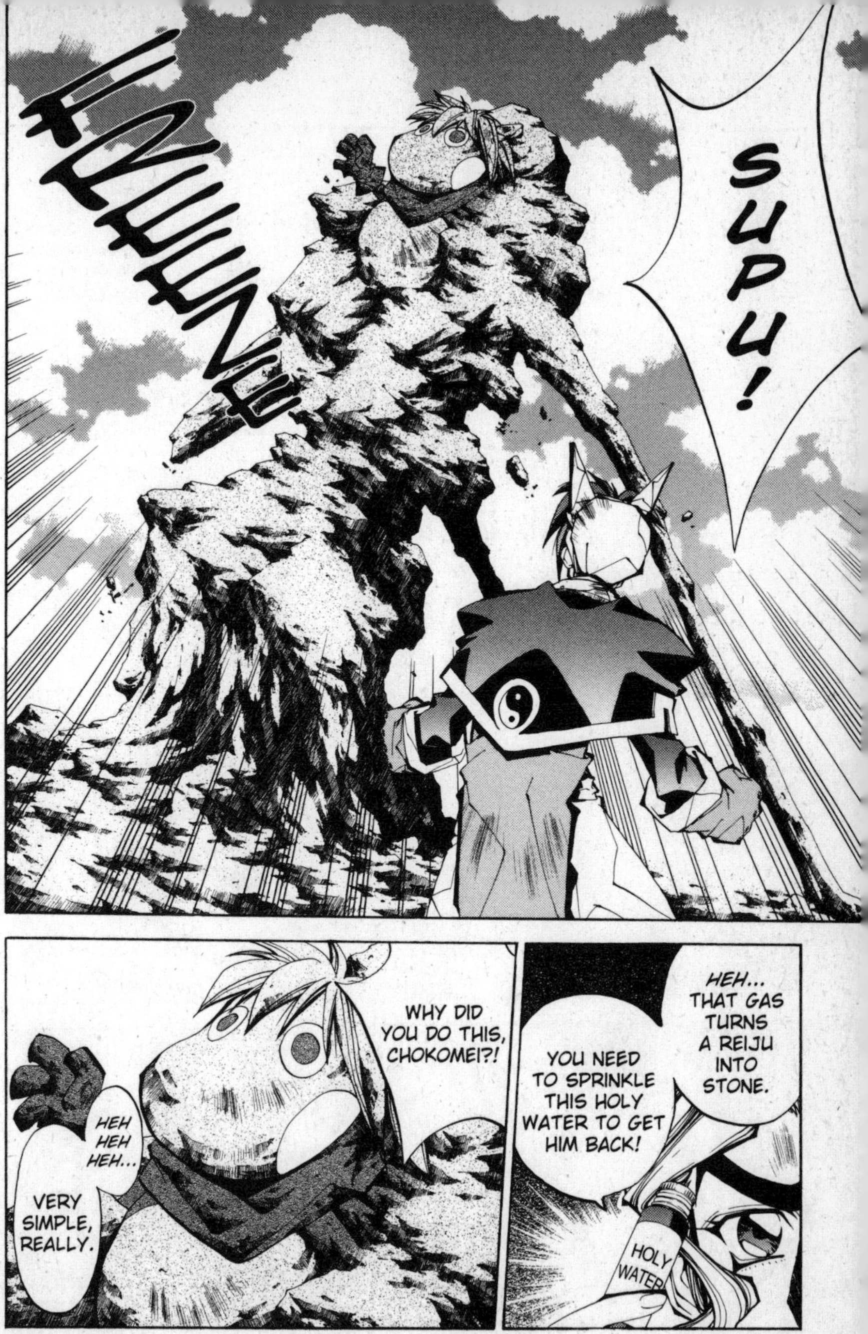
SUPU!
HEH... THAT GAS TURNS A REIJU INTO STONE.
YOU NEED TO SPRINKLE THIS HOLY WATER TO GET HIM BACK!
HOLY WATER
WHY DID YOU DO THIS, CHOKOMEI?!
HEH HEH HEH...
VERY SIMPLE, REALLY.

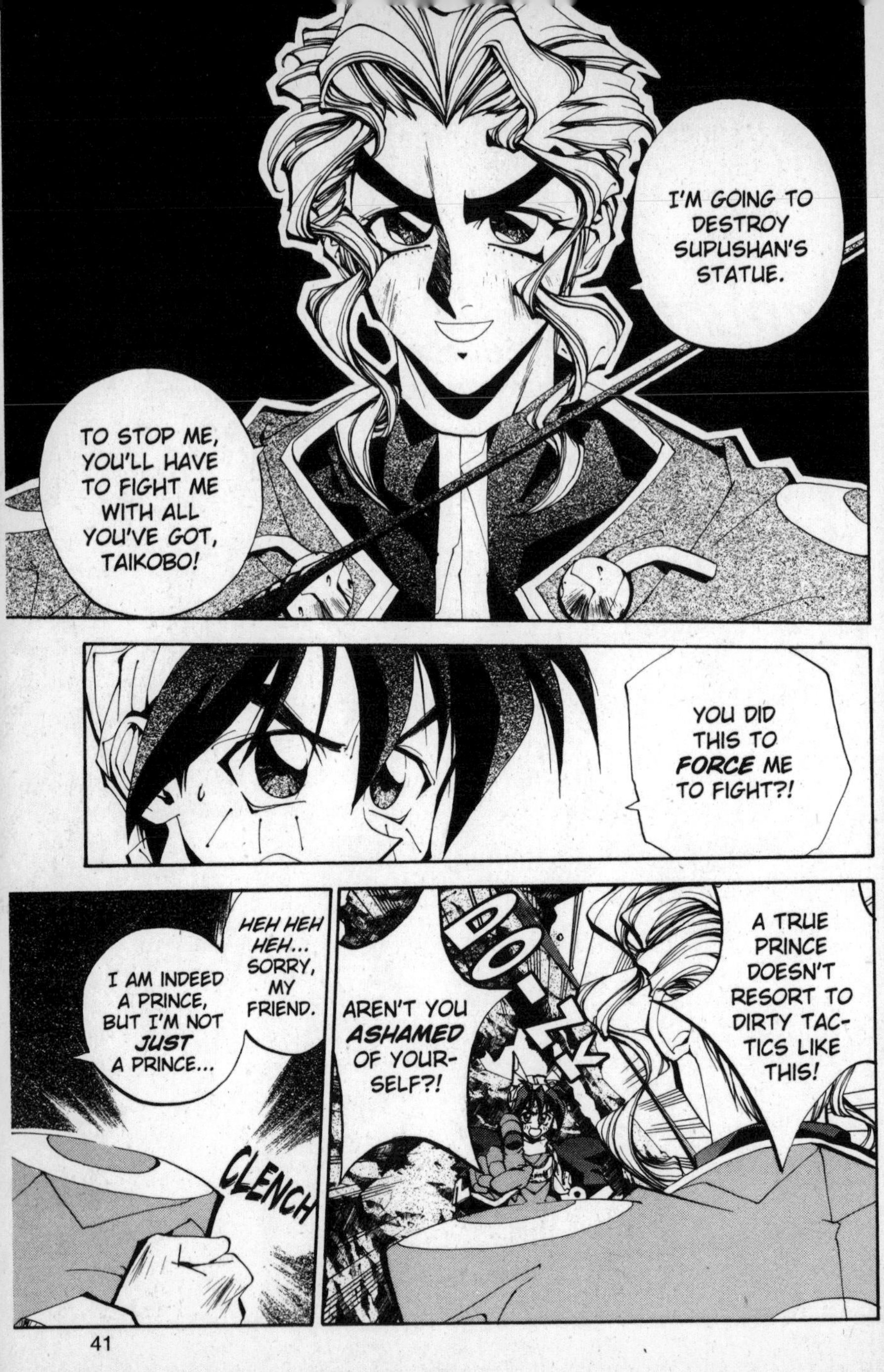
I'M GOING TO DESTROY SUPUSHAN'S STATUE.
TO STOP ME, YOU'LL HAVE TO FIGHT ME WITH ALL YOU'VE GOT, TAIKOBO!
YOU DID THIS TO *FORCE* ME TO FIGHT?!
A TRUE PRINCE DOESN'T RESORT TO DIRTY TAC-TICS LIKE THIS!
DO-Z
AREN'T YOU *ASHAMED* OF YOUR-SELF?!
HEH HEH HEH... SORRY, MY FRIEND.
I AM INDEED A PRINCE, BUT I'M NOT *JUST* A PRINCE...
CLENCH

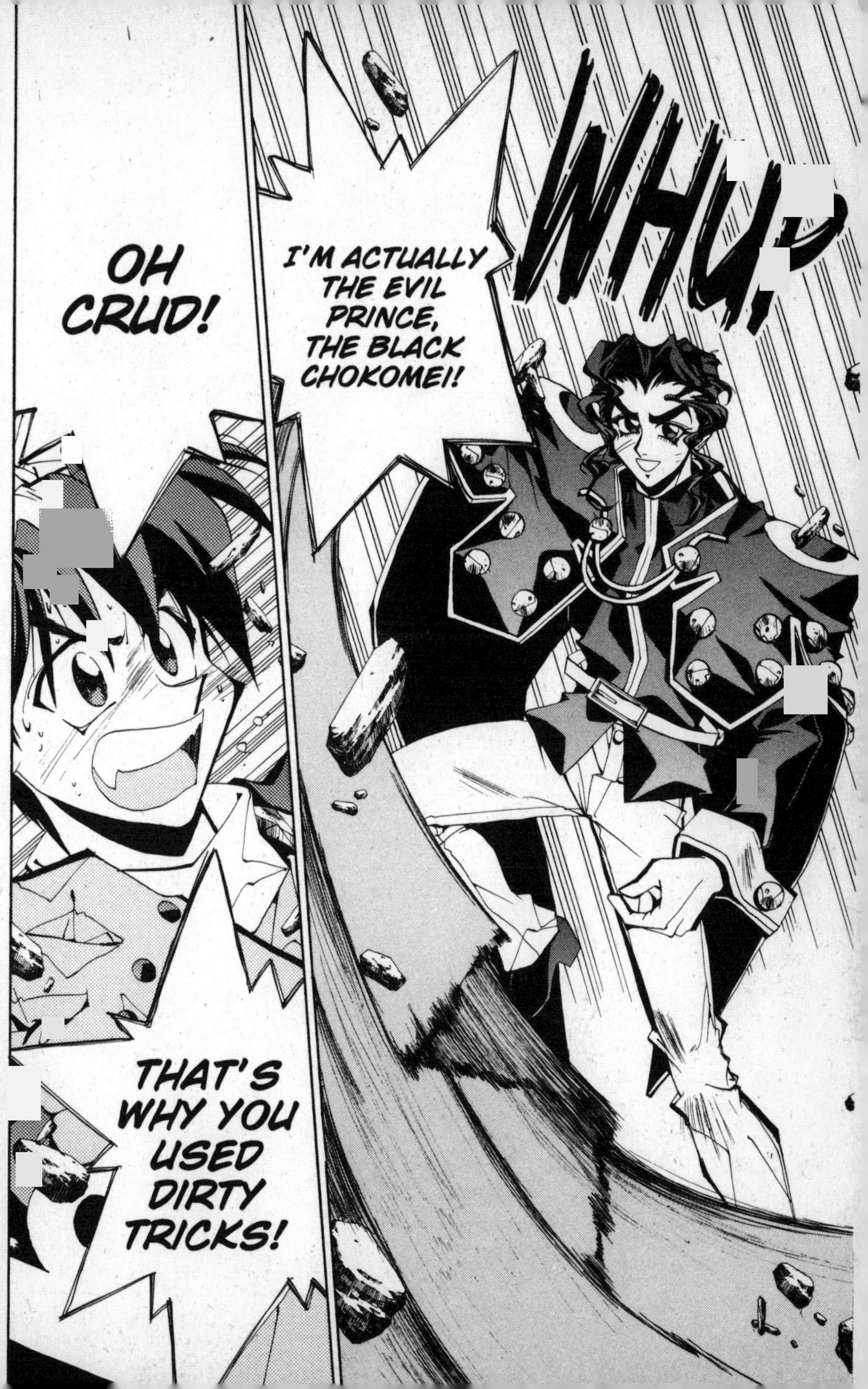
WHUP
I'M ACTUALLY THE EVIL PRINCE, THE BLACK CHOKOMEI!!
OH CRUD!
THAT'S WHY YOU USED DIRTY TRICKS!

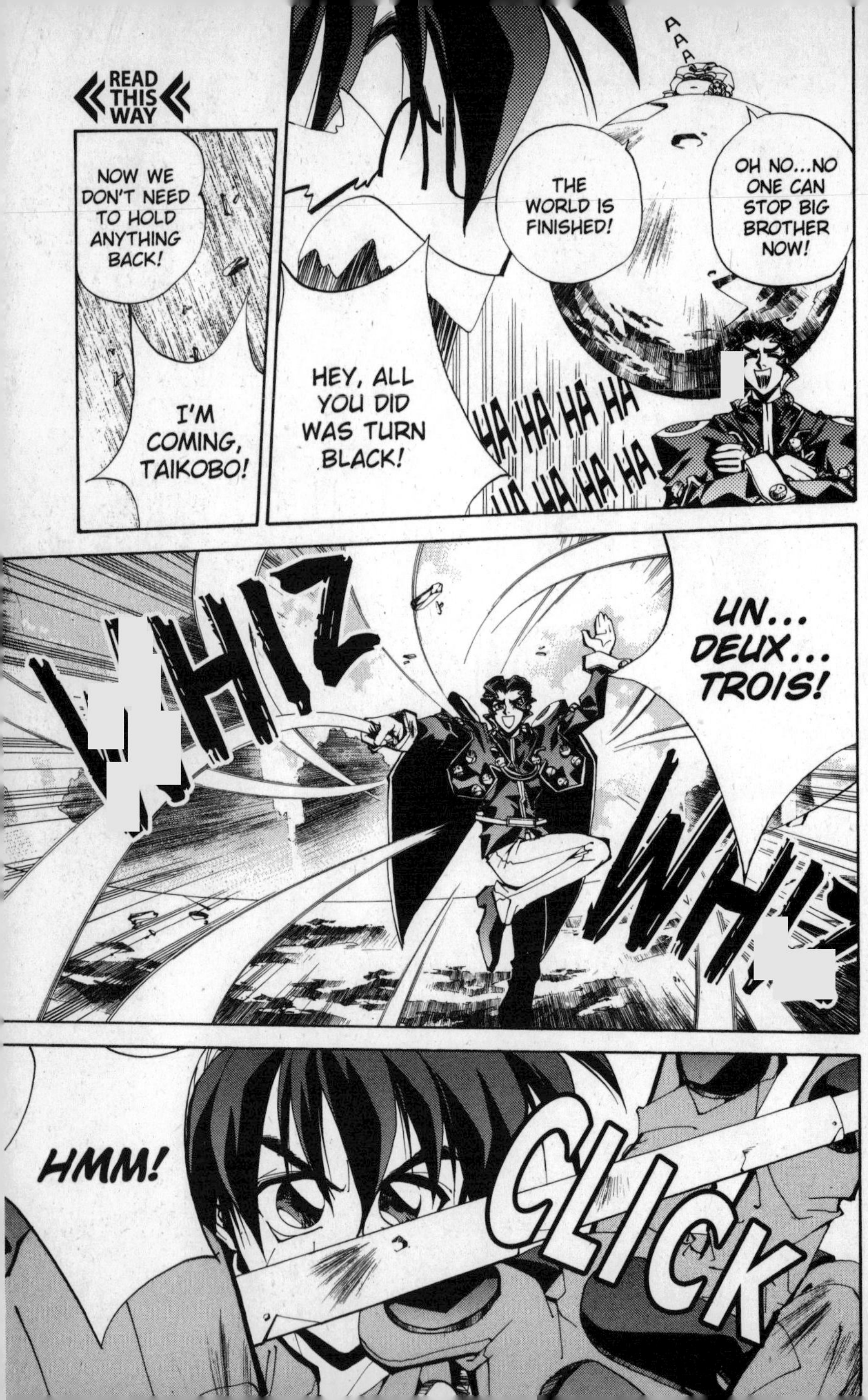
READ THIS WAY
AAA
OH NO...NO ONE CAN STOP BIG BROTHER NOW!
THE WORLD IS FINISHED!
HA HA HA HA
HA HA HA HA
HEY, ALL YOU DID WAS TURN BLACK!
NOW WE DON'T NEED TO HOLD ANYTHING BACK!
I'M COMING, TAIKOBO!
UN... DEUX... TROIS!
WHIZ
CLICK
HMM!

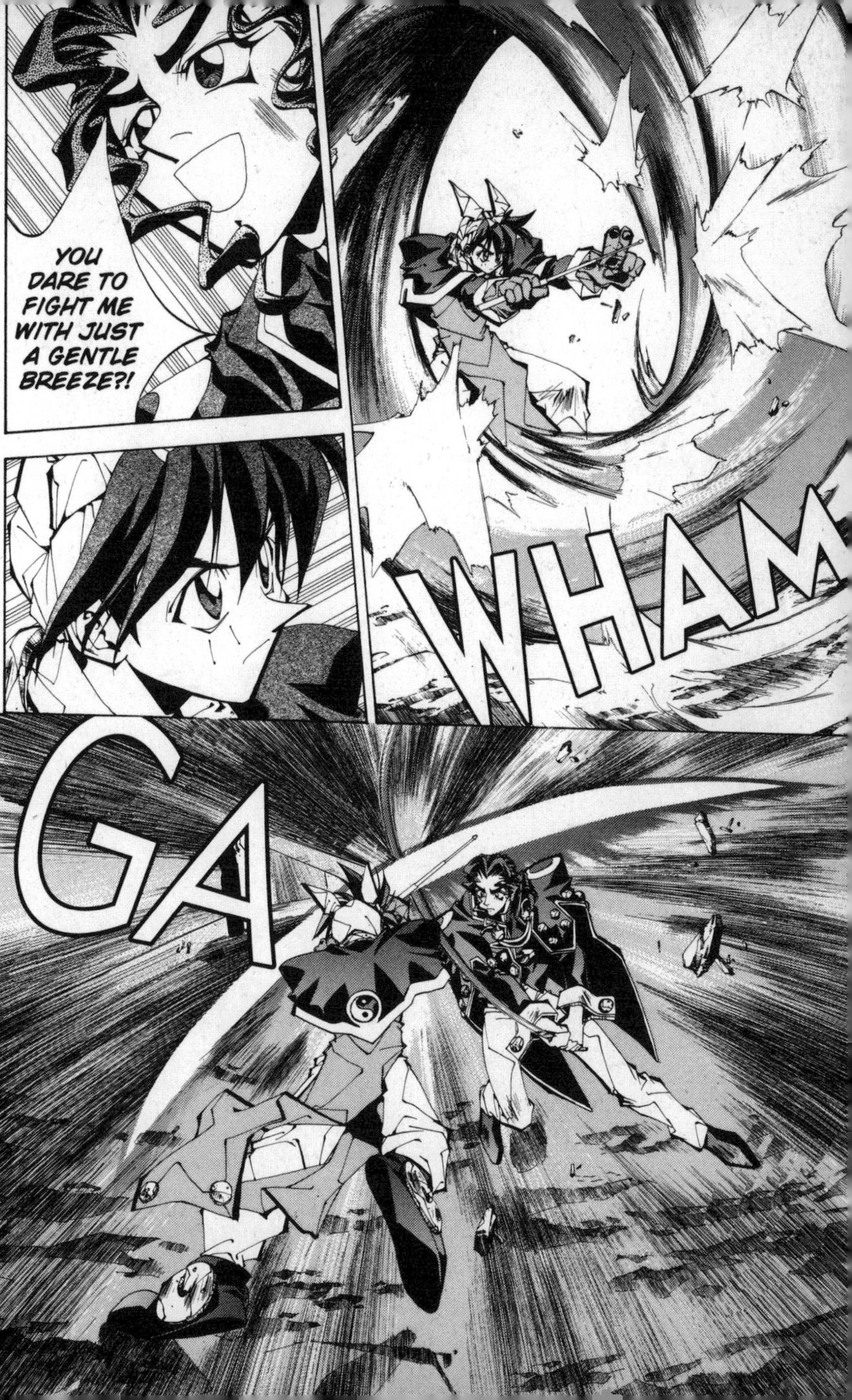
WHAM
YOU DARE TO FIGHT ME WITH JUST A GENTLE BREEZE?!
GA

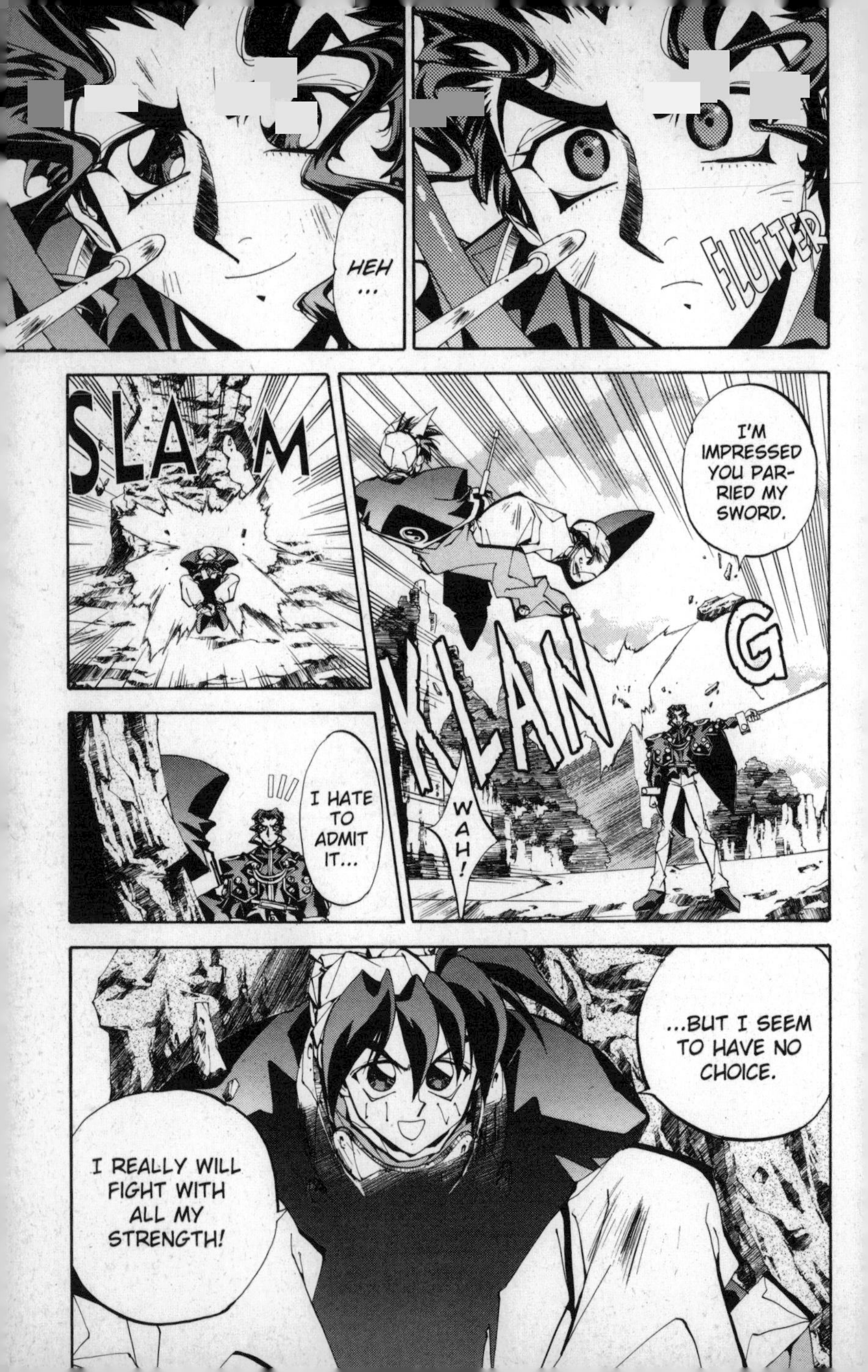
FLUTTER
HEH ...
I'M IMPRESSED YOU PAR-RIED MY SWORD.
KLANG
WAH!
SLAM
I HATE TO ADMIT IT...
...BUT I SEEM TO HAVE NO CHOICE.
I REALLY WILL FIGHT WITH ALL MY STRENGTH!

封神演義

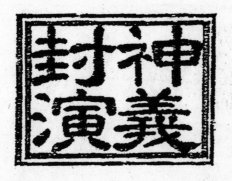

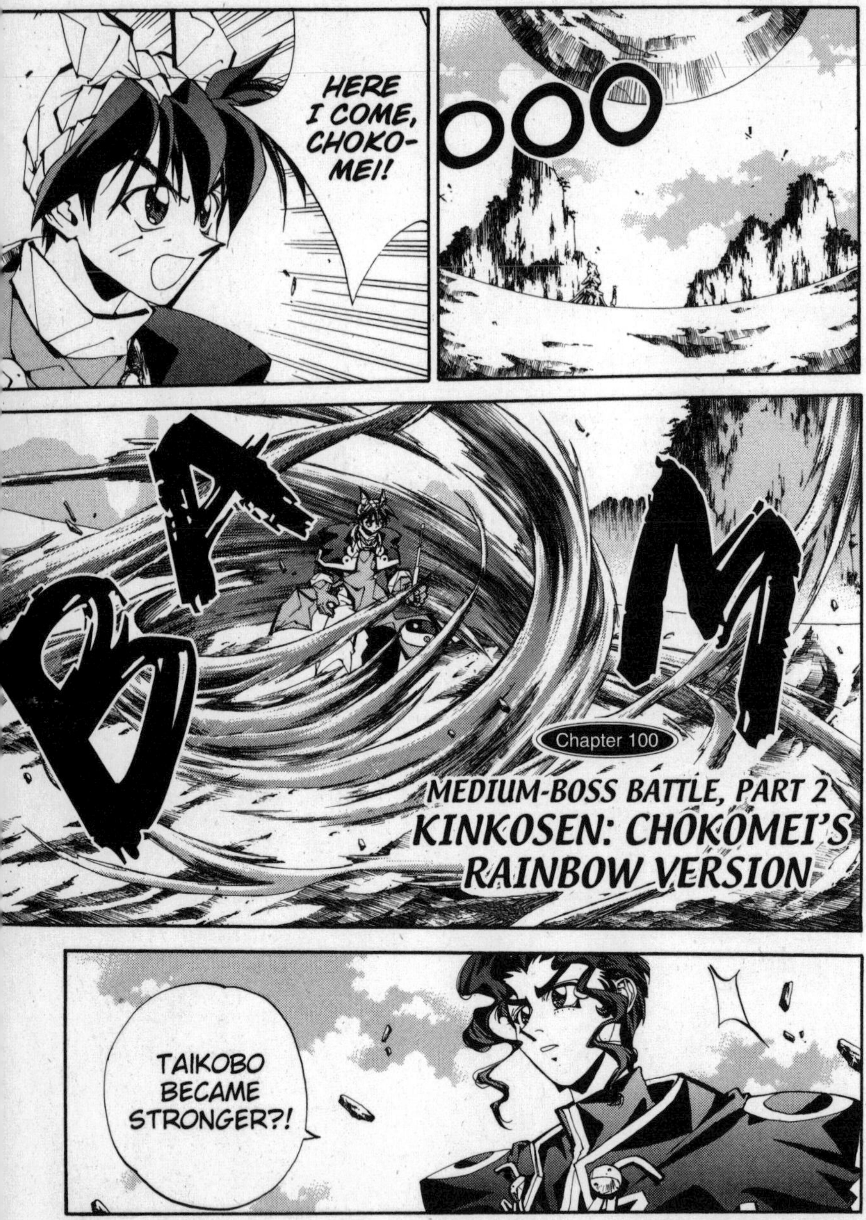
OOO
HERE I COME, CHOKO-MEI!
BAM
Chapter 100
MEDIUM-BOSS BATTLE, PART 2
KINKOSEN: CHOKOMEI'S RAINBOW VERSION
TAIKOBO BECAME STRONGER?!

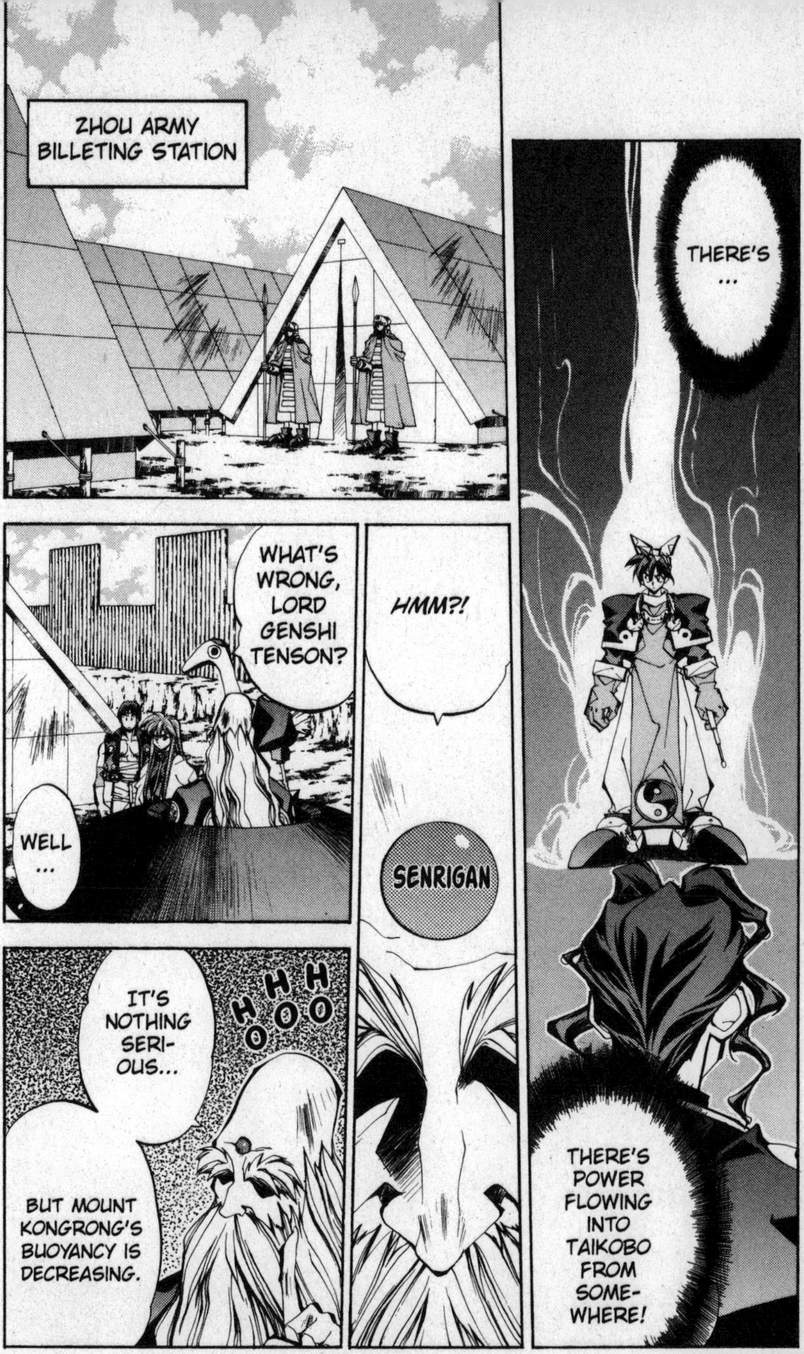
ZHOU ARMY BILLETING STATION
HMM?!
WHAT'S WRONG, LORD GENSHI TENSON?
WELL ...
SENRIGAN
HOHOHO
IT'S NOTHING SERI-OUS...
BUT MOUNT KONGRONG'S BUOYANCY IS DECREASING.
THERE'S ...
THERE'S POWER FLOWING INTO TAIKOBO FROM SOME-WHERE!

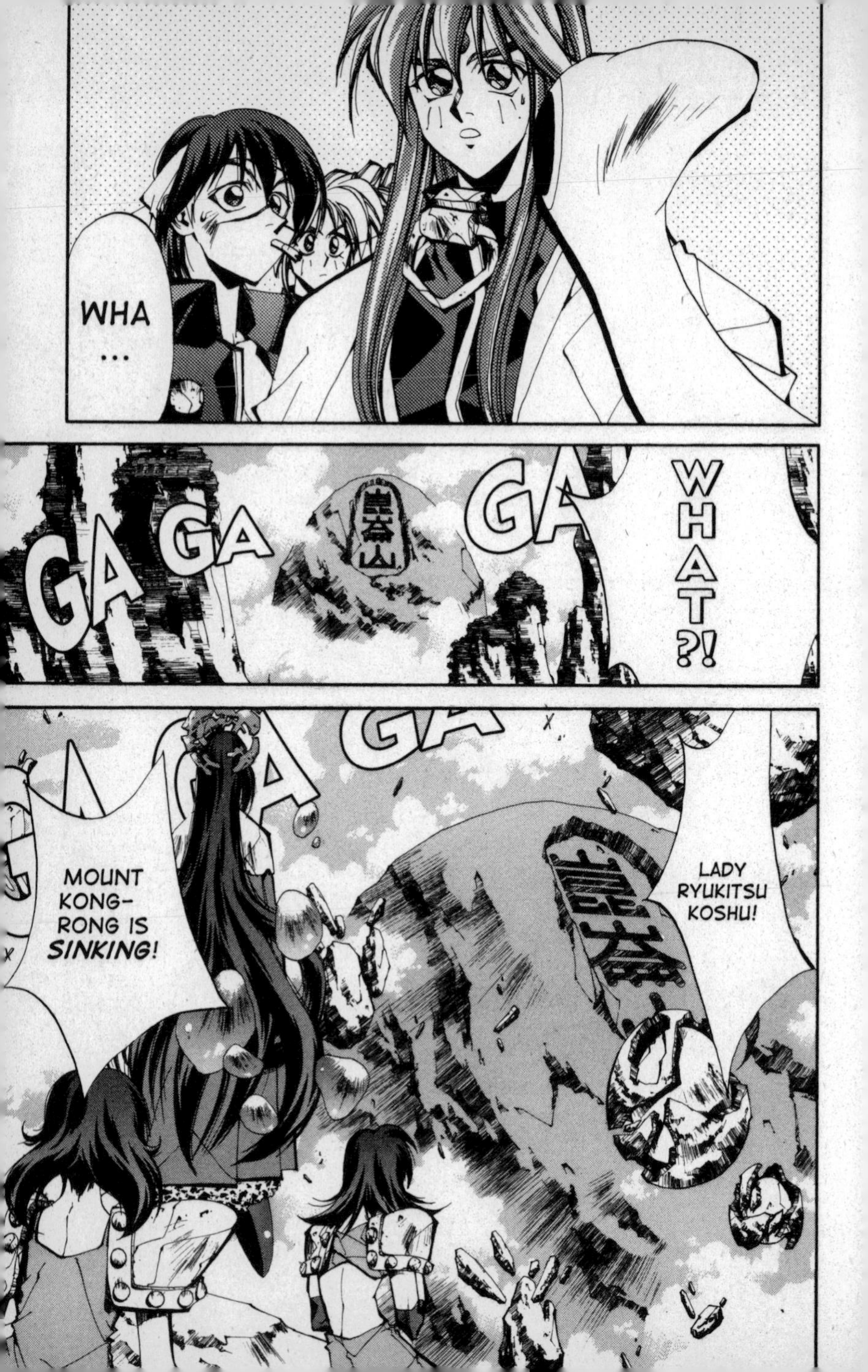
WHA ...
WHAT?!
GA GA
GA GA
LADY RYUKITSU KOSHU!
GA GA GA
MOUNT KONG-RONG IS SINKING!

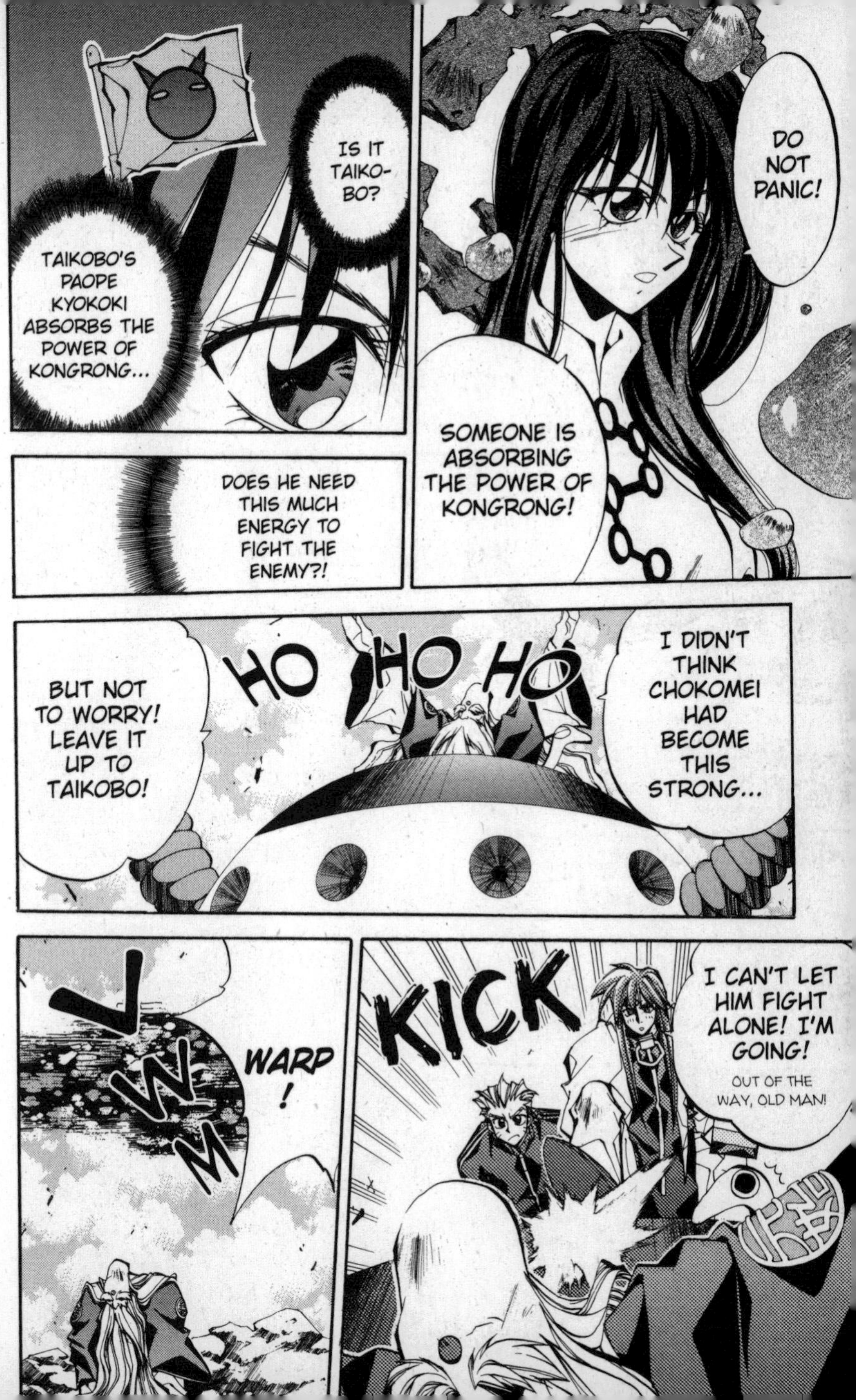
DO NOT PANIC!
SOMEONE IS ABSORBING THE POWER OF KONGRONG!
IS IT TAIKO-BO?
TAIKOBO'S PAOPE KYOKOKI ABSORBS THE POWER OF KONGRONG...
DOES HE NEED THIS MUCH ENERGY TO FIGHT THE ENEMY?!
I DIDN'T THINK CHOKOMEI HAD BECOME THIS STRONG...
HO HO HO
BUT NOT TO WORRY! LEAVE IT UP TO TAIKOBO!
I CAN'T LET HIM FIGHT ALONE! I'M GOING!
OUT OF THE WAY, OLD MAN!
KICK
WARP!
VWM

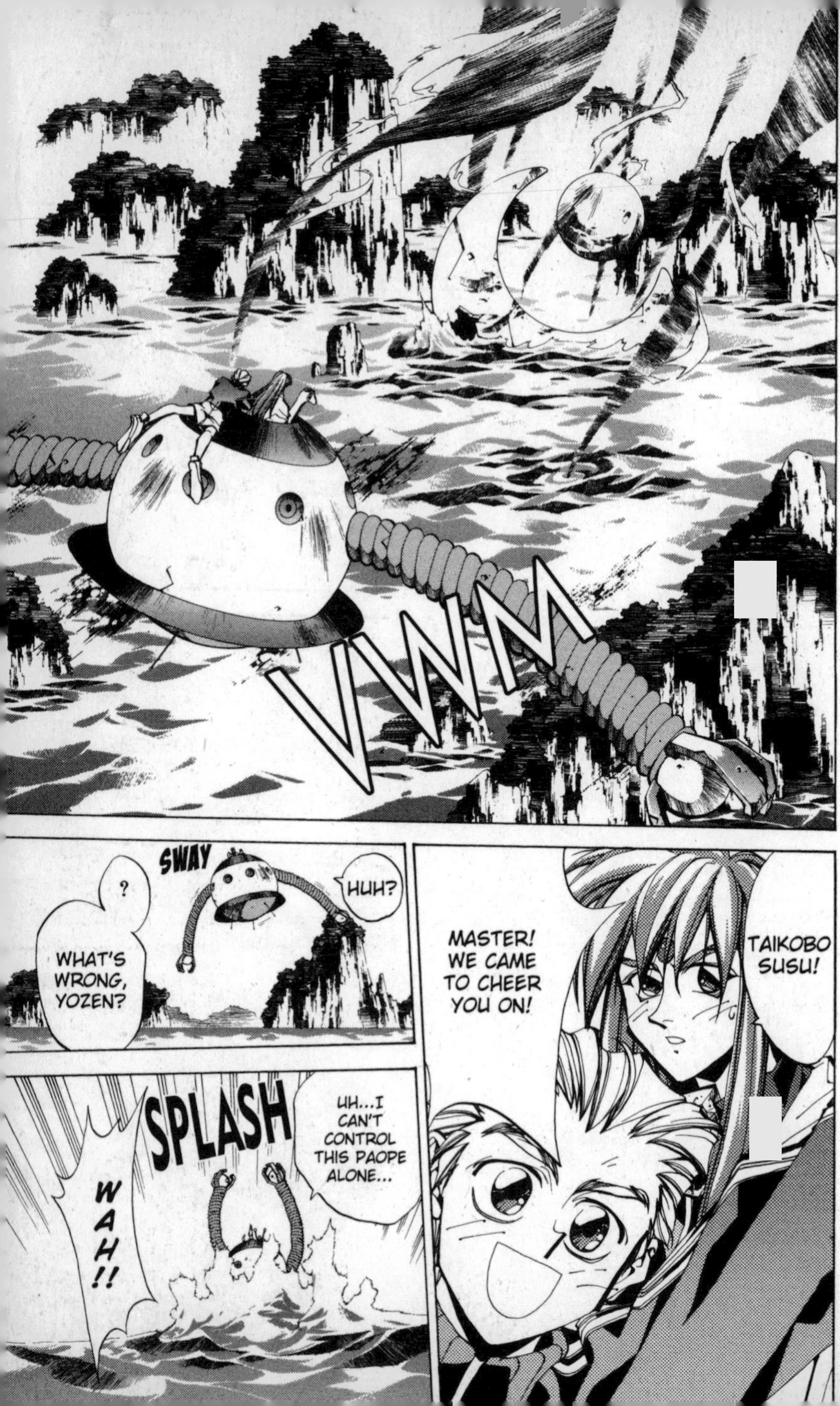
VWWM
TAIKOBO SUSU!
MASTER! WE CAME TO CHEER YOU ON!
SWAY
HUH?
?
WHAT'S WRONG, YOZEN?
SPLASH
UH...I CAN'T CONTROL THIS PAOPE ALONE...
WAH!!

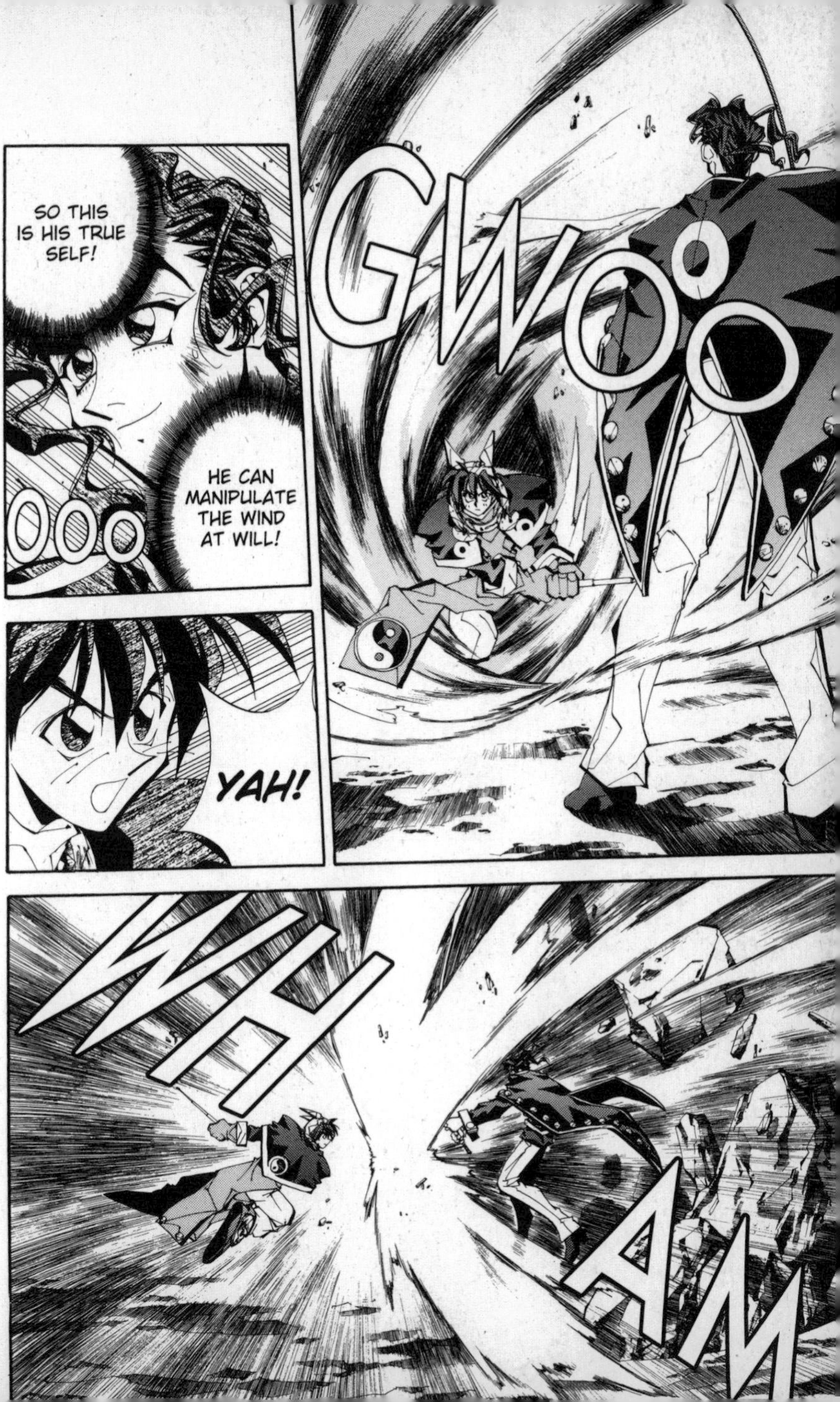
GWOOO
SO THIS IS HIS TRUE SELF!
HE CAN MANIPULATE THE WIND AT WILL!
OOO
YAH!
WH
AM

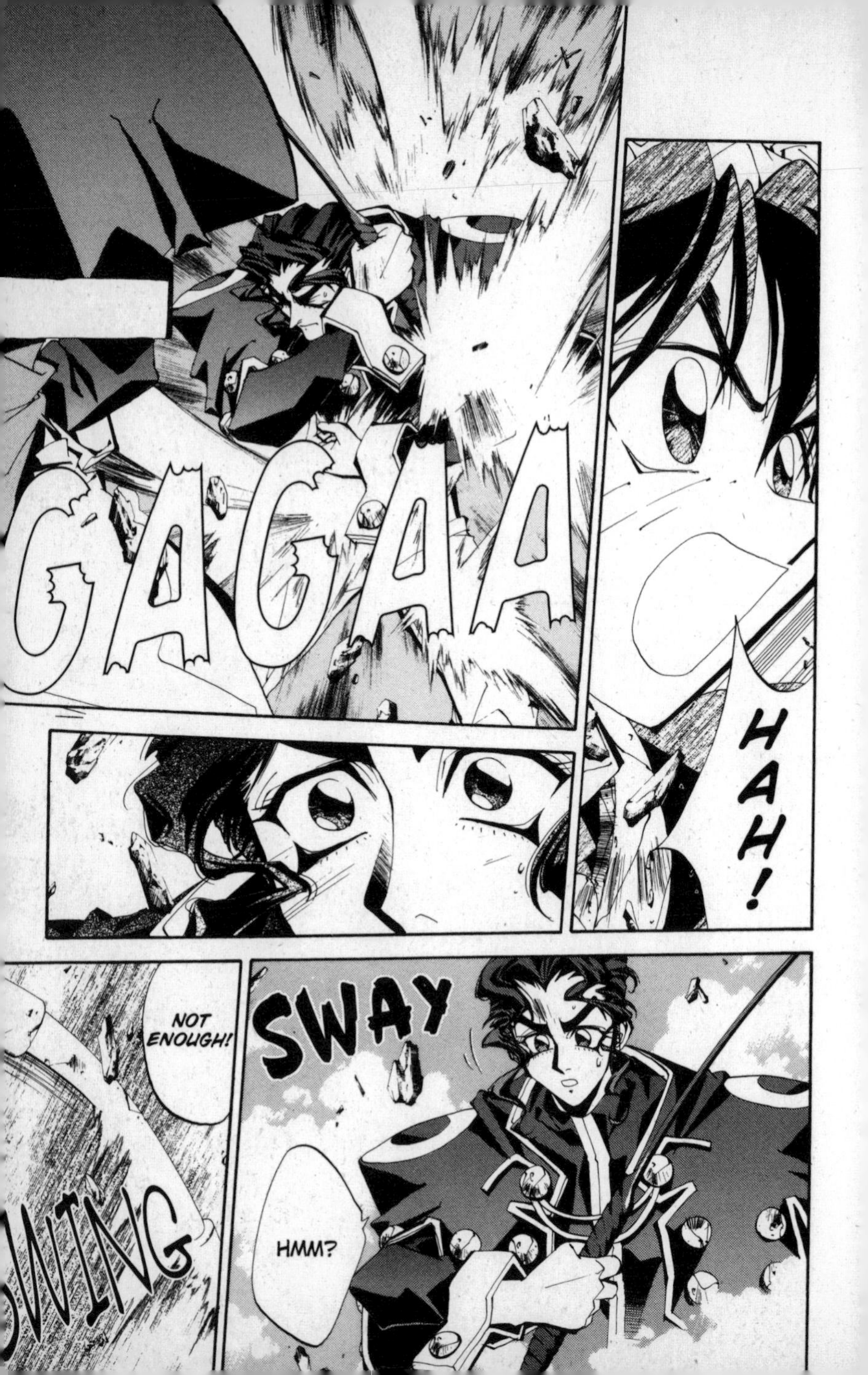
HAH!
GAGAA
SWAY
HMM?
NOT ENOUGH!
SWING

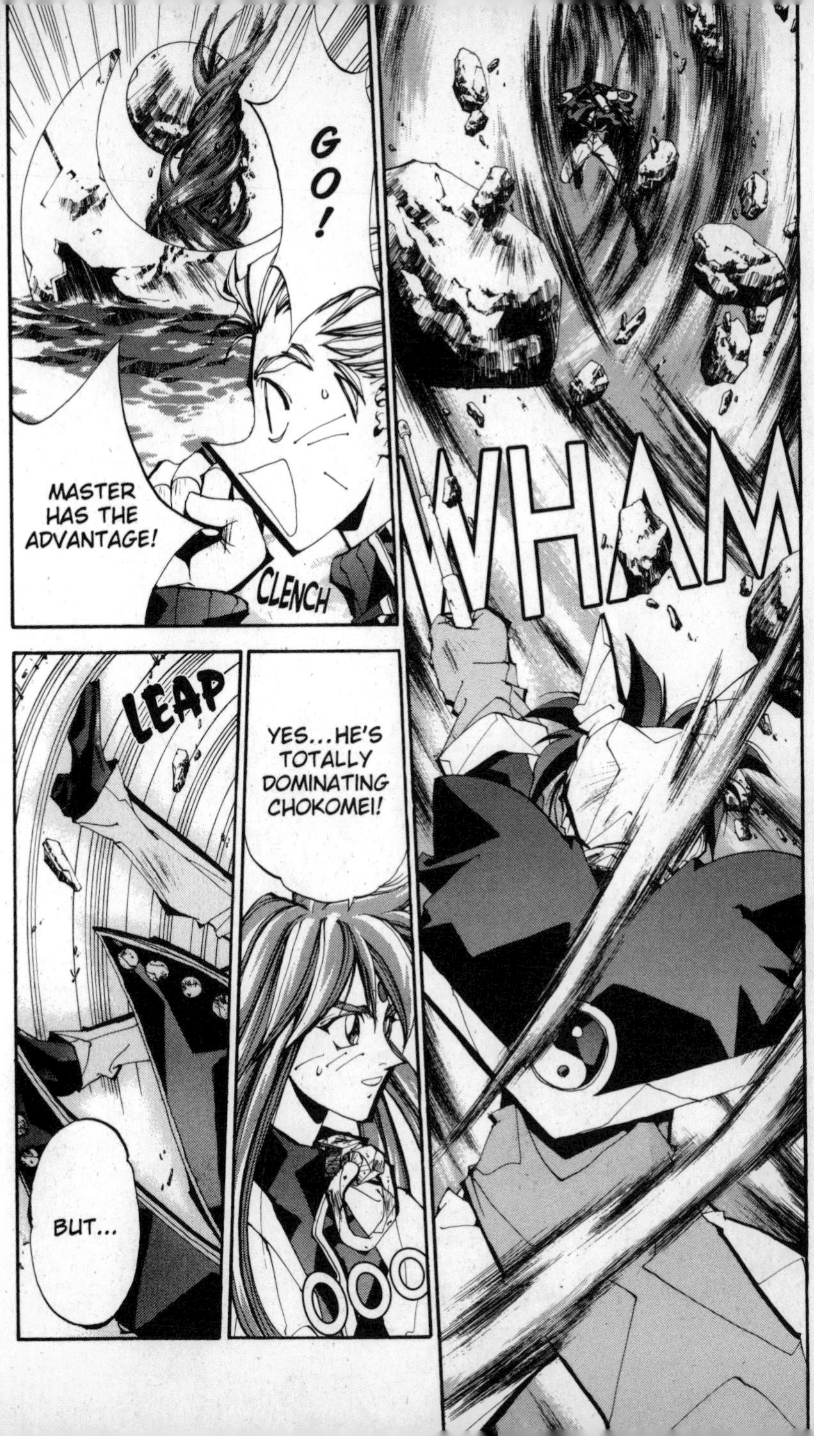
WHAM
GO!
MASTER HAS THE ADVANTAGE!
CLENCH
YES...HE'S TOTALLY DOMINATING CHOKOMEI!
LEAP
BUT...

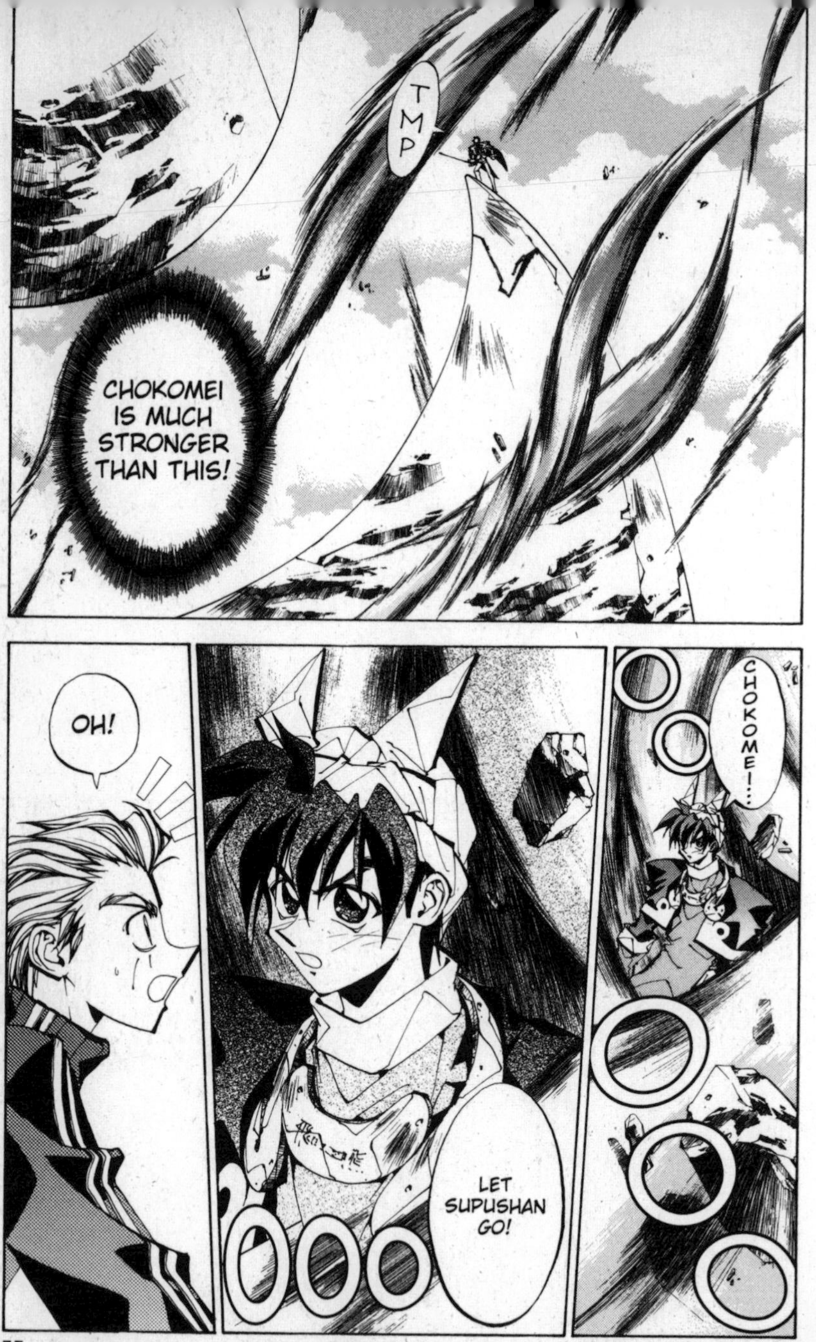
TMP
CHOKOMEI IS MUCH STRONGER THAN THIS!
CHOKOMEI...
LET SUPUSHAN GO!
OH!

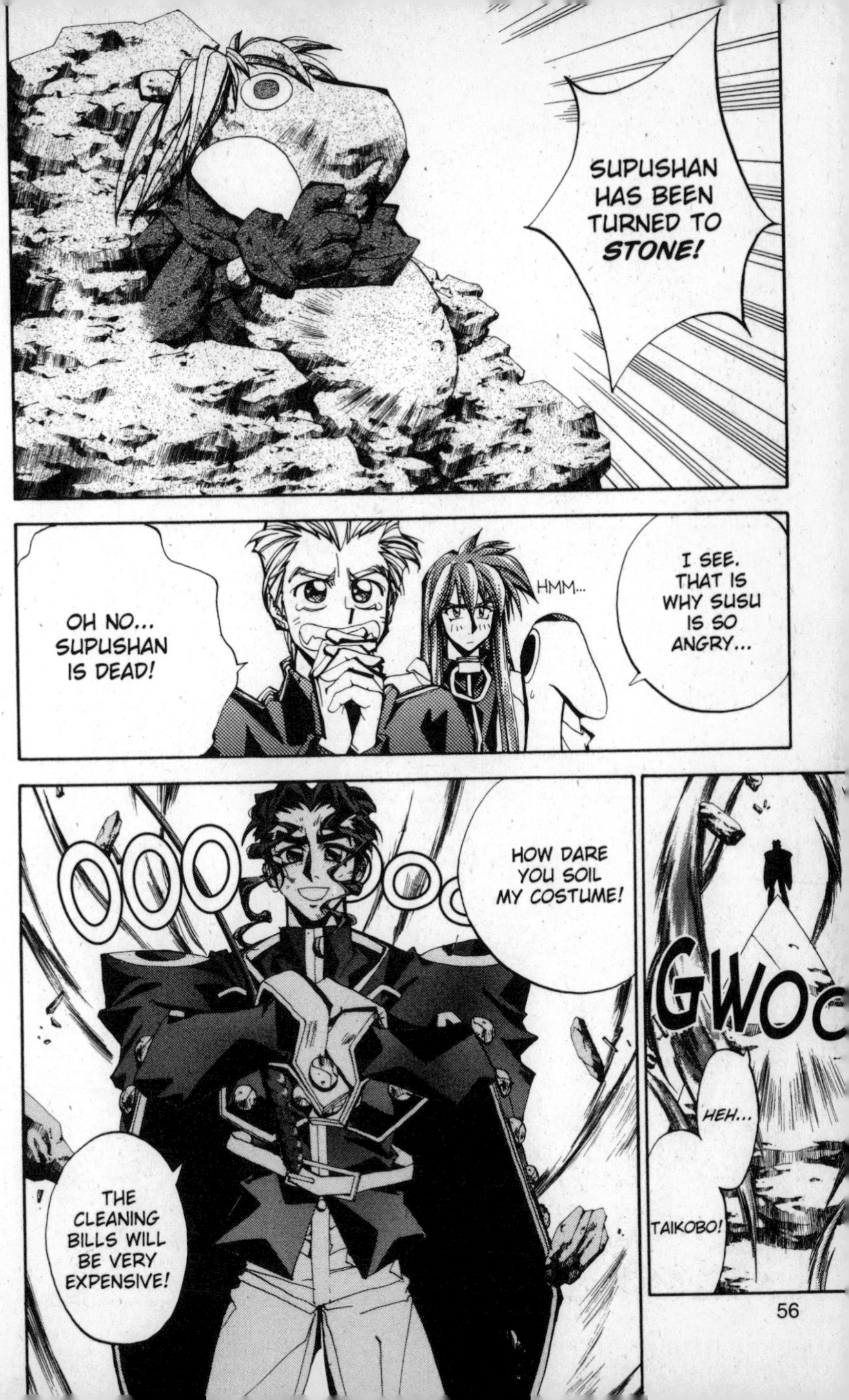
SUPUSHAN HAS BEEN TURNED TO STONE!
I SEE. THAT IS WHY SUSU IS SO ANGRY...
HMM...
OH NO... SUPUSHAN IS DEAD!
GWO
HEH...
TAIKOBO!
HOW DARE YOU SOIL MY COSTUME!
THE CLEANING BILLS WILL BE VERY EXPENSIVE!

READ THIS WAY

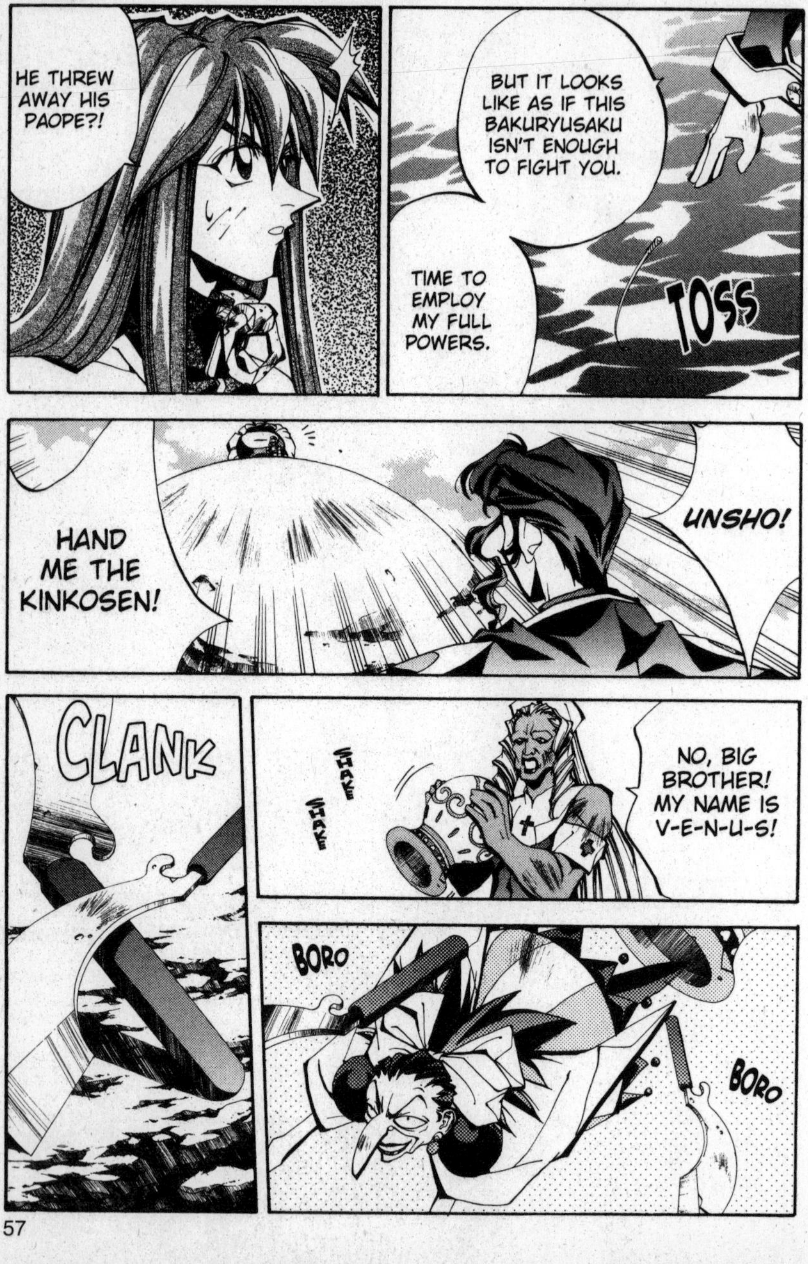
BUT IT LOOKS LIKE AS IF THIS BAKURYUSAKU ISN'T ENOUGH TO FIGHT YOU.
TIME TO EMPLOY MY FULL POWERS.
TOSS
HE THREW AWAY HIS PAOPE?!
UNSHO!
HAND ME THE KINKOSEN!
NO, BIG BROTHER! MY NAME IS V-E-N-U-S!
SHAKE
SHAKE
BORO
BORO
CLANK

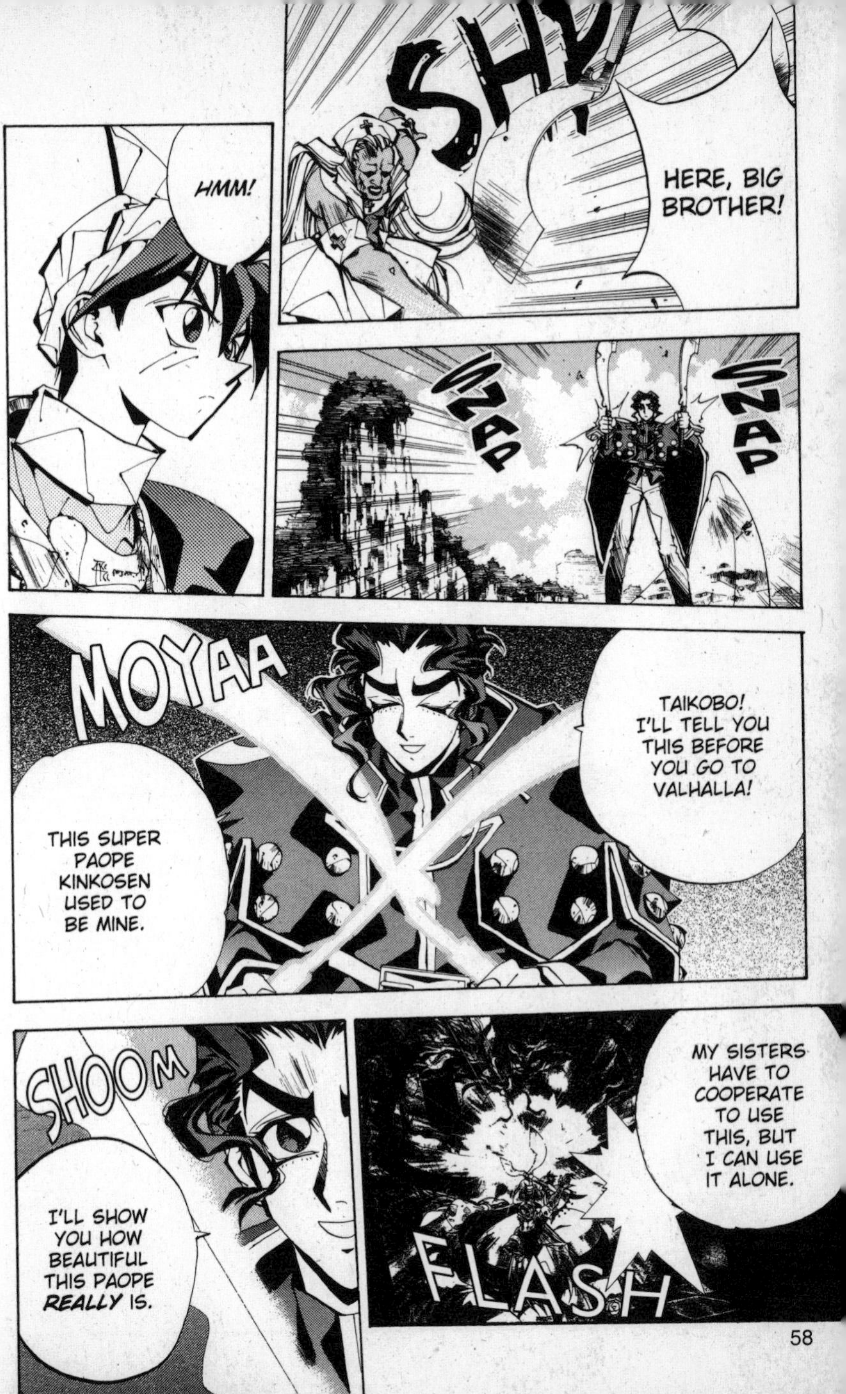
SHY
HERE, BIG BROTHER!
SNAP
SNAP
HMM!
TAIKOBO! I'LL TELL YOU THIS BEFORE YOU GO TO VALHALLA!
MOYAA
THIS SUPER PAOPE KINKOSEN USED TO BE MINE.
MY SISTERS HAVE TO COOPERATE TO USE THIS, BUT I CAN USE IT ALONE.
FLASH
SHOOM
I'LL SHOW YOU HOW BEAUTIFUL THIS PAOPE *REALLY* IS.

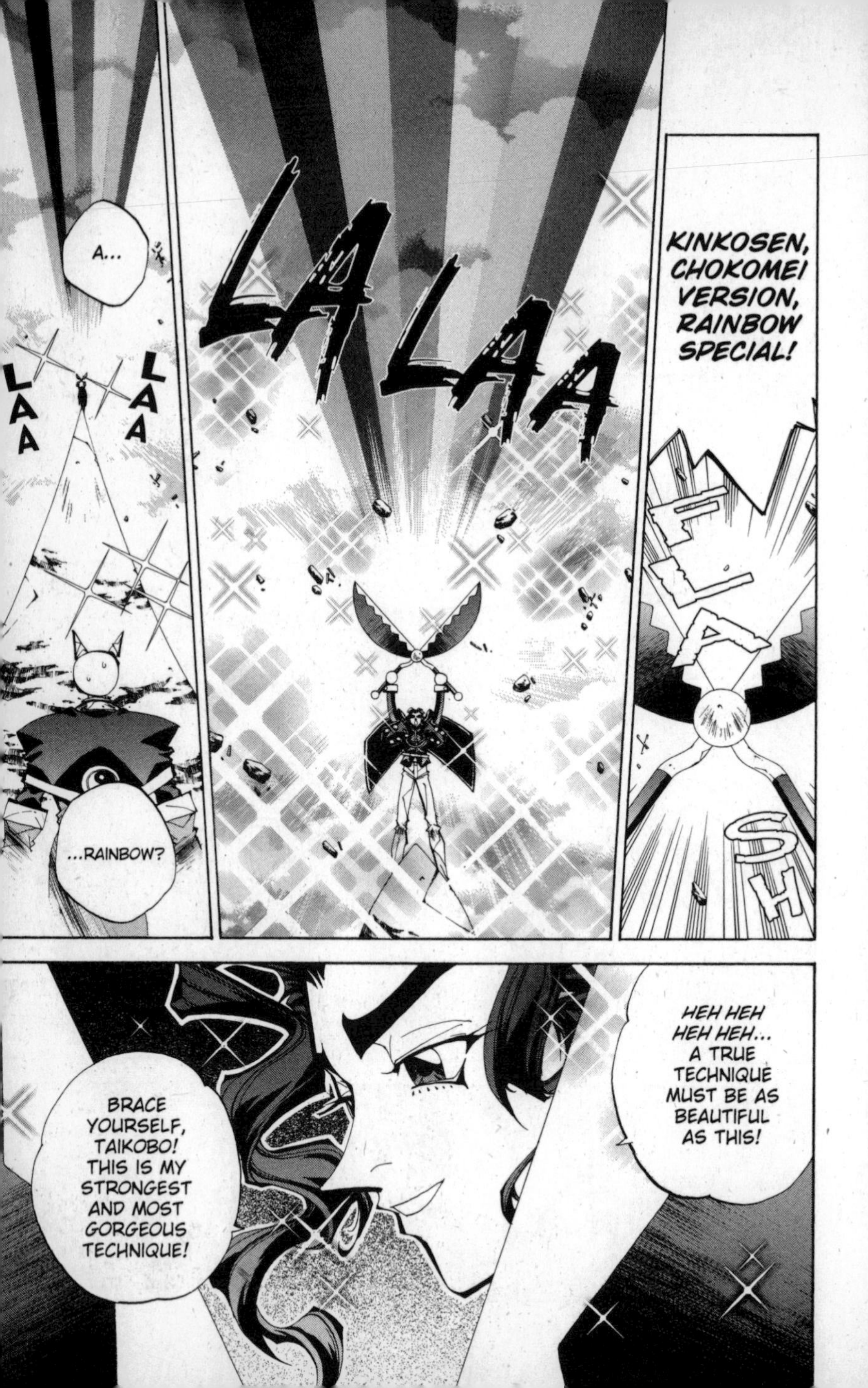
KINKOSEN, CHOKOMEI VERSION, RAINBOW SPECIAL!
FLASH
LALAA
A...
LAA
LAA
...RAINBOW?
HEH HEH HEH HEH... A TRUE TECHNIQUE MUST BE AS BEAUTIFUL AS THIS!
BRACE YOURSELF, TAIKOBO! THIS IS MY STRONGEST AND MOST GORGEOUS TECHNIQUE!

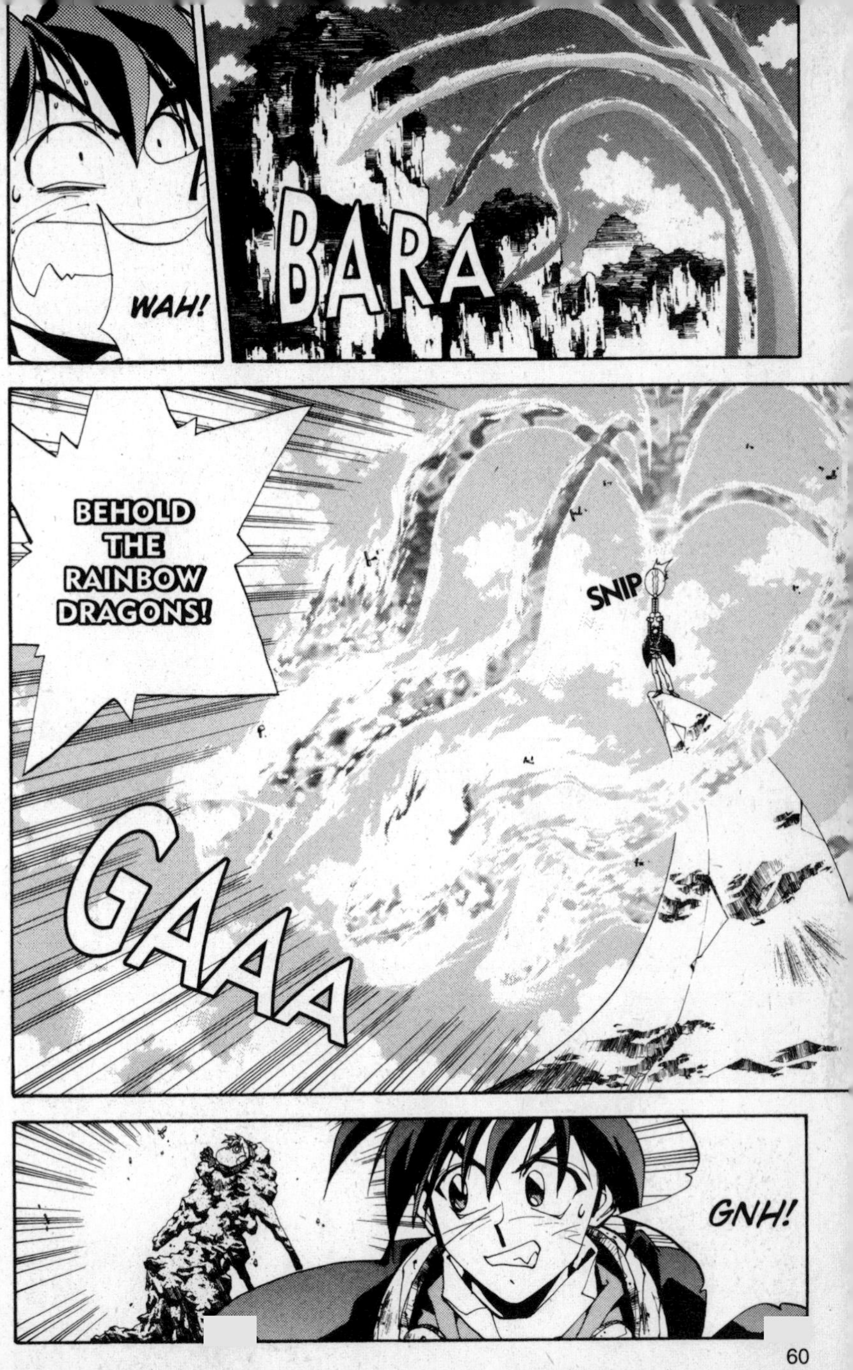
BARA
WAH!
BEHOLD THE RAINBOW DRAGONS!
SNIP
GAAA
GNH!

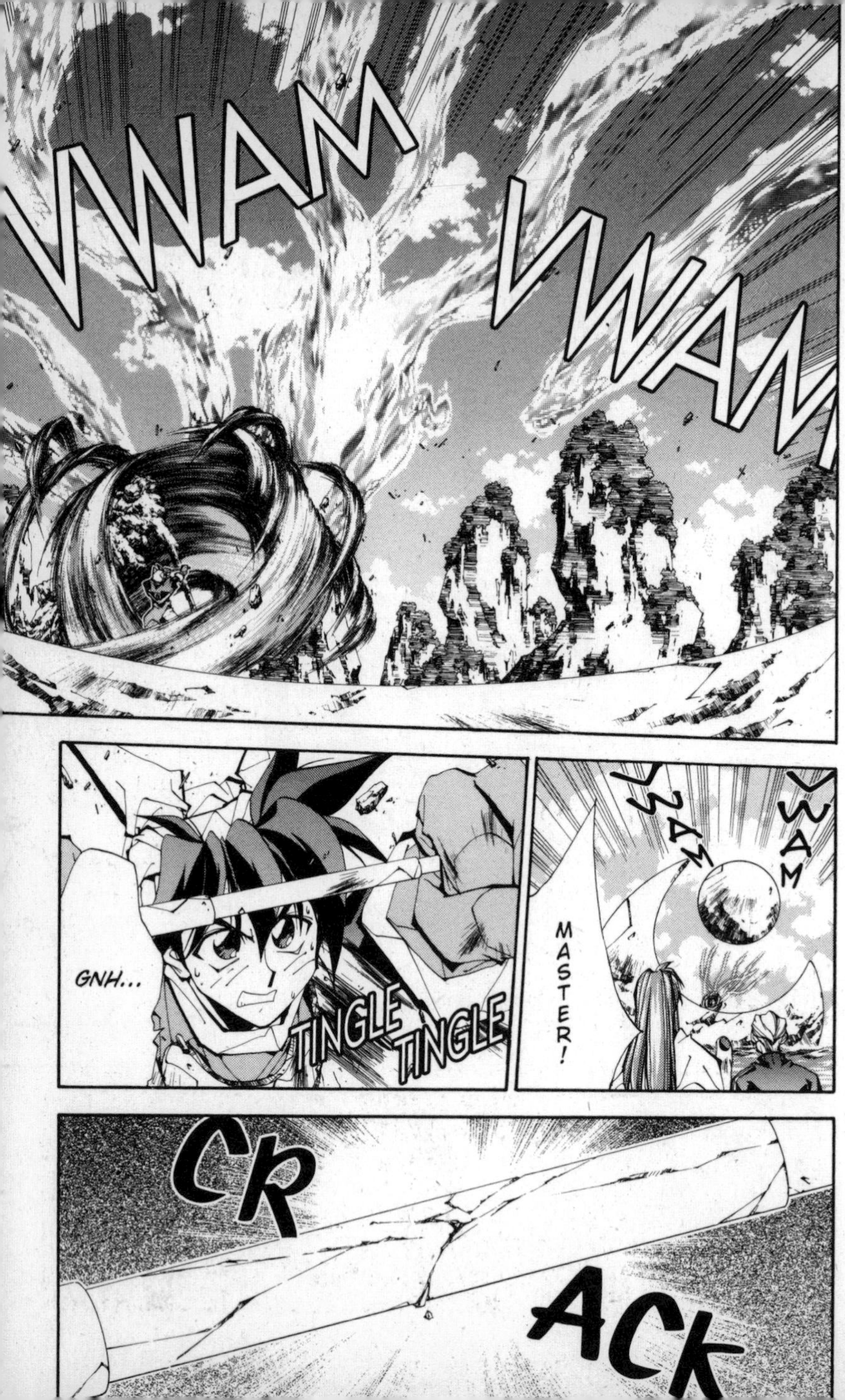
WWAM
WWAM
WWAM
WWAM
MASTER!
GNH...
TINGLE
TINGLE
CR
ACK

封神演義

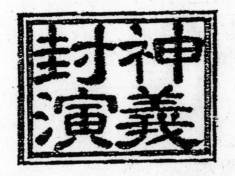

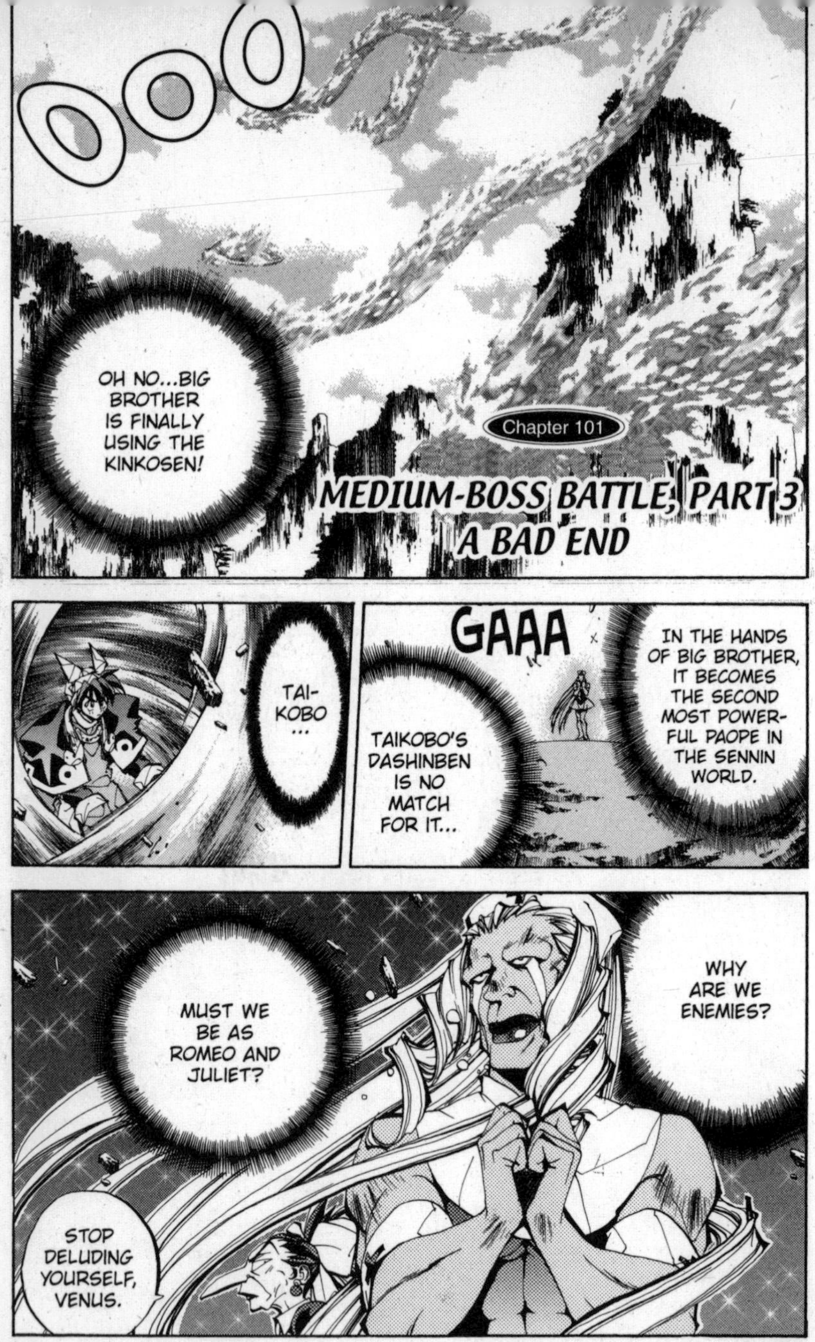
OOO
OH NO...BIG BROTHER IS FINALLY USING THE KINKOSEN!
Chapter 101
MEDIUM-BOSS BATTLE, PART 3
A BAD END
GAAA
IN THE HANDS OF BIG BROTHER, IT BECOMES THE SECOND MOST POWER-FUL PAOPE IN THE SENNIN WORLD.
TAIKOBO'S DASHINBEN IS NO MATCH FOR IT...
TAI-KOBO...
WHY ARE WE ENEMIES?
MUST WE BE AS ROMEO AND JULIET?
STOP DELUDING YOURSELF, VENUS.

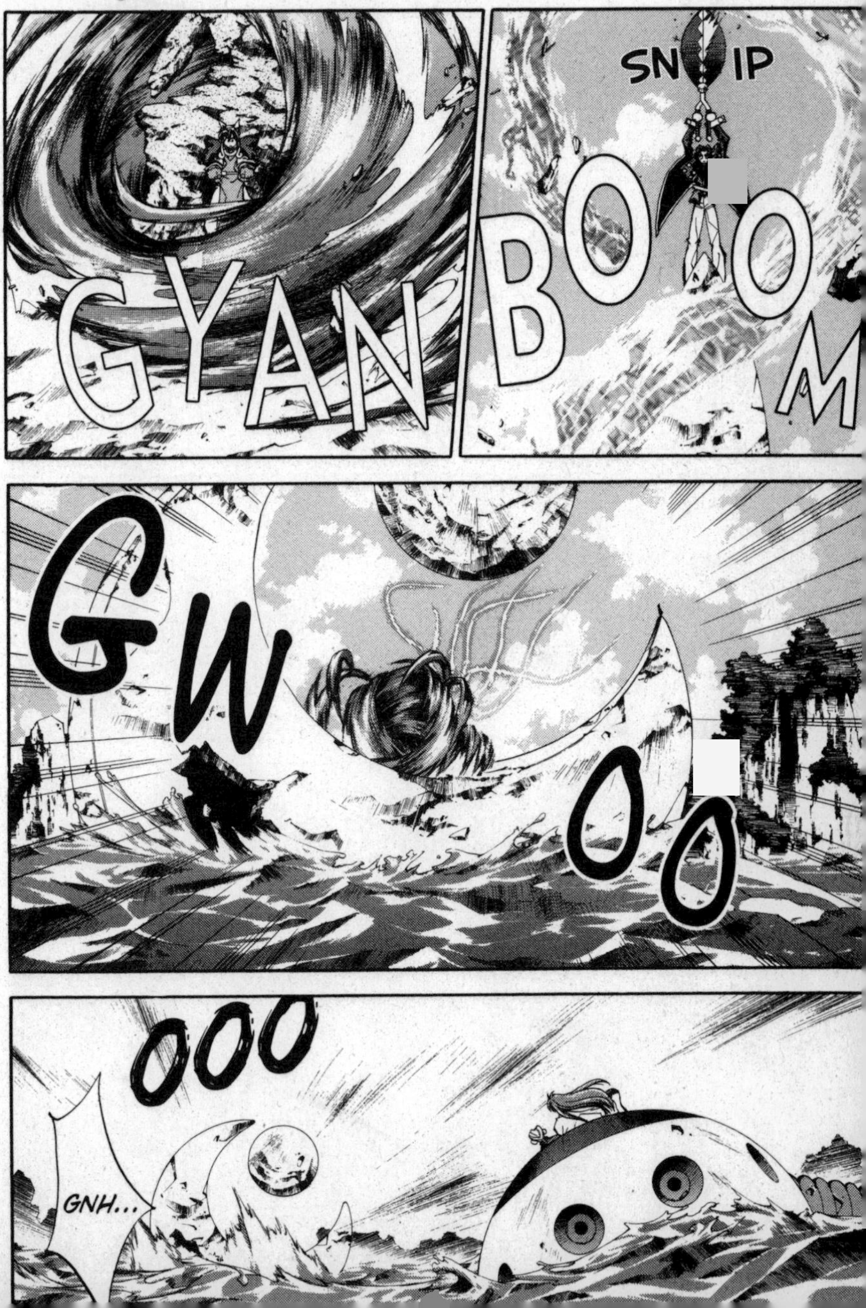
SN IP
BO O M
GYAN
GW OOO
OOOO
GNH...

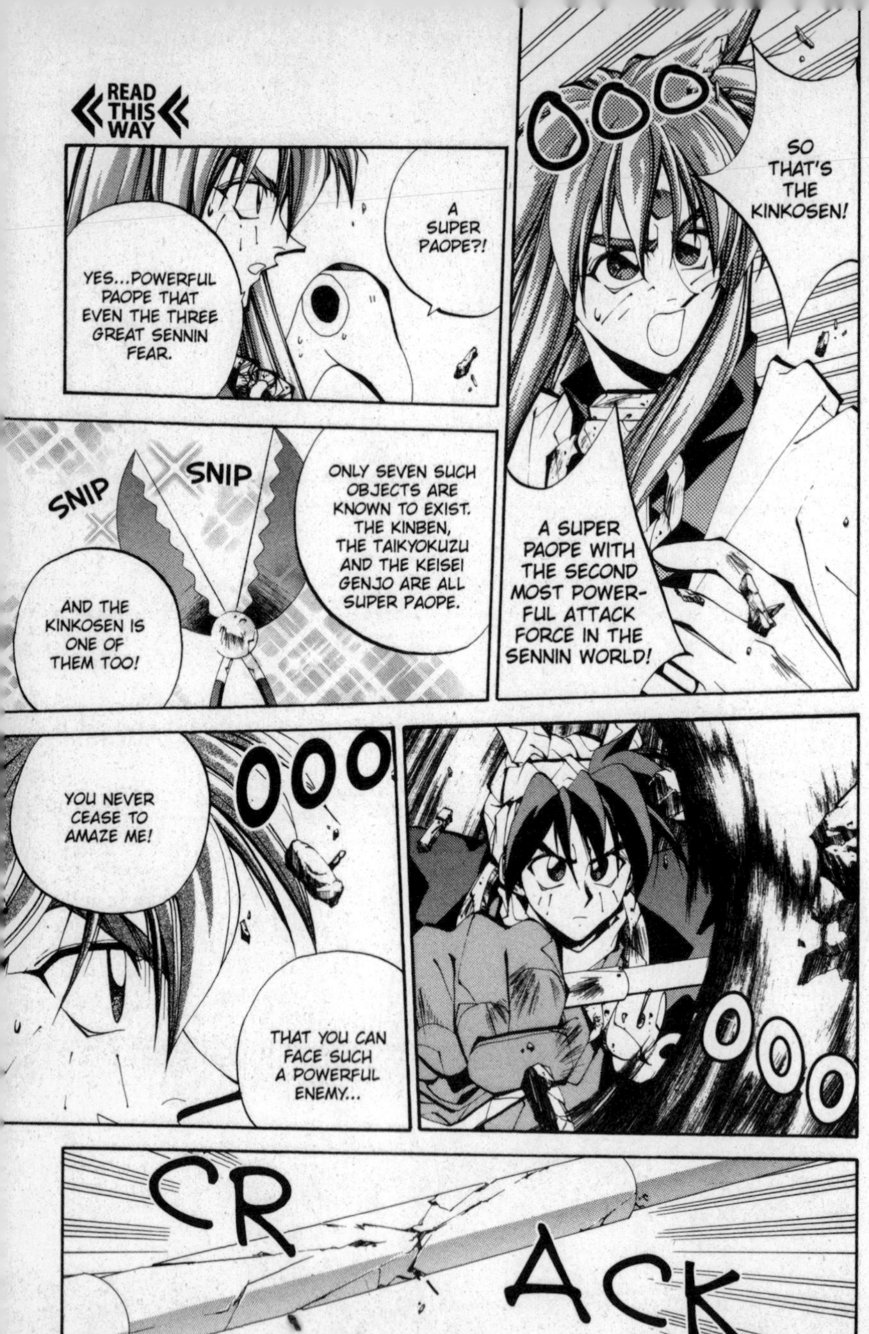

READ THIS WAY
OOO
SO THAT'S THE KINKOSEN!
A SUPER PAOPE WITH THE SECOND MOST POWERFUL ATTACK FORCE IN THE SENNIN WORLD!
A SUPER PAOPE?!
YES...POWERFUL PAOPE THAT EVEN THE THREE GREAT SENNIN FEAR.
ONLY SEVEN SUCH OBJECTS ARE KNOWN TO EXIST. THE KINBEN, THE TAIKYOKUZU AND THE KEISEI GENJO ARE ALL SUPER PAOPE.
SNIP
SNIP
AND THE KINKOSEN IS ONE OF THEM TOO!
OOO
OOO
YOU NEVER CEASE TO AMAZE ME!
THAT YOU CAN FACE SUCH A POWERFUL ENEMY...
CRACK

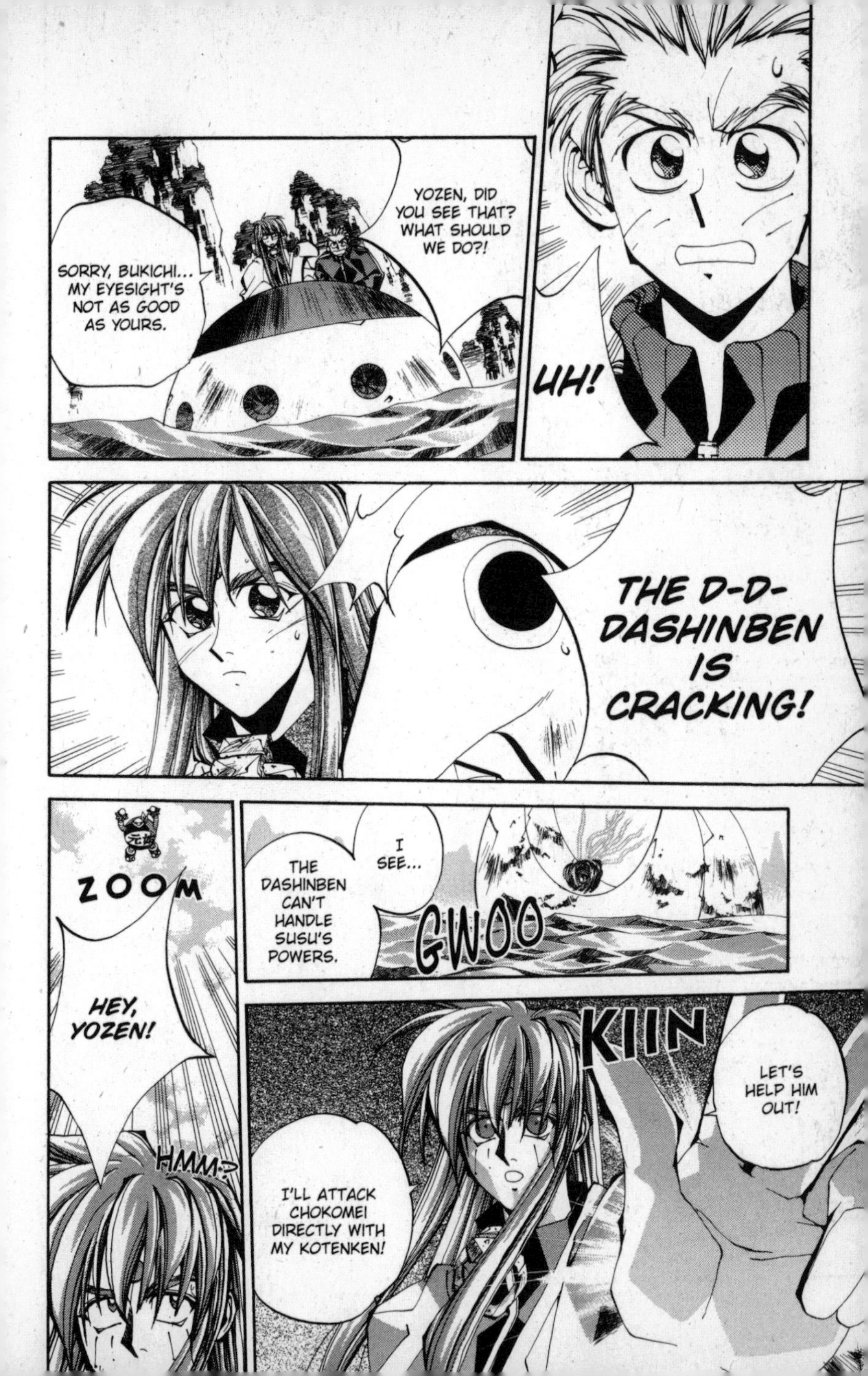
UH!
YOZEN, DID YOU SEE THAT? WHAT SHOULD WE DO?!
SORRY, BUKICHI... MY EYESIGHT'S NOT AS GOOD AS YOURS.
THE D-D-DASHINBEN IS CRACKING!
GWOO
I SEE...
THE DASHINBEN CAN'T HANDLE SUSU'S POWERS.
ZOOM
HEY, YOZEN!
KIIN
LET'S HELP HIM OUT!
I'LL ATTACK CHOKOMEI DIRECTLY WITH MY KOTENKEN!
HMM?

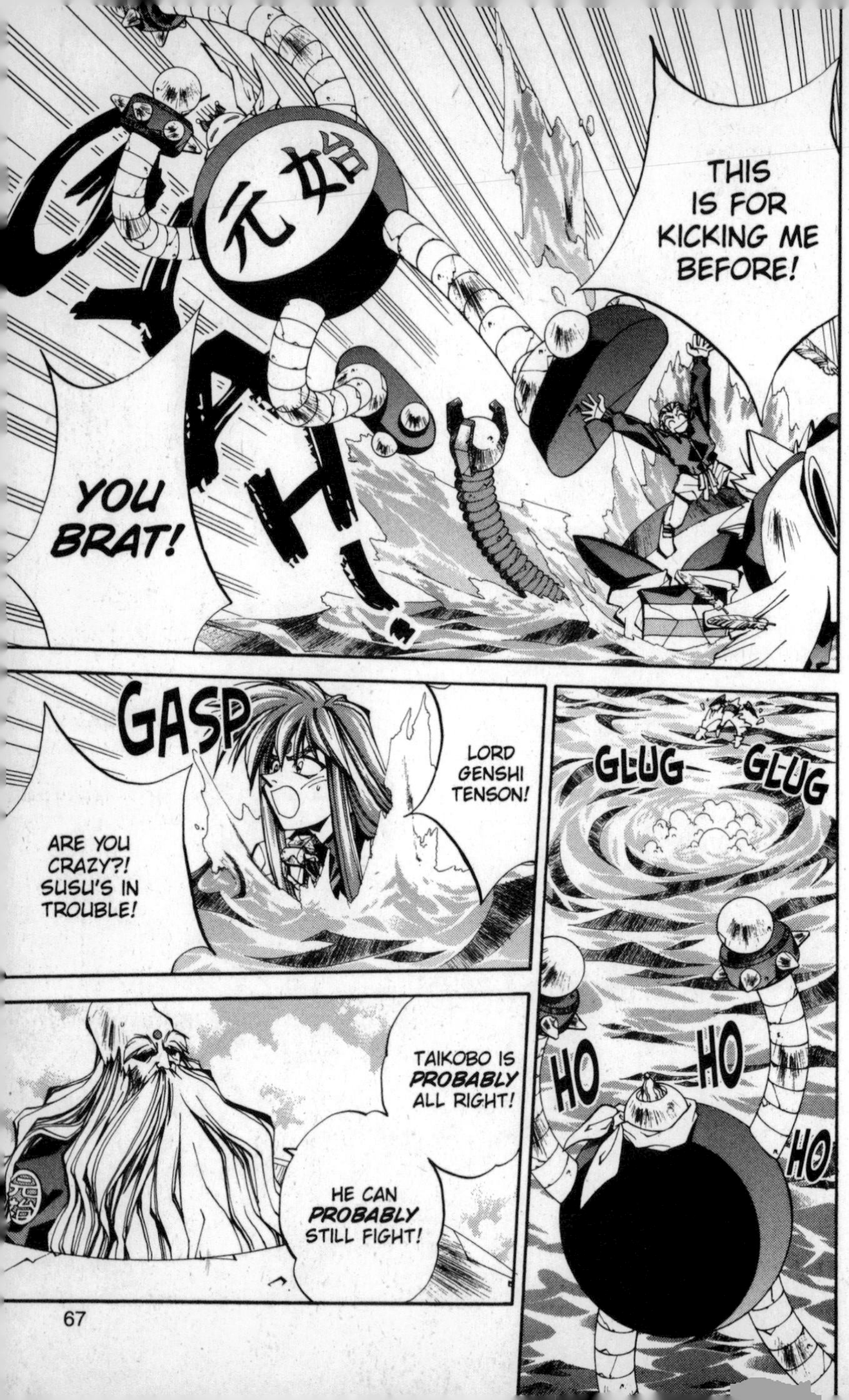
THIS IS FOR KICKING ME BEFORE!
YOU BRAT!
GLUG GLUG
GASP
LORD GENSHI TENSON!
ARE YOU CRAZY?! SUSU'S IN TROUBLE!
HO HO HO
TAIKOBO IS *PROBABLY* ALL RIGHT!
HE CAN *PROBABLY* STILL FIGHT!

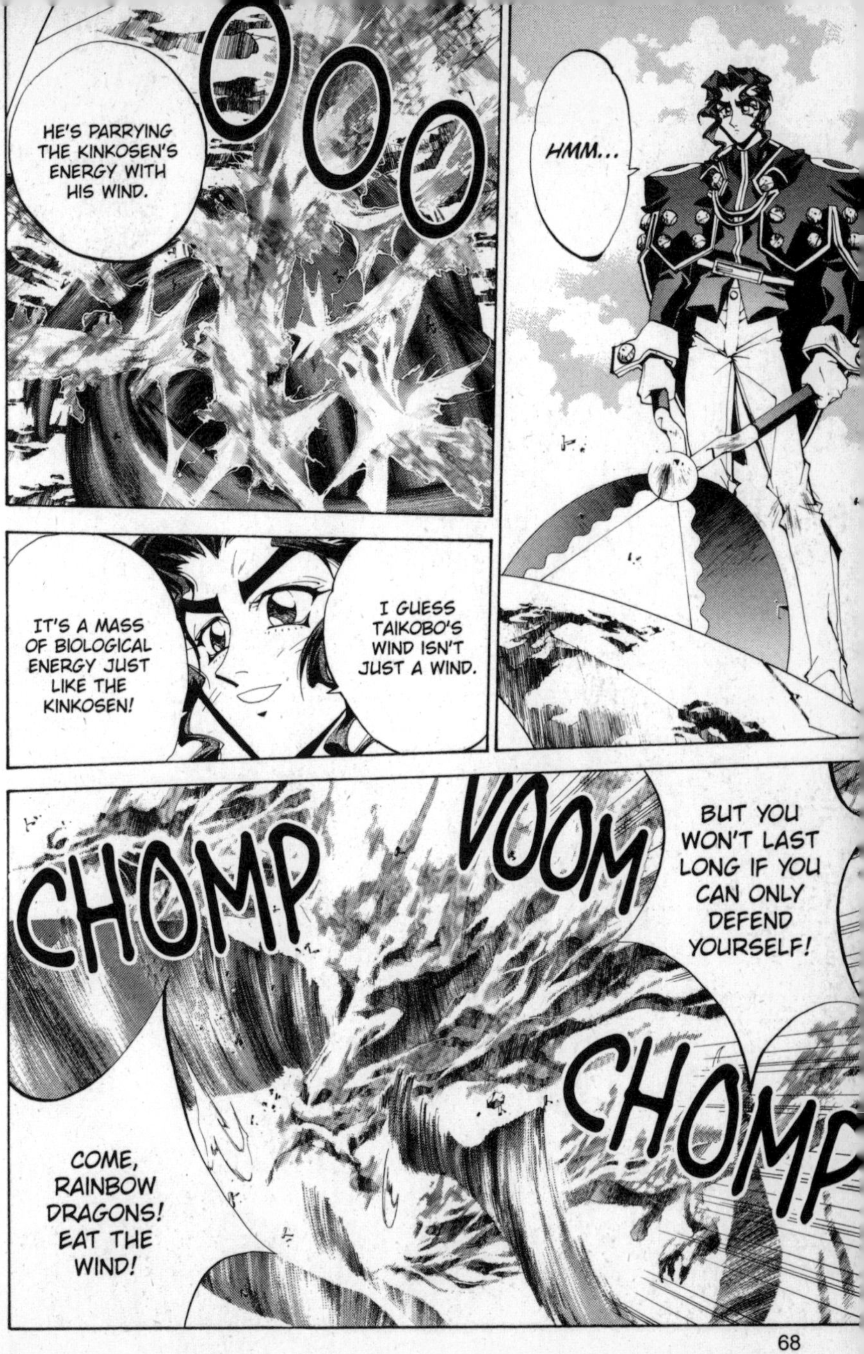
HMM...
OOO
HE'S PARRYING THE KINKOSEN'S ENERGY WITH HIS WIND.
I GUESS TAIKOBO'S WIND ISN'T JUST A WIND.
IT'S A MASS OF BIOLOGICAL ENERGY JUST LIKE THE KINKOSEN!
BUT YOU WON'T LAST LONG IF YOU CAN ONLY DEFEND YOURSELF!
VOOM
CHOMP
CHOMP
COME, RAINBOW DRAGONS! EAT THE WIND!

READ THIS WAY

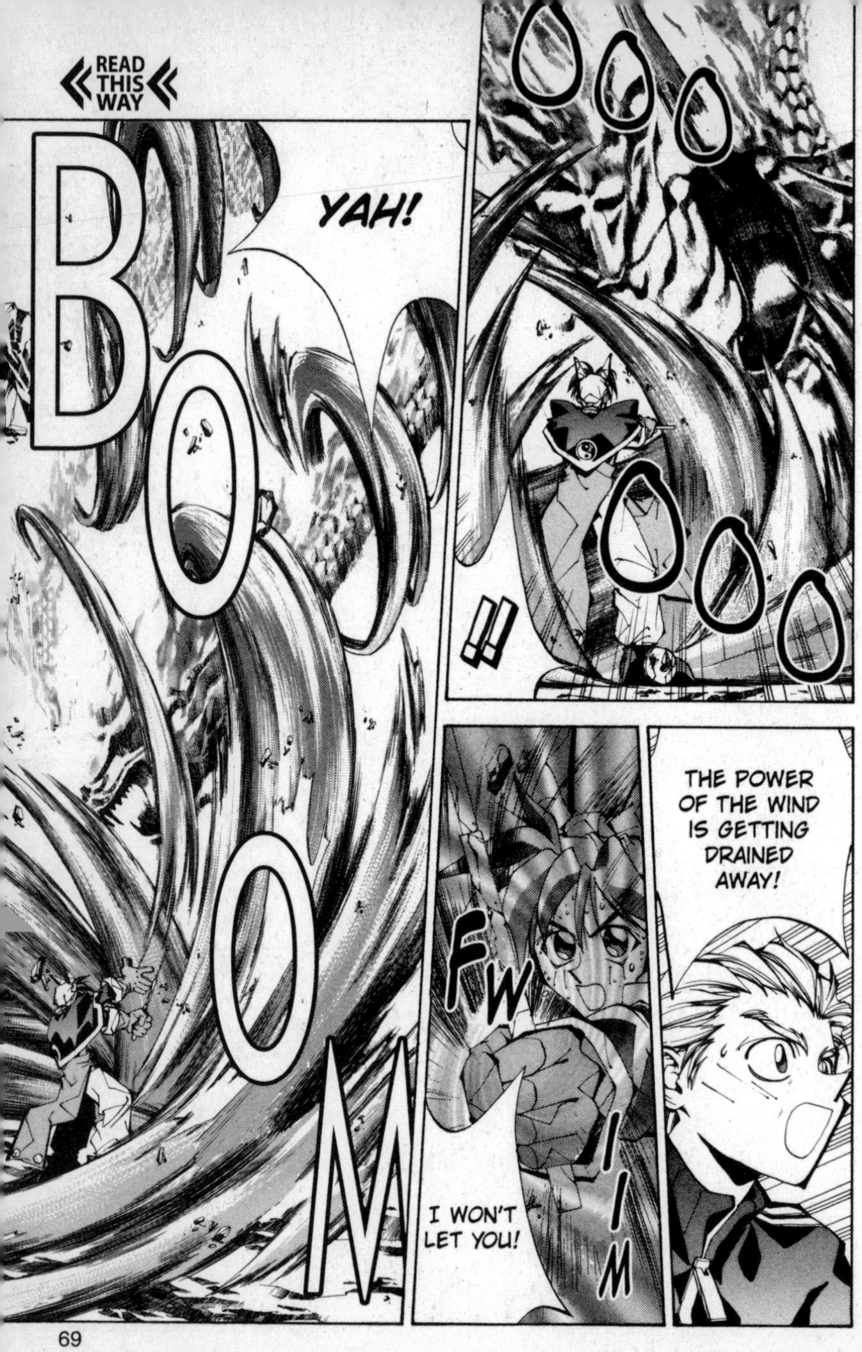
OOOOOO
!!
THE POWER OF THE WIND IS GETTING DRAINED AWAY!
FWIIM
I WON'T LET YOU!
BOOOOM
YAH!

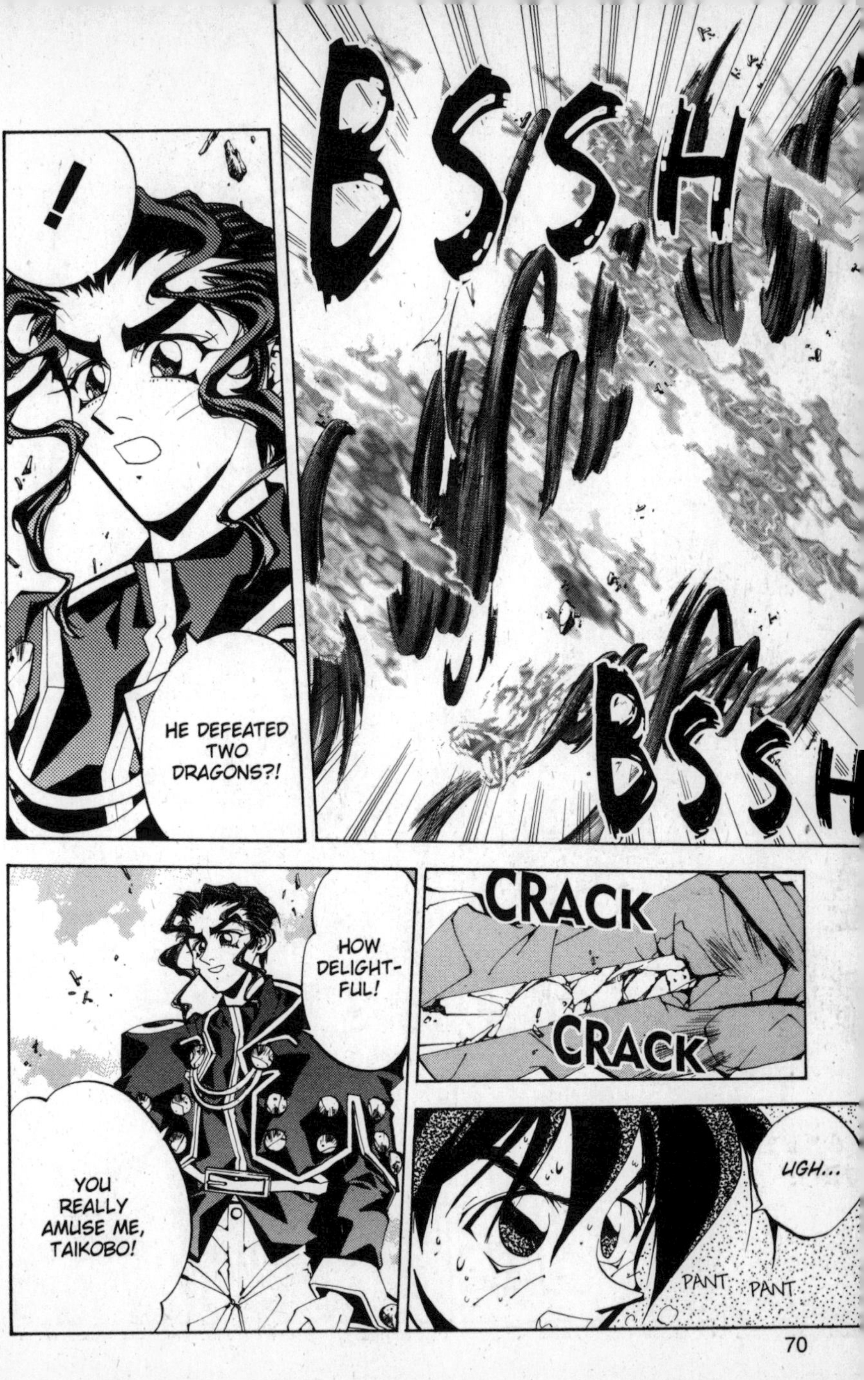
BSSSH
BSSH
!
HE DEFEATED TWO DRAGONS?!
CRACK
CRACK
UGH...
PANT PANT
HOW DELIGHT-FUL!
YOU REALLY AMUSE ME, TAIKOBO!

READ THIS WAY

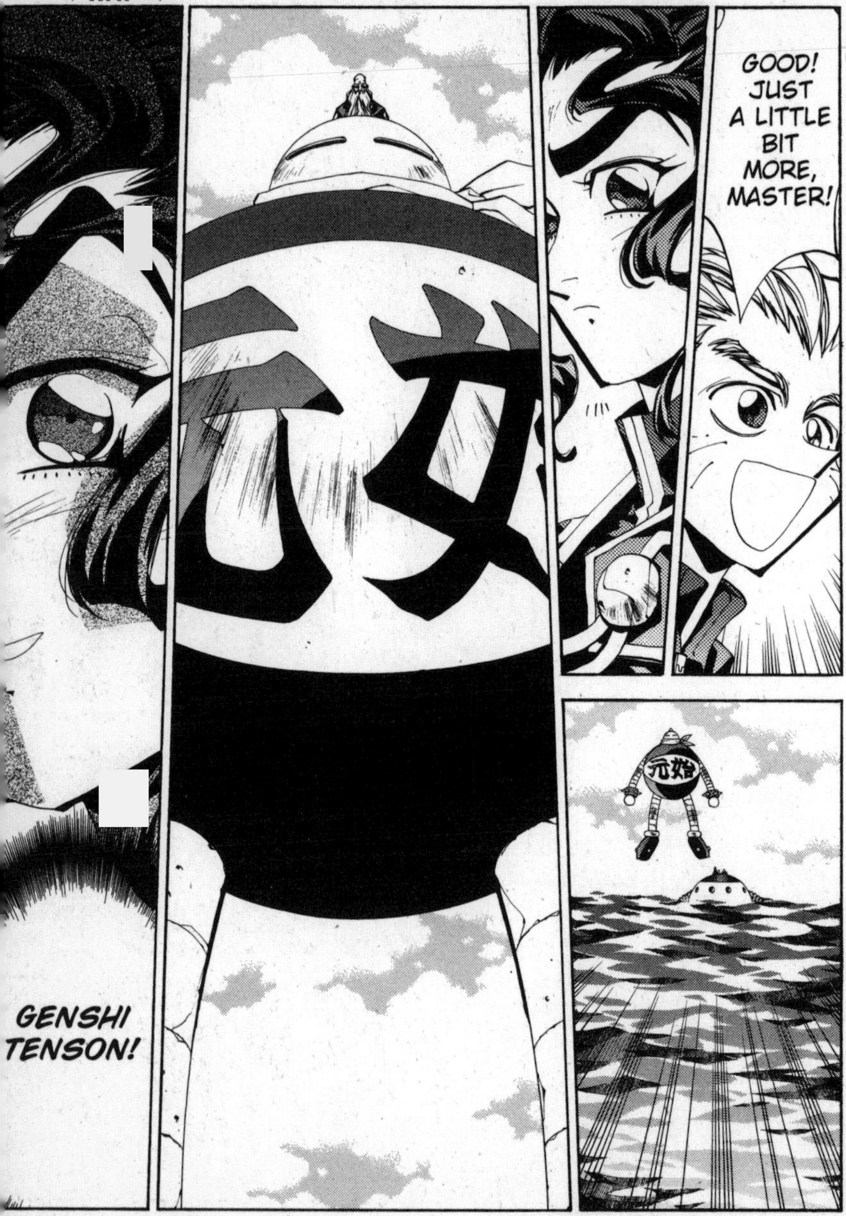
GOOD! JUST A LITTLE BIT MORE, MASTER!
GENSHI TENSON!

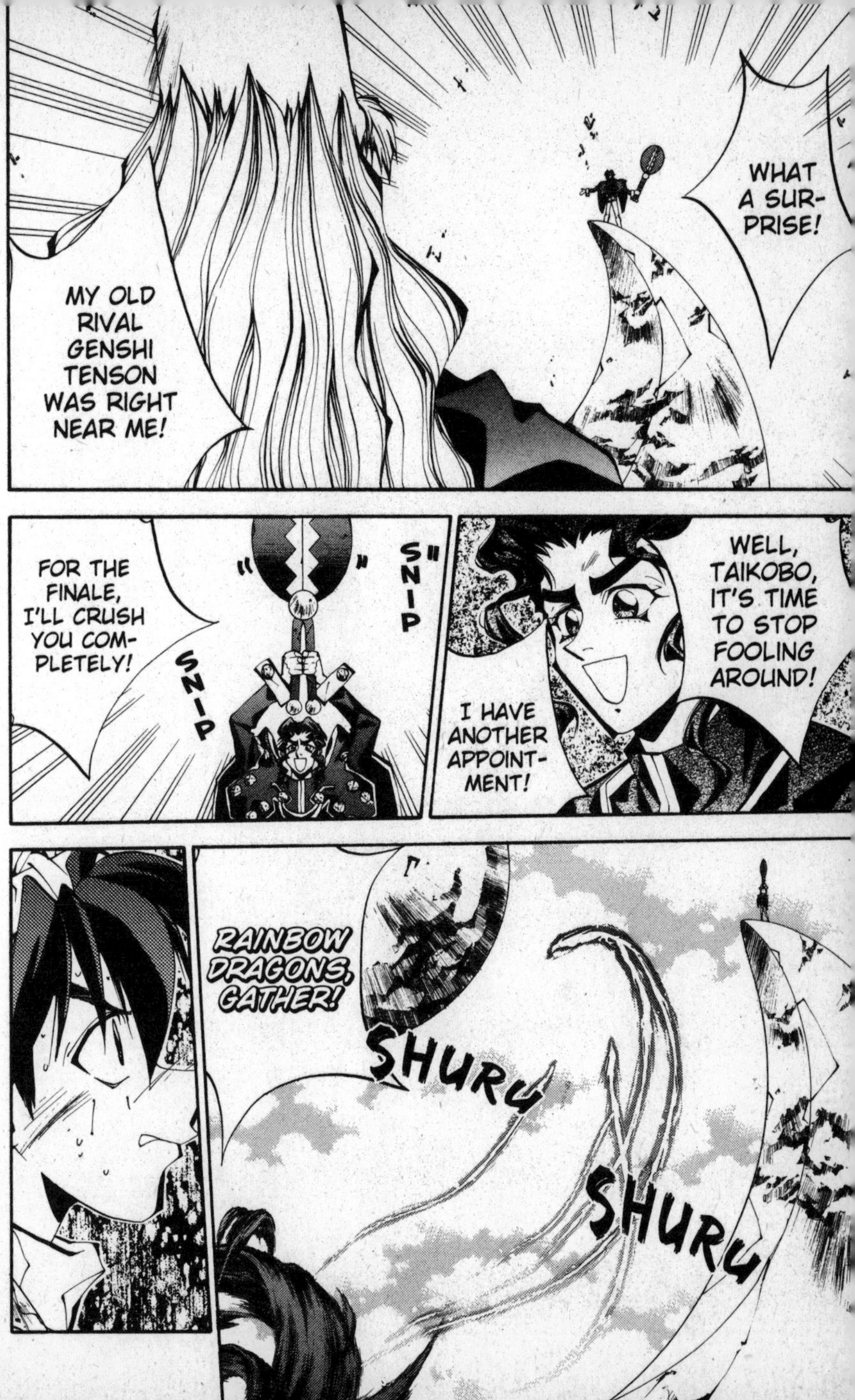
WHAT A SUR-PRISE!
MY OLD RIVAL GENSHI TENSON WAS RIGHT NEAR ME!
WELL, TAIKOBO, IT'S TIME TO STOP FOOLING AROUND!
I HAVE ANOTHER APPOINT-MENT!
SNIP
FOR THE FINALE, I'LL CRUSH YOU COM-PLETELY!
SNIP
RAINBOW DRAGONS, GATHER!
SHURU
SHURU

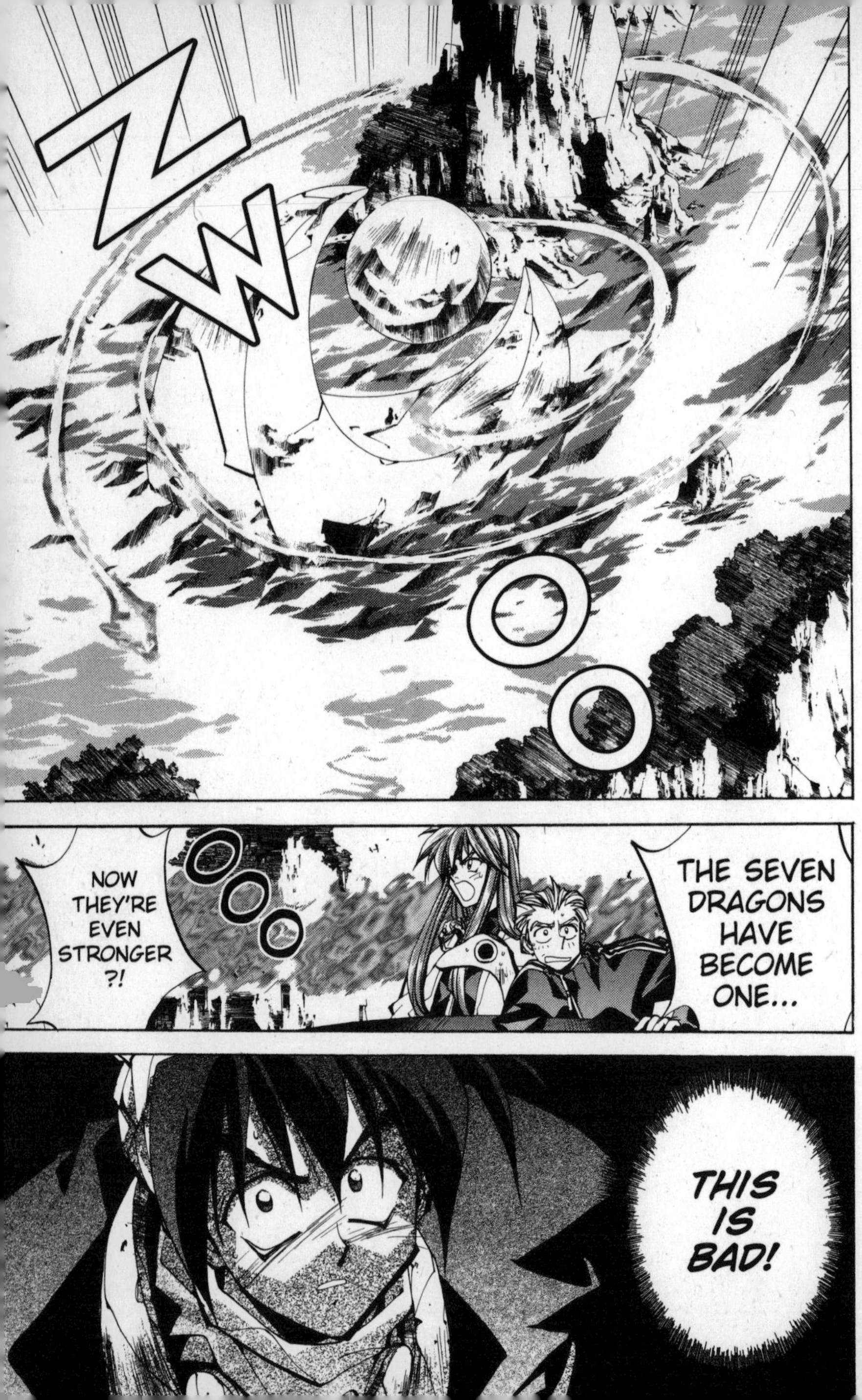
ZWOO
THE SEVEN DRAGONS HAVE BECOME ONE...
OOO
NOW THEY'RE EVEN STRONGER ?!
THIS IS BAD!

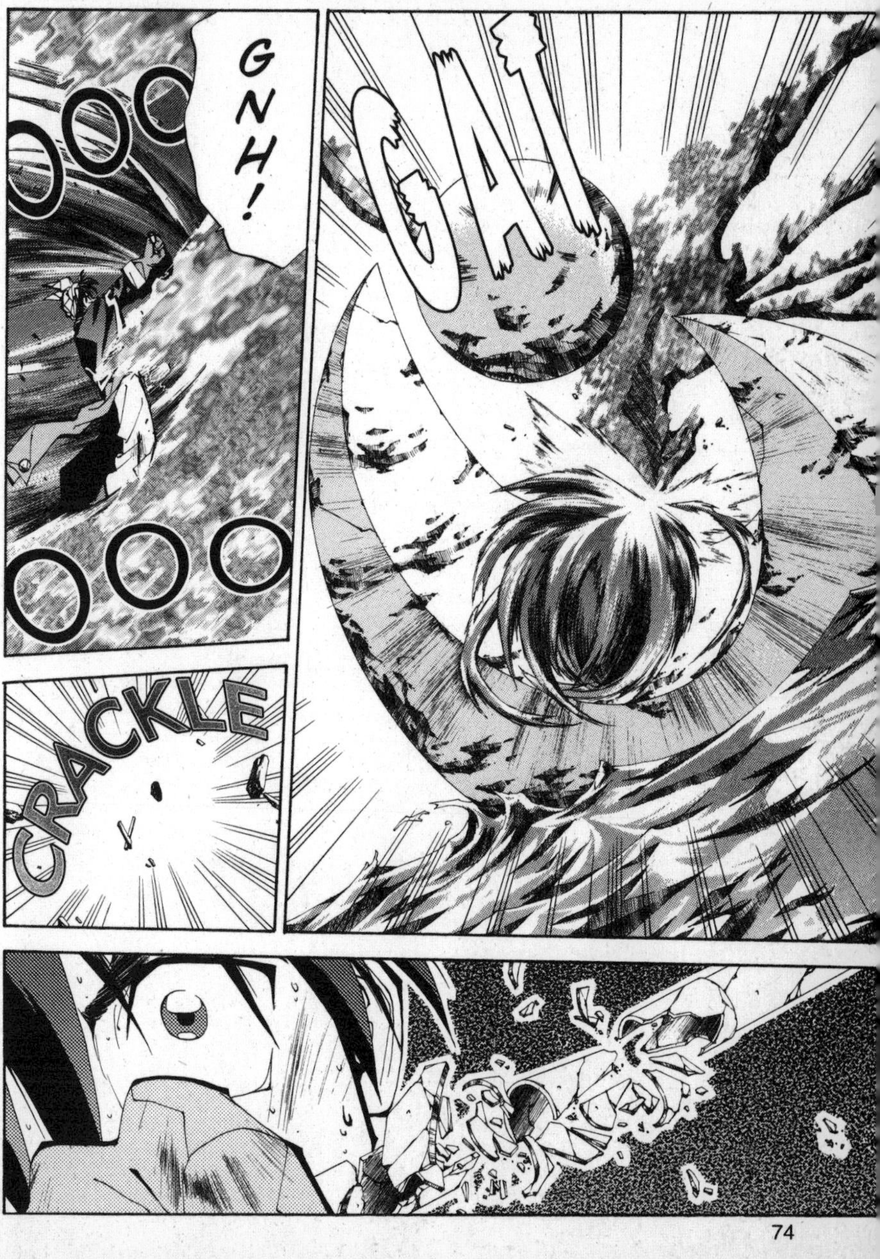
GAI
GNH!
CRACKLE

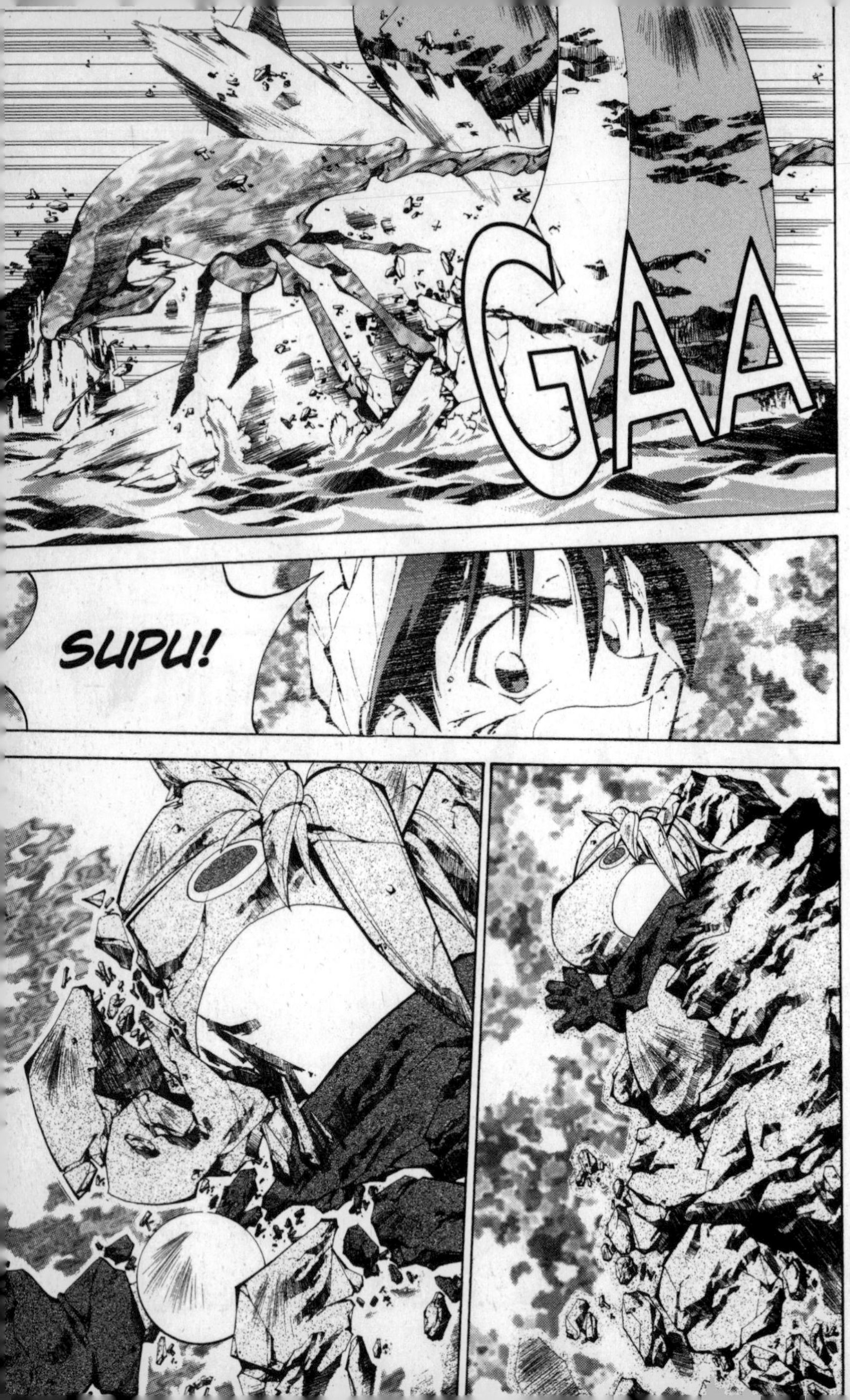
GAA
SUPU!

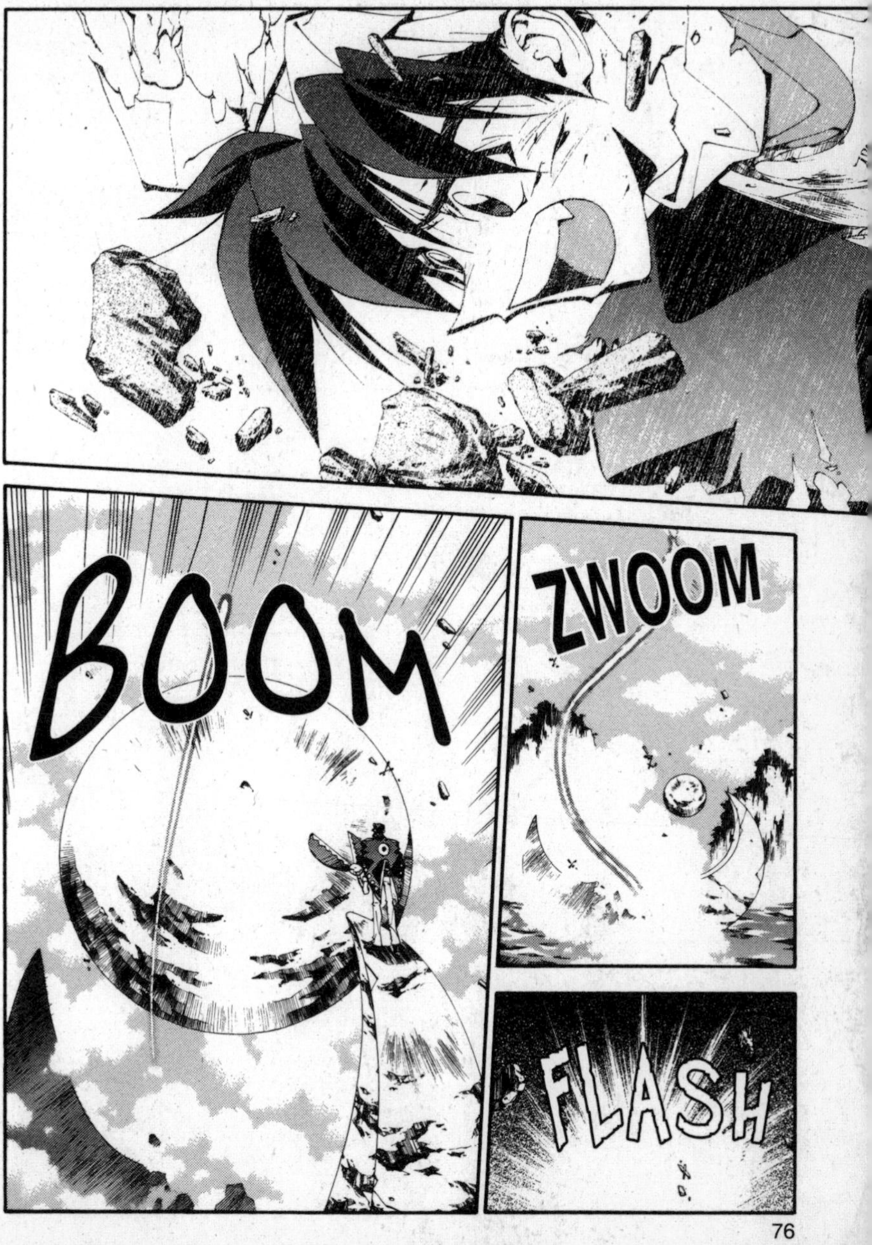
ZWOOM
FLASH
BOOM

READ THIS WAY

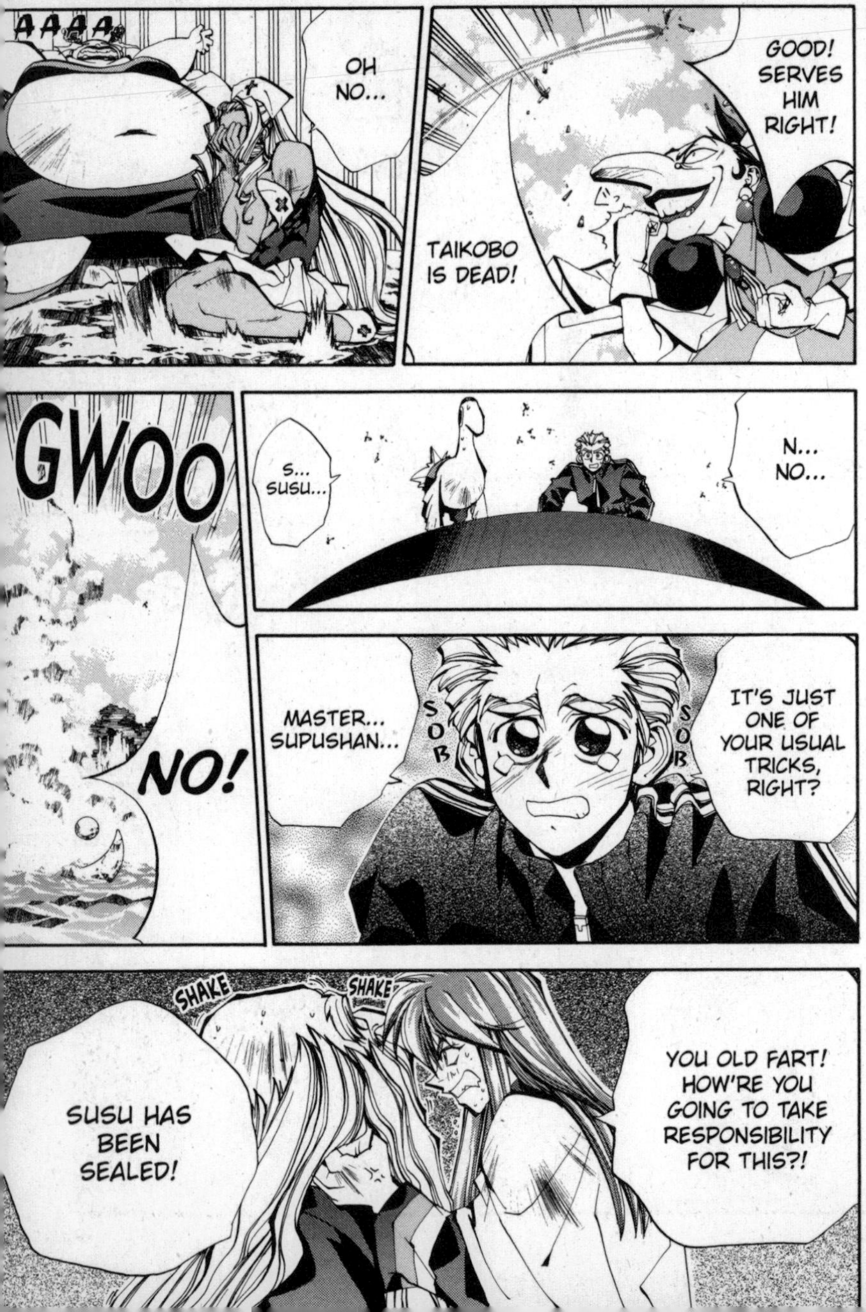
GOOD! SERVES HIM RIGHT!
TAIKOBO IS DEAD!
AAAA
OH NO...
N... NO...
S... SUSU...
SOB
SOB
MASTER... SUPUSHAN...
IT'S JUST ONE OF YOUR USUAL TRICKS, RIGHT?
GWOO
NO!
SHAKE
SHAKE
YOU OLD FART! HOW'RE YOU GOING TO TAKE RESPONSIBILITY FOR THIS?!
SUSU HAS BEEN SEALED!

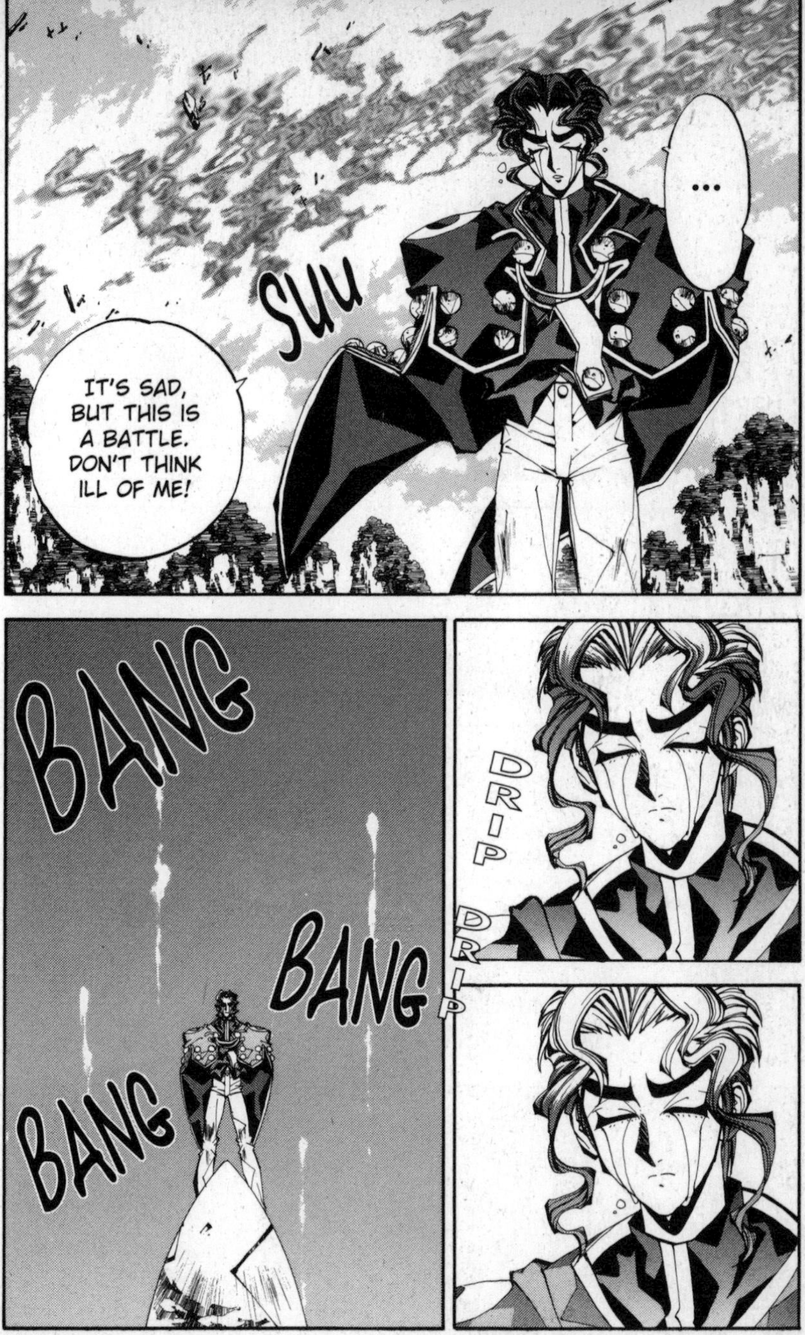
...
SUU
IT'S SAD, BUT THIS IS A BATTLE. DON'T THINK ILL OF ME!
DRIP
DRIP
BANG
BANG
BANG

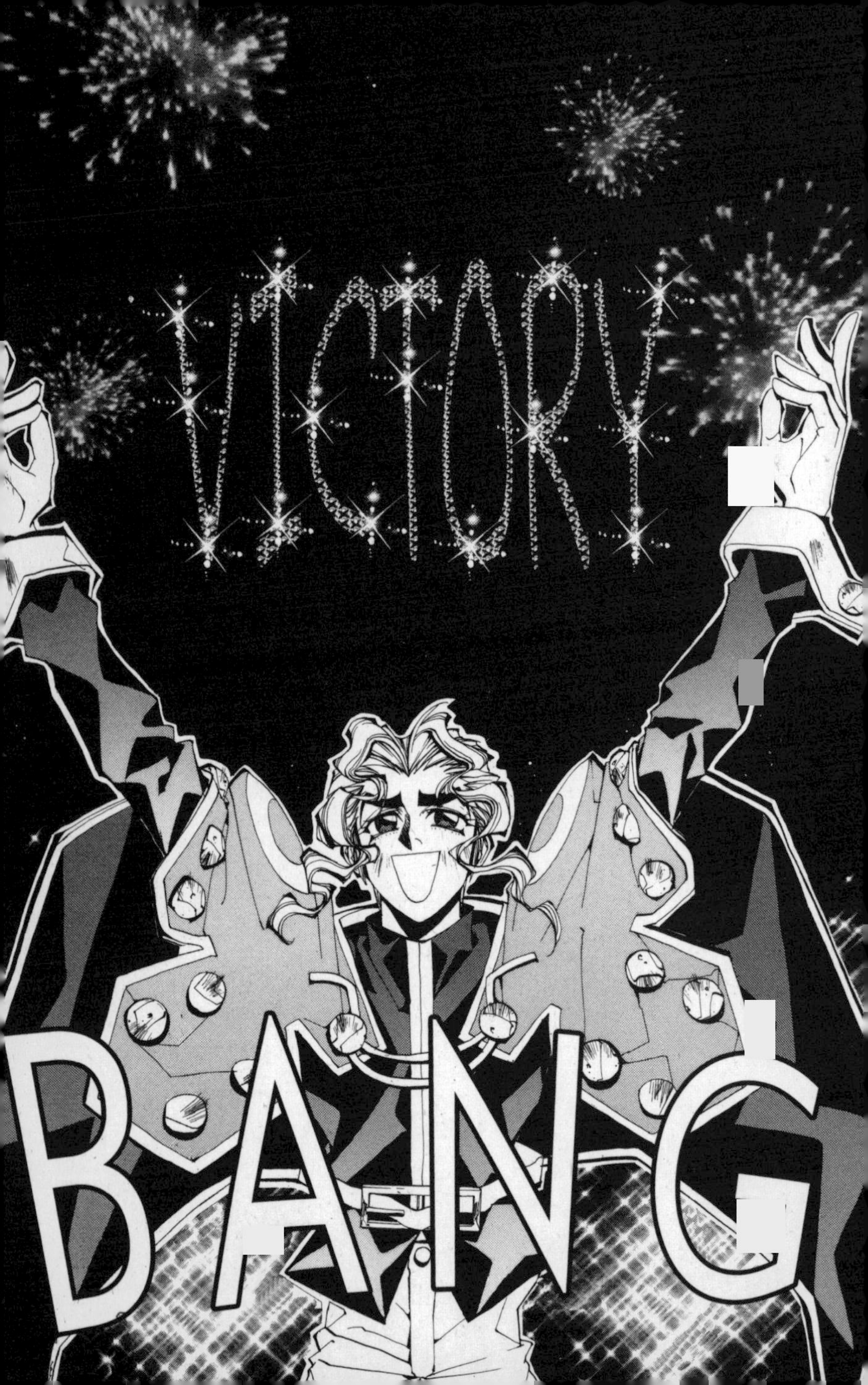
VICTORY
BANG

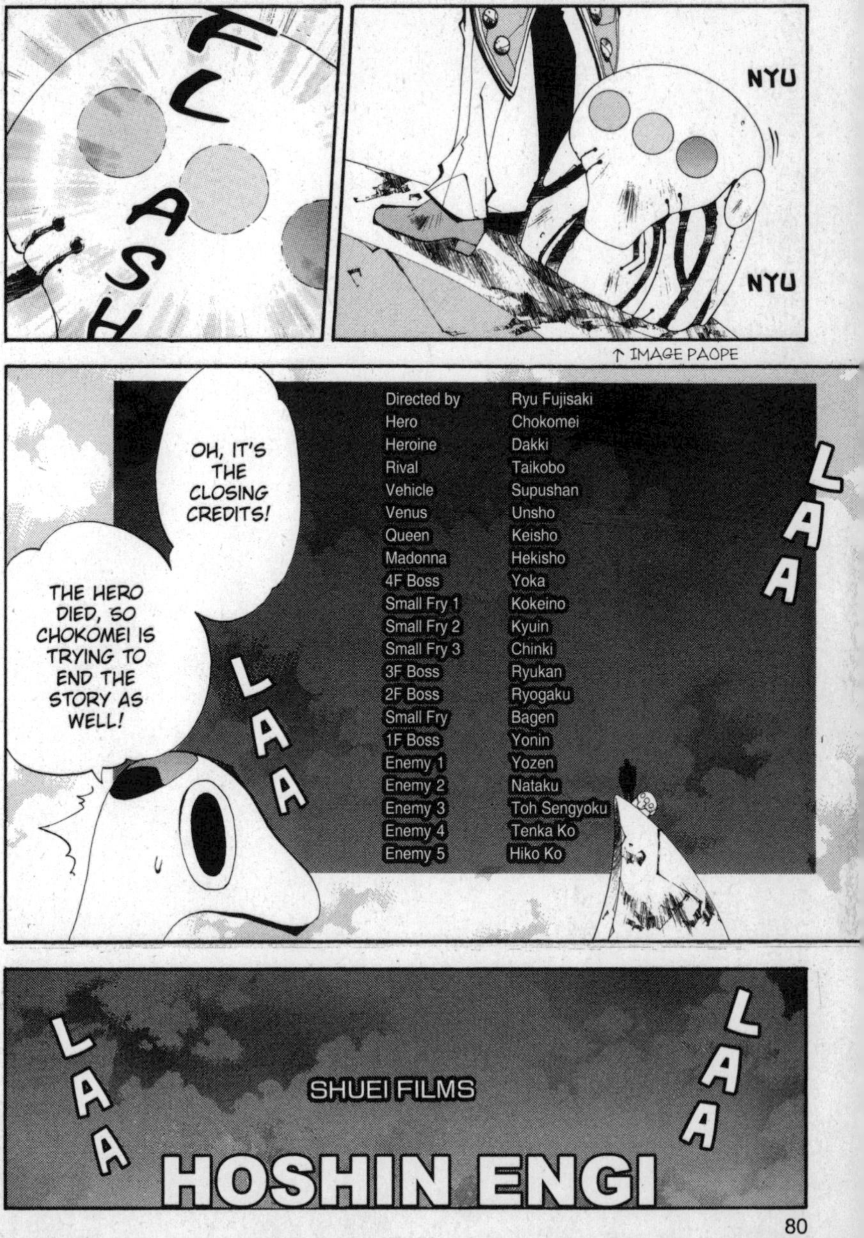
NYU
NYU
FLASH
↑ IMAGE PAOPE
LAA
Directed by Ryu Fujisaki
Hero Chokomei
Heroine Dakki
Rival Taikobo
Vehicle Supushan
Venus Unsho
Queen Keisho
Madonna Hekisho
4F Boss Yoka
Small Fry 1 Kokeino
Small Fry 2 Kyuin
Small Fry 3 Chinki
3F Boss Ryukan
2F Boss Ryogaku
Small Fry Bagen
1F Boss Yonin
Enemy 1 Yozen
Enemy 2 Nataku
Enemy 3 Toh Sengyoku
Enemy 4 Tenka Ko
Enemy 5 Hiko Ko
OH, IT'S THE CLOSING CREDITS!
THE HERO DIED, SO CHOKOMEI IS TRYING TO END THE STORY AS WELL!
LAA
LAA
SHUEI FILMS
HOSHIN ENGI
LAA

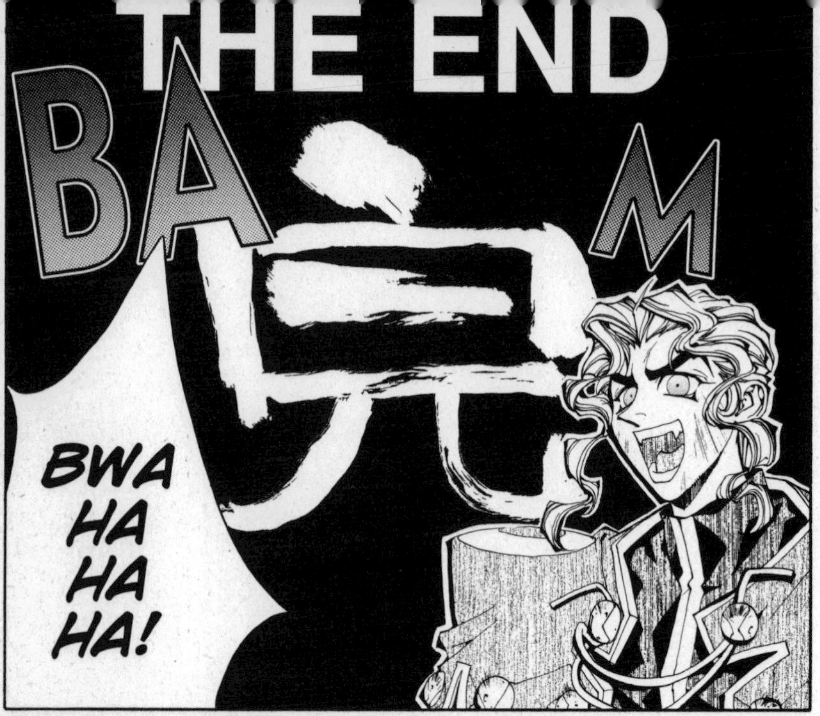
THE END
BAM
BWA HA HA HA!

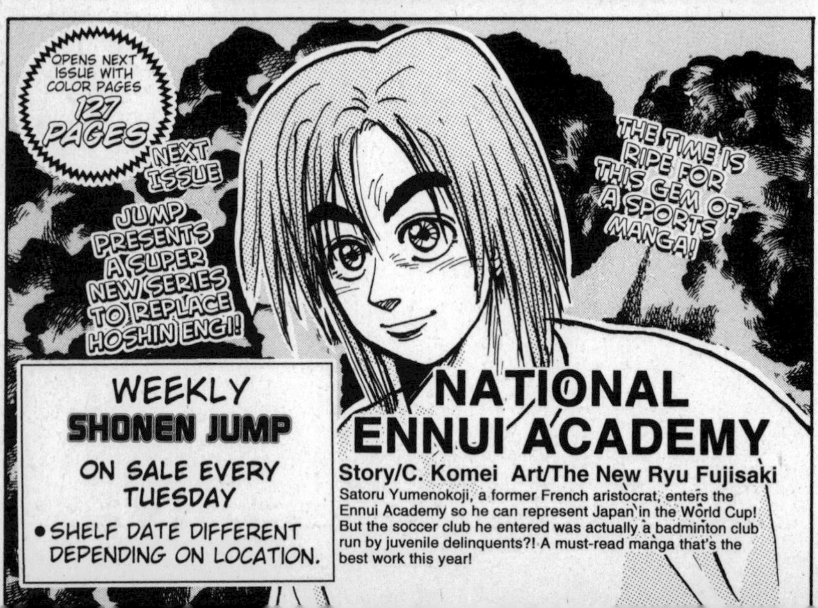
OPENS NEXT ISSUE WITH COLOR PAGES 127 PAGES
NEXT ISSUE
JUMP PRESENTS A SUPER NEW SERIES TO REPLACE HOSHIN ENGI!
THE TIME IS RIPE FOR THIS GEM OF A SPORTS MANGA!
WEEKLY SHONEN JUMP
ON SALE EVERY TUESDAY
• SHELF DATE DIFFERENT DEPENDING ON LOCATION.
NATIONAL ENNUI ACADEMY
Story/C. Komei Art/The New Ryu Fujisaki
Satoru Yumenokoji, a former French aristocrat, enters the Ennui Academy so he can represent Japan in the World Cup! But the soccer club he entered was actually a badminton club run by juvenile delinquents?! A must-read manga that's the best work this year!

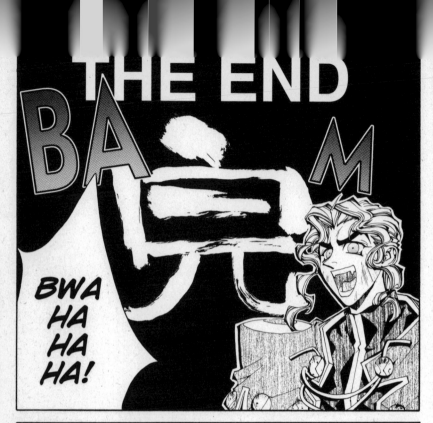

封神演義

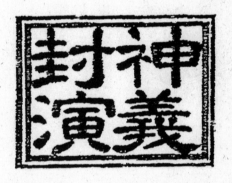

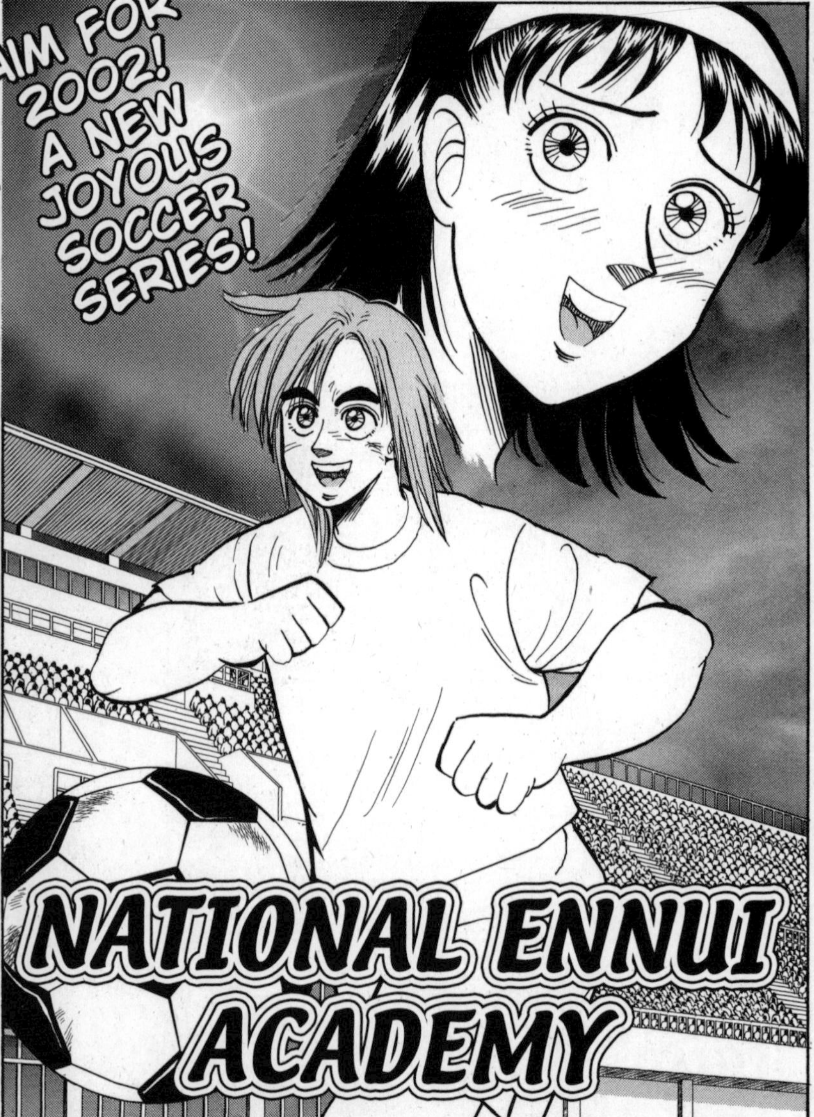
AIM FOR 2002! A NEW JOYOUS SOCCER SERIES!
NATIONAL ENNUI ACADEMY
Chapter 1: LOTS OF RIVALS!

Yo! I'm Satoru Yumenokoji, the new hero that replaces Taikobo! Howdy!

Story By C. Komei *Art By The New Ryu Fujisaki*

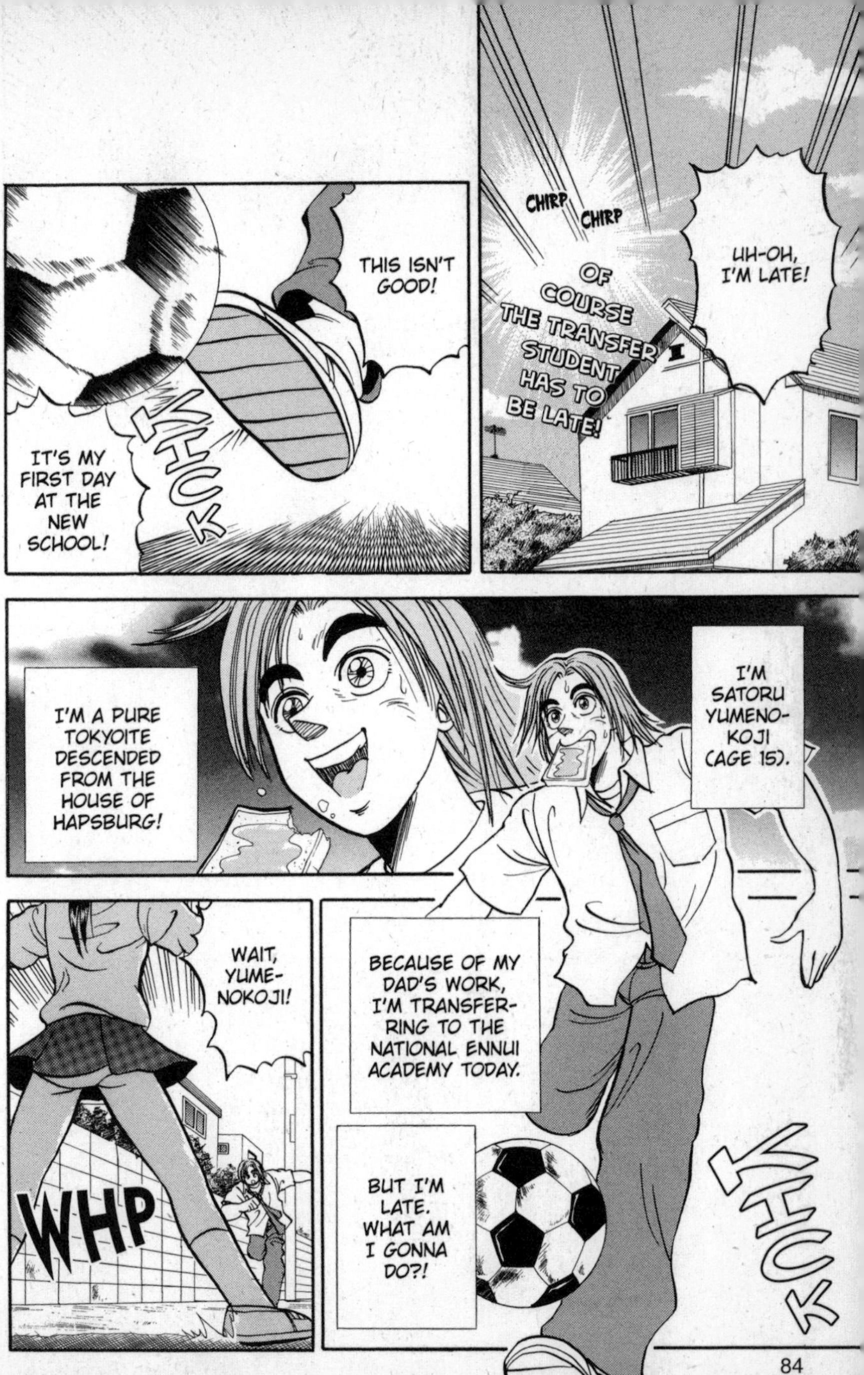
UH-OH, I'M LATE!
CHIRP
CHIRP
OF COURSE THE TRANSFER STUDENT HAS TO BE LATE!
THIS ISN'T GOOD!
KICK
IT'S MY FIRST DAY AT THE NEW SCHOOL!
I'M SATORU YUMENO-KOJI (AGE 15).
I'M A PURE TOKYOITE DESCENDED FROM THE HOUSE OF HAPSBURG!
BECAUSE OF MY DAD'S WORK, I'M TRANSFER-RING TO THE NATIONAL ENNUI ACADEMY TODAY.
KICK
BUT I'M LATE. WHAT AM I GONNA DO?!
WAIT, YUME-NOKOJI!
WHP

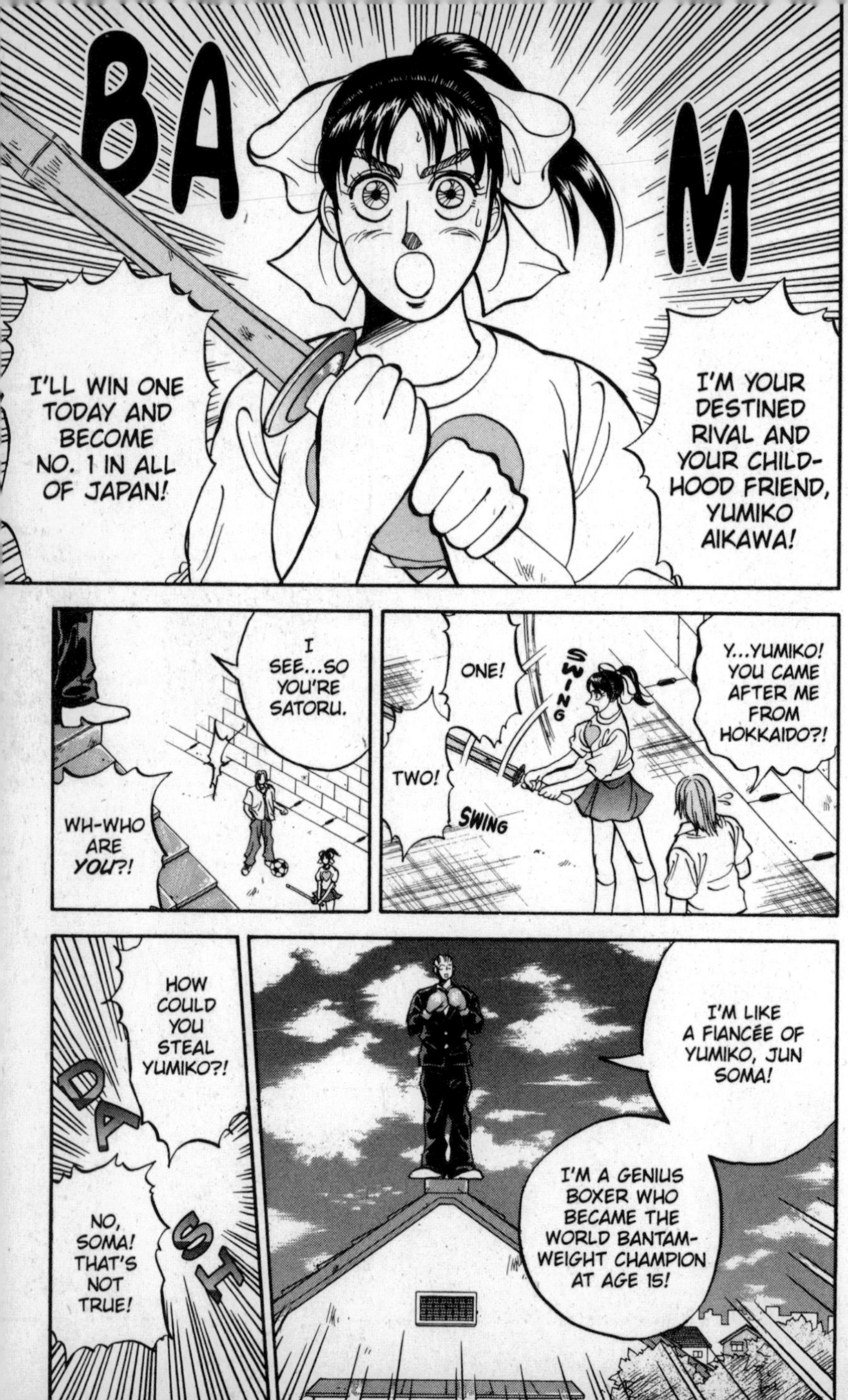
BAM
I'M YOUR DESTINED RIVAL AND YOUR CHILDHOOD FRIEND, YUMIKO AIKAWA!
I'LL WIN ONE TODAY AND BECOME NO. 1 IN ALL OF JAPAN!
Y...YUMIKO! YOU CAME AFTER ME FROM HOKKAIDO?!
ONE!
SWING
TWO!
SWING
I SEE...SO YOU'RE SATORU.
WH-WHO ARE *YOU*?!
I'M LIKE A FIANCÉE OF YUMIKO, JUN SOMA!
I'M A GENIUS BOXER WHO BECAME THE WORLD BANTAMWEIGHT CHAMPION AT AGE 15!
HOW COULD YOU STEAL YUMIKO?!
DASH
NO, SOMA! THAT'S NOT TRUE!

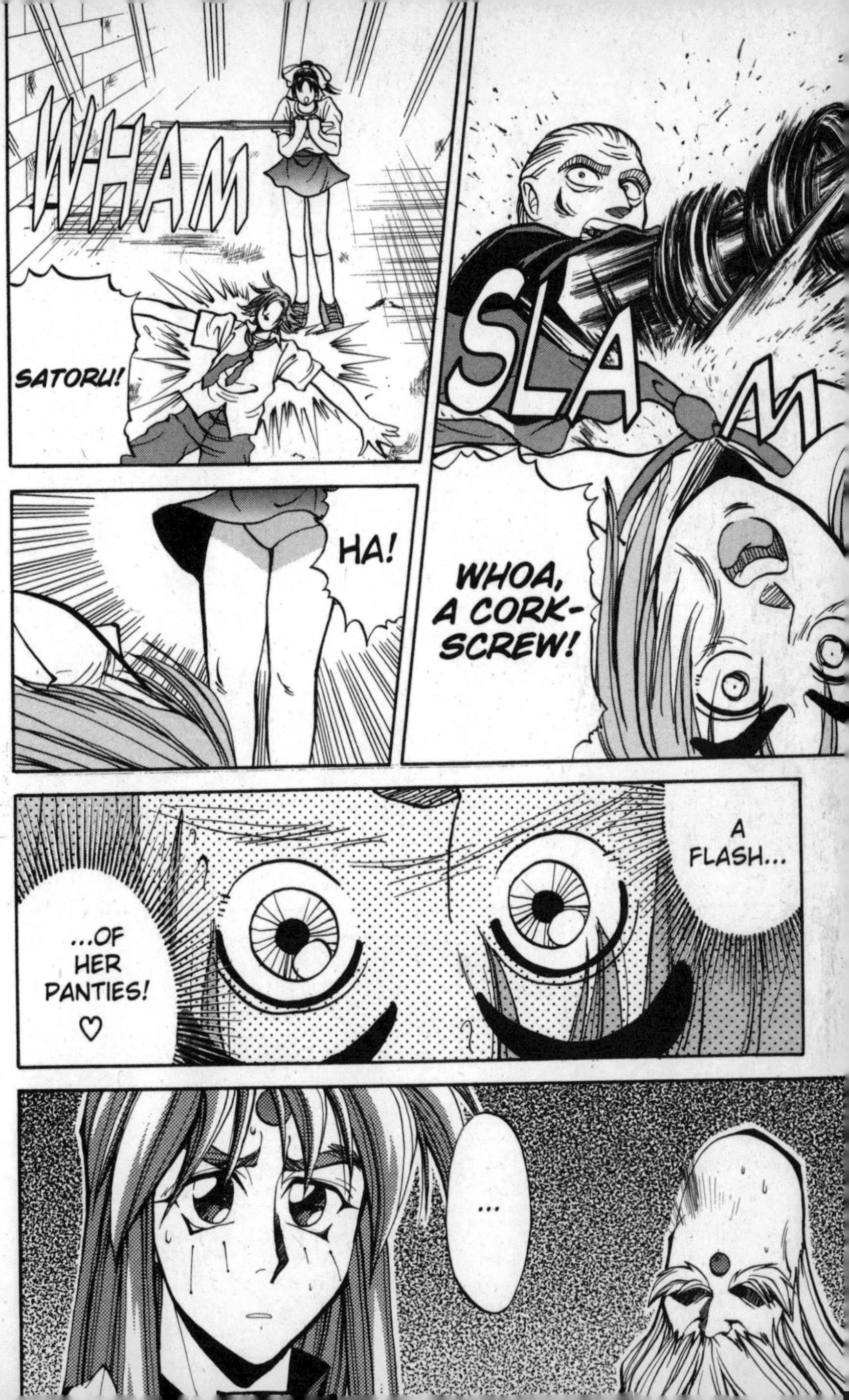
SLAM
WHAM
SATORU!
WHOA, A CORK-SCREW!
HA!
A FLASH...
...OF HER PANTIES! ♡
...

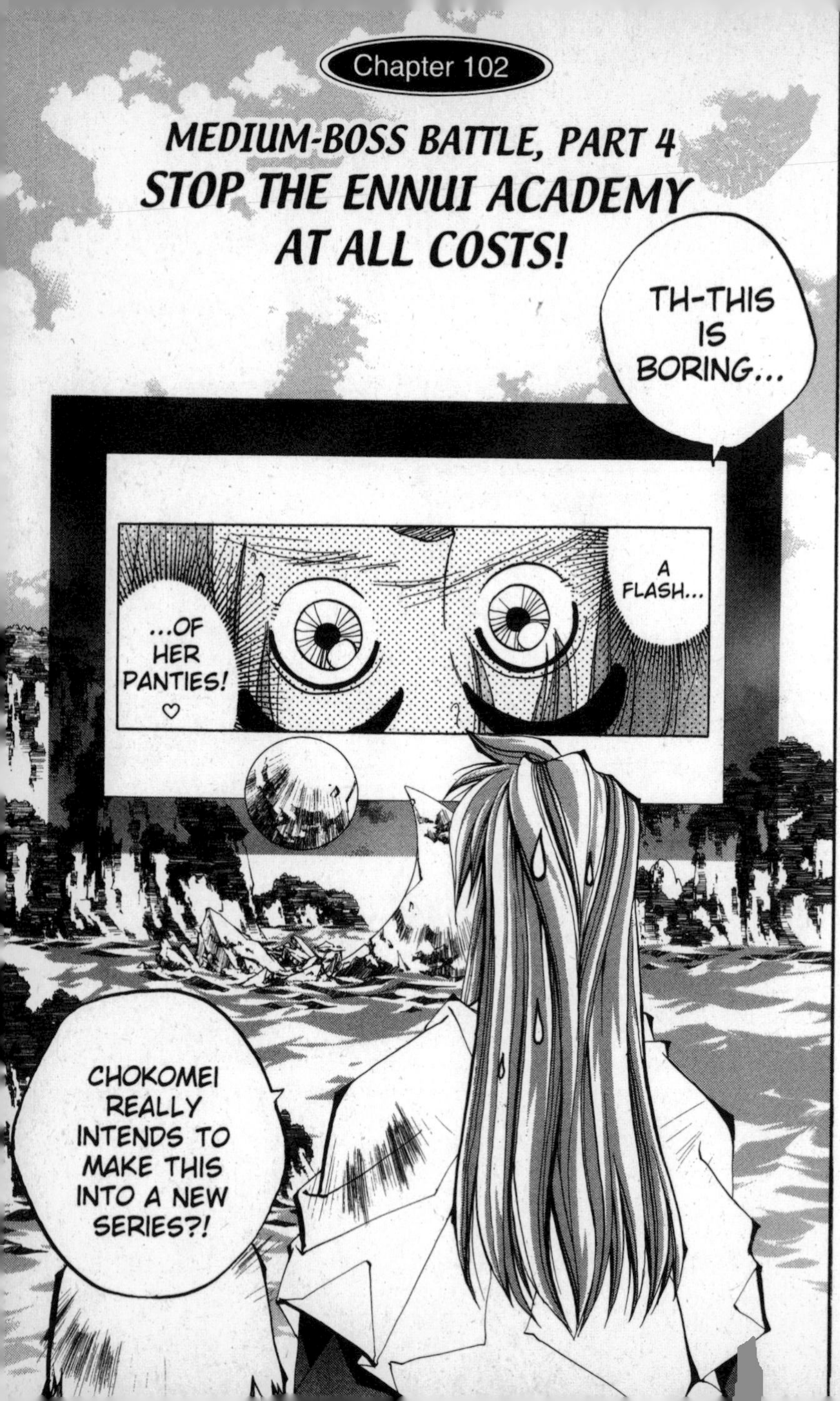
Chapter 102
MEDIUM-BOSS BATTLE, PART 4
STOP THE ENNUI ACADEMY AT ALL COSTS!
TH-THIS IS BORING...
A FLASH...
...OF HER PANTIES! ♡
CHOKOMEI REALLY INTENDS TO MAKE THIS INTO A NEW SERIES?!

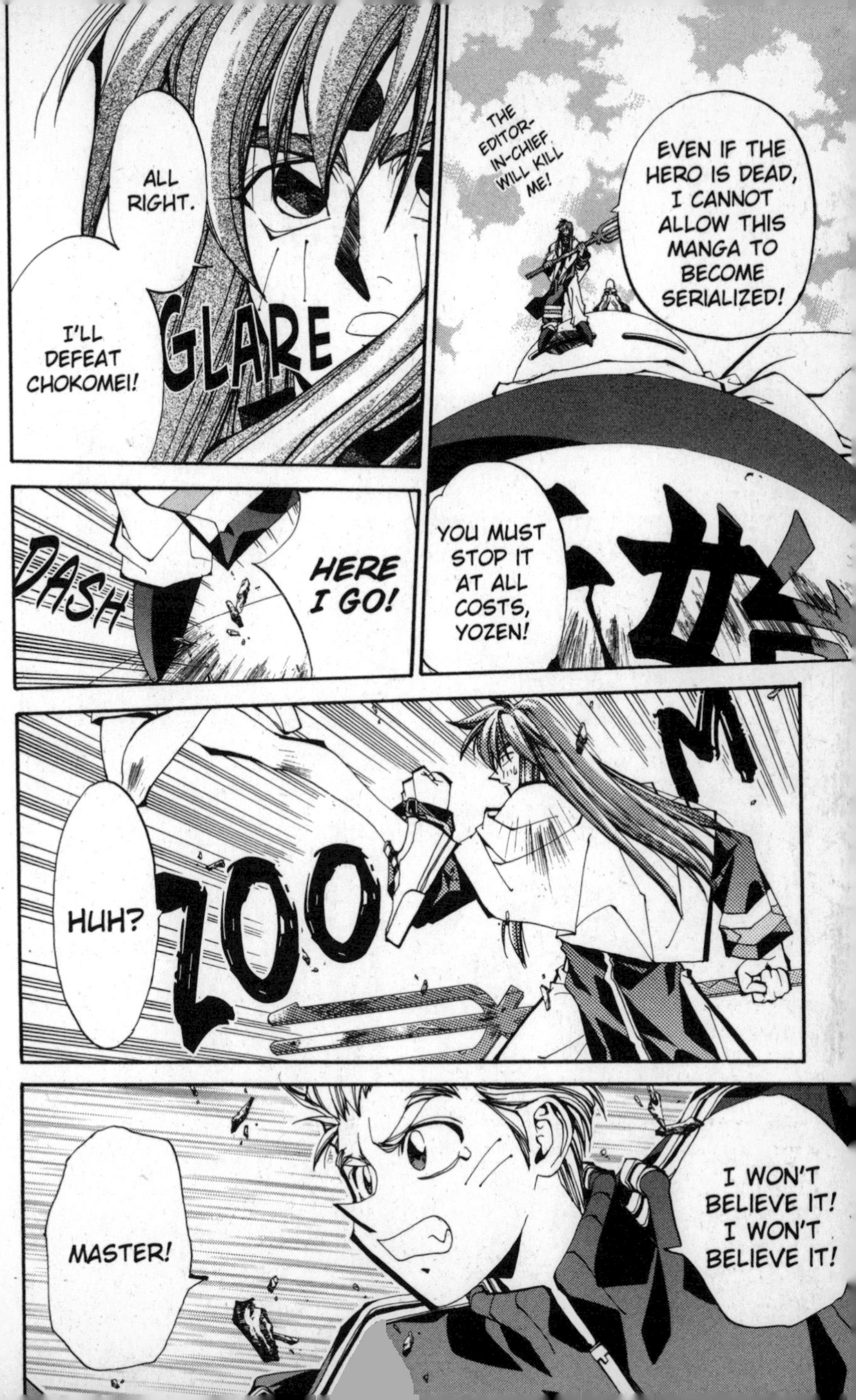
EVEN IF THE HERO IS DEAD, I CANNOT ALLOW THIS MANGA TO BECOME SERIALIZED!
THE EDITOR-IN-CHIEF WILL KILL ME!
ALL RIGHT.
GLARE
I'LL DEFEAT CHOKOMEI!
YOU MUST STOP IT AT ALL COSTS, YOZEN!
HERE I GO!
DASH
M
ZOO
HUH?
I WON'T BELIEVE IT! I WON'T BELIEVE IT!
MASTER!

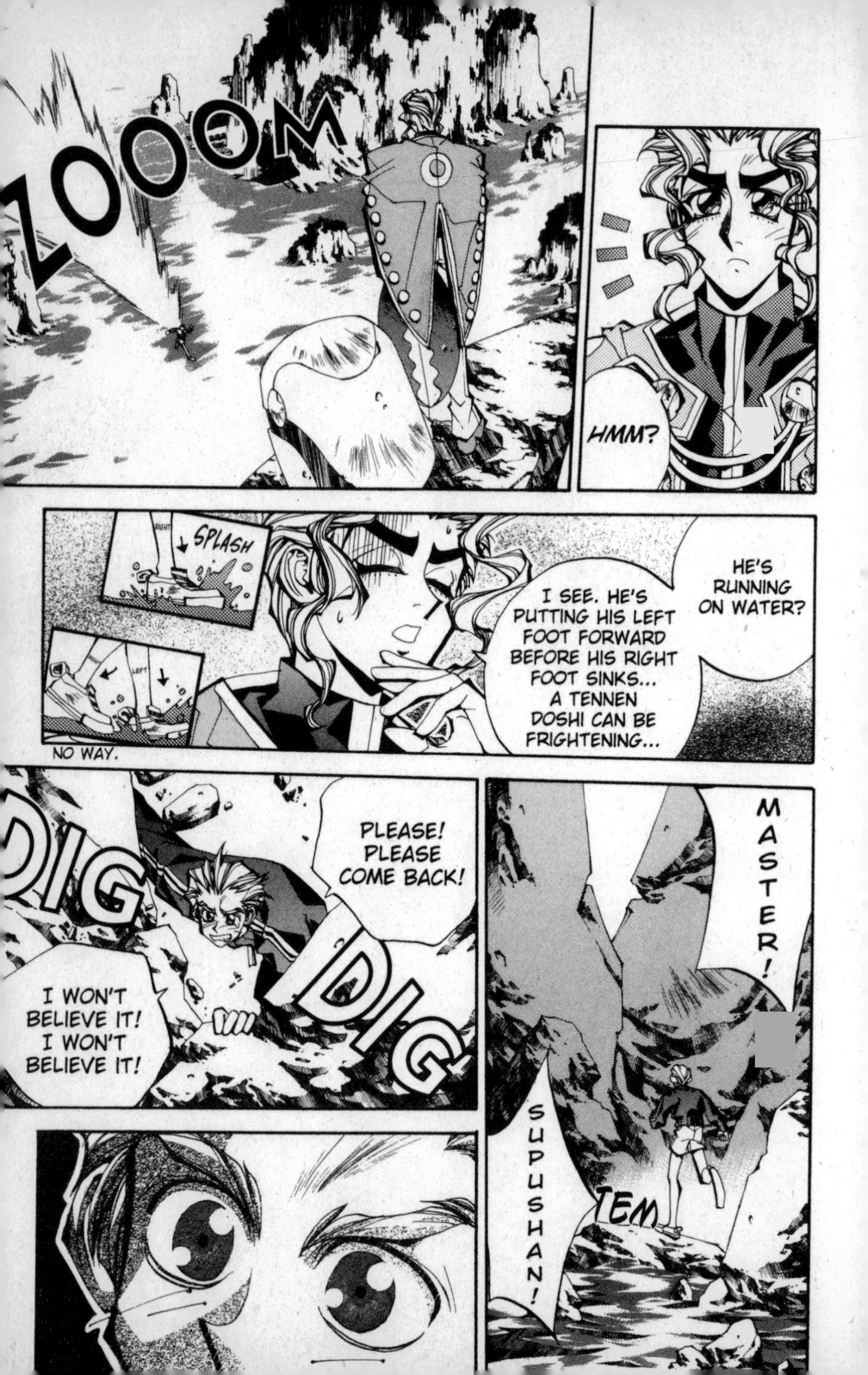
HMM?
ZOOOM
HE'S RUNNING ON WATER?
I SEE. HE'S PUTTING HIS LEFT FOOT FORWARD BEFORE HIS RIGHT FOOT SINKS... A TENNEN DOSHI CAN BE FRIGHTENING...
RIGHT
SPLASH
LEFT
NO WAY.
MASTER!
SUPUSHAN!
TEM
PLEASE! PLEASE COME BACK!
DIG
I WON'T BELIEVE IT! I WON'T BELIEVE IT!
DIG

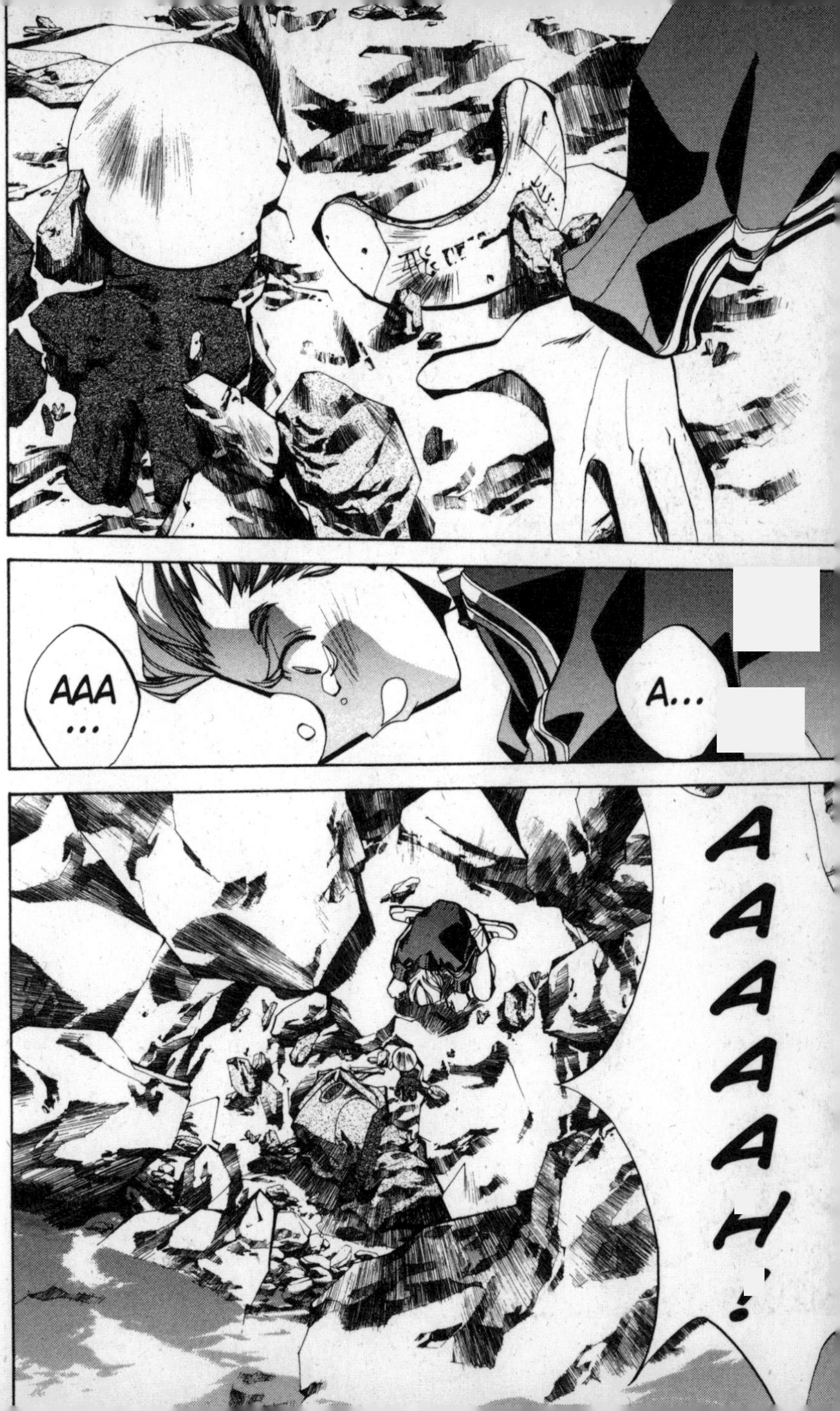
A...
AAA ...
AAAAAAH!

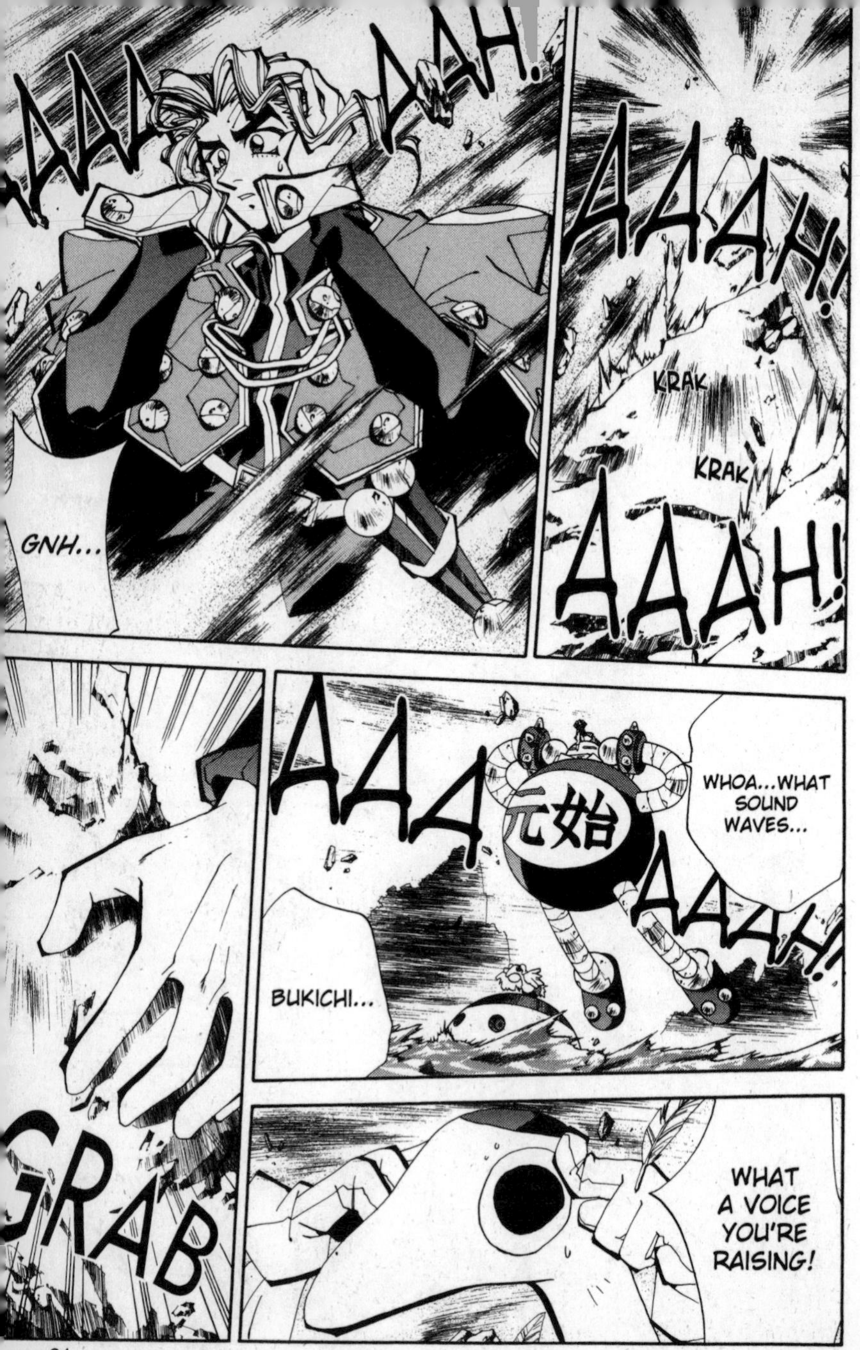
AAAAH!
KRAK
KRAK
AAAAH!
AAAA DAAH!
GNH...
AAAAAAAH!!
WHOA...WHAT SOUND WAVES...
BUKICHI...
WHAT A VOICE YOU'RE RAISING!
GRAB

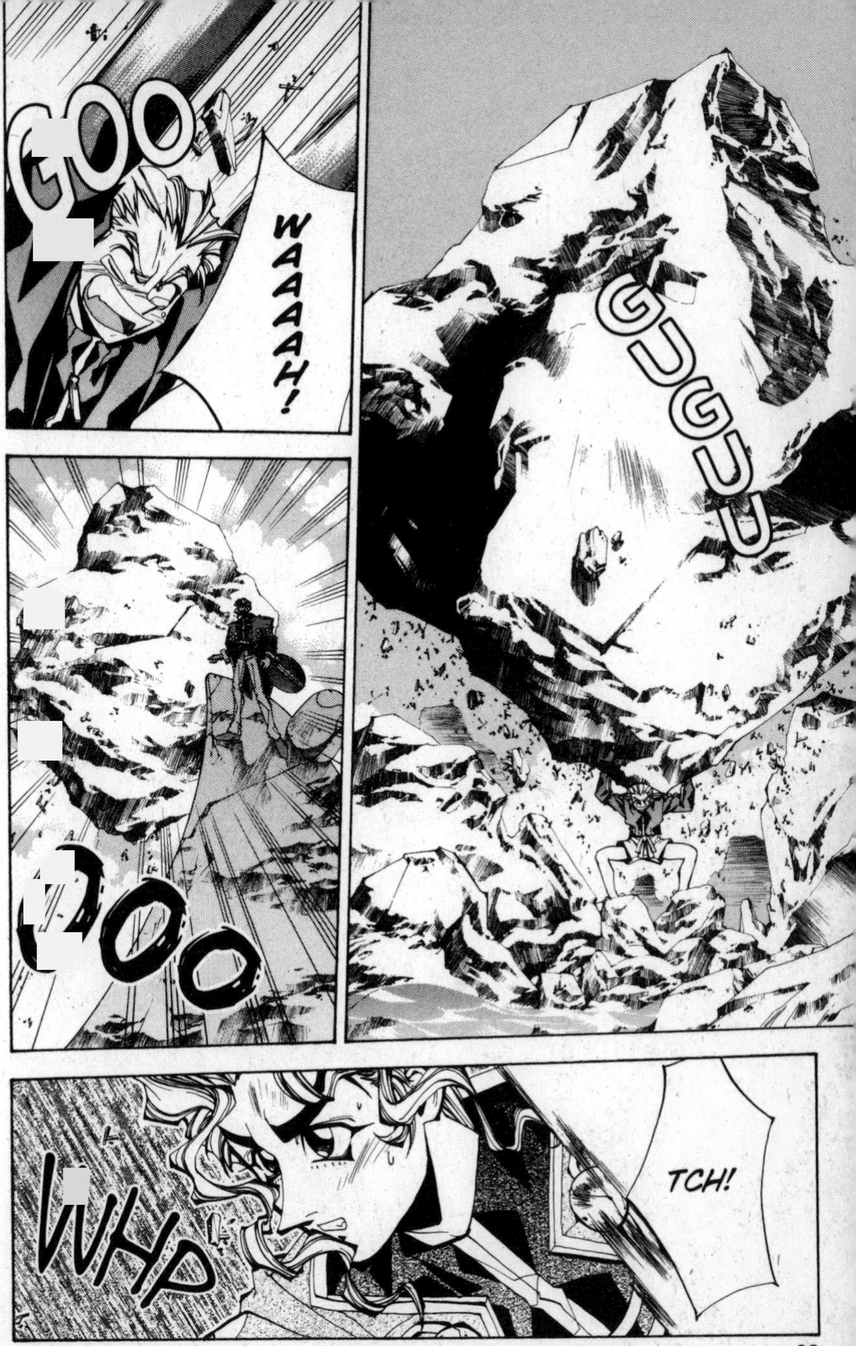
GUGUU
GOO
WAAAAH!
OOO
TCH!
WHP

READ THIS WAY

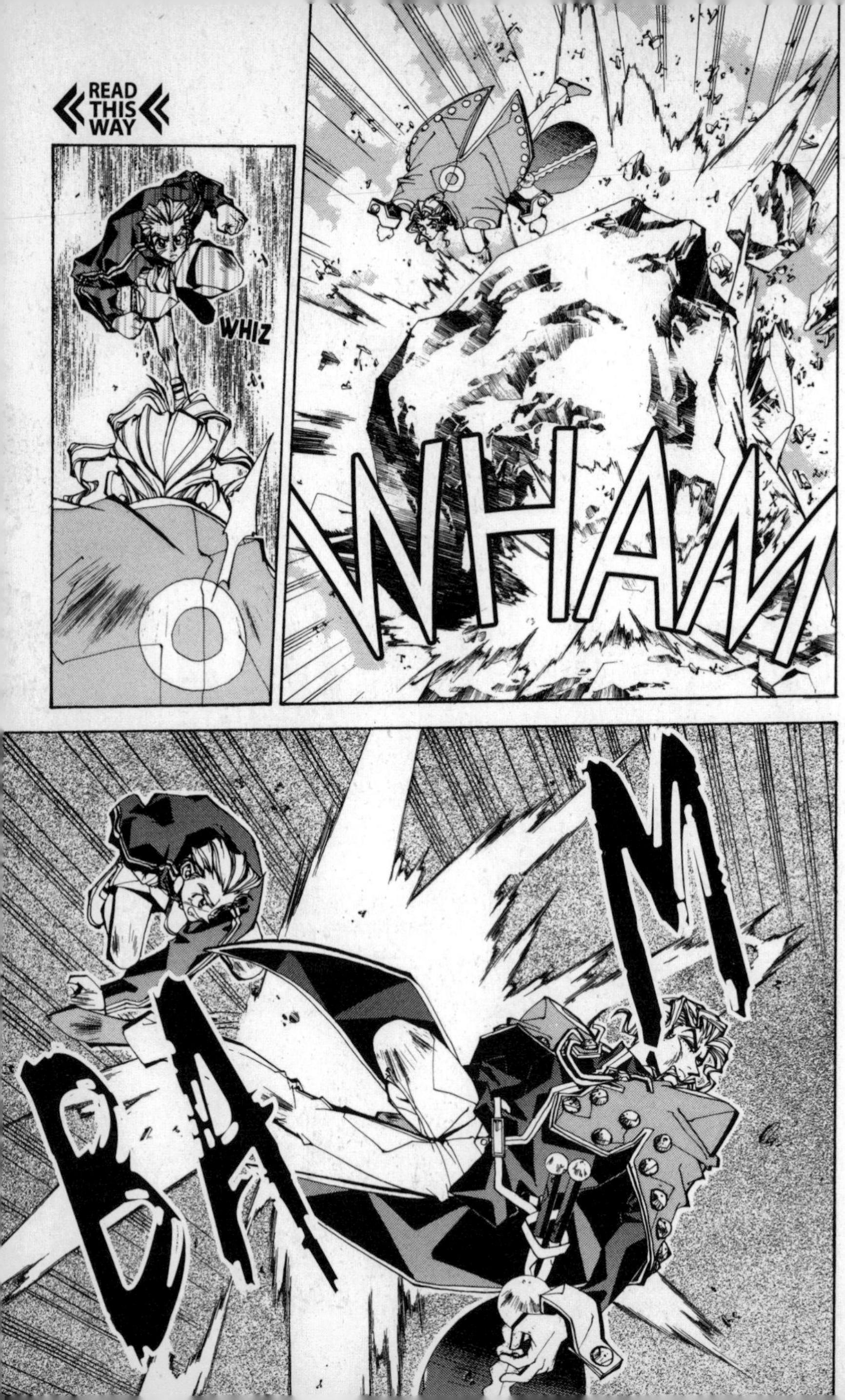
WHAM
WHIZ
BAM

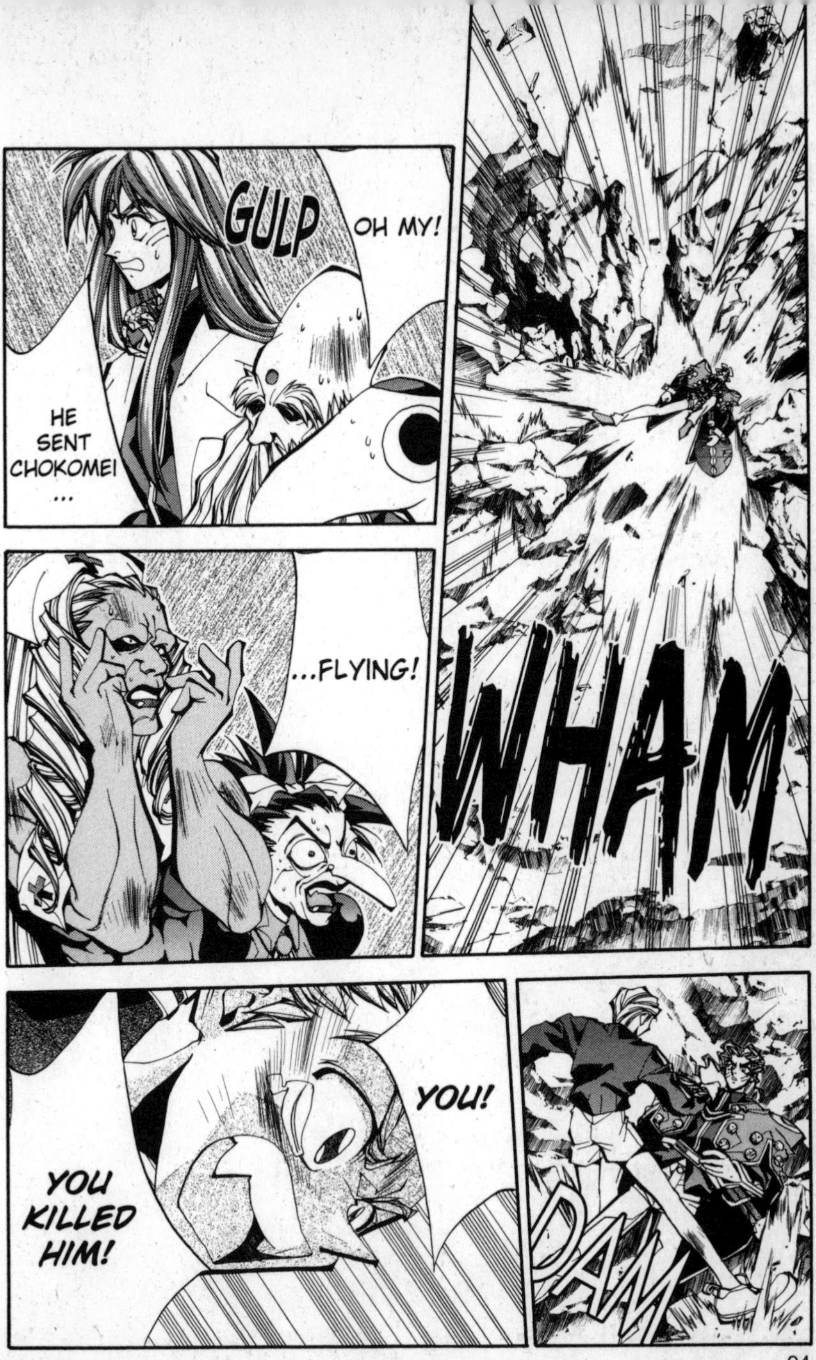
WHAM
OH MY!
GULP
HE SENT CHOKOMEI ...
...FLYING!
DAM
YOU!
YOU KILLED HIM!

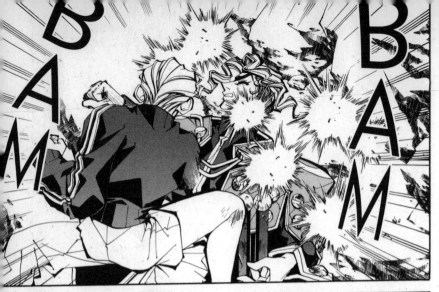

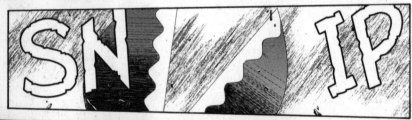

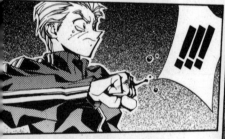

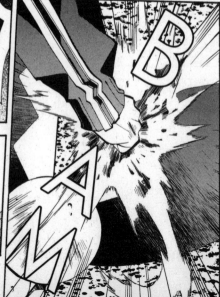

I DIDN'T FORESEE THIS HAPPENING.

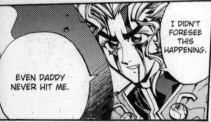

EVEN DADDY NEVER HIT ME.

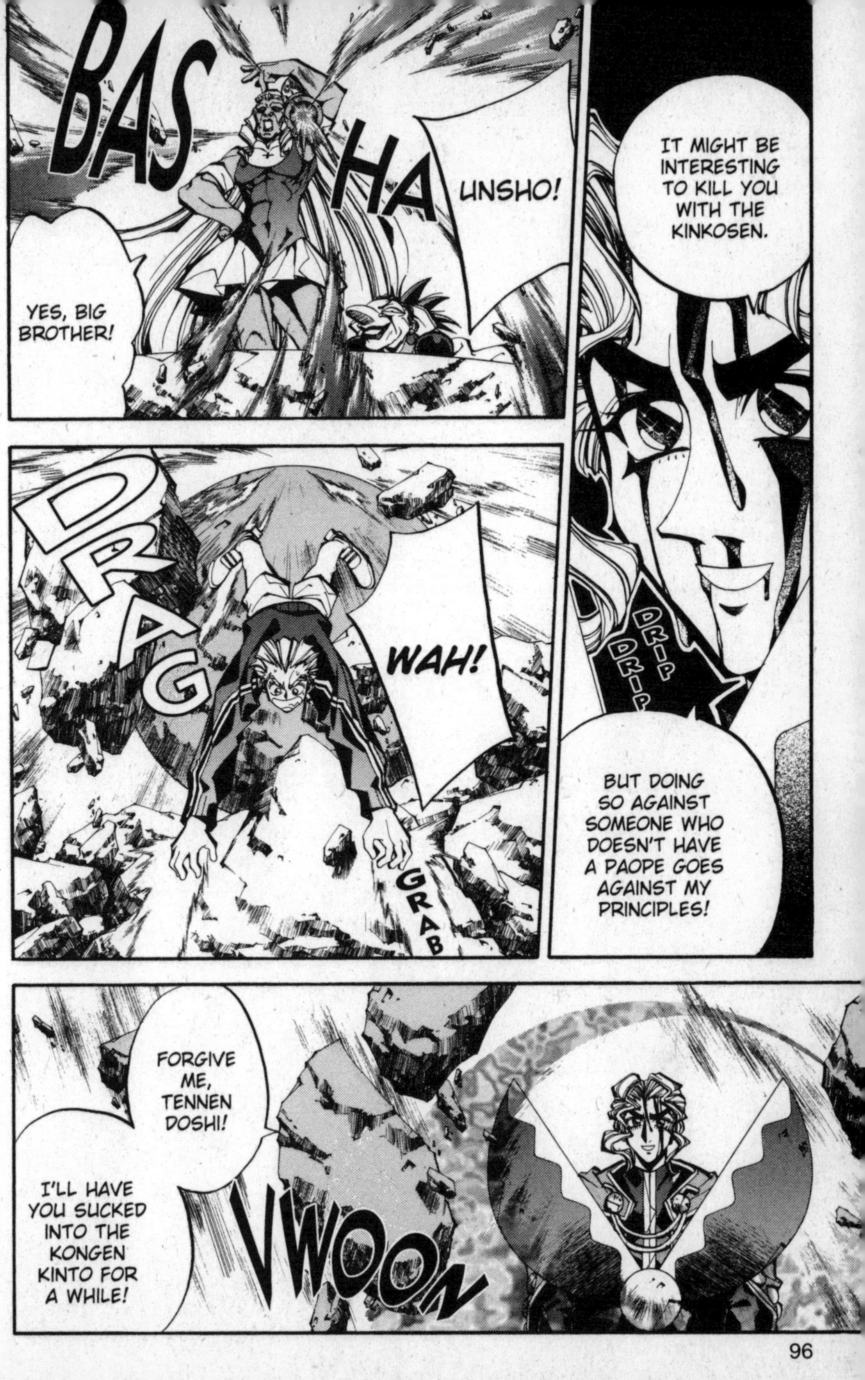
IT MIGHT BE INTERESTING TO KILL YOU WITH THE KINKOSEN.
DRIP DRIP
BUT DOING SO AGAINST SOMEONE WHO DOESN'T HAVE A PAOPE GOES AGAINST MY PRINCIPLES!
UNSHO!
BASHA
YES, BIG BROTHER!
WAH!
DRAG
GRAB
FORGIVE ME, TENNEN DOSHI!
I'LL HAVE YOU SUCKED INTO THE KONGEN KINTO FOR A WHILE!
VWOON

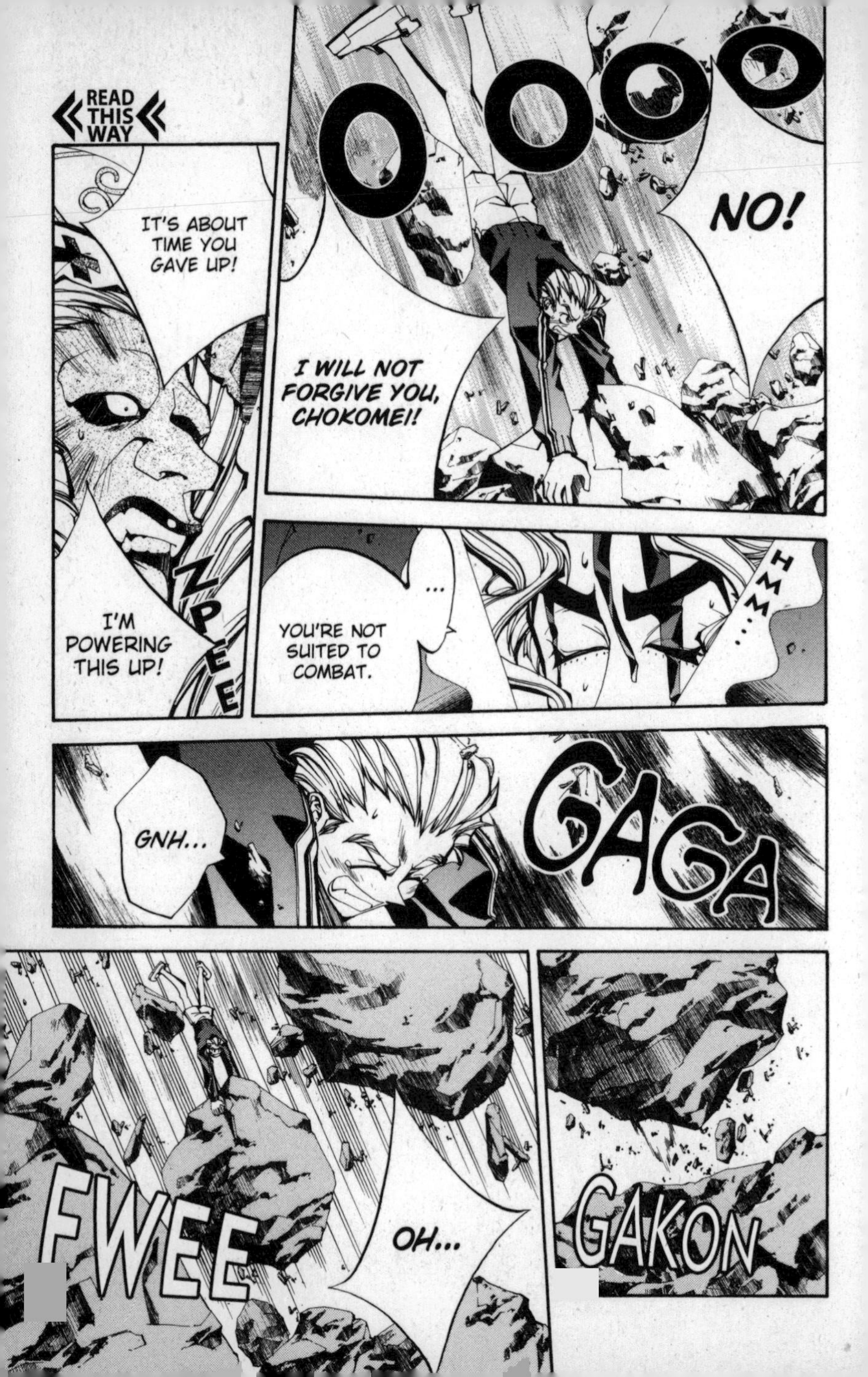
READ THIS WAY
OOOO NO!
I WILL NOT FORGIVE YOU, CHOKOME!!
HMM...
...
YOU'RE NOT SUITED TO COMBAT.
IT'S ABOUT TIME YOU GAVE UP!
ZPEE
I'M POWERING THIS UP!
GAGA
GNH...
GAKON
OH...
FWEE

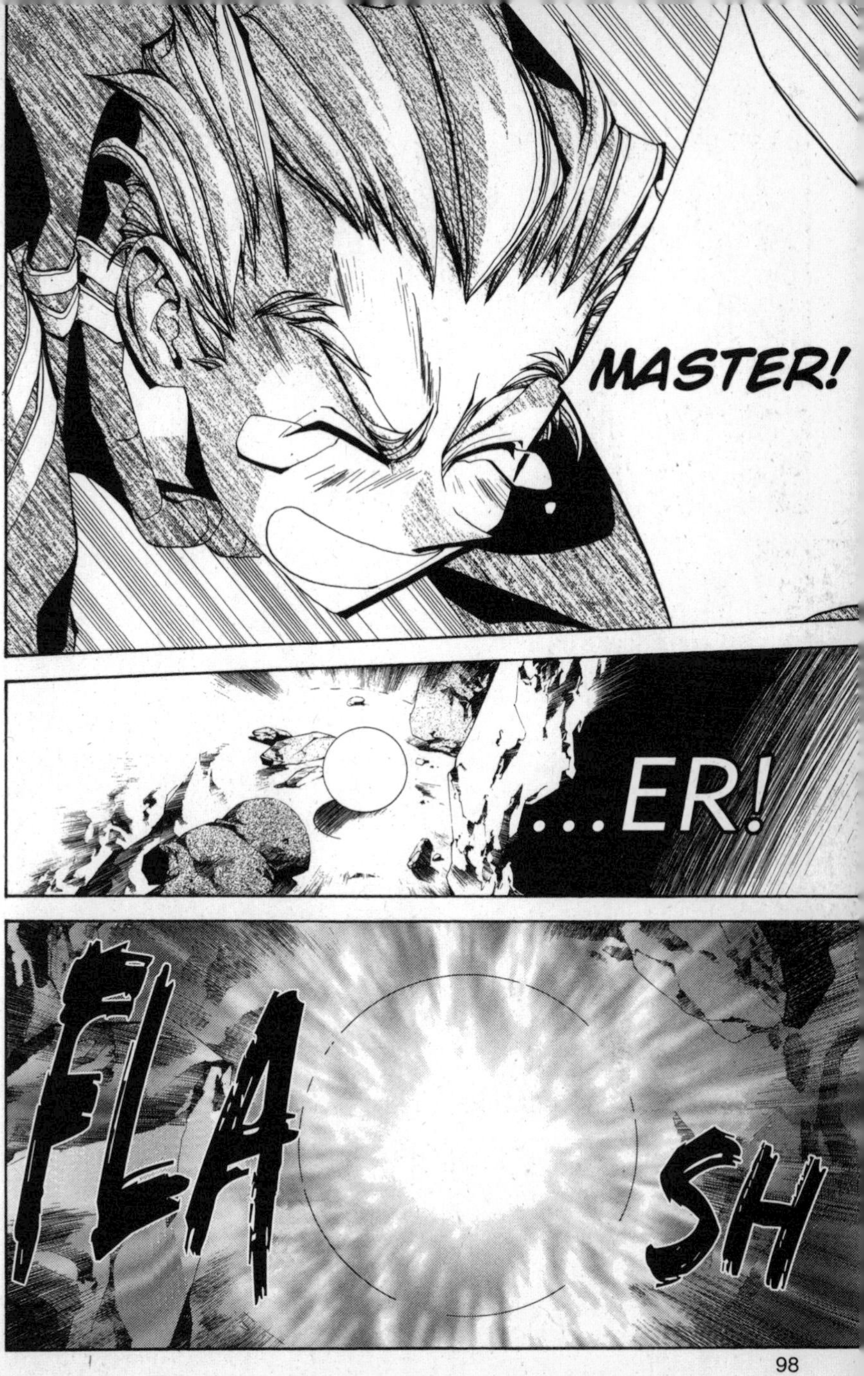
MASTER!
...ER!
FLASH

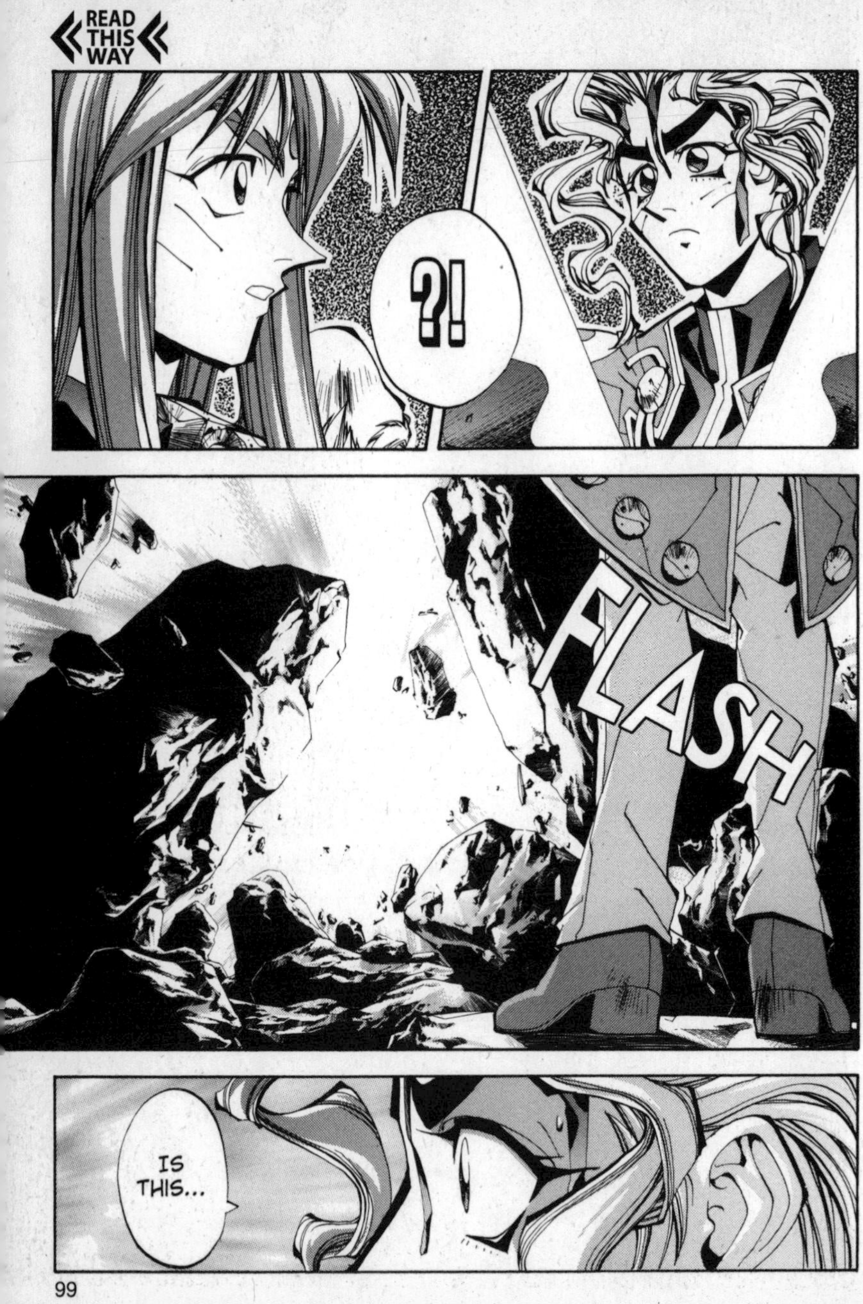
?!
FLASH
IS THIS...

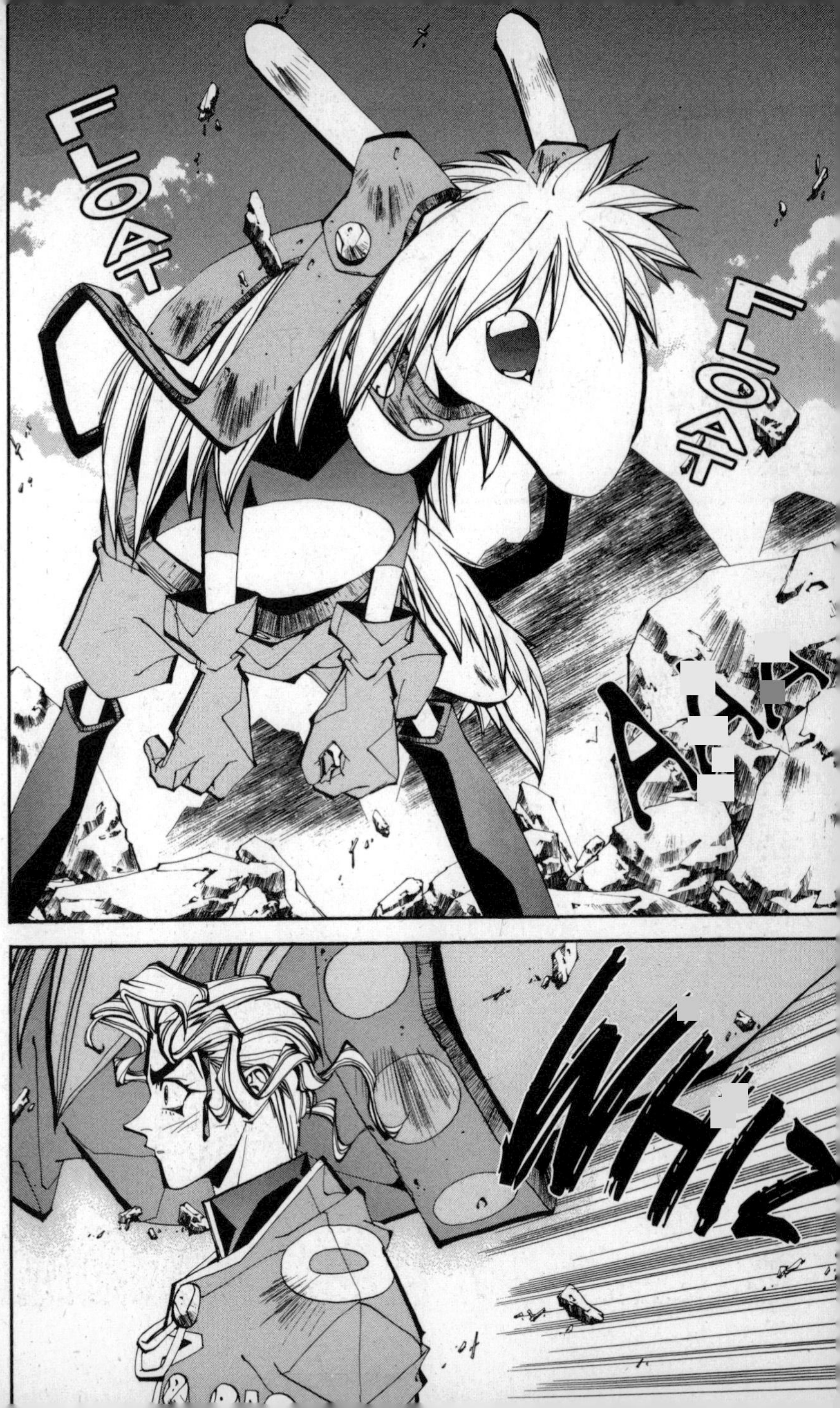
FLOAT
FLOAT
AH
WHIZ

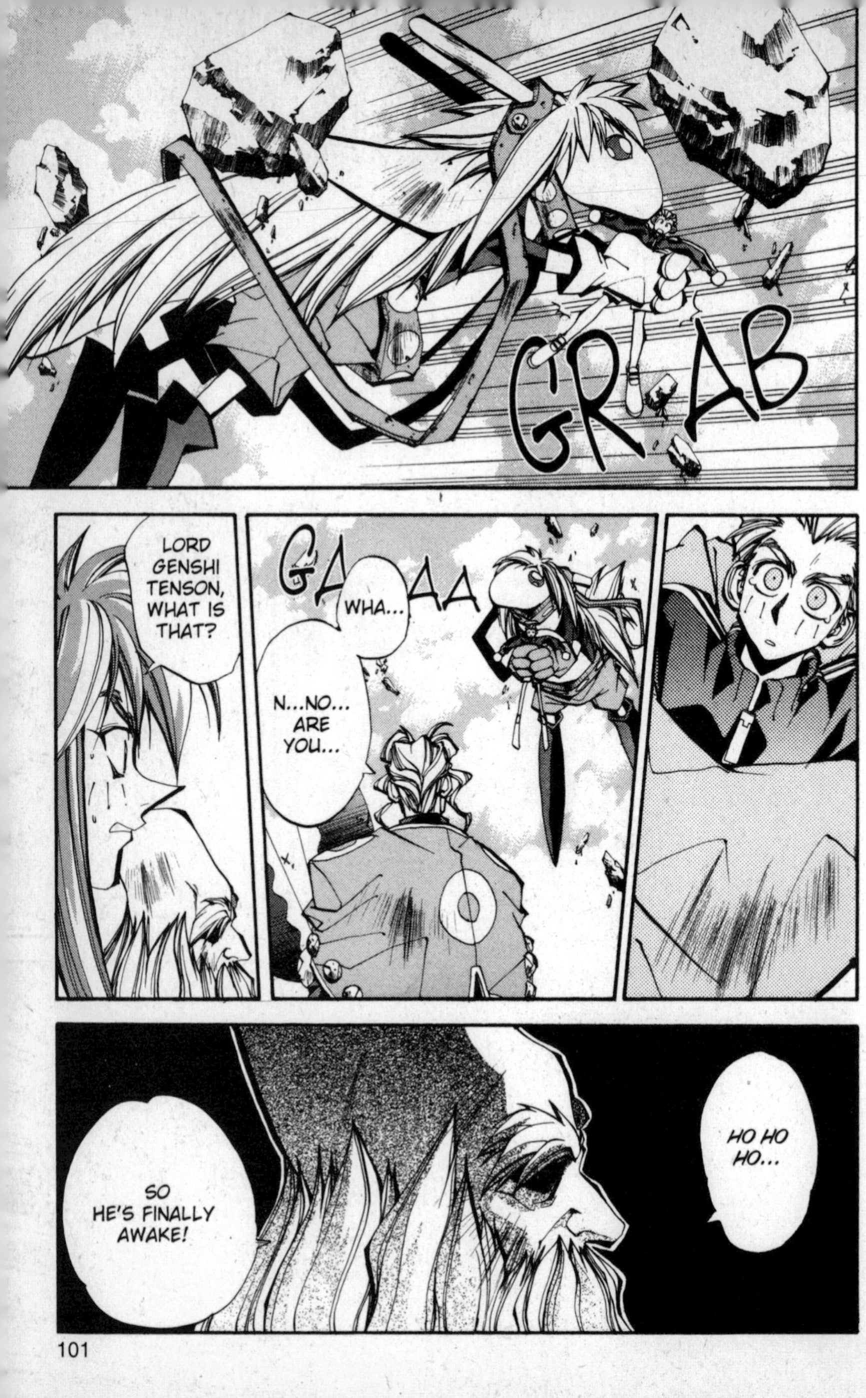
GRAB
GAAA
WHA...
N...NO... ARE YOU...
LORD GENSHI TENSON, WHAT IS THAT?
HO HO HO...
SO HE'S FINALLY AWAKE!

封神演義

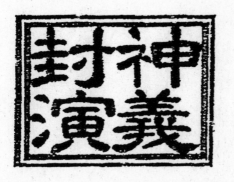

Chapter 103

MEDIUM-BOSS BATTLE, PART 5
THE SUPU VALLEY

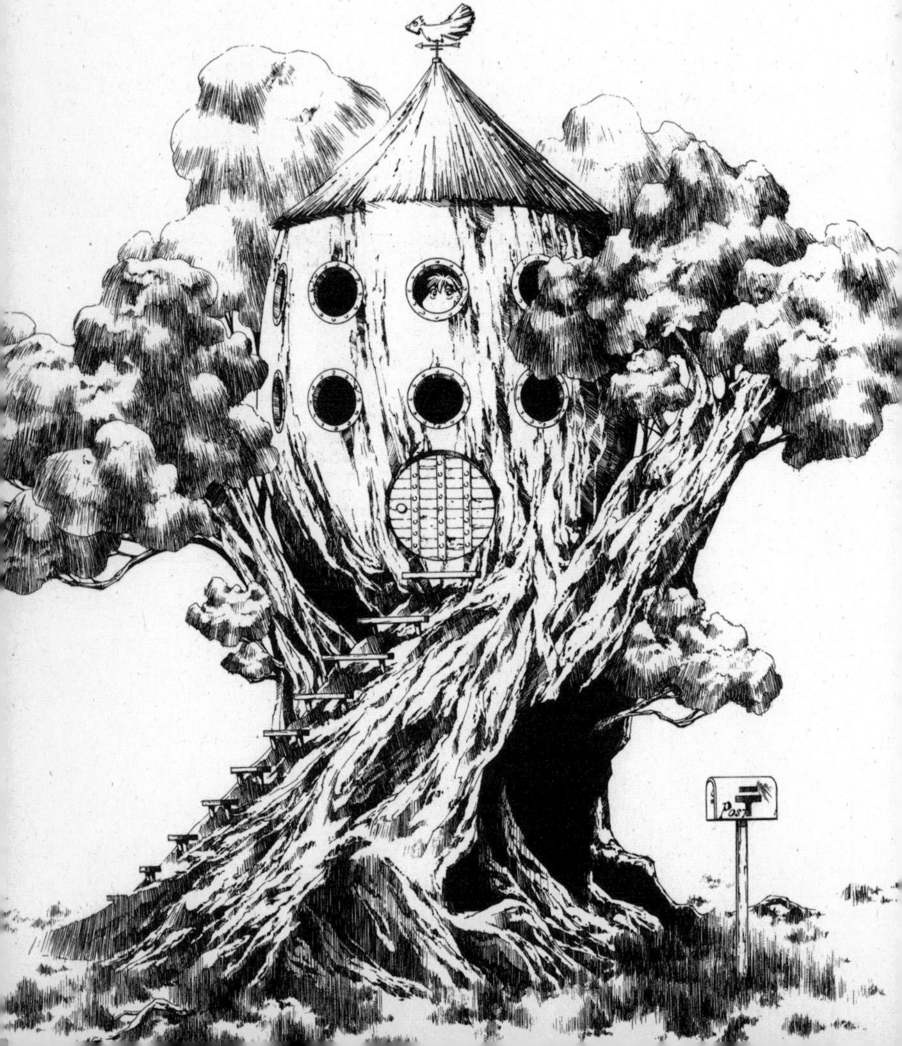
Post

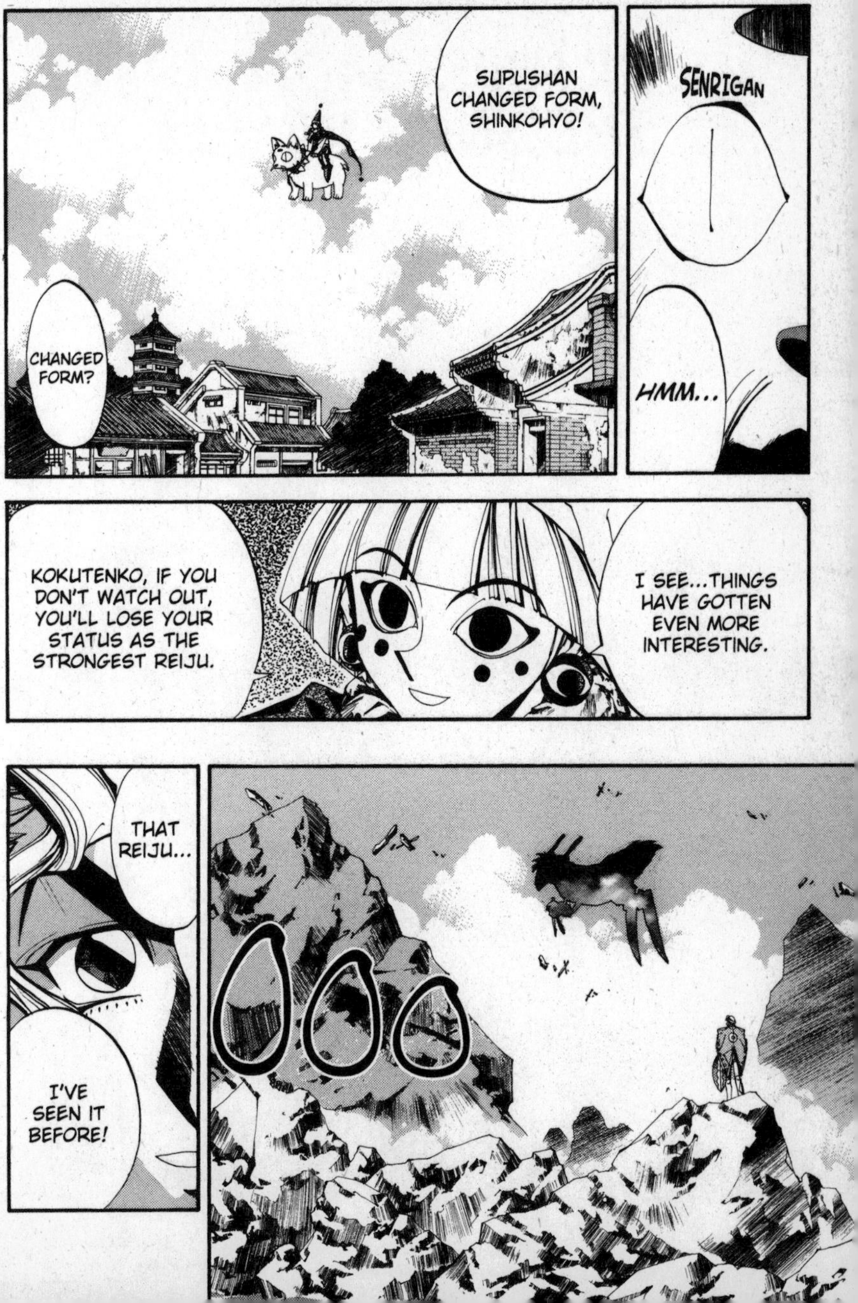
SENRIGAN
HMM...
SUPUSHAN CHANGED FORM, SHINKOHYO!
CHANGED FORM?
I SEE...THINGS HAVE GOTTEN EVEN MORE INTERESTING.
KOKUTENKO, IF YOU DON'T WATCH OUT, YOU'LL LOSE YOUR STATUS AS THE STRONGEST REIJU.
THAT REIJU...
I'VE SEEN IT BEFORE!

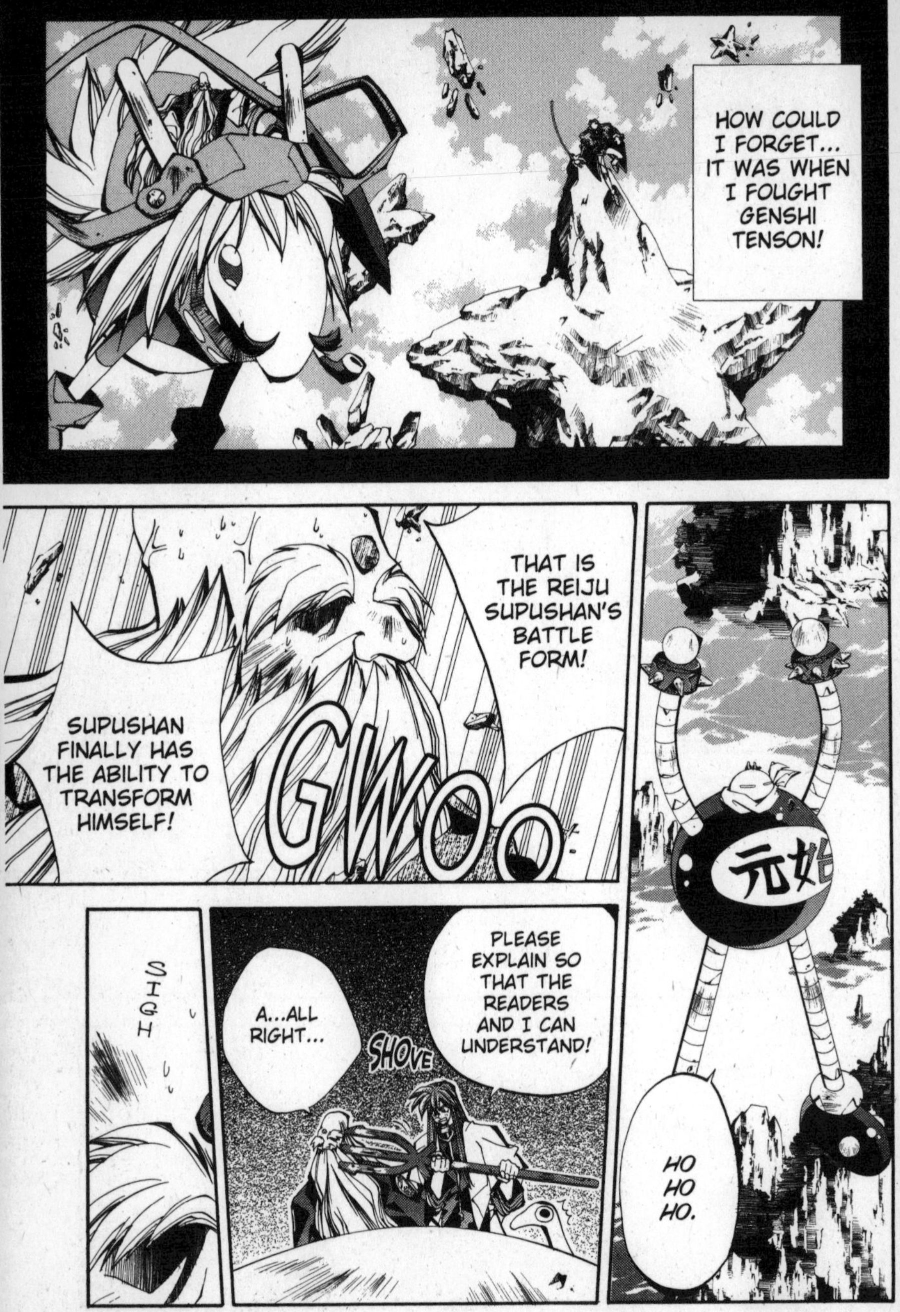
HOW COULD I FORGET... IT WAS WHEN I FOUGHT GENSHI TENSON!
元始
HO HO HO.
THAT IS THE REIJU SUPUSHAN'S BATTLE FORM!
SUPUSHAN FINALLY HAS THE ABILITY TO TRANSFORM HIMSELF!
GWOO
PLEASE EXPLAIN SO THAT THE READERS AND I CAN UNDERSTAND!
A...ALL RIGHT...
SHOVE
SIGH

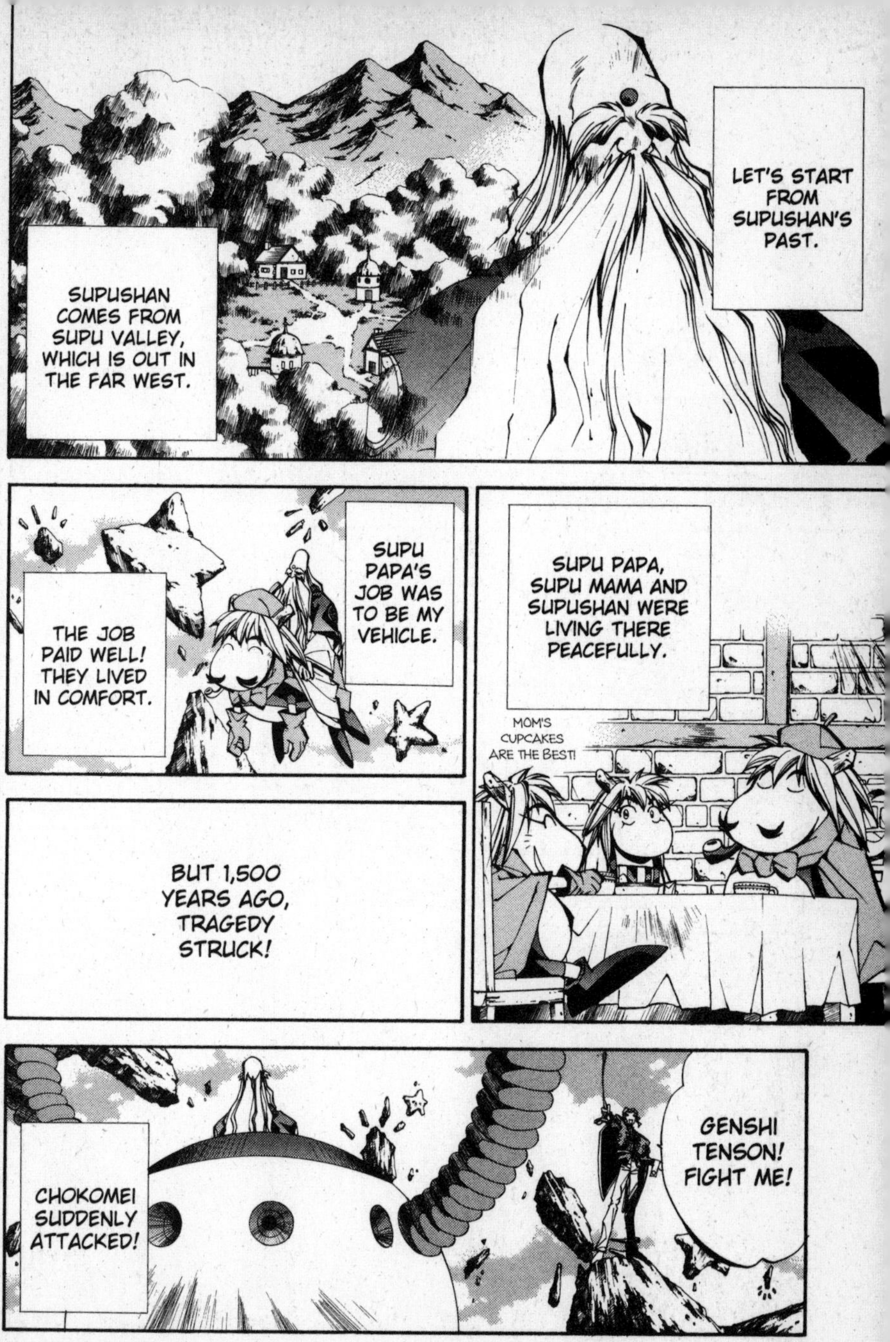
LET'S START FROM SUPUSHAN'S PAST.
SUPUSHAN COMES FROM SUPU VALLEY, WHICH IS OUT IN THE FAR WEST.
SUPU PAPA, SUPU MAMA AND SUPUSHAN WERE LIVING THERE PEACEFULLY.
MOM'S CUPCAKES ARE THE BEST!
SUPU PAPA'S JOB WAS TO BE MY VEHICLE.
THE JOB PAID WELL! THEY LIVED IN COMFORT.
BUT 1,500 YEARS AGO, TRAGEDY STRUCK!
GENSHI TENSON! FIGHT ME!
CHOKOMEI SUDDENLY ATTACKED!

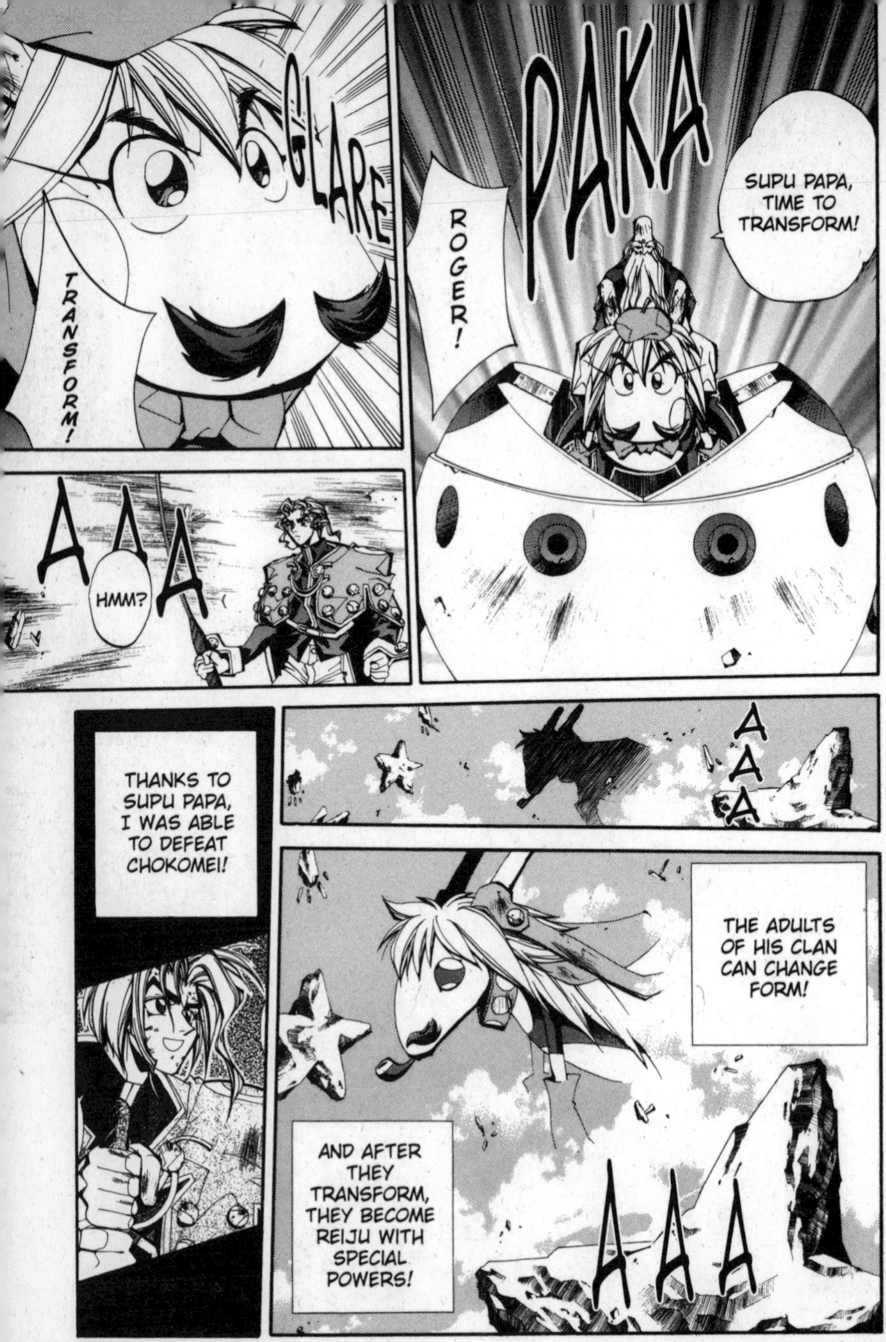
SUPU PAPA, TIME TO TRANSFORM!
PAKA
ROGER!
GLARE
TRANSFORM!
HMM?
AAA
AAA
THE ADULTS OF HIS CLAN CAN CHANGE FORM!
AND AFTER THEY TRANSFORM, THEY BECOME REIJU WITH SPECIAL POWERS!
PAAA
THANKS TO SUPU PAPA, I WAS ABLE TO DEFEAT CHOKOMEI!

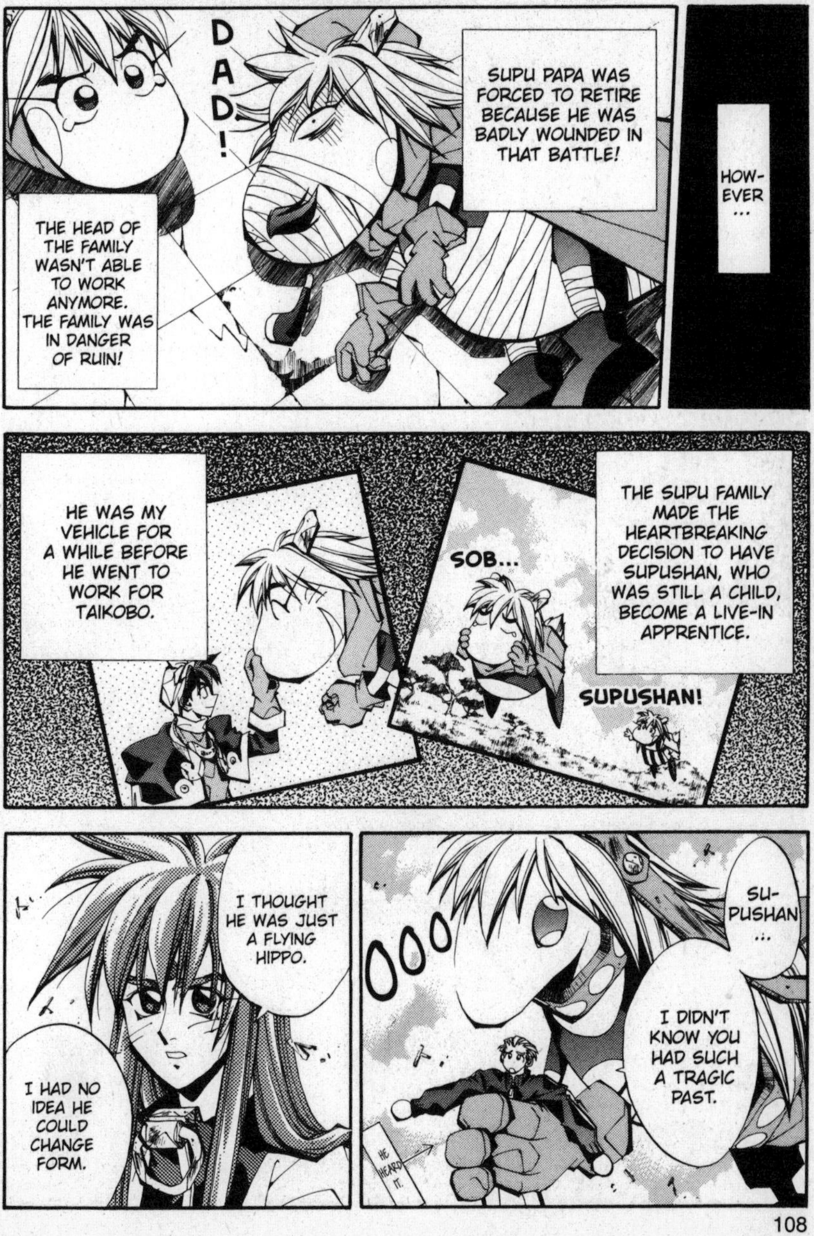
HOW-EVER...
SUPU PAPA WAS FORCED TO RETIRE BECAUSE HE WAS BADLY WOUNDED IN THAT BATTLE!
DAD!
THE HEAD OF THE FAMILY WASN'T ABLE TO WORK ANYMORE. THE FAMILY WAS IN DANGER OF RUIN!
THE SUPU FAMILY MADE THE HEARTBREAKING DECISION TO HAVE SUPUSHAN, WHO WAS STILL A CHILD, BECOME A LIVE-IN APPRENTICE.
SOB...
SUPUSHAN!
HE WAS MY VEHICLE FOR A WHILE BEFORE HE WENT TO WORK FOR TAIKOBO.
SU-PUSHAN...
OOO
I DIDN'T KNOW YOU HAD SUCH A TRAGIC PAST.
HE HEARD IT.
I THOUGHT HE WAS JUST A FLYING HIPPO.
I HAD NO IDEA HE COULD CHANGE FORM.

READ THIS WAY

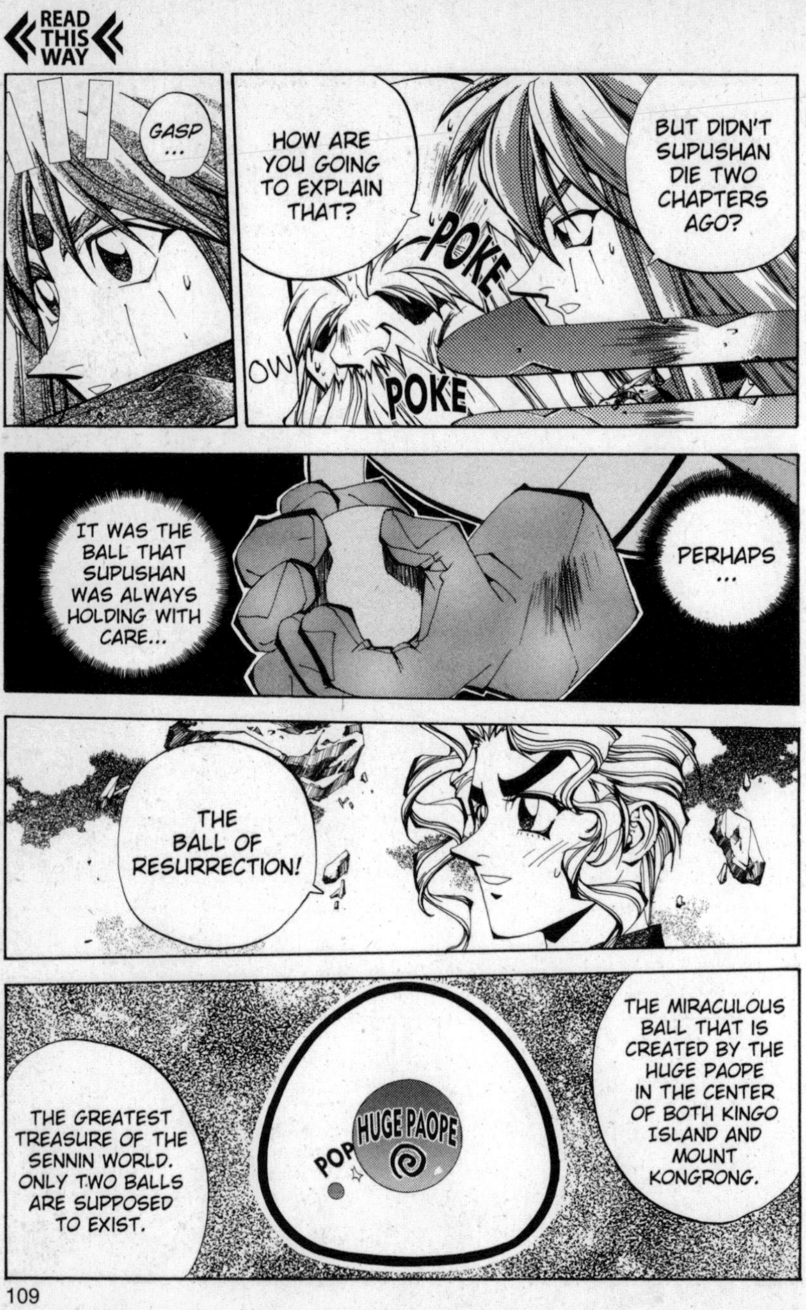

BUT DIDN'T SUPUSHAN DIE TWO CHAPTERS AGO?
HOW ARE YOU GOING TO EXPLAIN THAT?
POKE
POKE
OW
GASP ...
PERHAPS ...
IT WAS THE BALL THAT SUPUSHAN WAS ALWAYS HOLDING WITH CARE...
THE BALL OF RESURRECTION!
THE MIRACULOUS BALL THAT IS CREATED BY THE HUGE PAOPE IN THE CENTER OF BOTH KINGO ISLAND AND MOUNT KONGRONG.
HUGE PAOPE
POP
THE GREATEST TREASURE OF THE SENNIN WORLD. ONLY TWO BALLS ARE SUPPOSED TO EXIST.

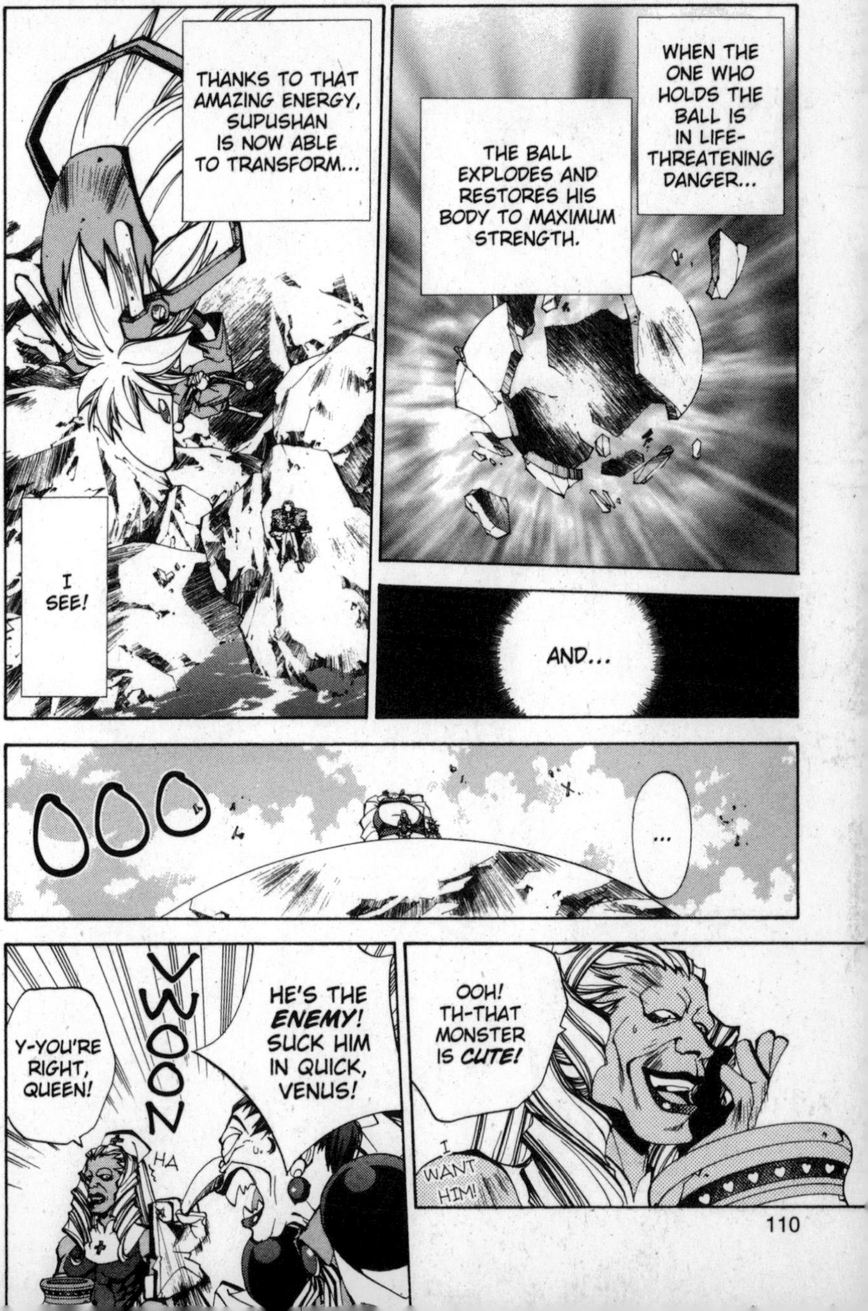

WHEN THE ONE WHO HOLDS THE BALL IS IN LIFE-THREATENING DANGER...
THE BALL EXPLODES AND RESTORES HIS BODY TO MAXIMUM STRENGTH.
AND...
THANKS TO THAT AMAZING ENERGY, SUPUSHAN IS NOW ABLE TO TRANSFORM...
I SEE!
...
OOO
OOH! TH-THAT MONSTER IS ***CUTE!***
I WANT HIM!
HE'S THE ***ENEMY!*** SUCK HIM IN QUICK, VENUS!
VWOON
Y-YOU'RE RIGHT, QUEEN!
HA

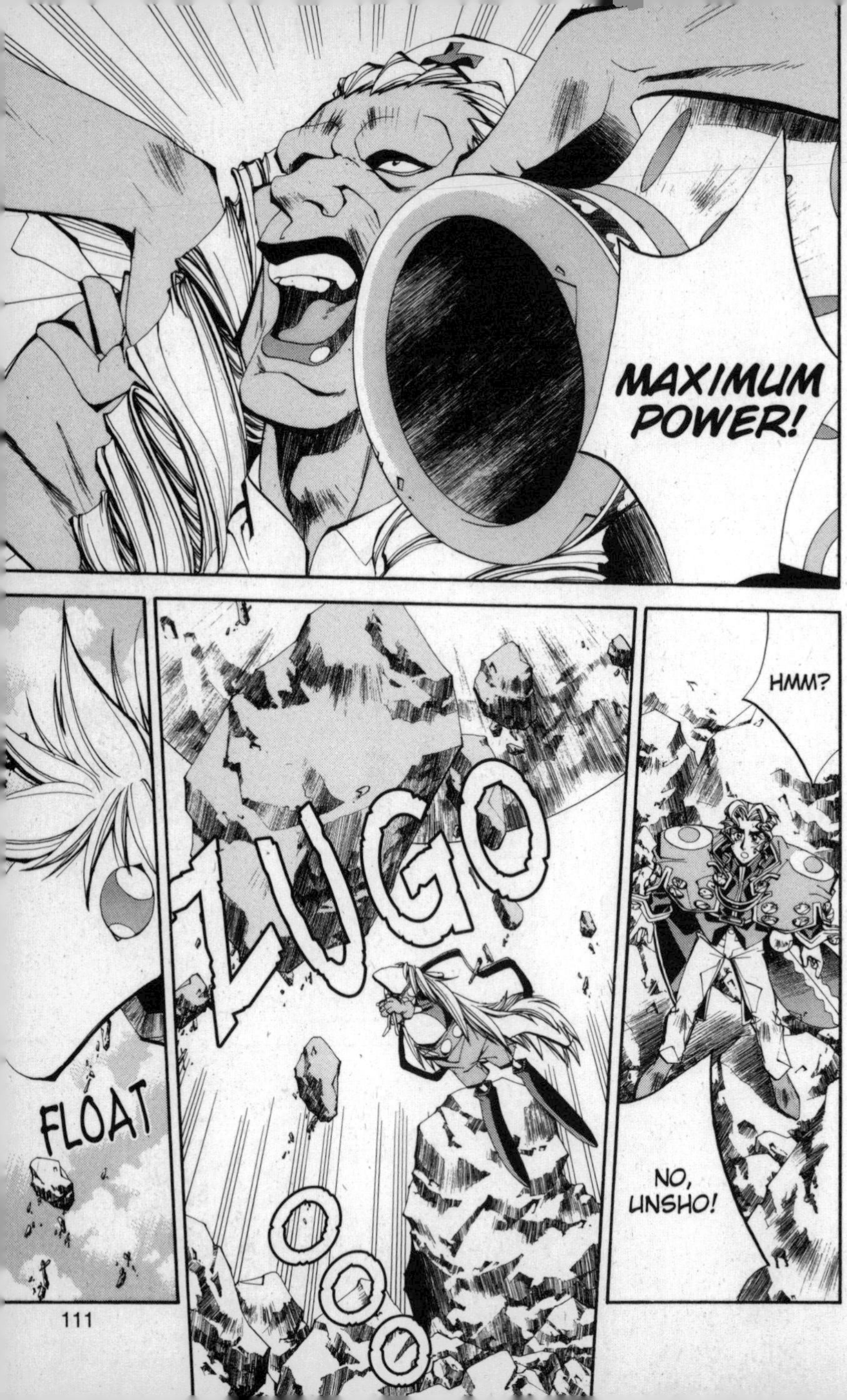
MAXIMUM POWER!
HMM?
NO, UNSHO!
ZUGO
OOOO
FLOAT

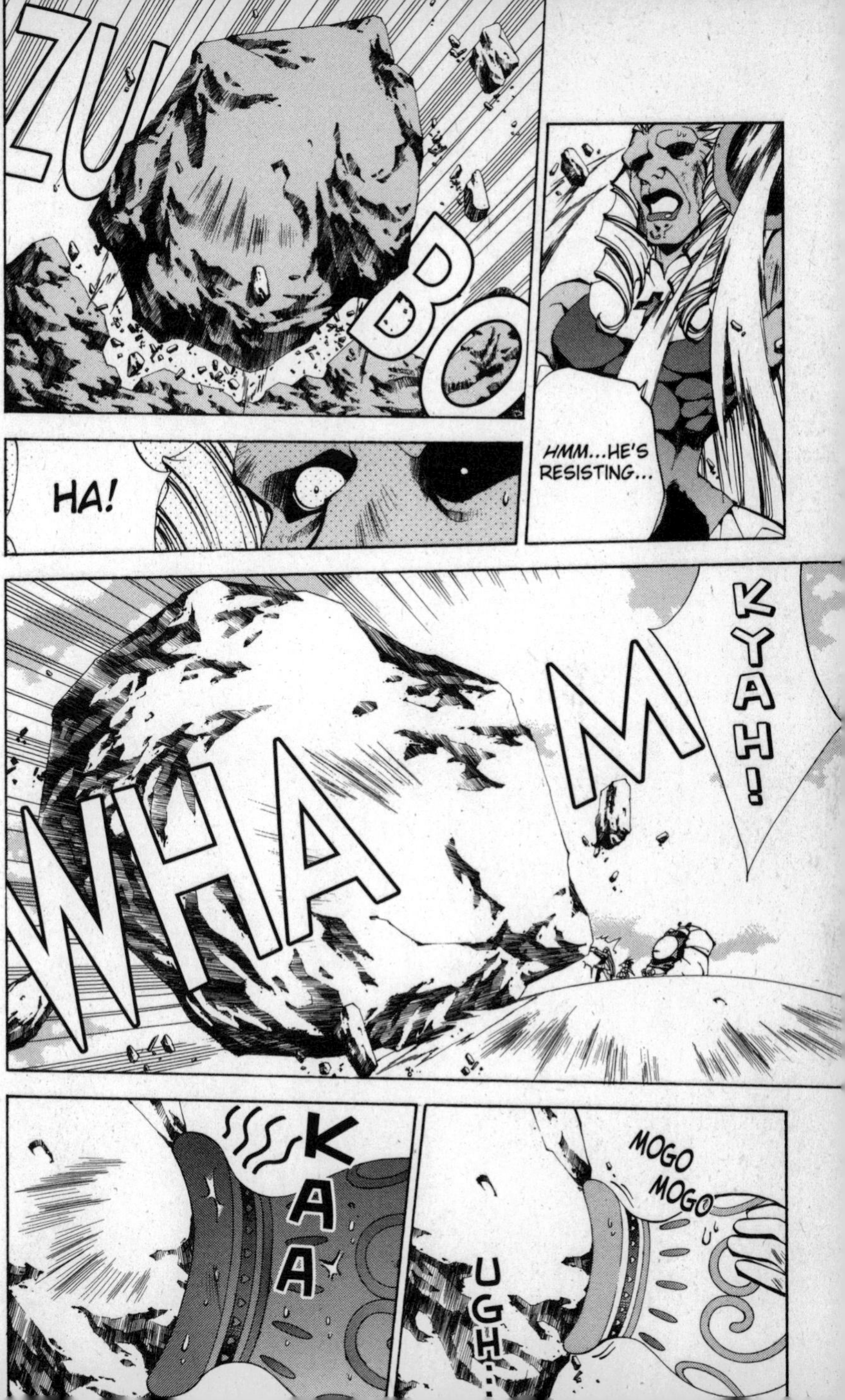
HMM...HE'S RESISTING...
ZU
BO
HA!
KYAH!
WHAM
MOGO MOGO
UGH...
KAA

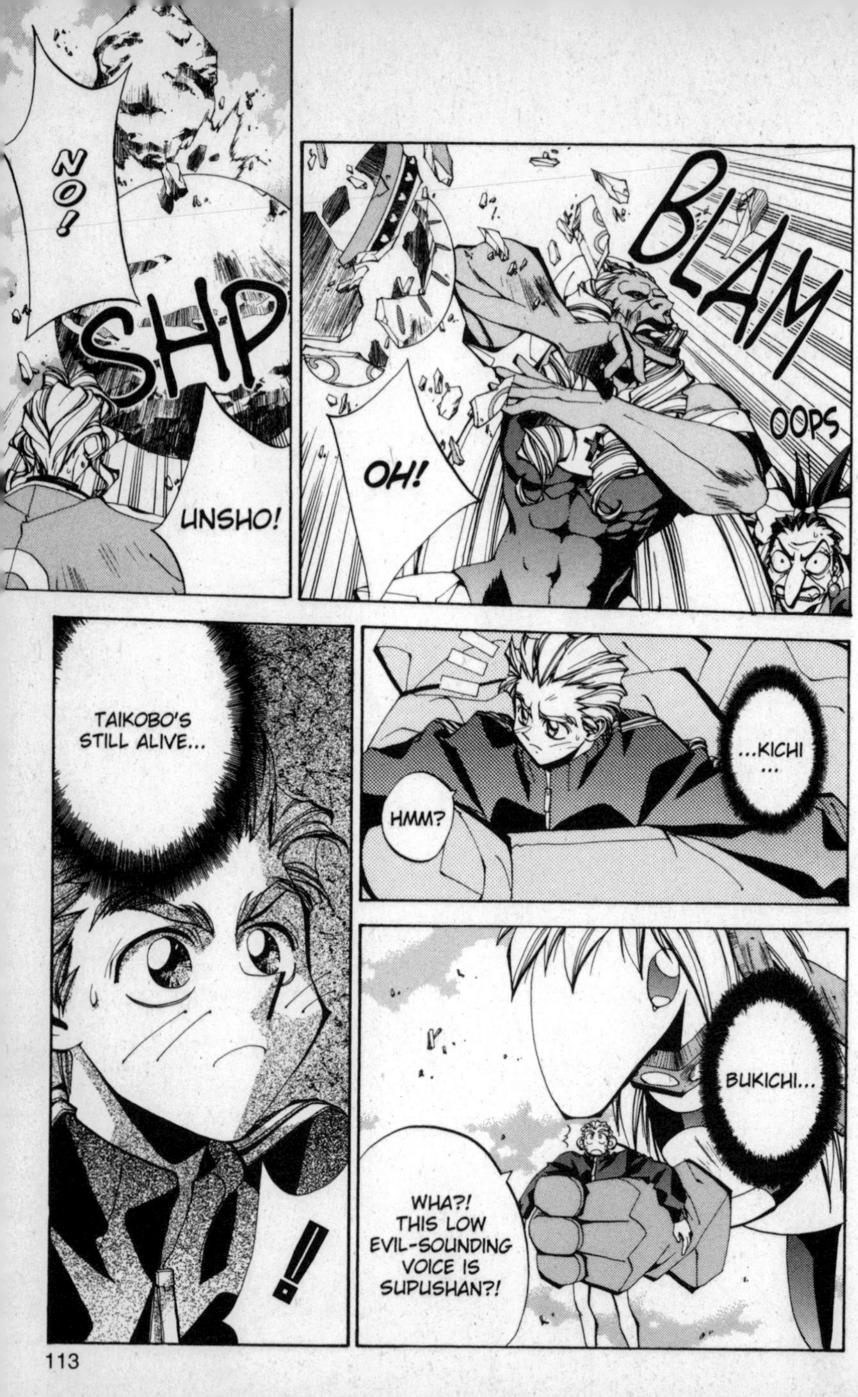
BLAM
OOPS
OH!
NO!
SHP
UNSHO!
...KICHI ...
HMM?
BUKICHI...
WHA?! THIS LOW EVIL-SOUNDING VOICE IS SUPUSHAN?!
TAIKOBO'S STILL ALIVE...
!

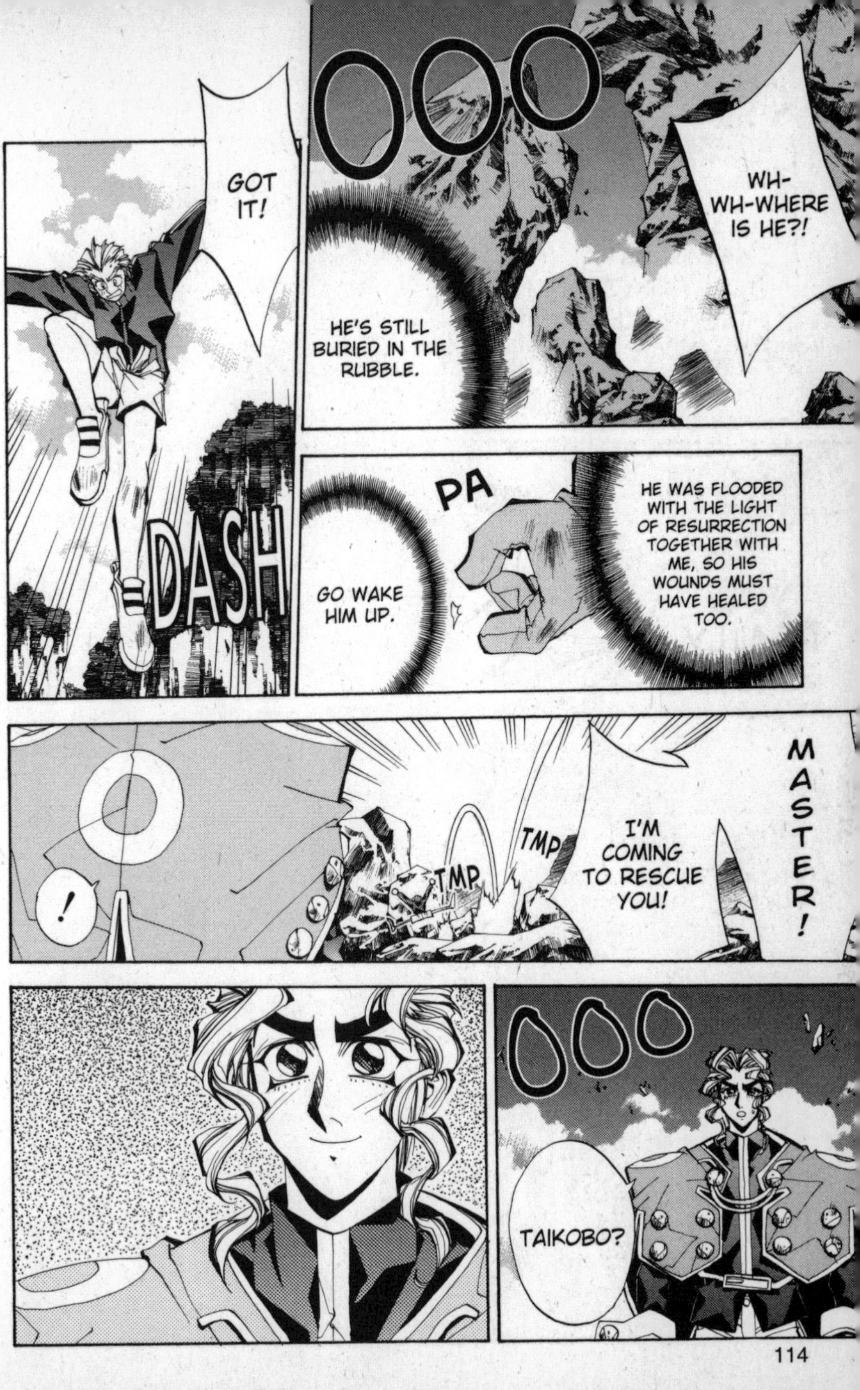
WH- WH-WHERE IS HE?!
OOO
HE'S STILL BURIED IN THE RUBBLE.
HE WAS FLOODED WITH THE LIGHT OF RESURRECTION TOGETHER WITH ME, SO HIS WOUNDS MUST HAVE HEALED TOO.
PA
GO WAKE HIM UP.
GOT IT!
DASH
MASTER!
I'M COMING TO RESCUE YOU!
TMP
TMP
!
OOO
TAIKOBO?

READ THIS WAY

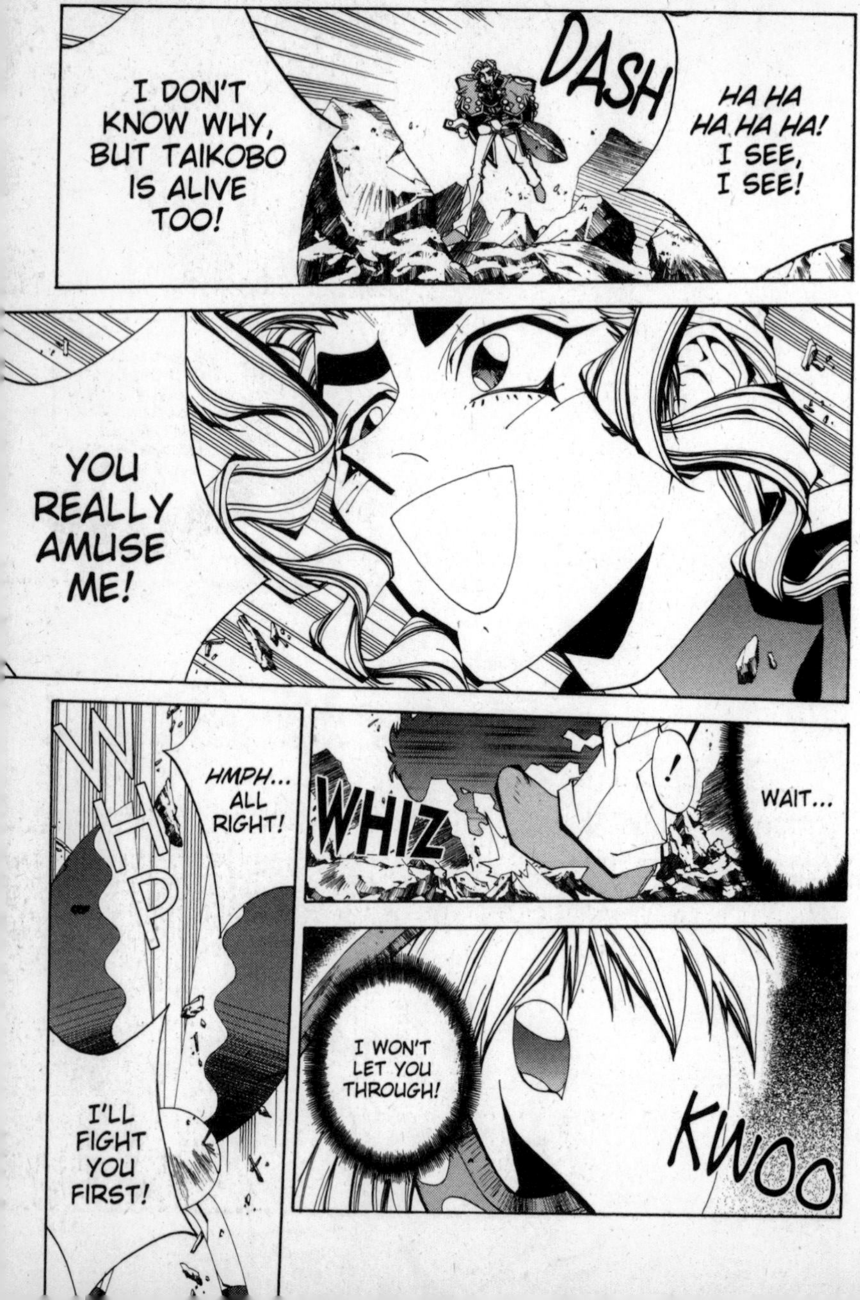
DASH
HA HA HA HA HA! I SEE, I SEE!
I DON'T KNOW WHY, BUT TAIKOBO IS ALIVE TOO!
YOU REALLY AMUSE ME!
WAIT...
!
WHIZ
KWOO
I WON'T LET YOU THROUGH!
HMPH... ALL RIGHT!
WHIP
I'LL FIGHT YOU FIRST!

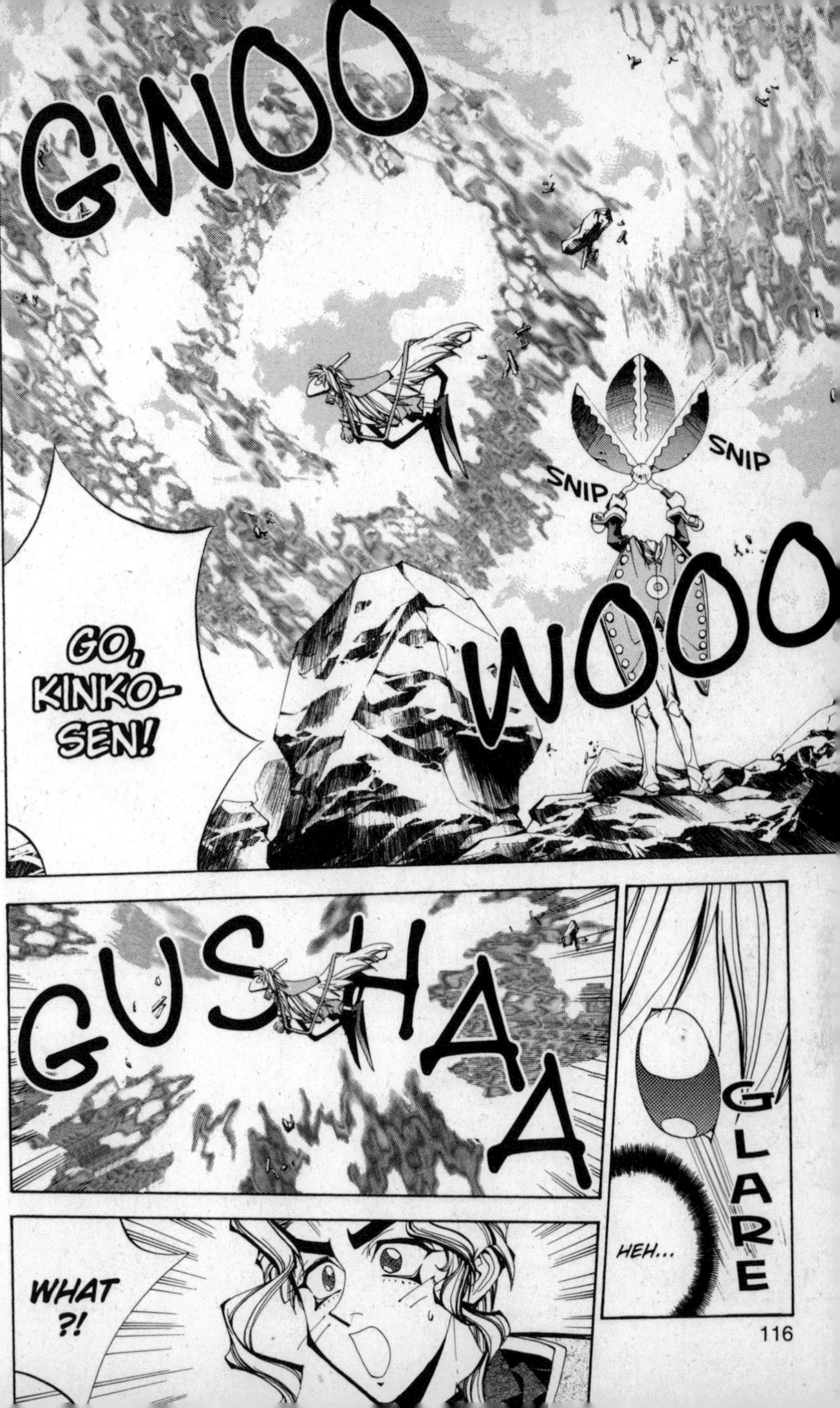
GWOO
SNIP
SNIP
WOOOO
GO, KINKO-SEN!
GLARE
HEH...
GUSHA
WHAT ?!

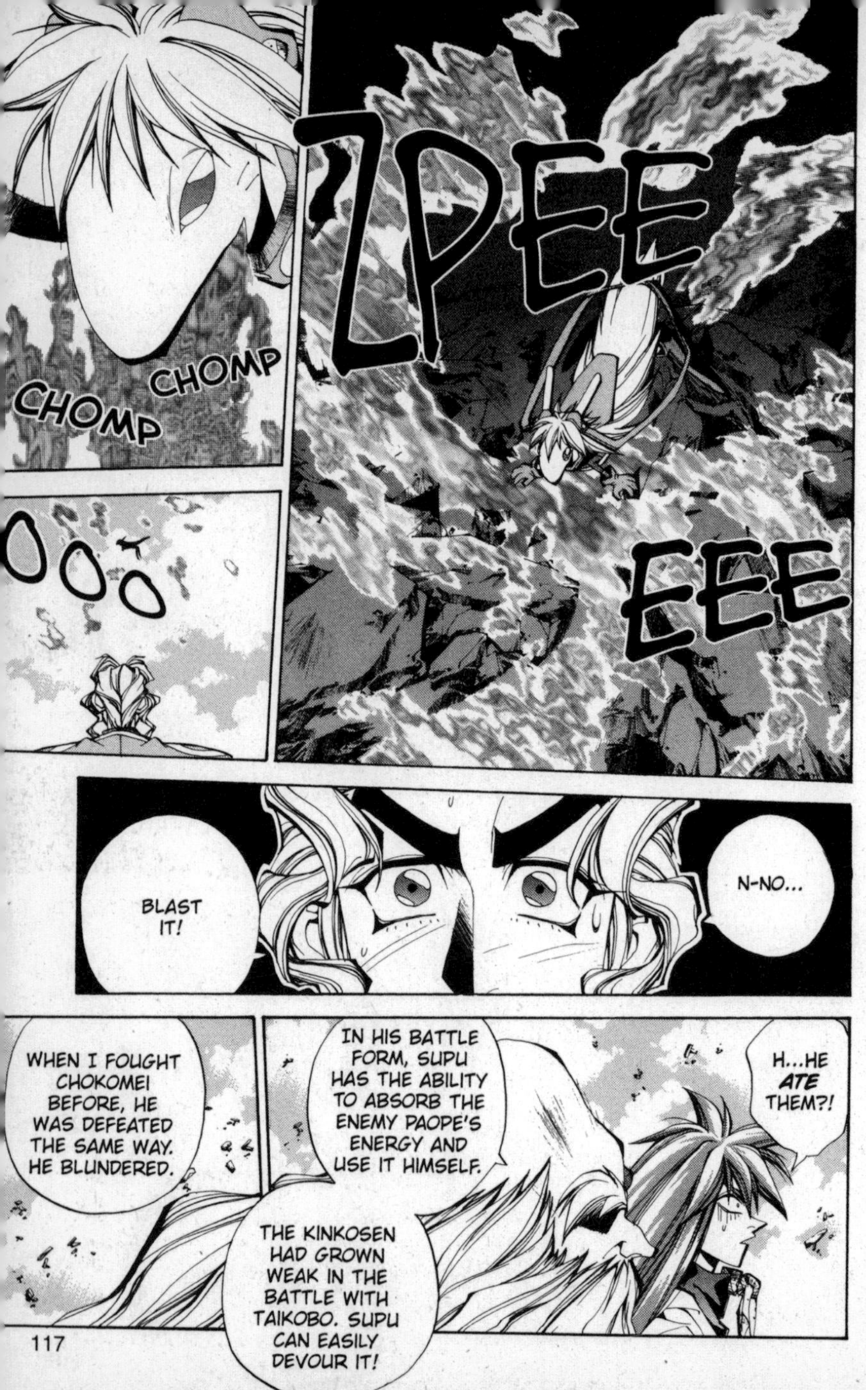
ZPEE
EEE
CHOMP
CHOMP
OOO
N-NO...
BLAST IT!
H...HE ATE THEM?!
IN HIS BATTLE FORM, SUPU HAS THE ABILITY TO ABSORB THE ENEMY PAOPE'S ENERGY AND USE IT HIMSELF.
THE KINKOSEN HAD GROWN WEAK IN THE BATTLE WITH TAIKOBO. SUPU CAN EASILY DEVOUR IT!
WHEN I FOUGHT CHOKOMEI BEFORE, HE WAS DEFEATED THE SAME WAY. HE BLUNDERED.

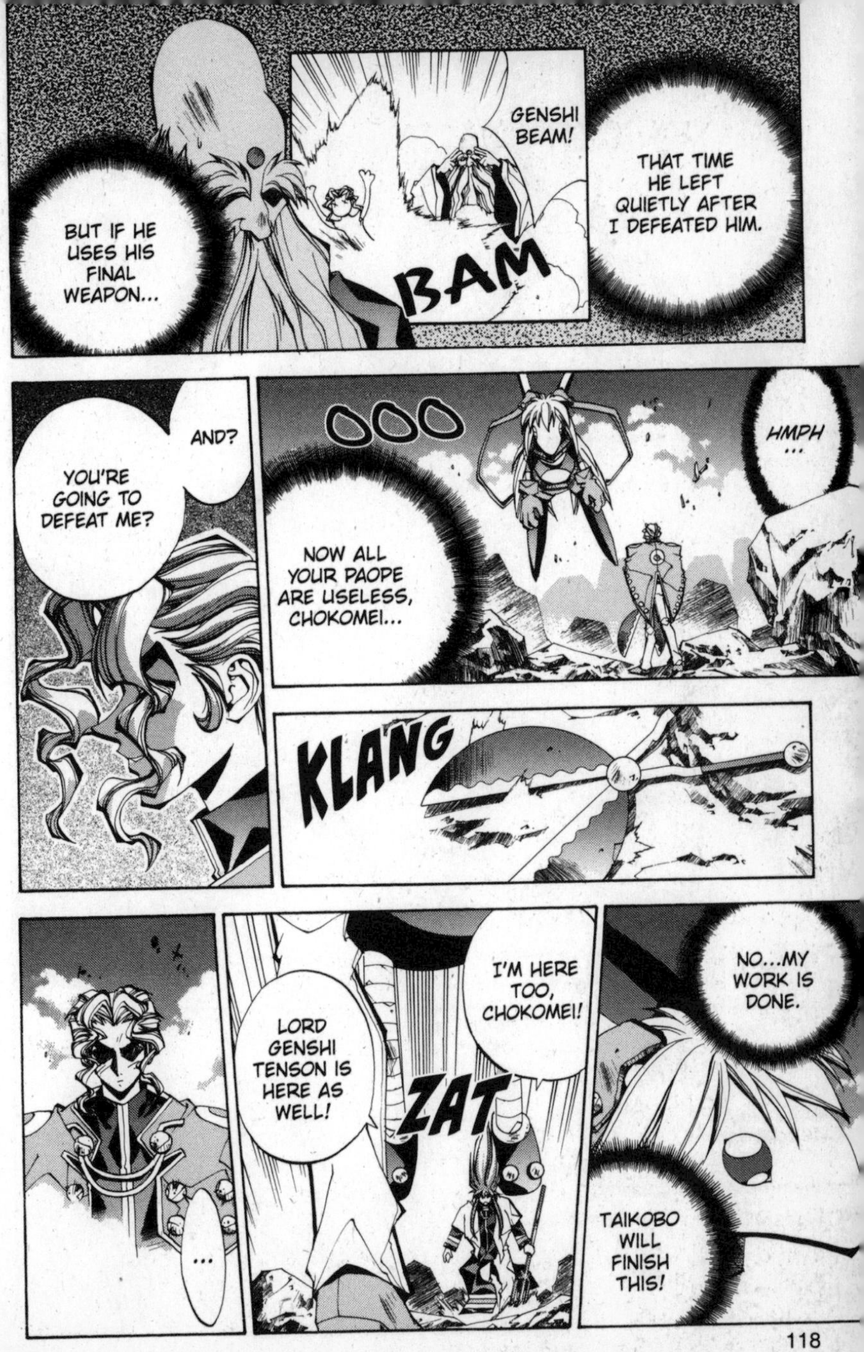
THAT TIME HE LEFT QUIETLY AFTER I DEFEATED HIM.
GENSHI BEAM!
BAM
BUT IF HE USES HIS FINAL WEAPON...
HMPH ...
OOO
NOW ALL YOUR PAOPE ARE USELESS, CHOKOMEI...
KLANG
AND?
YOU'RE GOING TO DEFEAT ME?
NO...MY WORK IS DONE.
TAIKOBO WILL FINISH THIS!
I'M HERE TOO, CHOKOMEI!
LORD GENSHI TENSON IS HERE AS WELL!
ZAT
...

READ THIS WAY

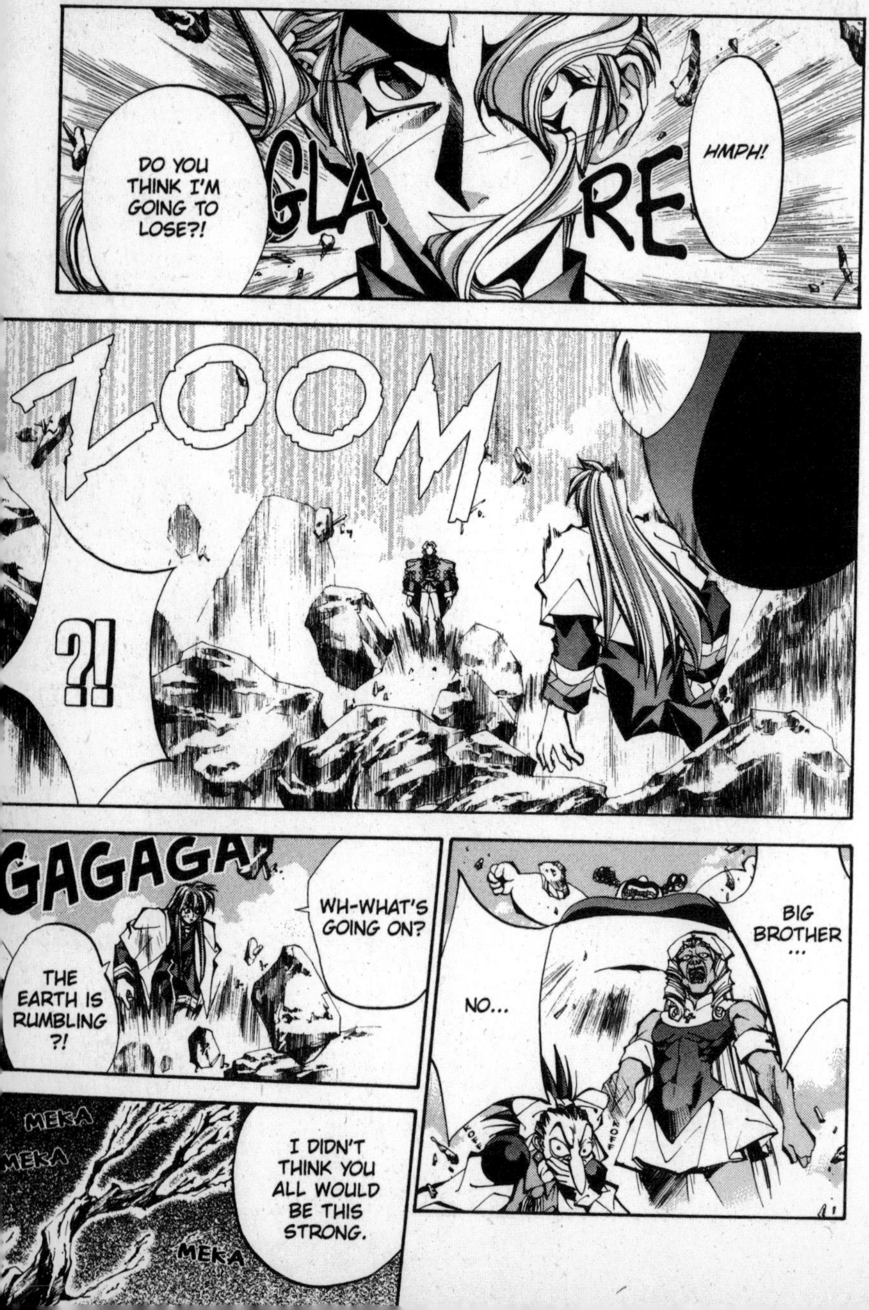
HMPH!
GLARE
DO YOU THINK I'M GOING TO LOSE?!
ZOOM
?!
BIG BROTHER...
NO...
KOFF
KOFF
GAGAGA
WH-WHAT'S GOING ON?
THE EARTH IS RUMBLING?!
I DIDN'T THINK YOU ALL WOULD BE THIS STRONG.
MEKA
MEKA
MEKA

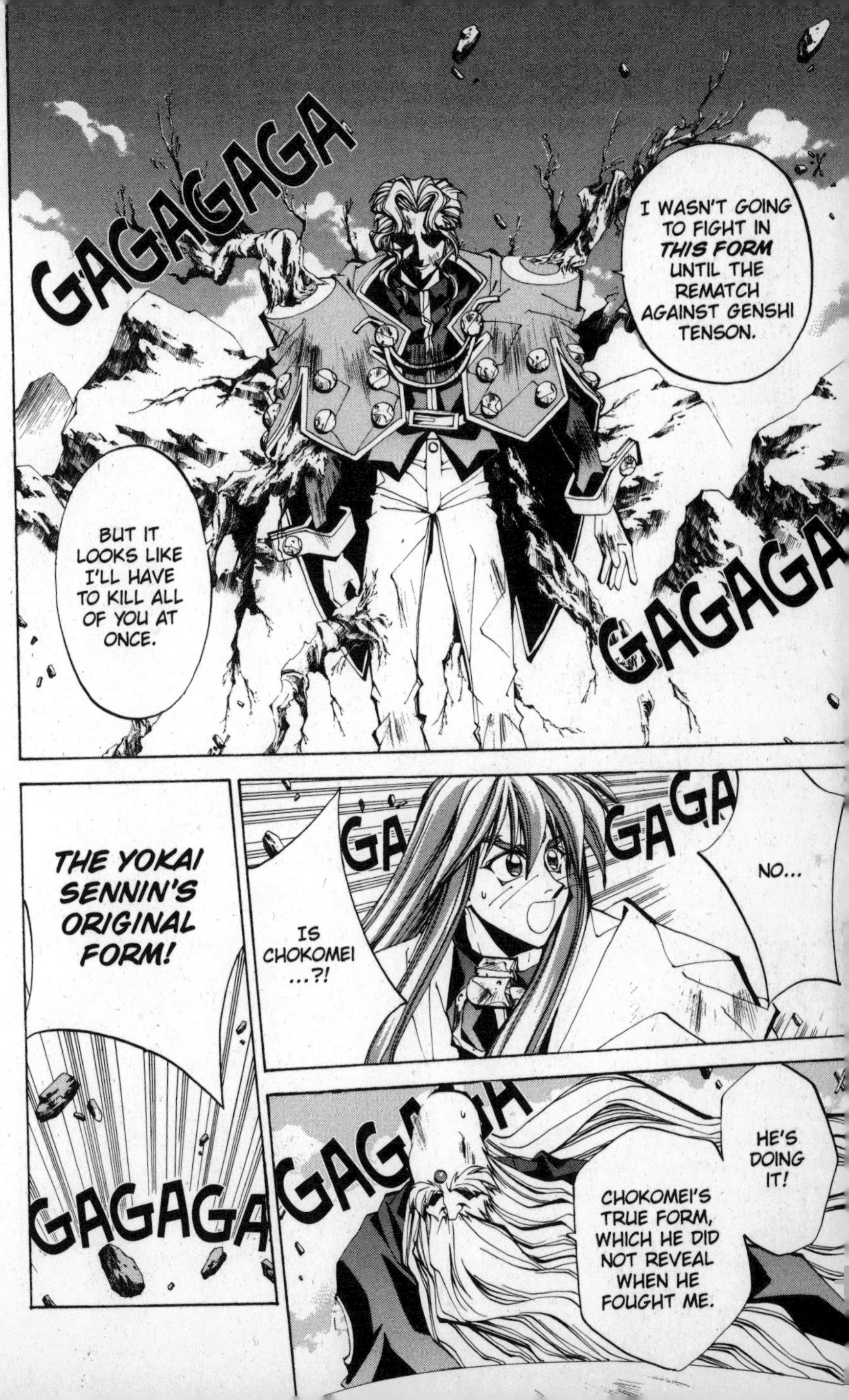
GAGAGAGA
I WASN'T GOING TO FIGHT IN THIS FORM UNTIL THE REMATCH AGAINST GENSHI TENSON.
BUT IT LOOKS LIKE I'LL HAVE TO KILL ALL OF YOU AT ONCE.
GAGAGA
GA GA GA
NO...
IS CHOKOMEI ...?!
GAGAGA
HE'S DOING IT!
CHOKOMEI'S TRUE FORM, WHICH HE DID NOT REVEAL WHEN HE FOUGHT ME.
THE YOKAI SENNIN'S ORIGINAL FORM!
GAGAGA

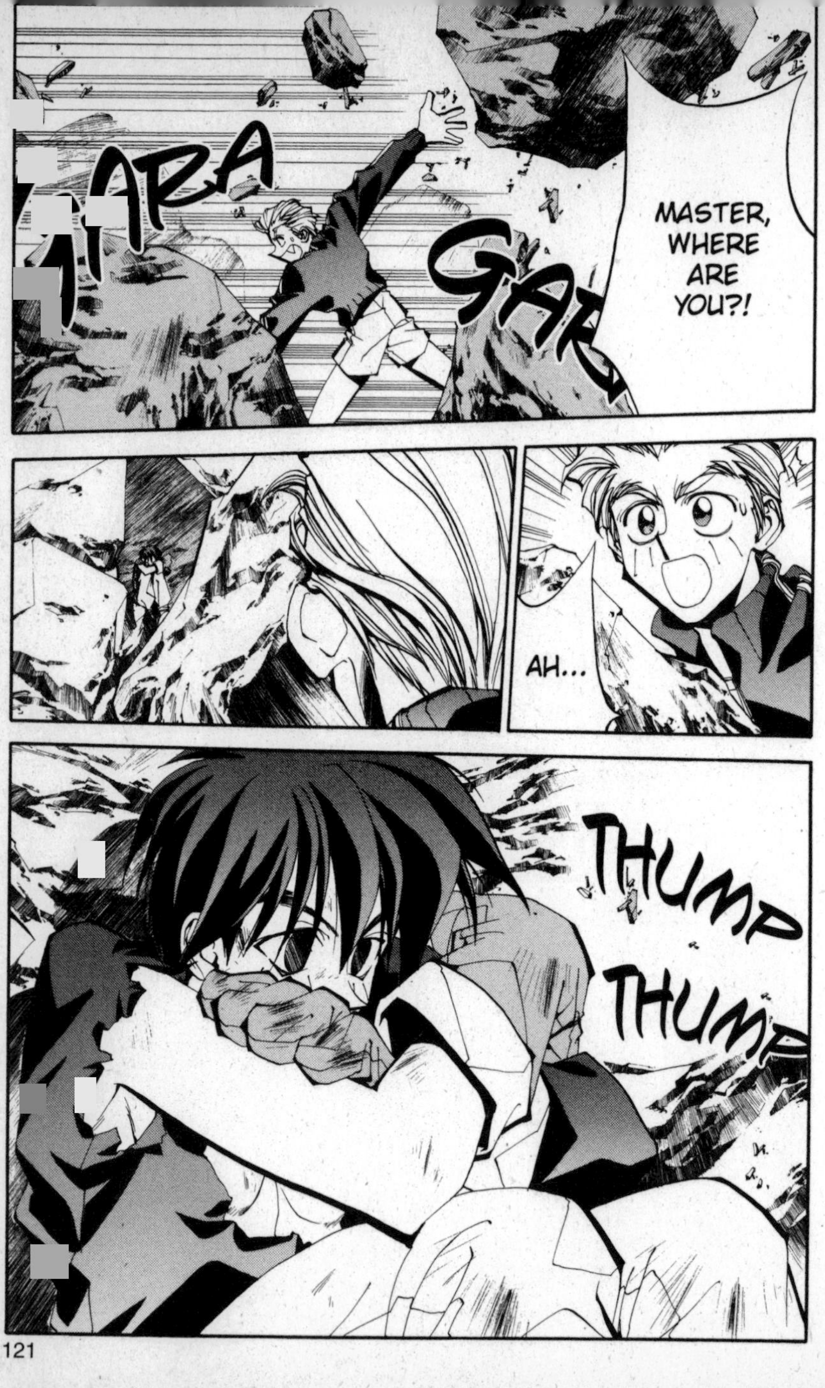
MASTER, WHERE ARE YOU?!
AH...
THUMP
THUMP

封神演義

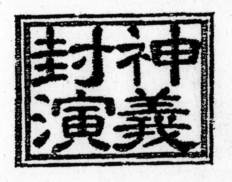

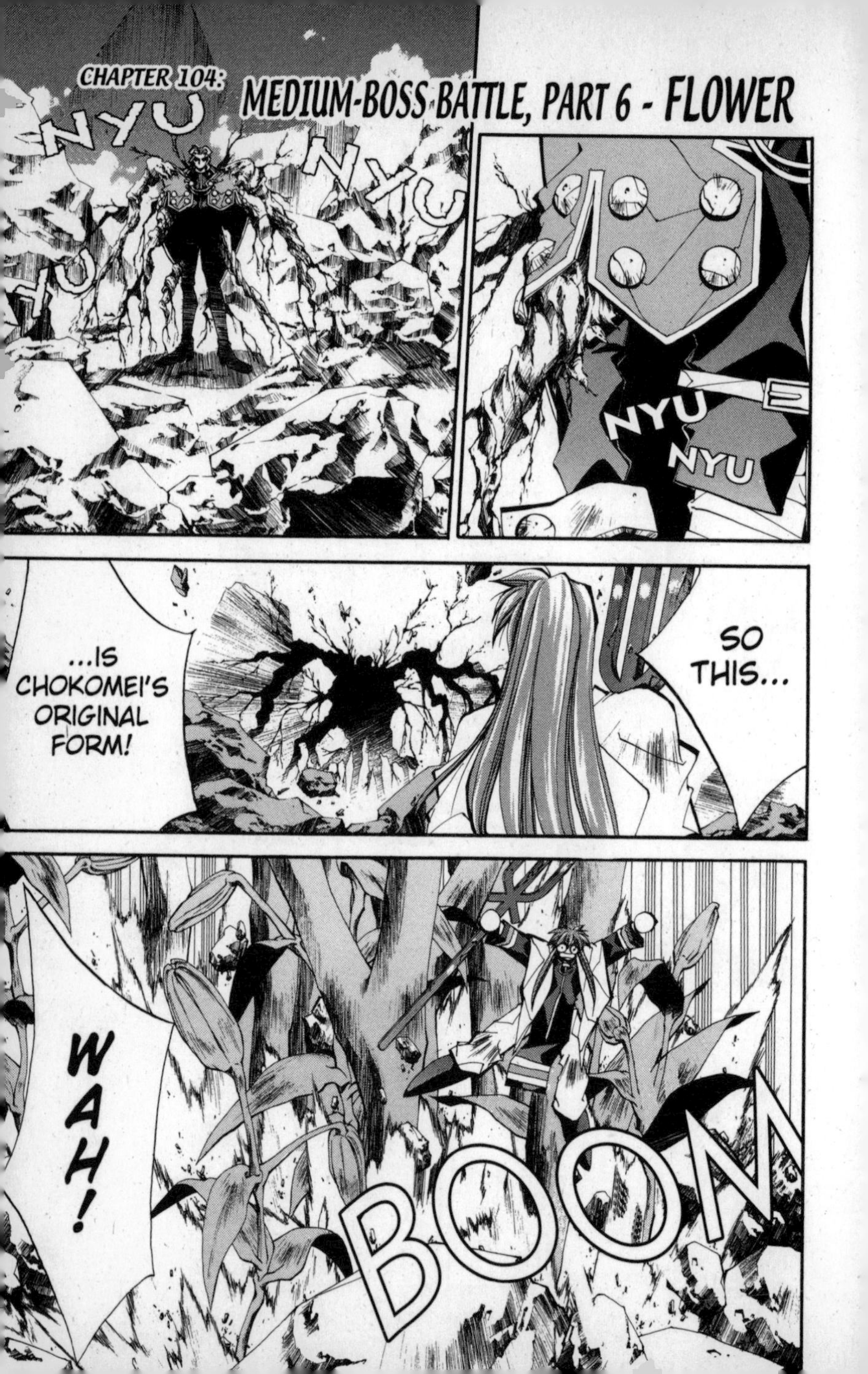
CHAPTER 104: MEDIUM-BOSS BATTLE, PART 6 - FLOWER
NYU
NYU
NYU
NYU
NYU
YU
SO THIS...
...IS CHOKOMEI'S ORIGINAL FORM!
BOOM
WAH!

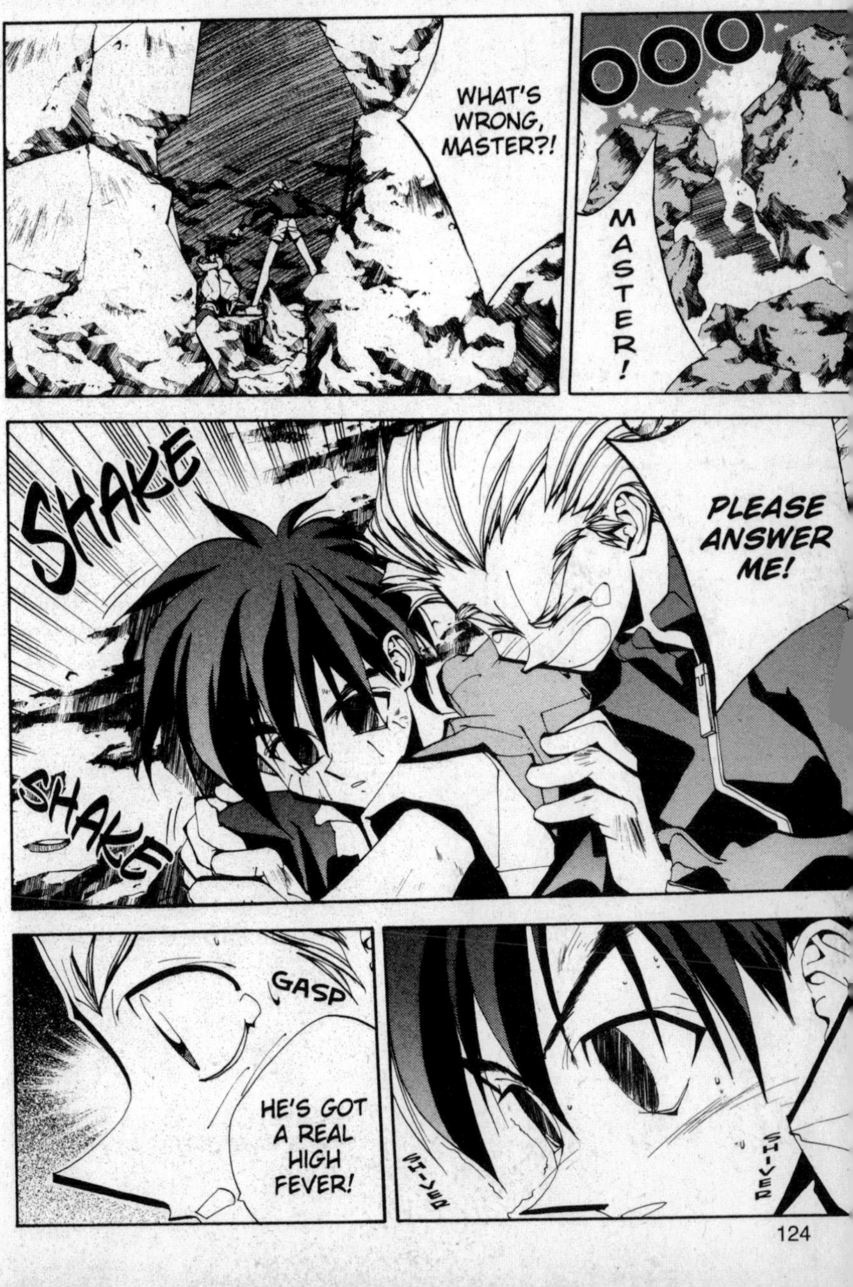
OOO
MASTER!
WHAT'S WRONG, MASTER?!
PLEASE ANSWER ME!
SHAKE
SHAKE
SHIVER
SHIVER
GASP
HE'S GOT A REAL HIGH FEVER!

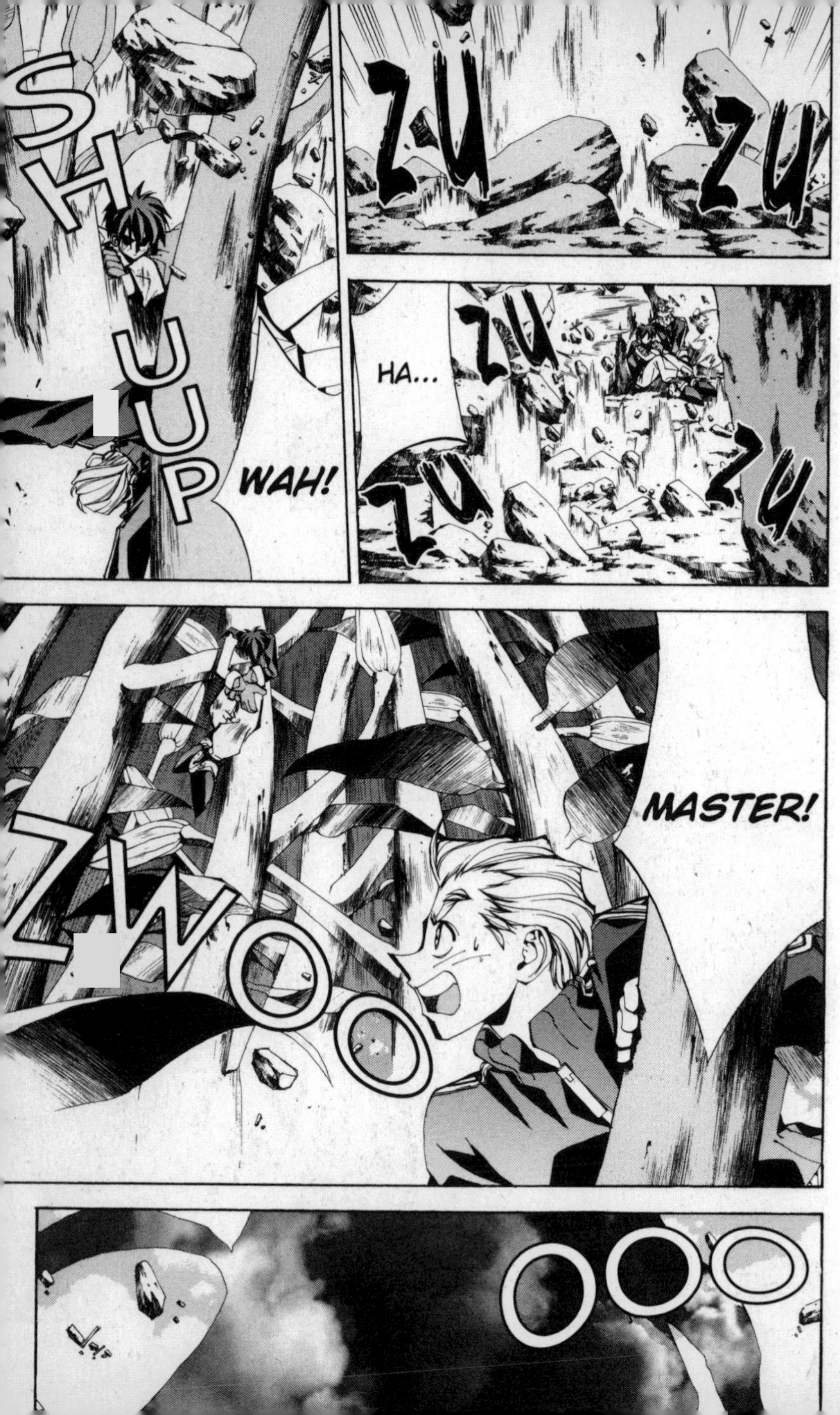
ZU ZU
HA...
ZU ZU
ZU ZU
SHUUP
WAH!
MASTER!
ZWOOO
OOO

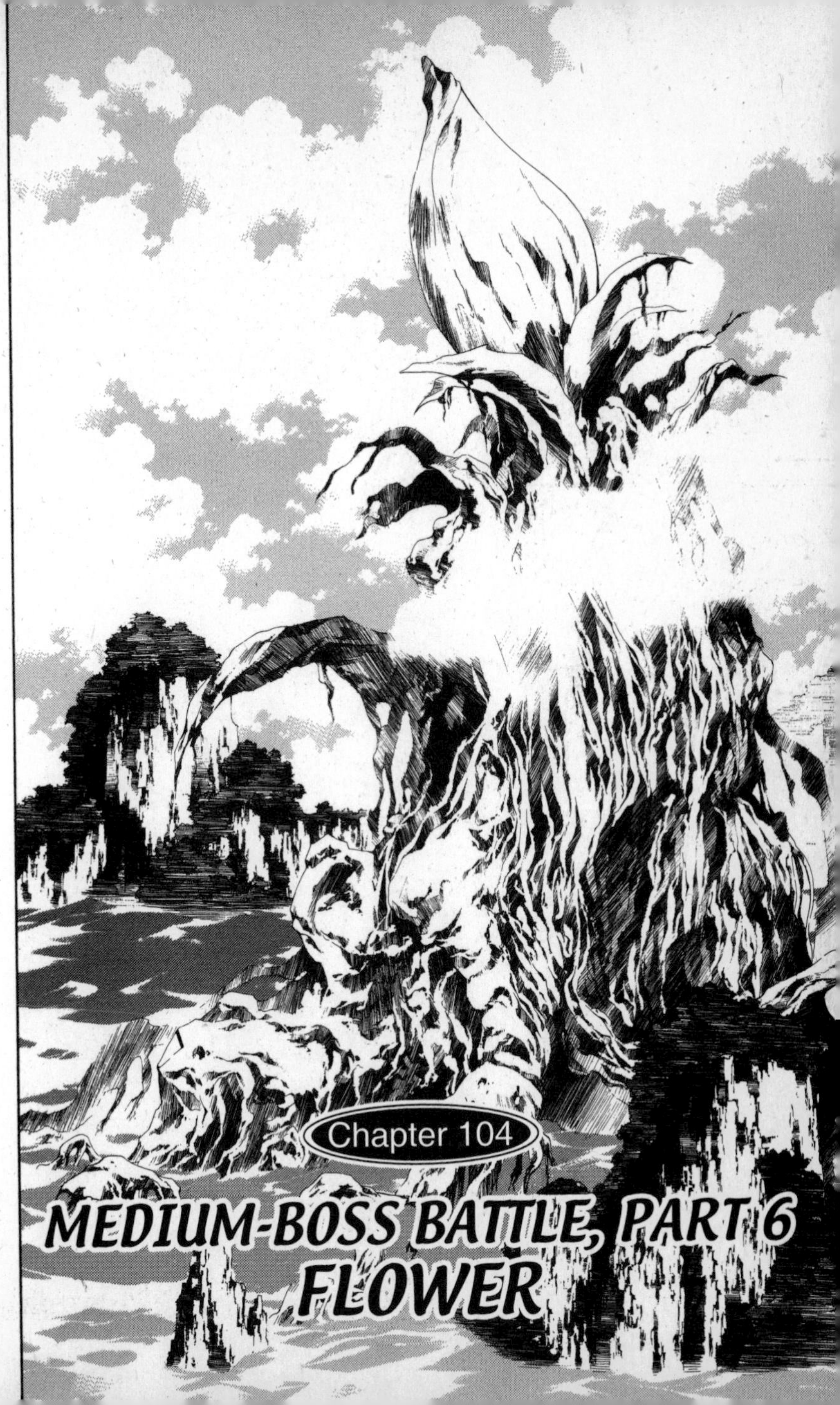
Chapter 104
MEDIUM-BOSS BATTLE, PART 6
FLOWER

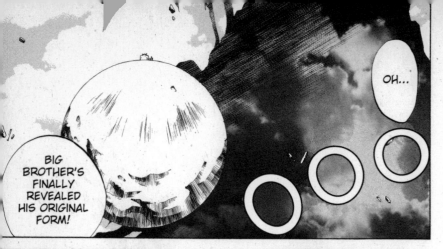

OH...
BIG BROTHER'S FINALLY REVEALED HIS ORIGINAL FORM!
THE LEGENDARY HUGE FLOWER... THAT IS BIG BROTHER'S TRUE SELF.
NO ONE CAN STOP HIM NOW.
HE WILL CONSUME ALL THE NUTRIENTS OF THE EARTH, AND THIS ENTIRE AREA WILL BECOME A DESERT.
GLUB
GLUB
WHAT AN ABSURDLY HUGE FLOWER.
I SUPPOSE IT SUITS CHOKOMEI RATHER WELL.
WHIZ
WHIZ

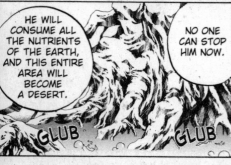

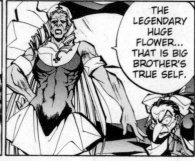

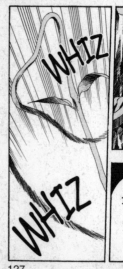

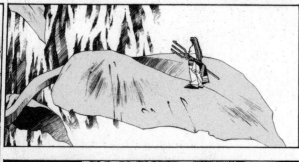

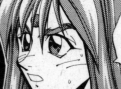

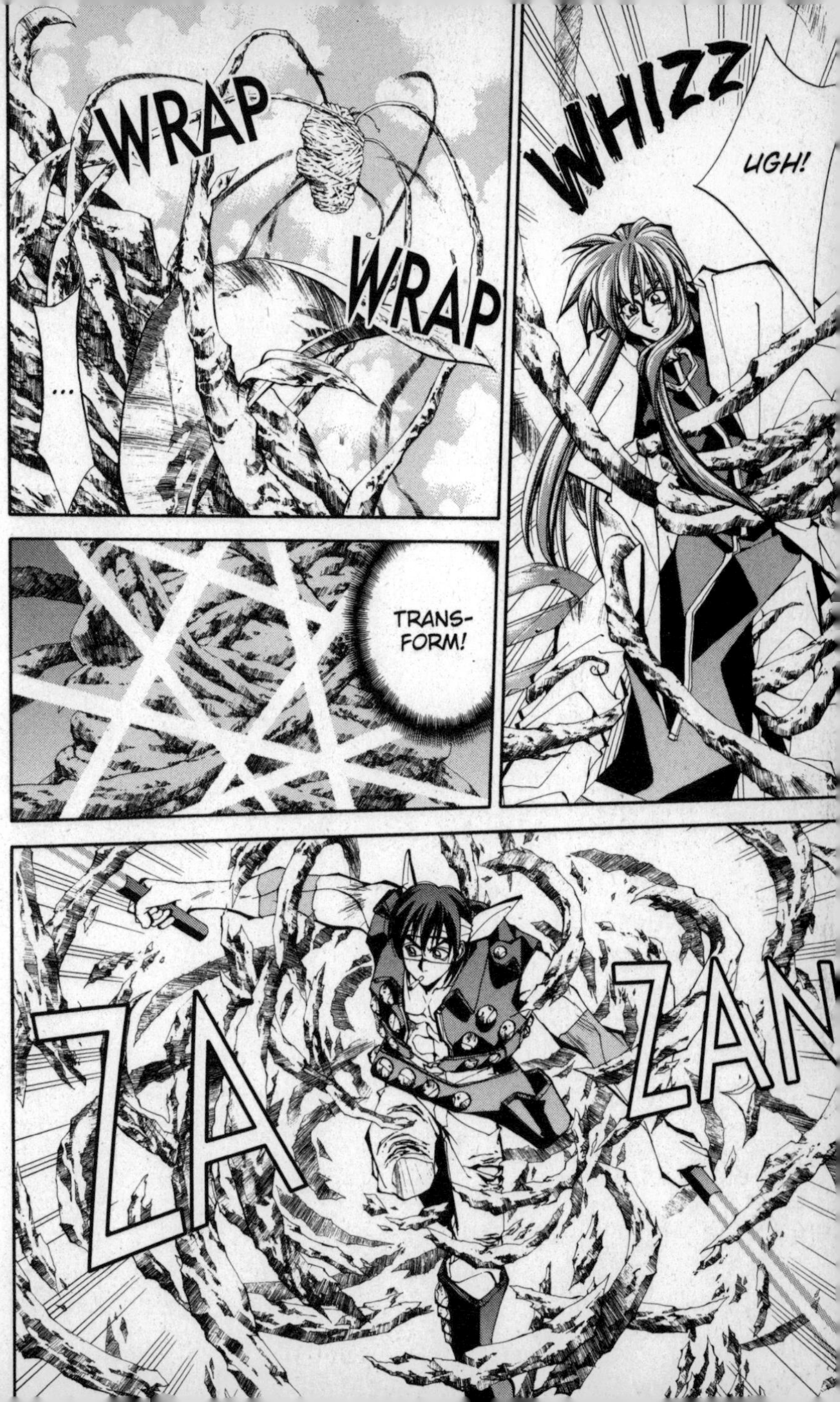
WHIZZ
UGH!
WRAP
WRAP
...
TRANS-
FORM!
ZA
ZAN

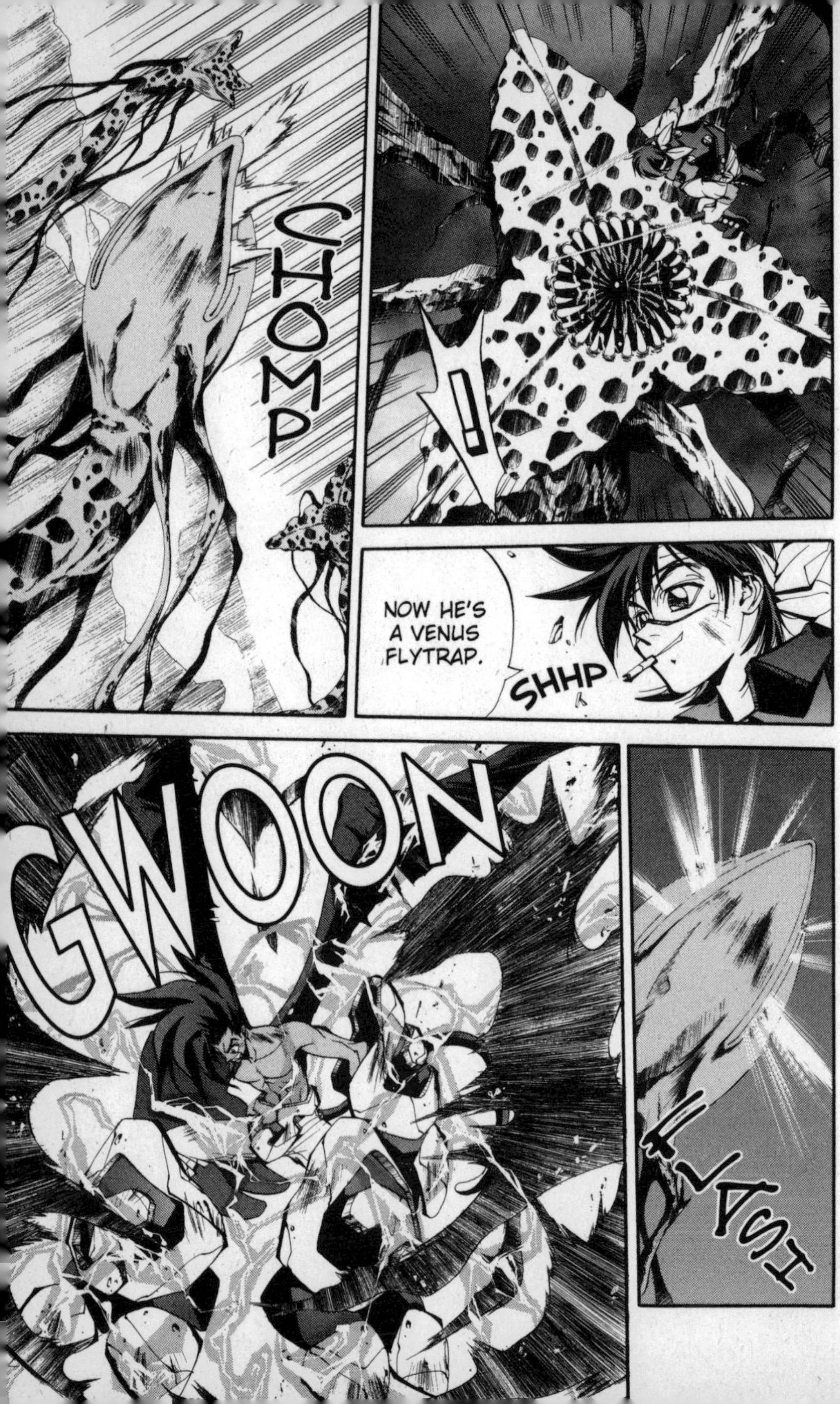
!
NOW HE'S A VENUS FLYTRAP.
SHHP
CHOMP
FLASH
GWOON

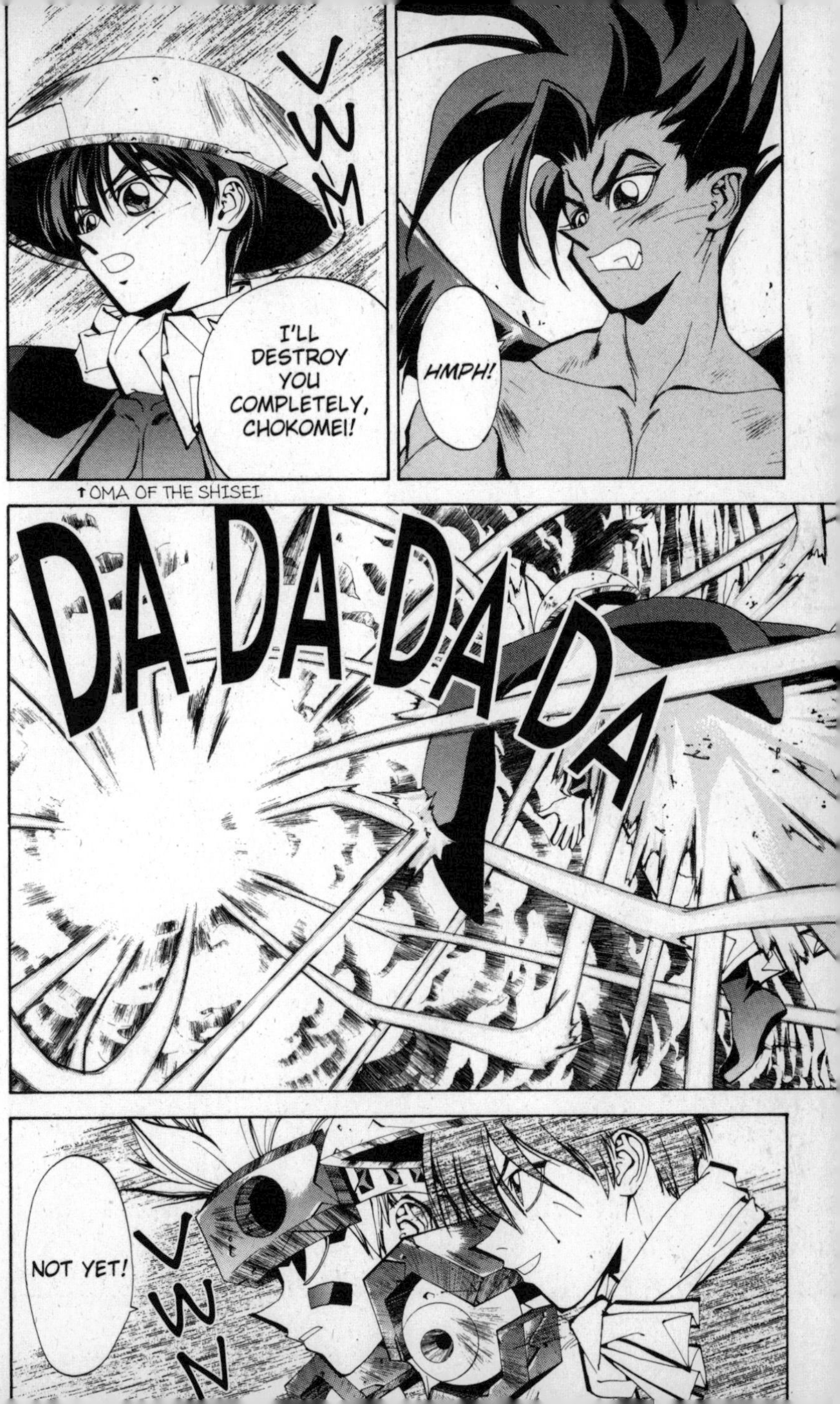
HMPH!
VWM
I'LL DESTROY YOU COMPLETELY, CHOKOMEI!
↑OMA OF THE SHISEI.
DA DA DA DA DA
NOT YET!
VWN

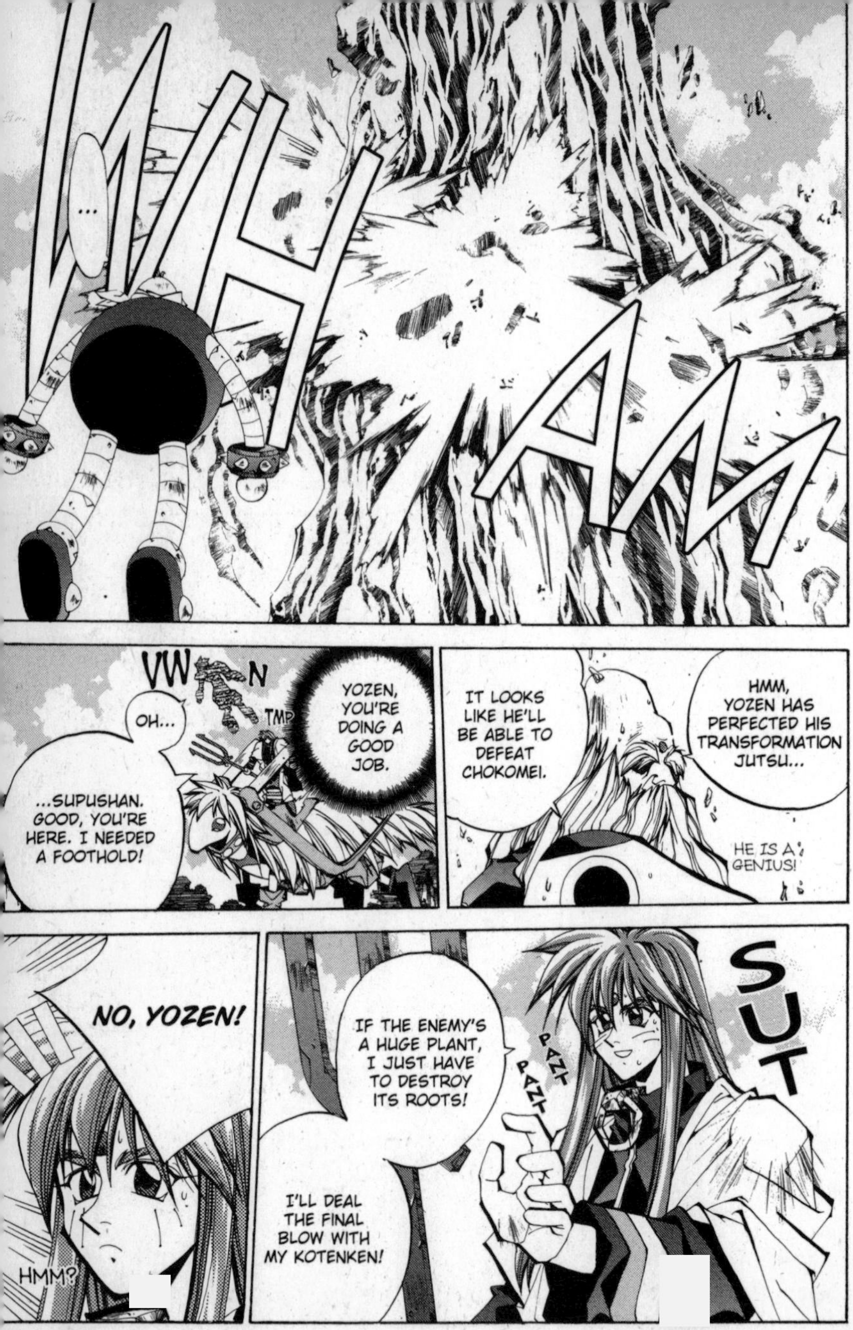
...
WHAM
HMM, YOZEN HAS PERFECTED HIS TRANSFORMATION JUTSU...
HE IS A GENIUS!
IT LOOKS LIKE HE'LL BE ABLE TO DEFEAT CHOKOMEI.
YOZEN, YOU'RE DOING A GOOD JOB.
VWN
TMP
OH...
...SUPUSHAN. GOOD, YOU'RE HERE. I NEEDED A FOOTHOLD!
SUT
PANT PANT
IF THE ENEMY'S A HUGE PLANT, I JUST HAVE TO DESTROY ITS ROOTS!
I'LL DEAL THE FINAL BLOW WITH MY KOTENKEN!
NO, YOZEN!
HMM?

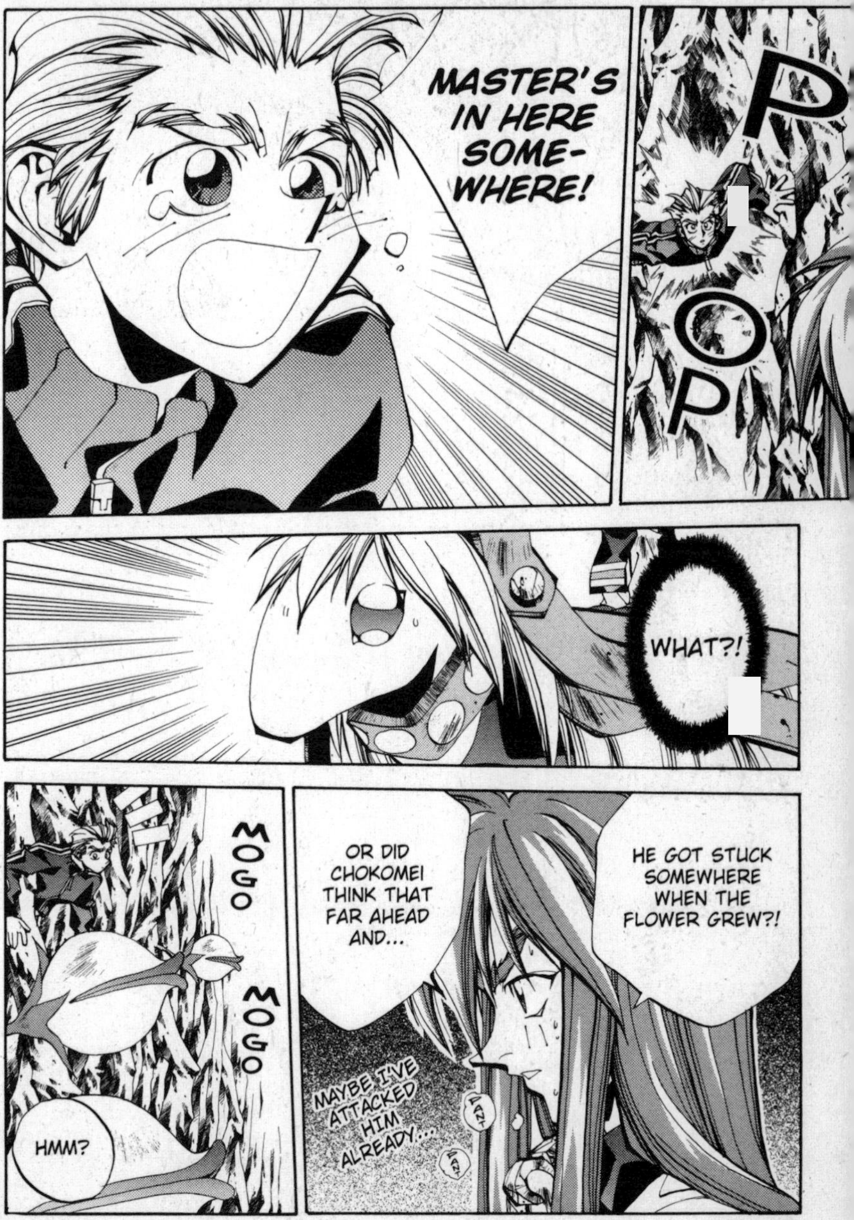
POP
MASTER'S IN HERE SOME-WHERE!
WHAT?!
HE GOT STUCK SOMEWHERE WHEN THE FLOWER GREW?!
OR DID CHOKOMEI THINK THAT FAR AHEAD AND...
MAYBE I'VE ATTACKED HIM ALREADY...
PANT
PANT
MOGO
MOGO
HMM?

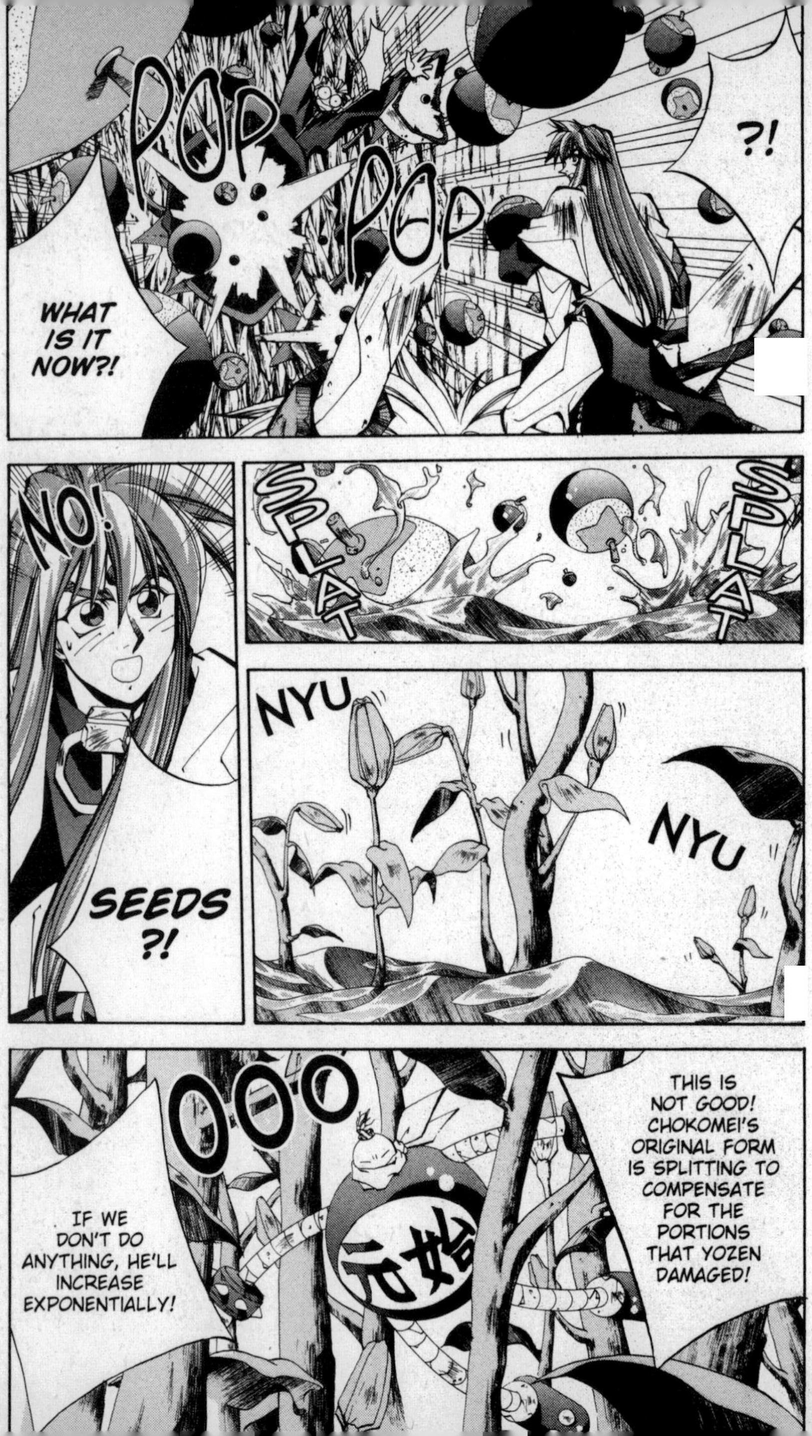
?!
POP
POP
WHAT IS IT NOW?!
SPLAT
SPLAT
NYU
NYU
NO!
SEEDS ?!
THIS IS NOT GOOD! CHOKOMEI'S ORIGINAL FORM IS SPLITTING TO COMPENSATE FOR THE PORTIONS THAT YOZEN DAMAGED!
OOO
IF WE DON'T DO ANYTHING, HE'LL INCREASE EXPONENTIALLY!

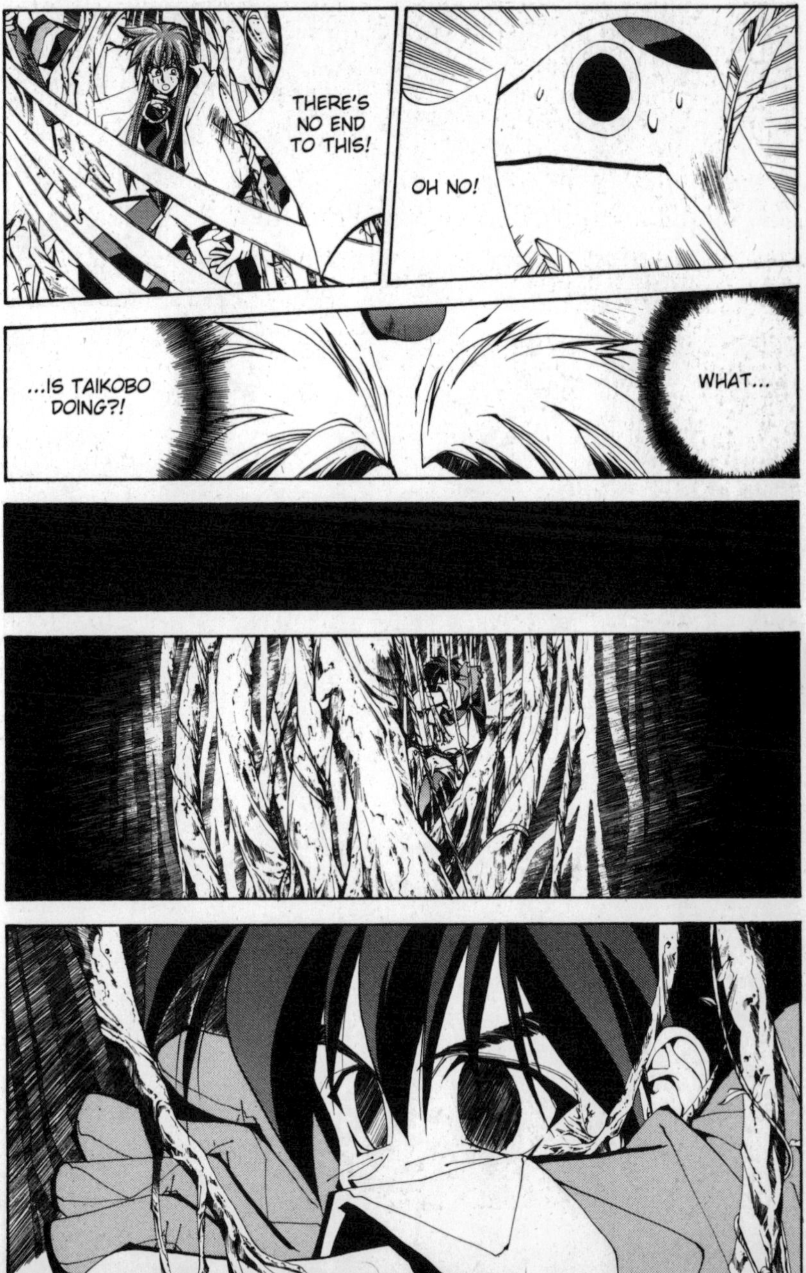
OH NO!
THERE'S NO END TO THIS!
WHAT...
...IS TAIKOBO DOING?!

READ THIS WAY

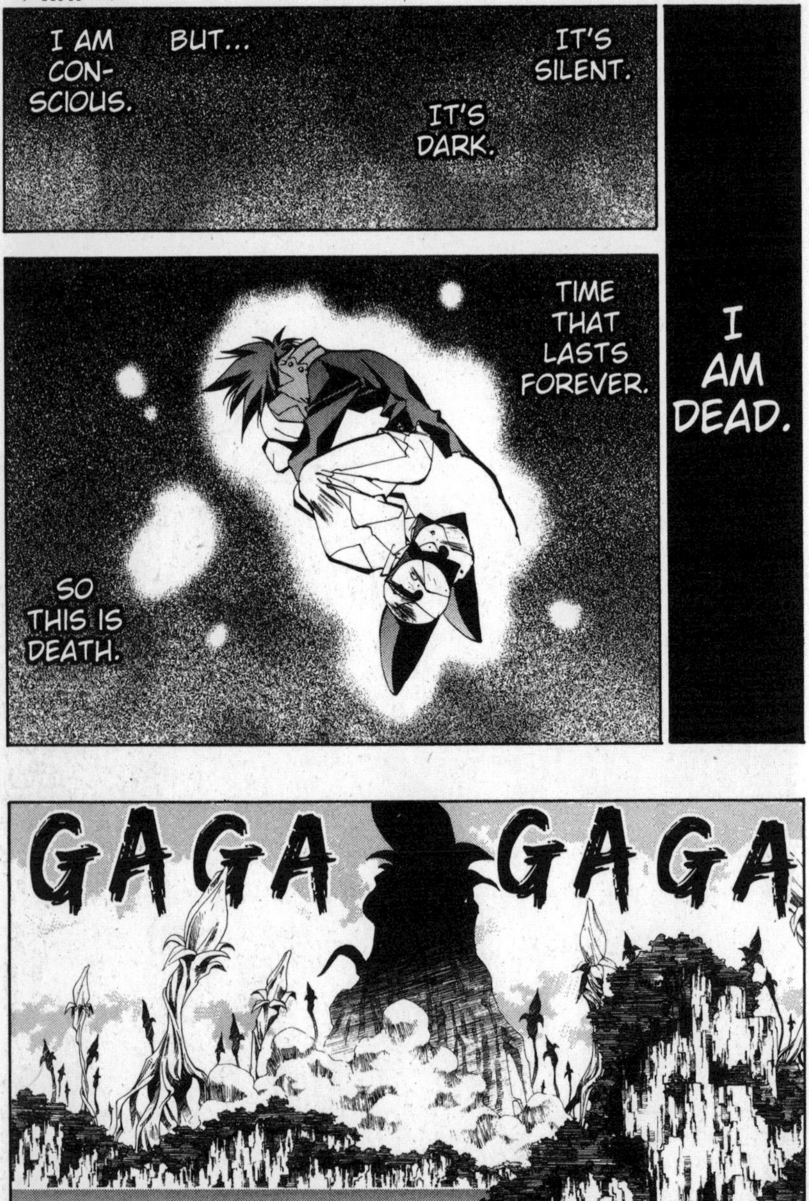
I AM DEAD.
IT'S SILENT.
IT'S DARK.
BUT...
I AM CONSCIOUS.
TIME THAT LASTS FOREVER.
SO THIS IS DEATH.
GAGA GAGA

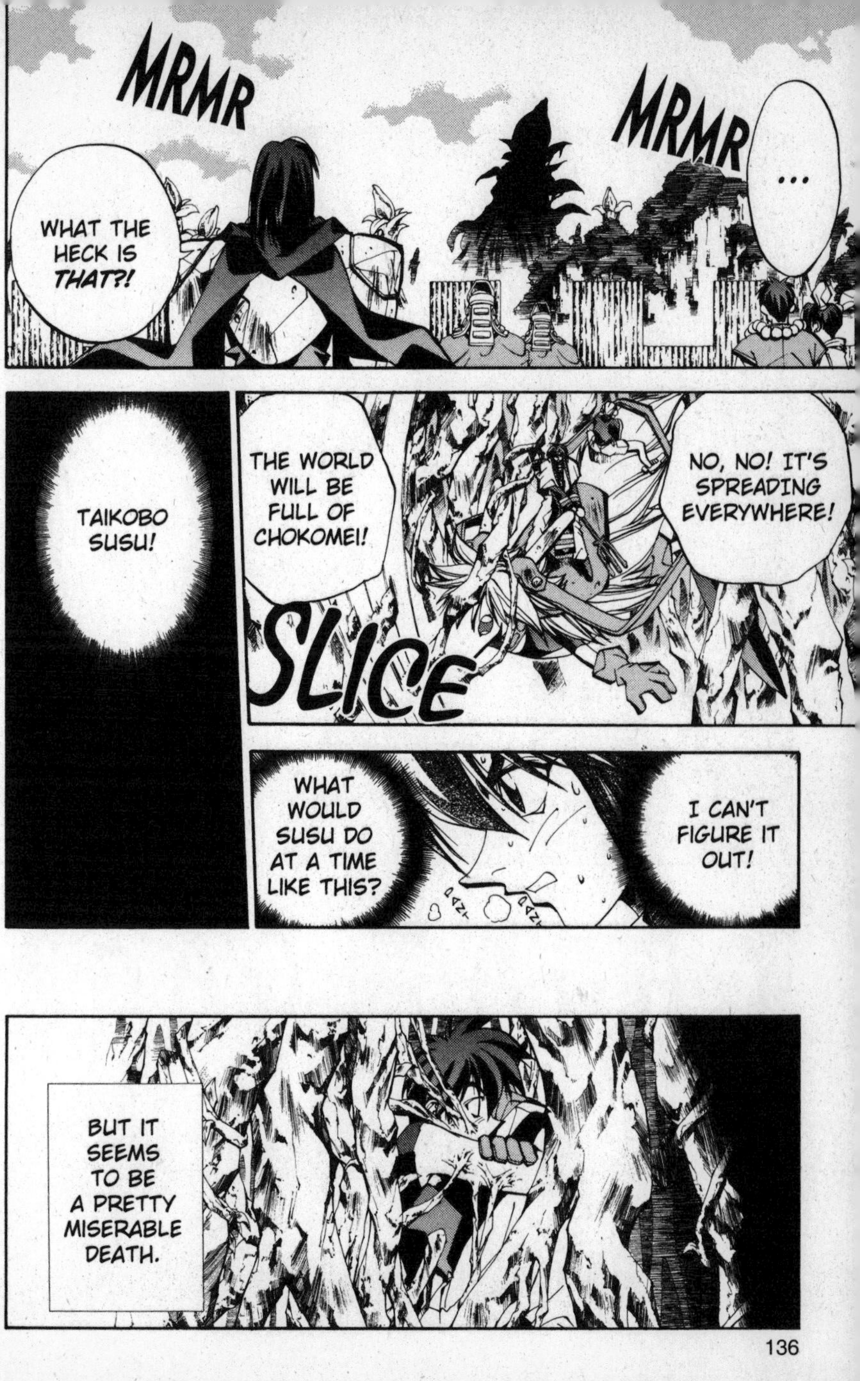
...
MRMR
MRMR
WHAT THE HECK IS *THAT?!*
NO, NO! IT'S SPREADING EVERYWHERE!
THE WORLD WILL BE FULL OF CHOKOMEI!
SLICE
I CAN'T FIGURE IT OUT!
WHAT WOULD SUSU DO AT A TIME LIKE THIS?
TAIKOBO SUSU!
BUT IT SEEMS TO BE A PRETTY MISERABLE DEATH.

READ THIS WAY

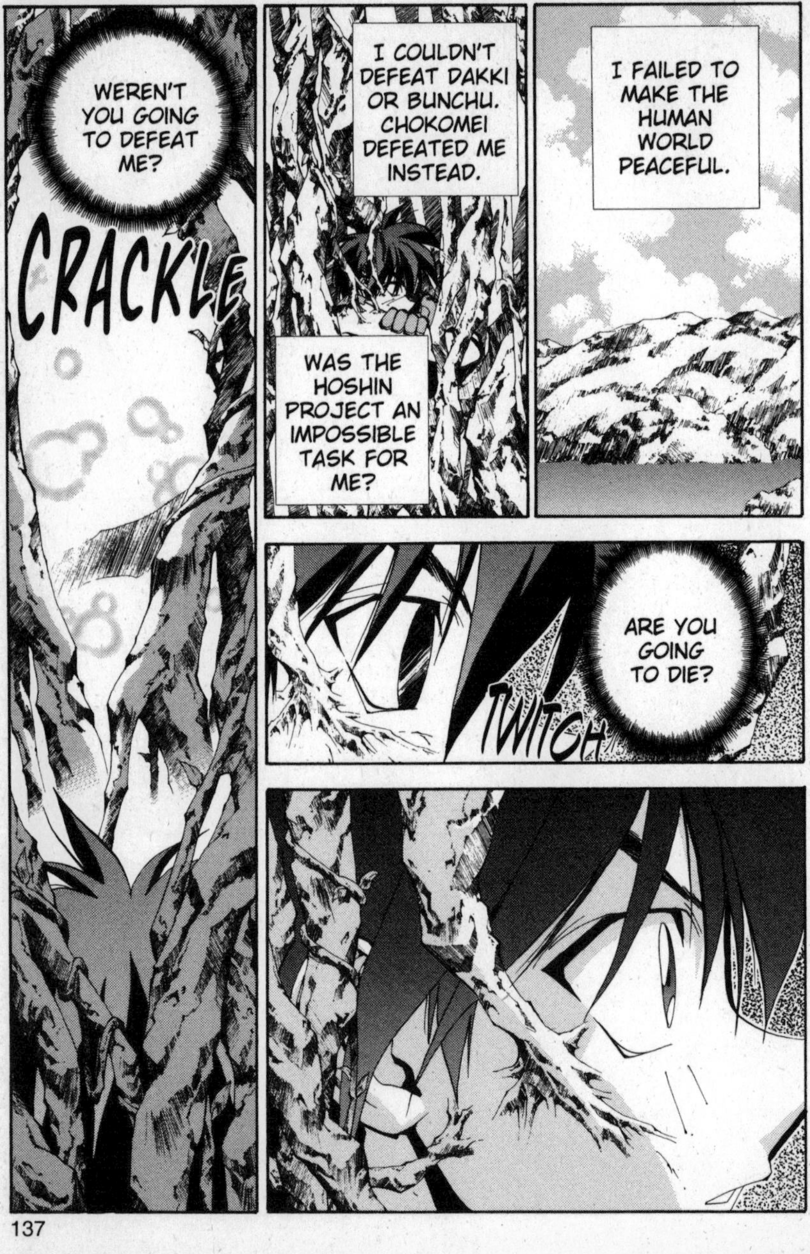
I FAILED TO MAKE THE HUMAN WORLD PEACEFUL.
I COULDN'T DEFEAT DAKKI OR BUNCHU. CHOKOMEI DEFEATED ME INSTEAD.
WAS THE HOSHIN PROJECT AN IMPOSSIBLE TASK FOR ME?
ARE YOU GOING TO DIE?
TWITCH
WEREN'T YOU GOING TO DEFEAT ME?
CRACKLE

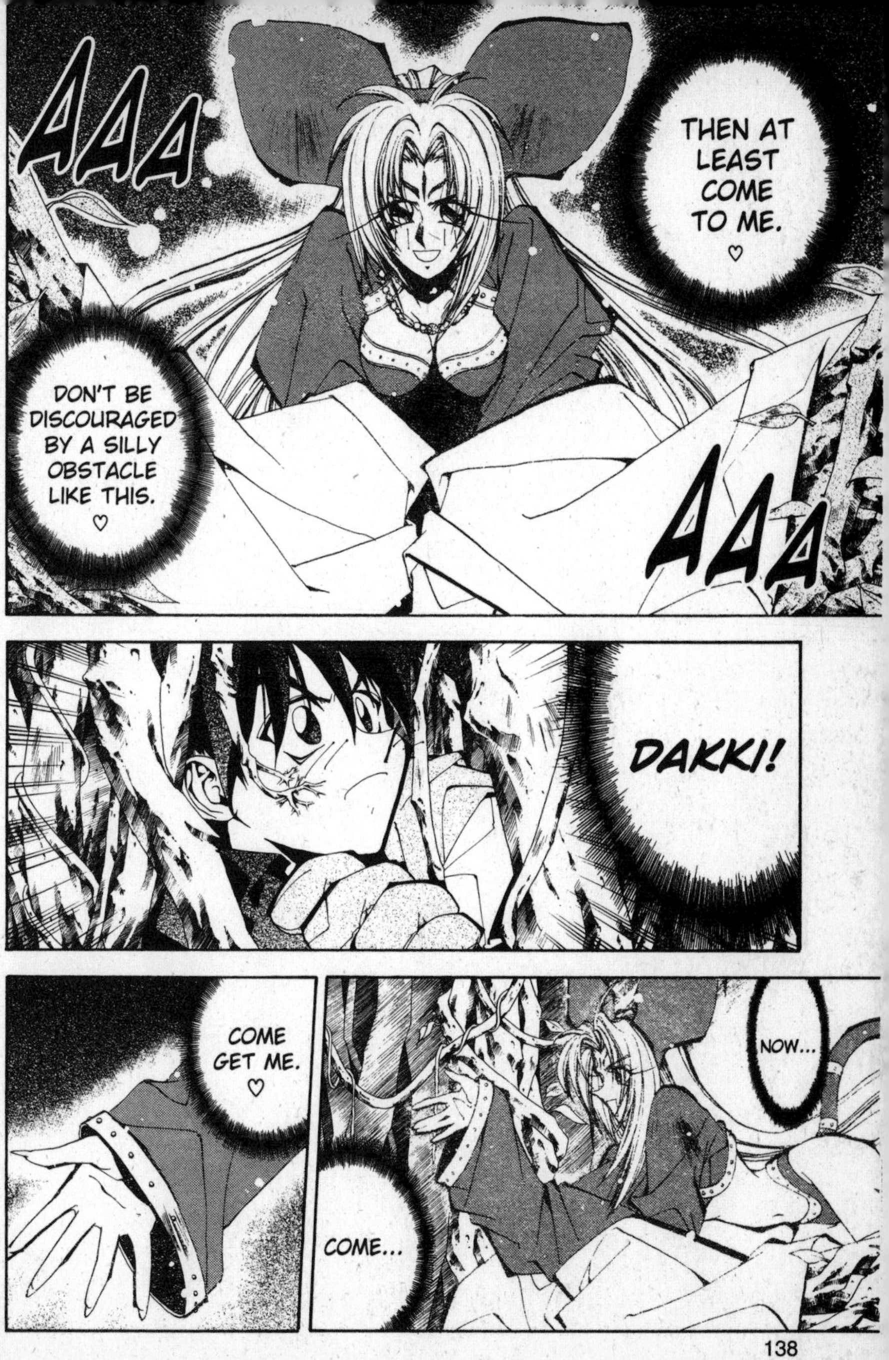
THEN AT LEAST COME TO ME. ♡
AAA
DON'T BE DISCOURAGED BY A SILLY OBSTACLE LIKE THIS. ♡
AAA
DAKKI!
NOW...
COME...
COME GET ME. ♡

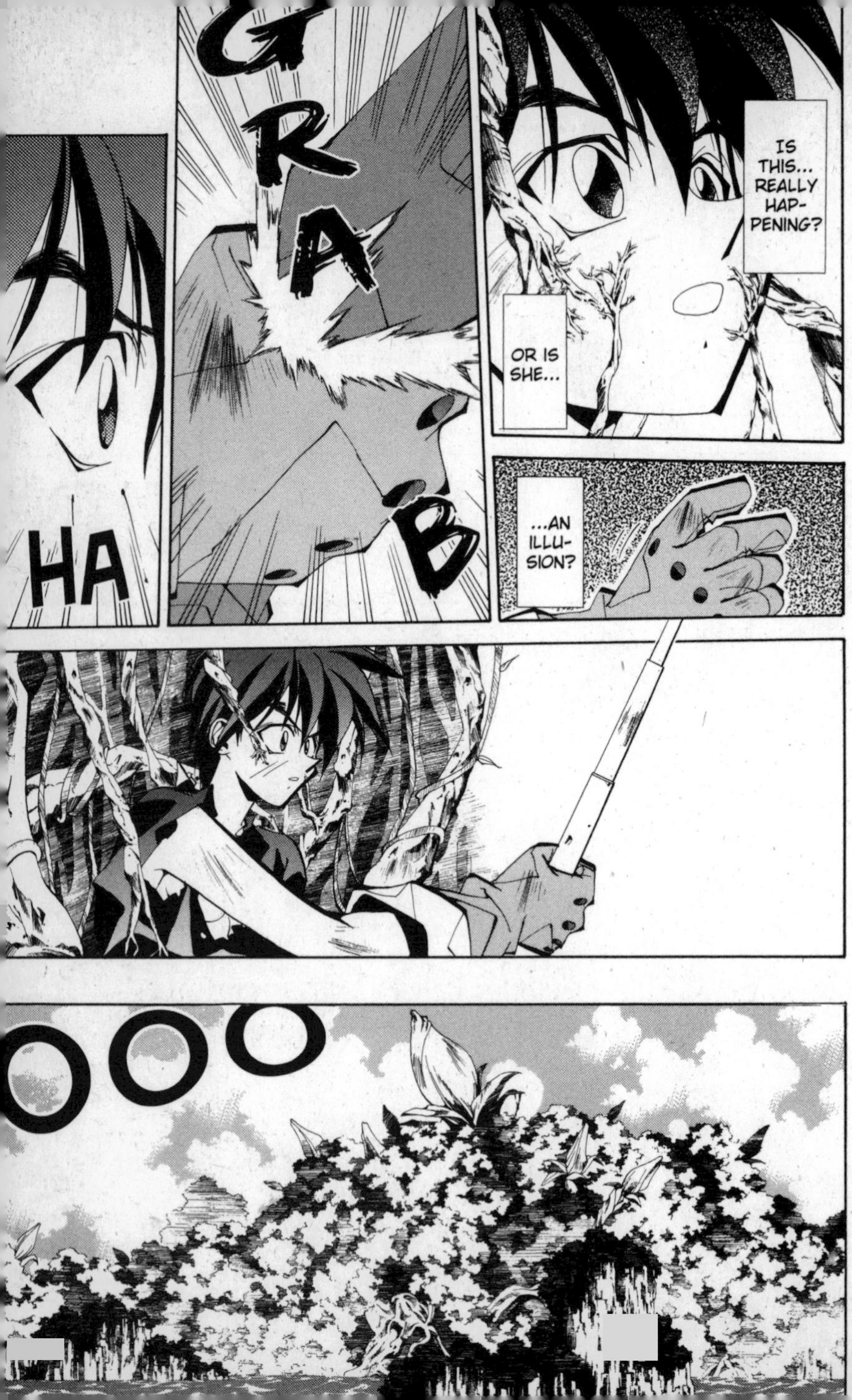
IS THIS... REALLY HAP-PENING?
OR IS SHE...
...AN ILLU-SION?
GRAB
HA
OOO

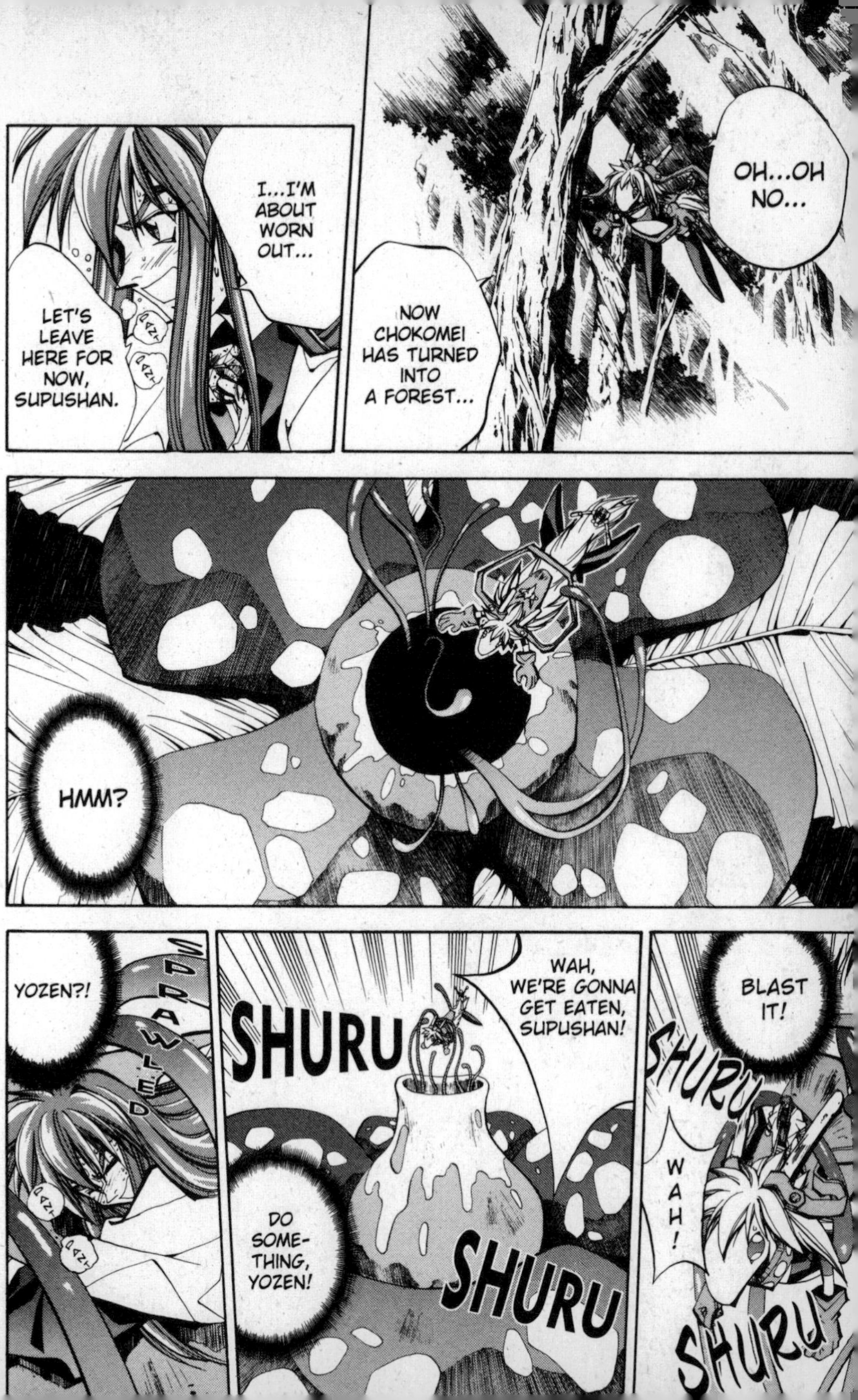
OH...OH NO...
NOW CHOKOMEI HAS TURNED INTO A FOREST...
I...I'M ABOUT WORN OUT...
LET'S LEAVE HERE FOR NOW, SUPUSHAN.
HMM?
BLAST IT!
SHURU
WAH!
SHURU
WAH, WE'RE GONNA GET EATEN, SUPUSHAN!
SHURU
DO SOME-THING, YOZEN!
SHURU
YOZEN?!
SPRAWLED

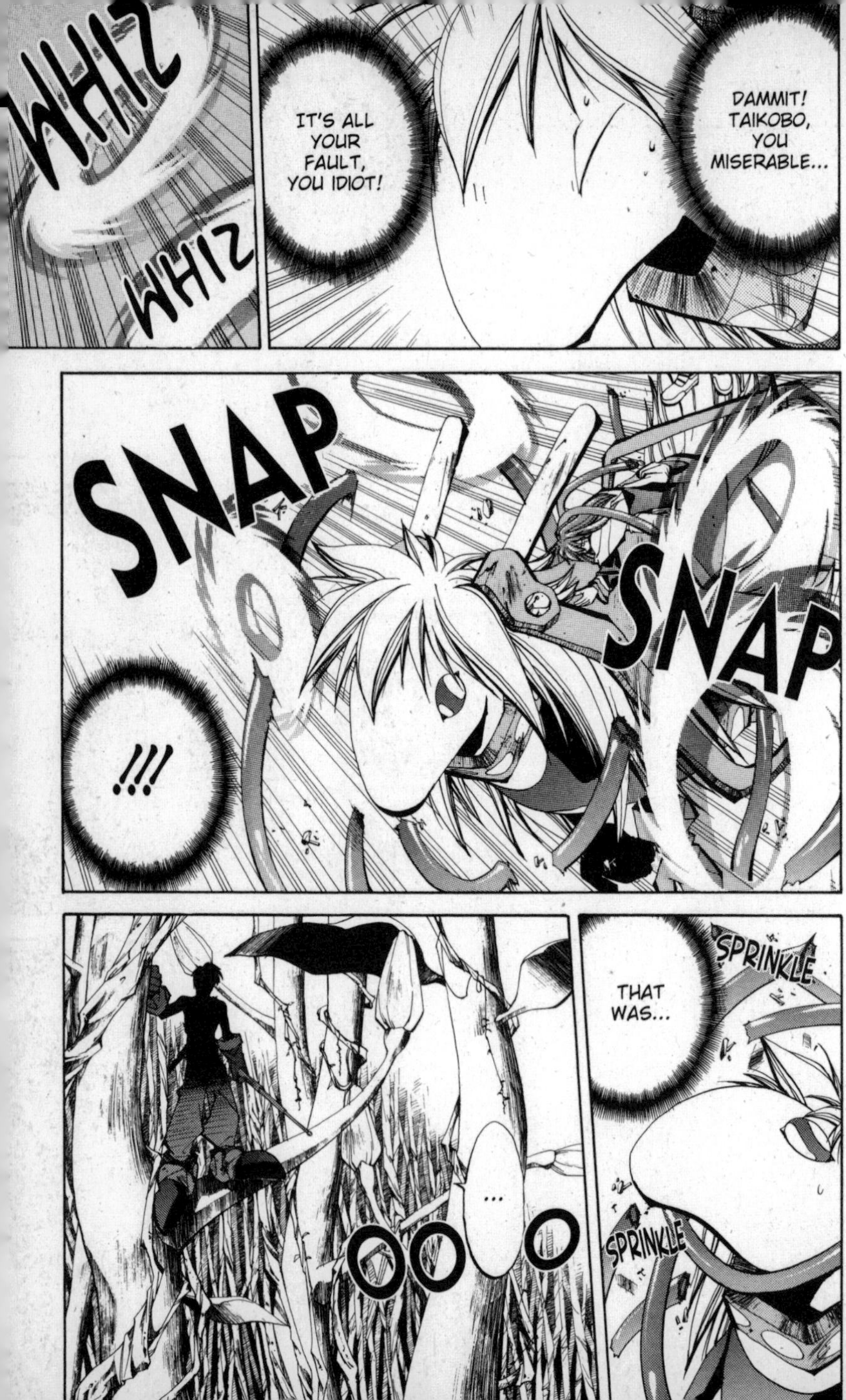
DAMMIT! TAIKOBO, YOU MISERABLE...
IT'S ALL YOUR FAULT, YOU IDIOT!
WHIZ
WHIZ
SNAP
SNAP
!!!
SPRINKLE
THAT WAS...
SPRINKLE
...

封神演義

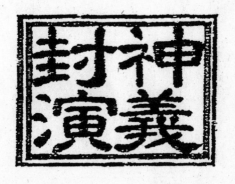

CHAPTER 105:

MEDIUM-BOSS BATTLE, PART 7 THE MESOSPHERE

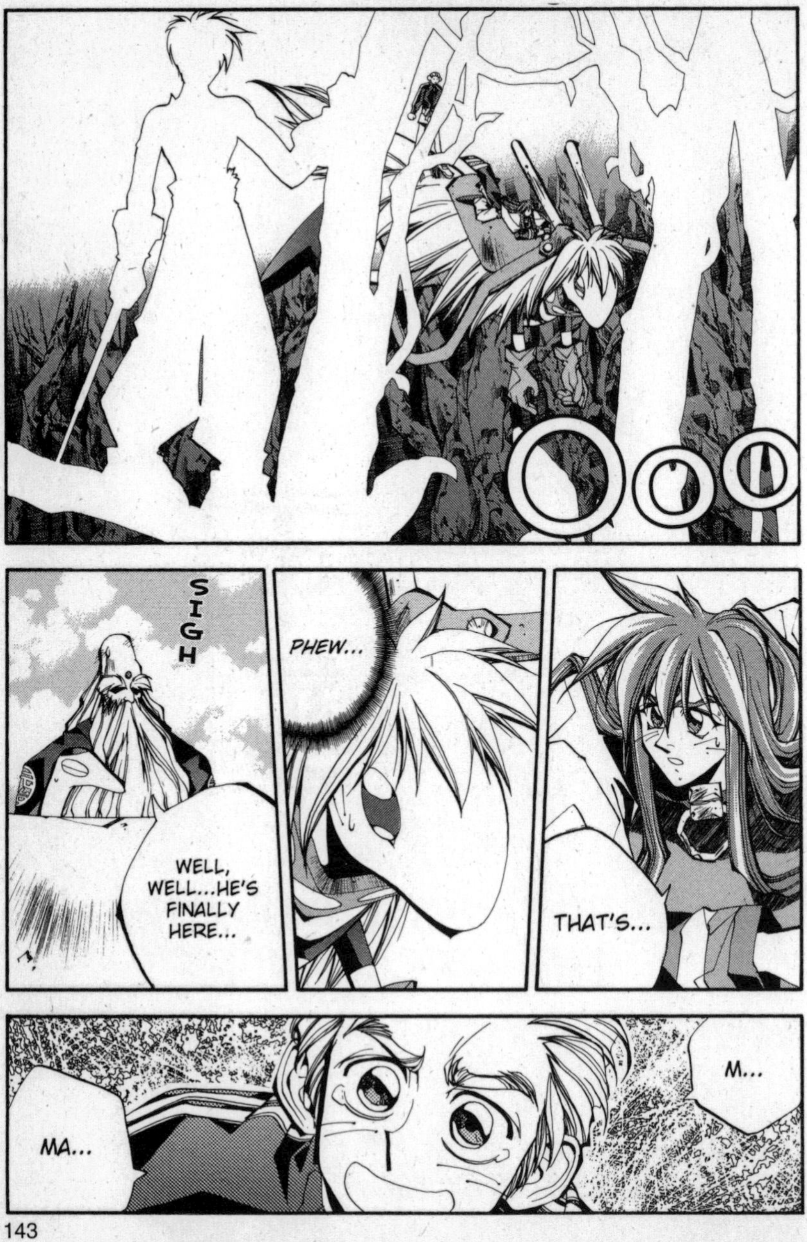
THAT'S...
PHEW...
SIGH
WELL, WELL...HE'S FINALLY HERE...
M...
MA...

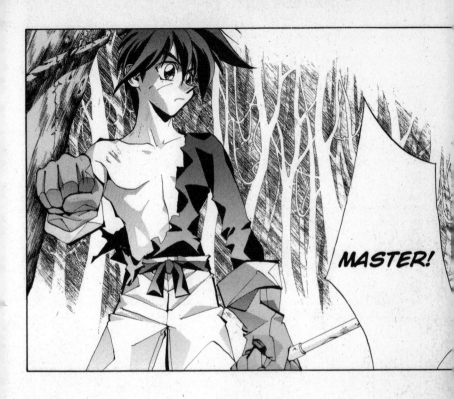

MASTER!

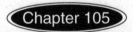

MEDIUM-BOSS BATTLE, PART 7
THE MESOSPHERE

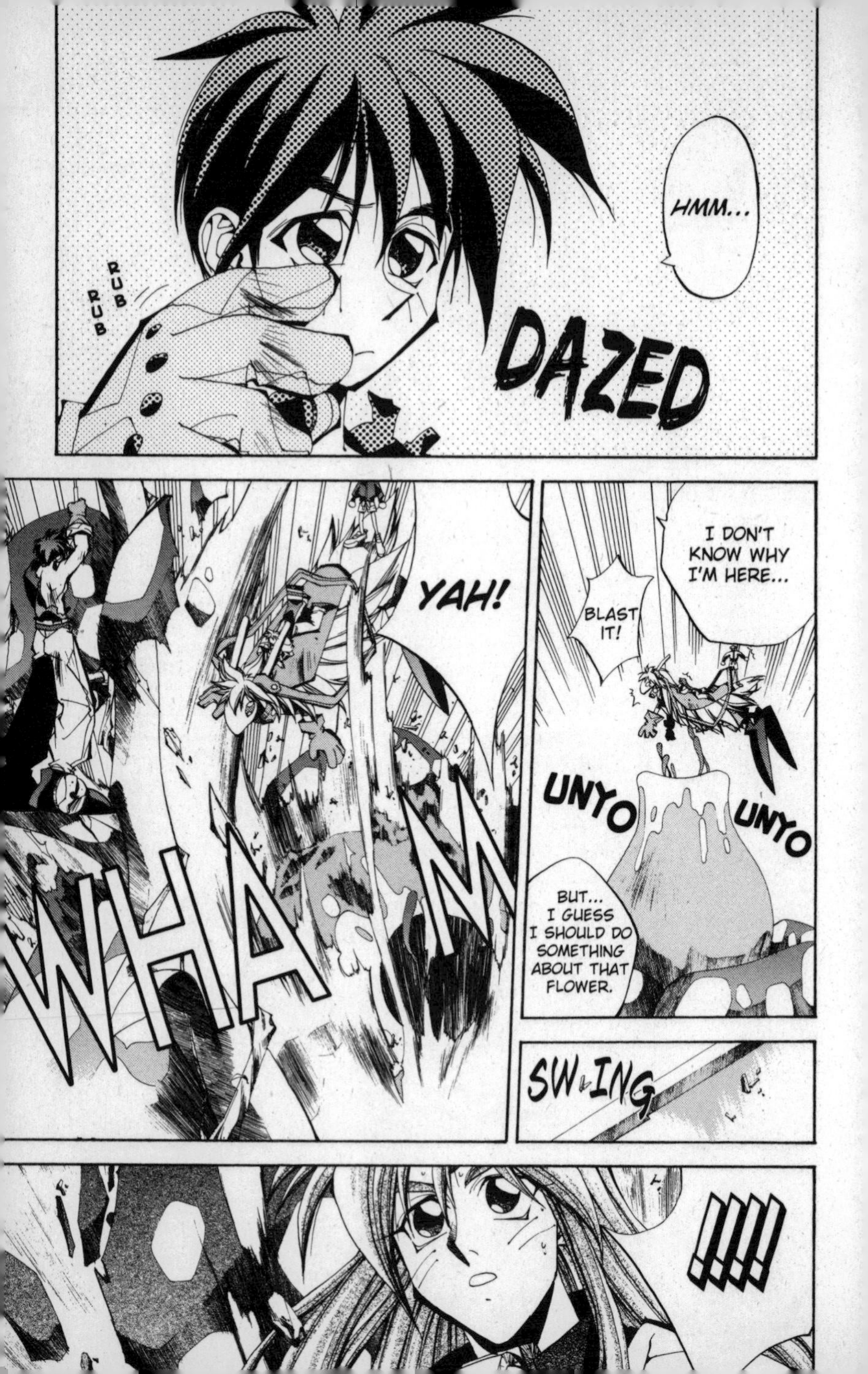
HMM...
DAZED
RUB RUB
I DON'T KNOW WHY I'M HERE...
BLAST IT!
UNYO
UNYO
BUT... I GUESS I SHOULD DO SOMETHING ABOUT THAT FLOWER.
SWING
YAH!
WHAM
!!!!!

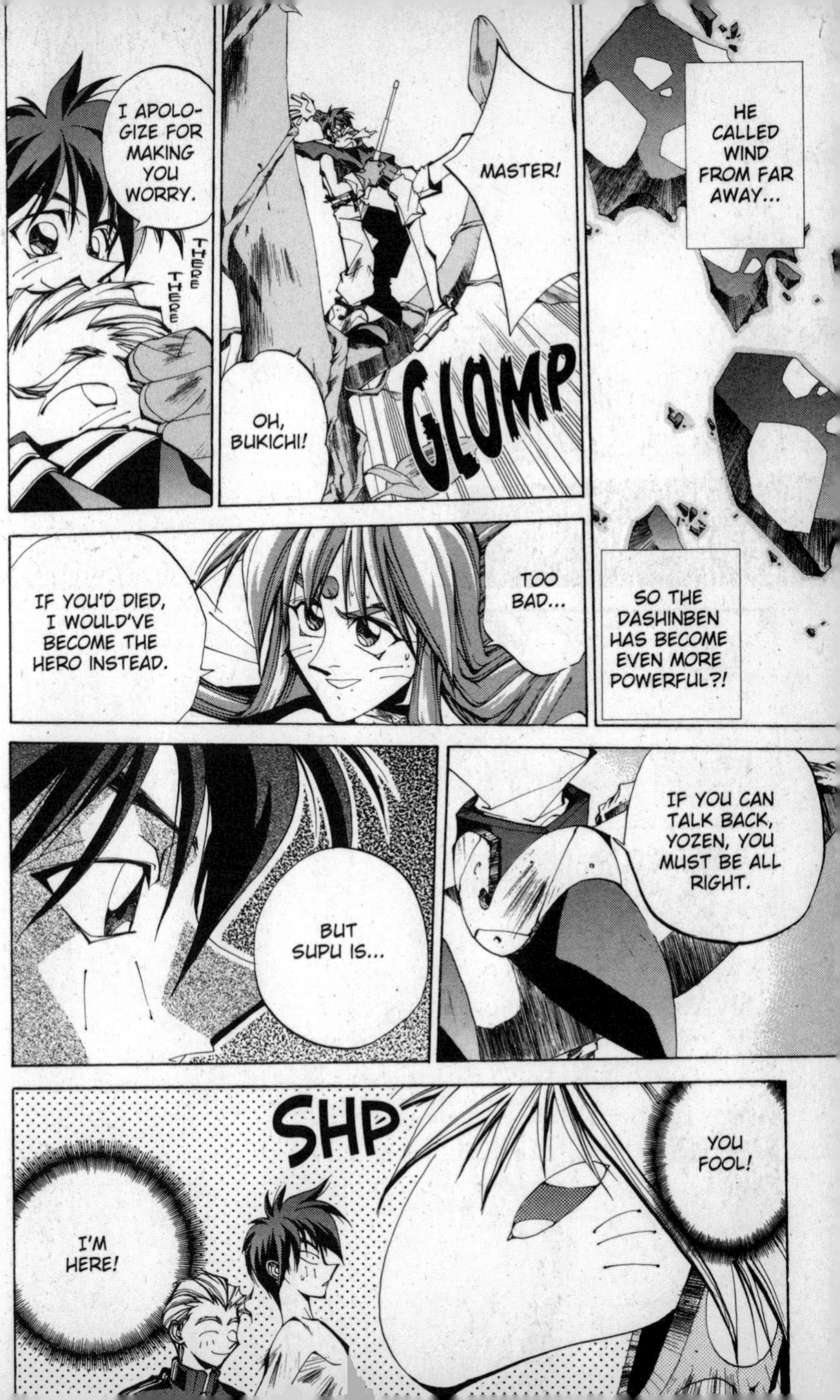
HE CALLED WIND FROM FAR AWAY...
SO THE DASHINBEN HAS BECOME EVEN MORE POWERFUL?!
MASTER!
GLOMP
OH, BUKICHI!
I APOLOGIZE FOR MAKING YOU WORRY.
THERE THERE
TOO BAD...
IF YOU'D DIED, I WOULD'VE BECOME THE HERO INSTEAD.
IF YOU CAN TALK BACK, YOZEN, YOU MUST BE ALL RIGHT.
BUT SUPU IS...
YOU FOOL!
SHP
I'M HERE!

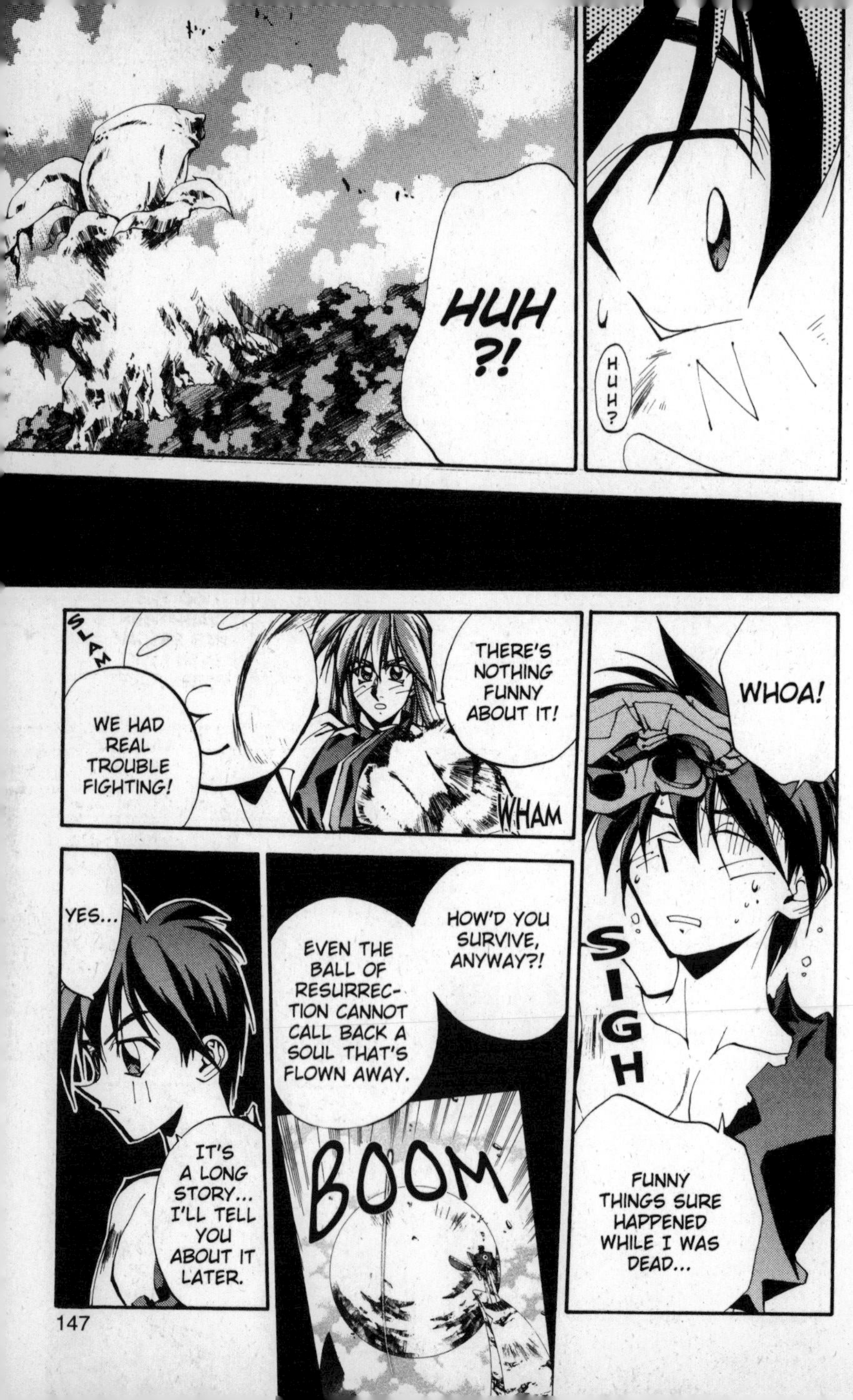
HUH?
HUH ?!
WHOA!
SIGH
FUNNY THINGS SURE HAPPENED WHILE I WAS DEAD...
SLAM
THERE'S NOTHING FUNNY ABOUT IT!
WE HAD REAL TROUBLE FIGHTING!
WHAM
HOW'D YOU SURVIVE, ANYWAY?!
EVEN THE BALL OF RESURREC-TION CANNOT CALL BACK A SOUL THAT'S FLOWN AWAY.
BOOM
YES...
IT'S A LONG STORY... I'LL TELL YOU ABOUT IT LATER.

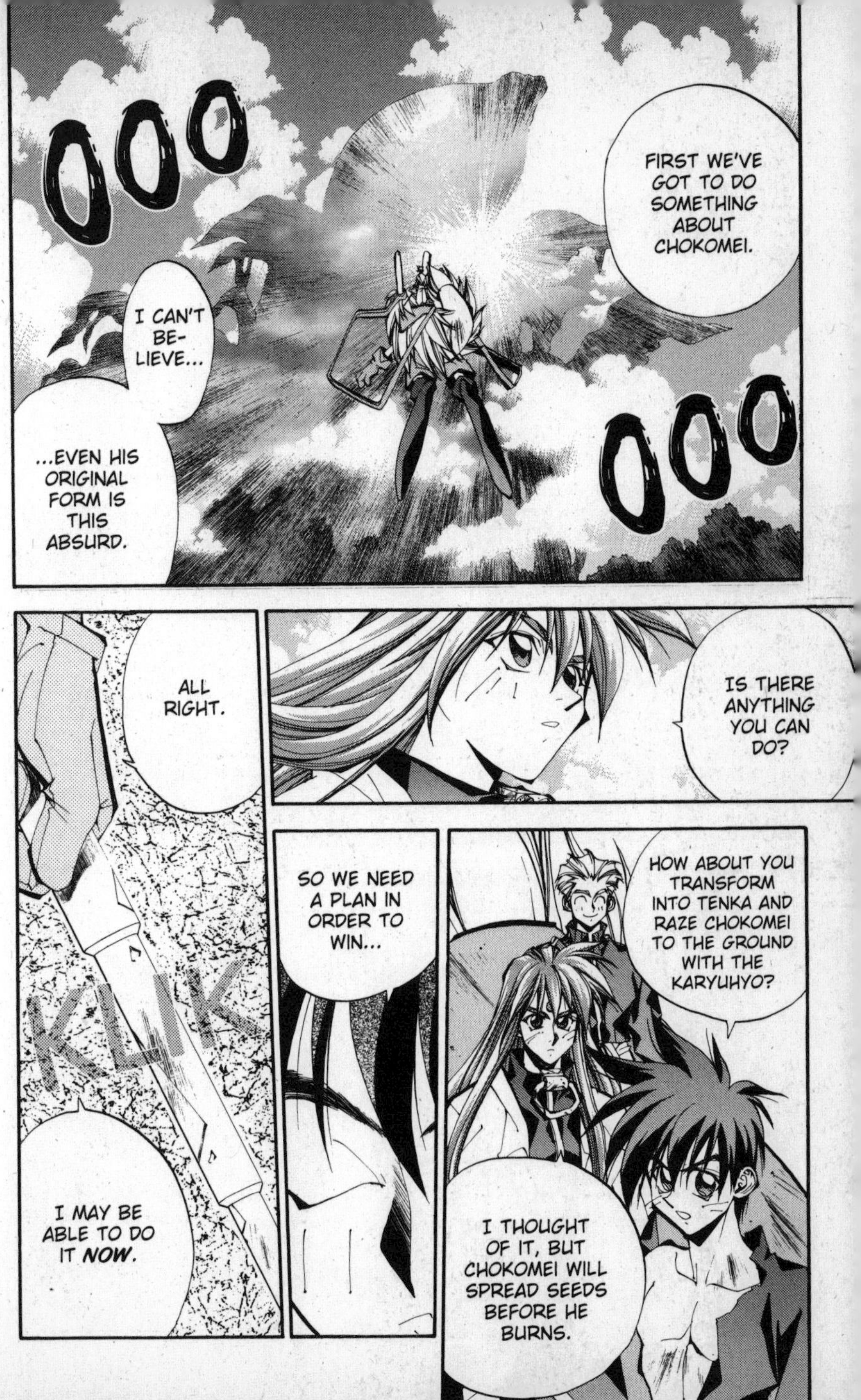
FIRST WE'VE GOT TO DO SOMETHING ABOUT CHOKOMEI.
OOO
I CAN'T BE-LIEVE...
...EVEN HIS ORIGINAL FORM IS THIS ABSURD.
OOO
IS THERE ANYTHING YOU CAN DO?
HOW ABOUT YOU TRANSFORM INTO TENKA AND RAZE CHOKOMEI TO THE GROUND WITH THE KARYUHYO?
I THOUGHT OF IT, BUT CHOKOMEI WILL SPREAD SEEDS BEFORE HE BURNS.
SO WE NEED A PLAN IN ORDER TO WIN...
ALL RIGHT.
KLIK
I MAY BE ABLE TO DO IT ***NOW***.

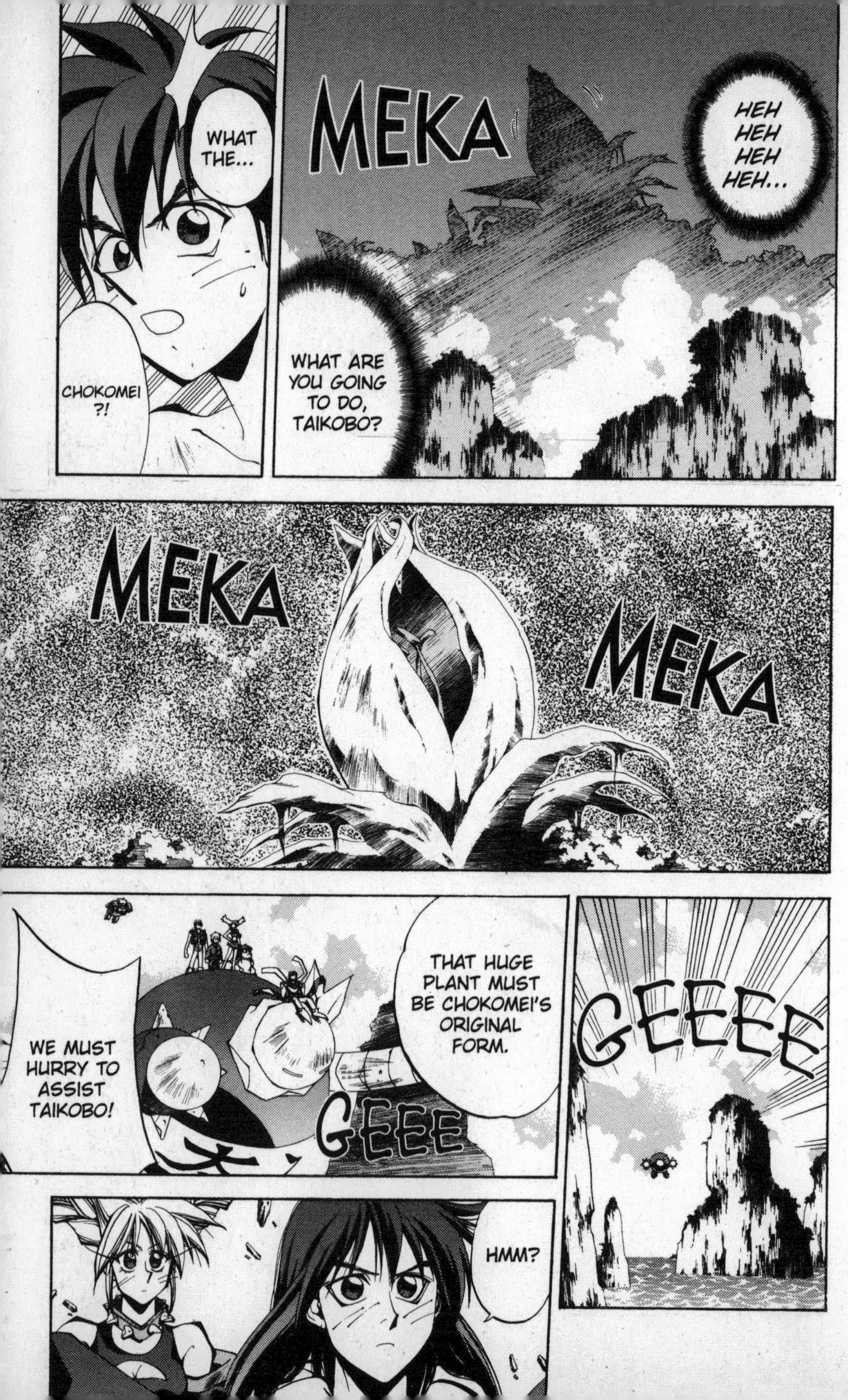
HEH HEH HEH HEH...
MEKA
WHAT ARE YOU GOING TO DO, TAIKOBO?
WHAT THE...
CHOKOMEI ?!
MEKA
MEKA
MEKA
GEEEE
THAT HUGE PLANT MUST BE CHOKOMEI'S ORIGINAL FORM.
GEEE
WE MUST HURRY TO ASSIST TAIKOBO!
HMM?

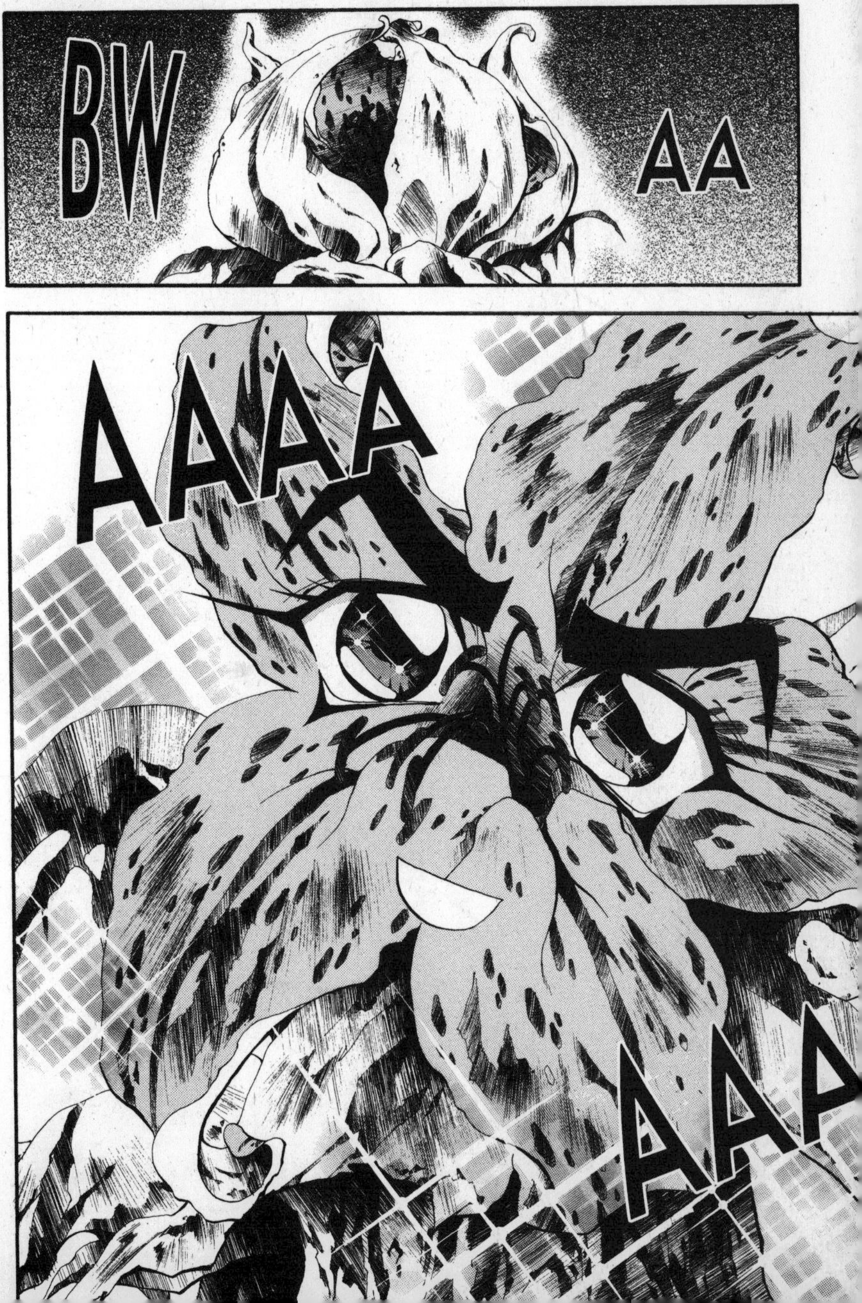
BW
AA
AAAA
AAA

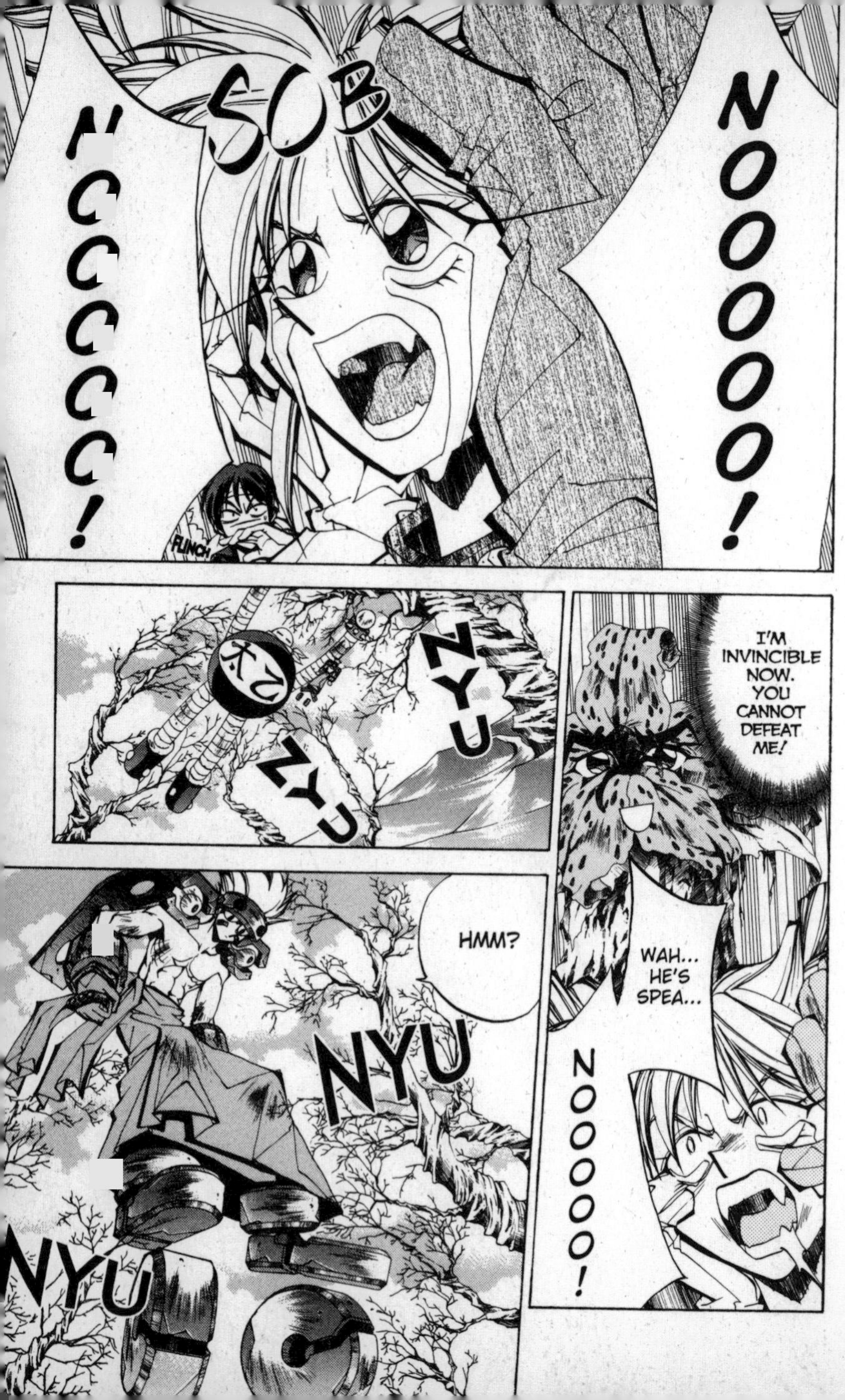
NOOOOOO!
SOB
NGGGGG!
FLINCH
I'M INVINCIBLE NOW. YOU CANNOT DEFEAT ME!
WAH... HE'S SPEA...
NOOOOOO!
NYU
ZYU
HMM?
NYU
NYU

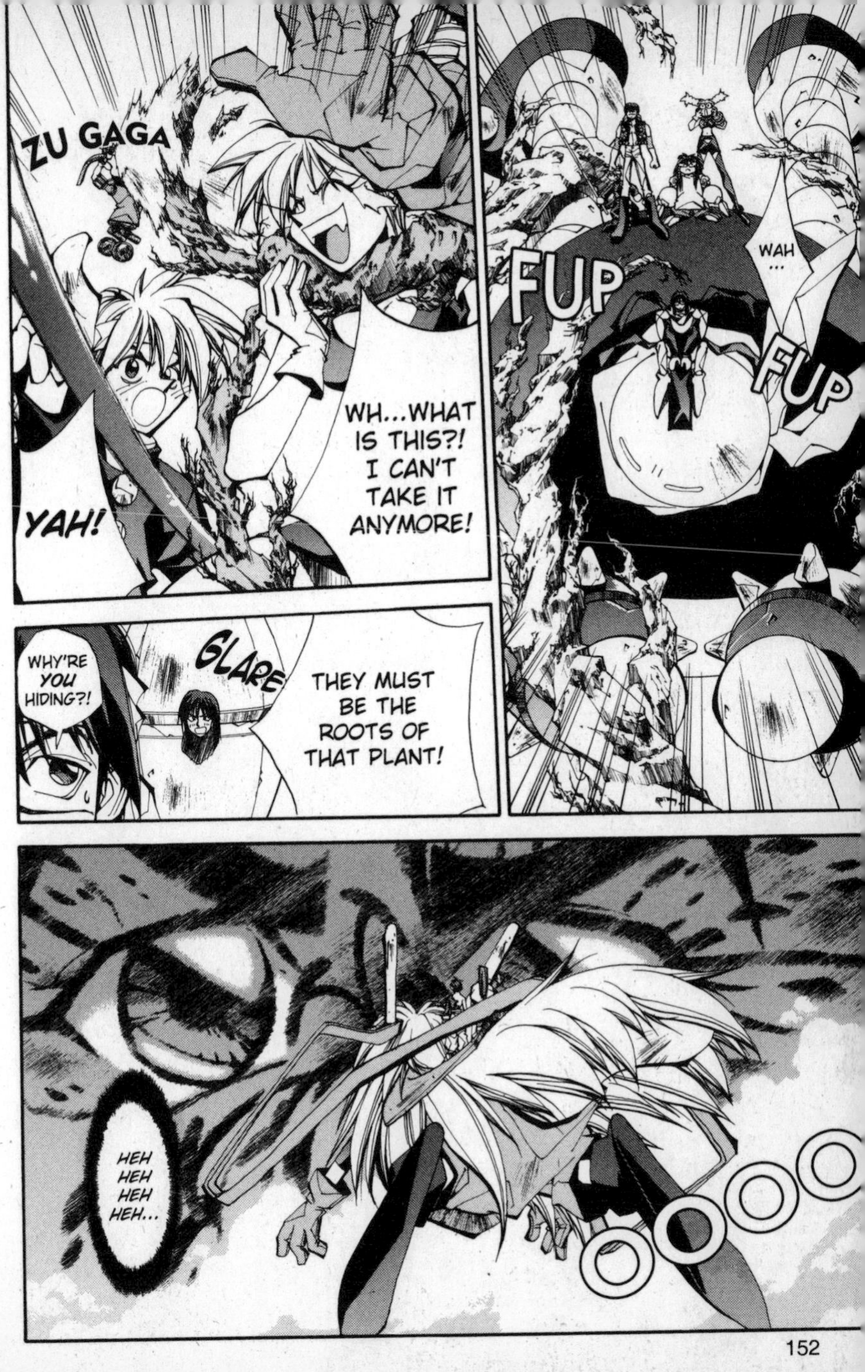
WAH ...
FUP
FUP
ZU GAGA
WH...WHAT IS THIS?! I CAN'T TAKE IT ANYMORE!
YAH!
THEY MUST BE THE ROOTS OF THAT PLANT!
GLARE
WHY'RE *YOU* HIDING?!
HEH HEH HEH HEH...

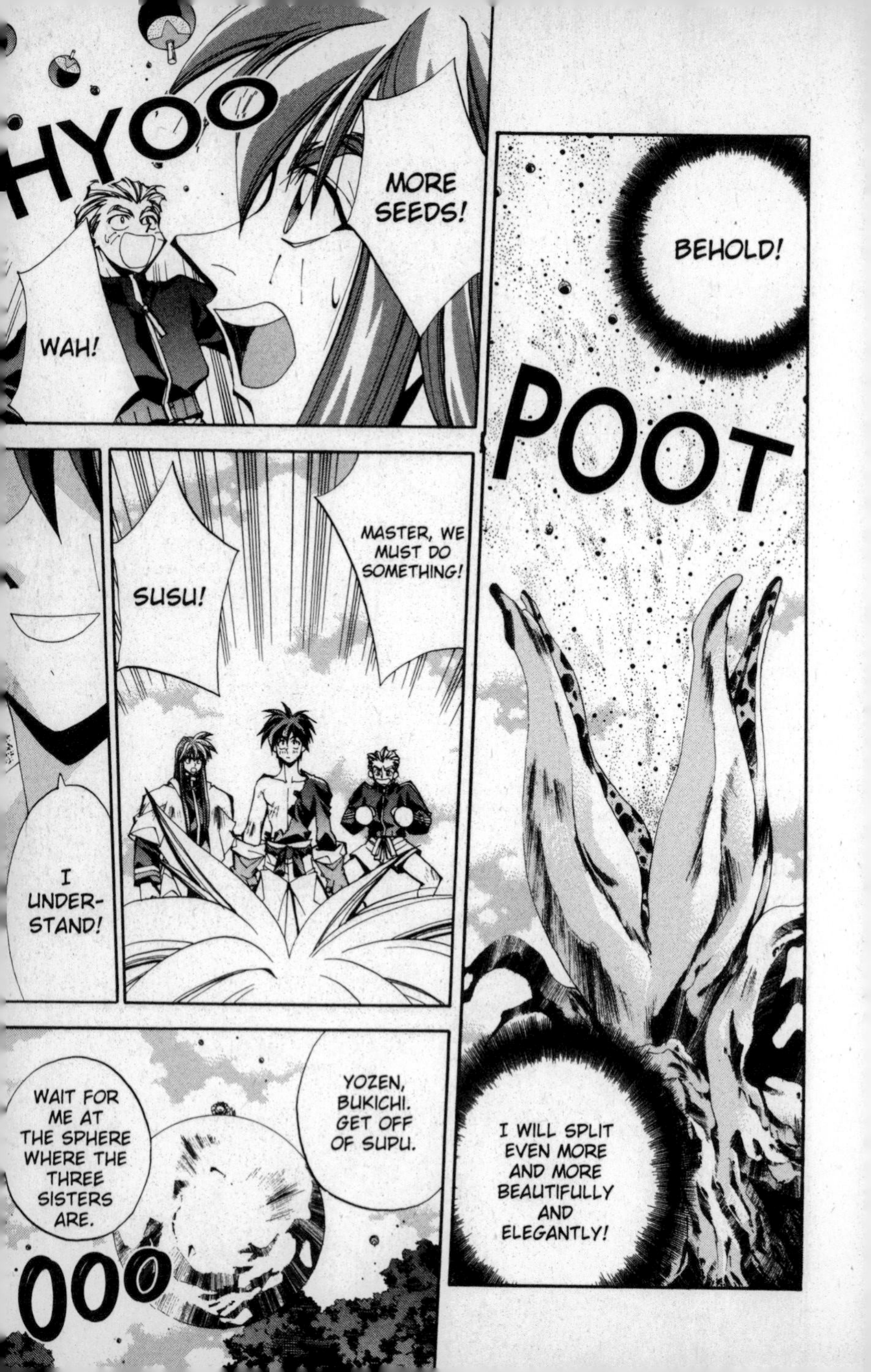
BEHOLD!
POOT
I WILL SPLIT EVEN MORE AND MORE BEAUTIFULLY AND ELEGANTLY!
HYOO
MORE SEEDS!
WAH!
MASTER, WE MUST DO SOMETHING!
SUSU!
I UNDER-STAND!
YOZEN, BUKICHI. GET OFF OF SUPU.
WAIT FOR ME AT THE SPHERE WHERE THE THREE SISTERS ARE.
OOO

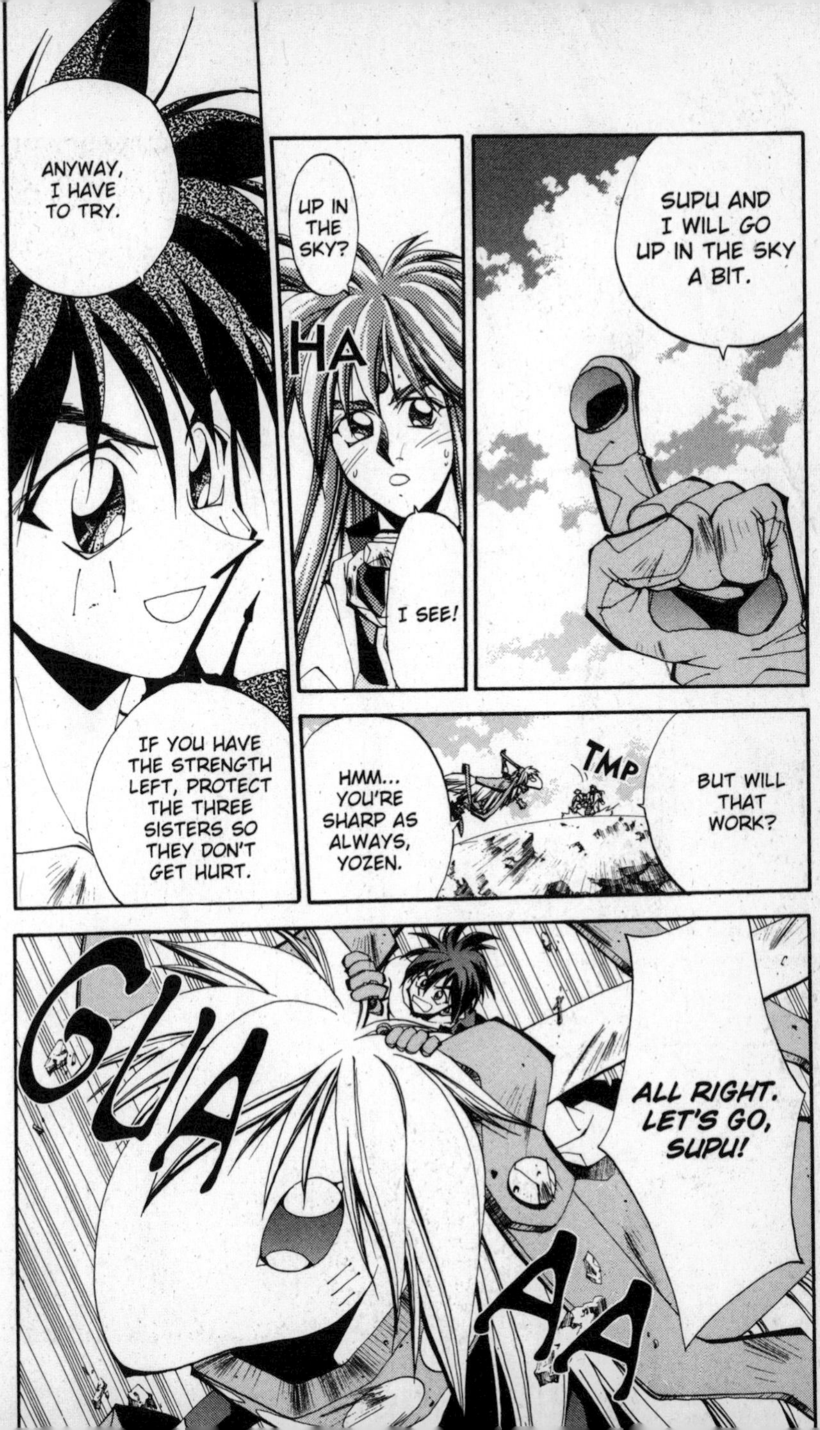
SUPU AND I WILL GO UP IN THE SKY A BIT.
UP IN THE SKY?
HA
I SEE!
BUT WILL THAT WORK?
TMP
HMM... YOU'RE SHARP AS ALWAYS, YOZEN.
ANYWAY, I HAVE TO TRY.
IF YOU HAVE THE STRENGTH LEFT, PROTECT THE THREE SISTERS SO THEY DON'T GET HURT.
ALL RIGHT. LET'S GO, SUPU!
GUA
AA

READ THIS WAY

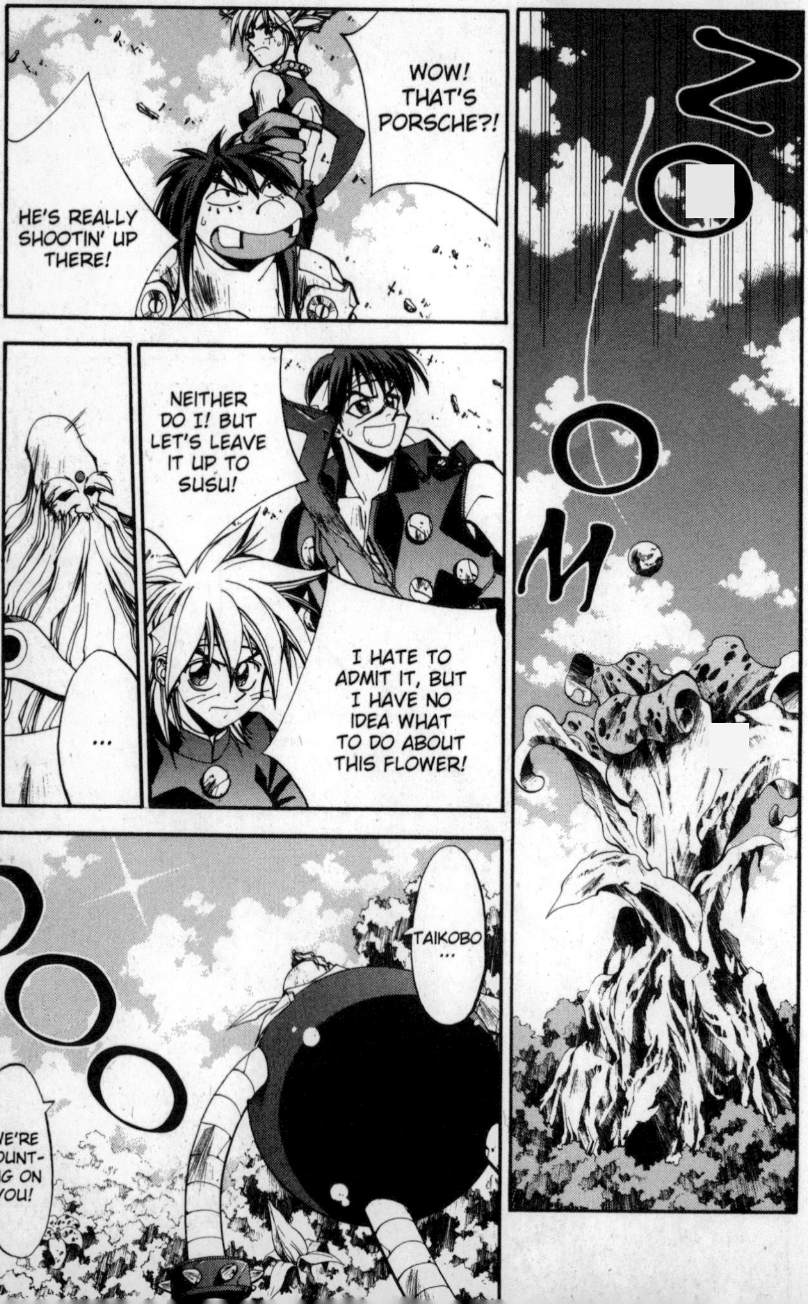
ZOOM
WOW! THAT'S PORSCHE?!
HE'S REALLY SHOOTIN' UP THERE!
I HATE TO ADMIT IT, BUT I HAVE NO IDEA WHAT TO DO ABOUT THIS FLOWER!
NEITHER DO I! BUT LET'S LEAVE IT UP TO SUSU!
...
OOO
TAIKOBO ...
WE'RE COUNT-ING ON YOU!

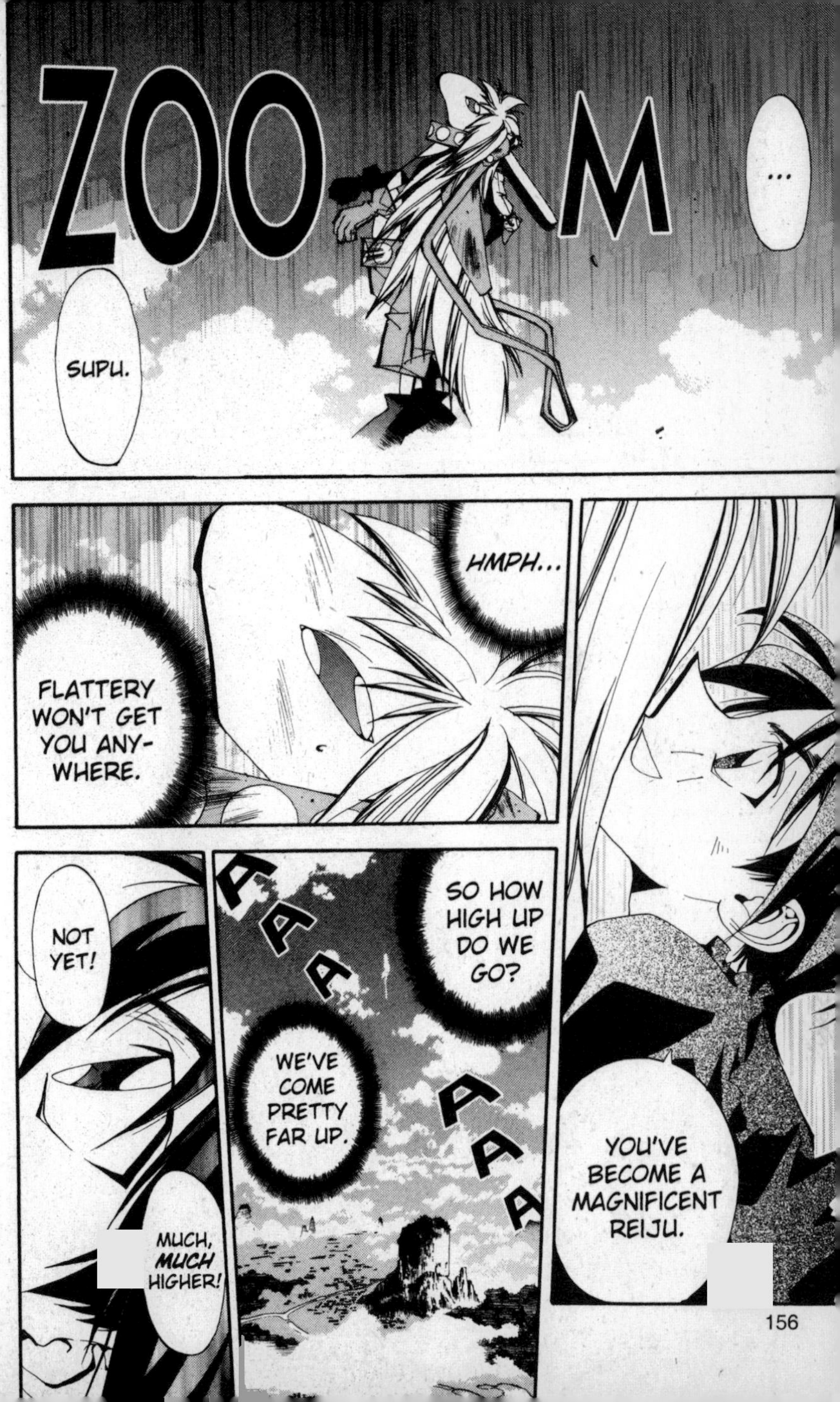
ZOOM
...
SUPU.
YOU'VE BECOME A MAGNIFICENT REIJU.
HMPH...
FLATTERY WON'T GET YOU ANYWHERE.
AAAAAAA
SO HOW HIGH UP DO WE GO?
WE'VE COME PRETTY FAR UP.
NOT YET!
MUCH, *MUCH* HIGHER!

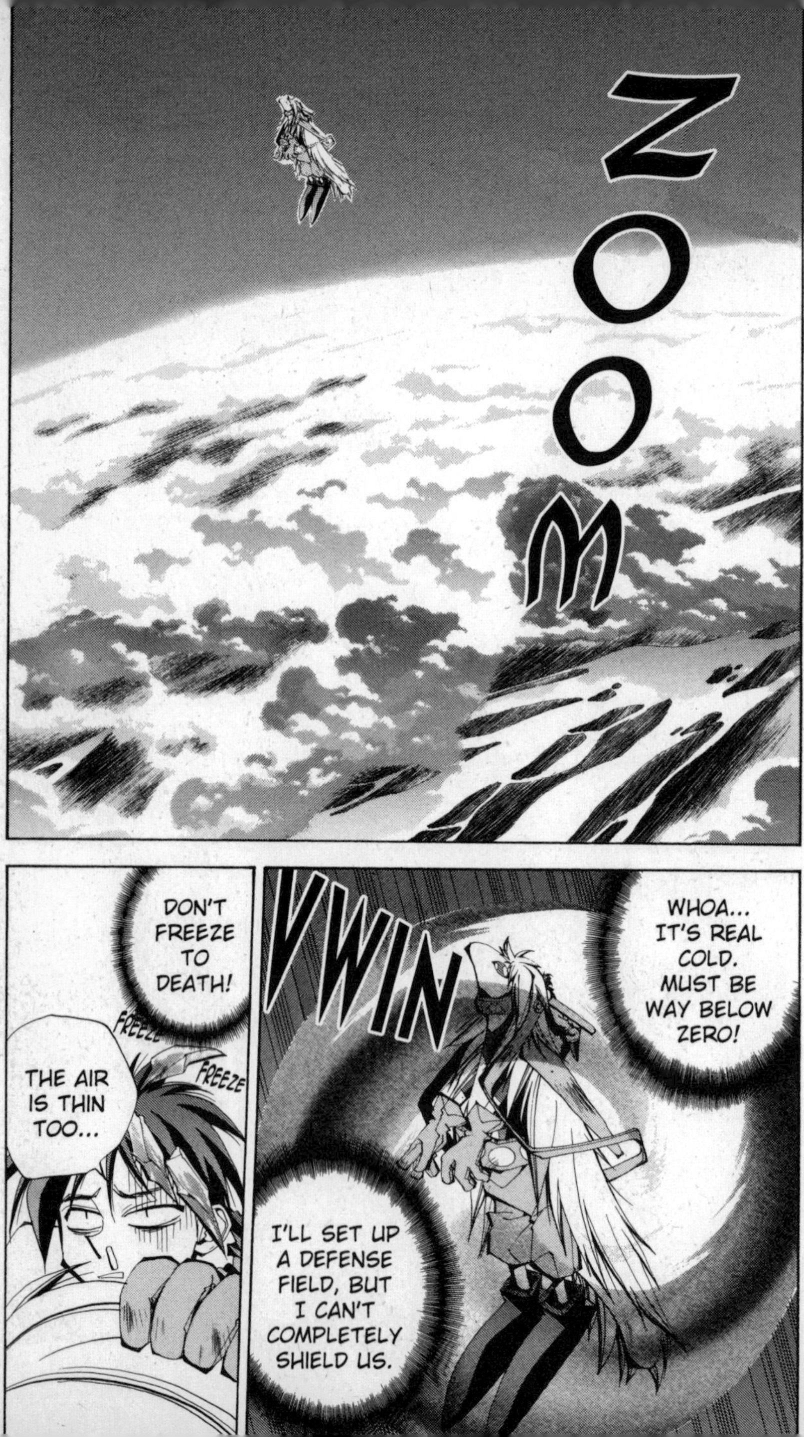
ZOOM
WHOA... IT'S REAL COLD. MUST BE WAY BELOW ZERO!
VWIN
I'LL SET UP A DEFENSE FIELD, BUT I CAN'T COMPLETELY SHIELD US.
DON'T FREEZE TO DEATH!
FREEZE
FREEZE
THE AIR IS THIN TOO...

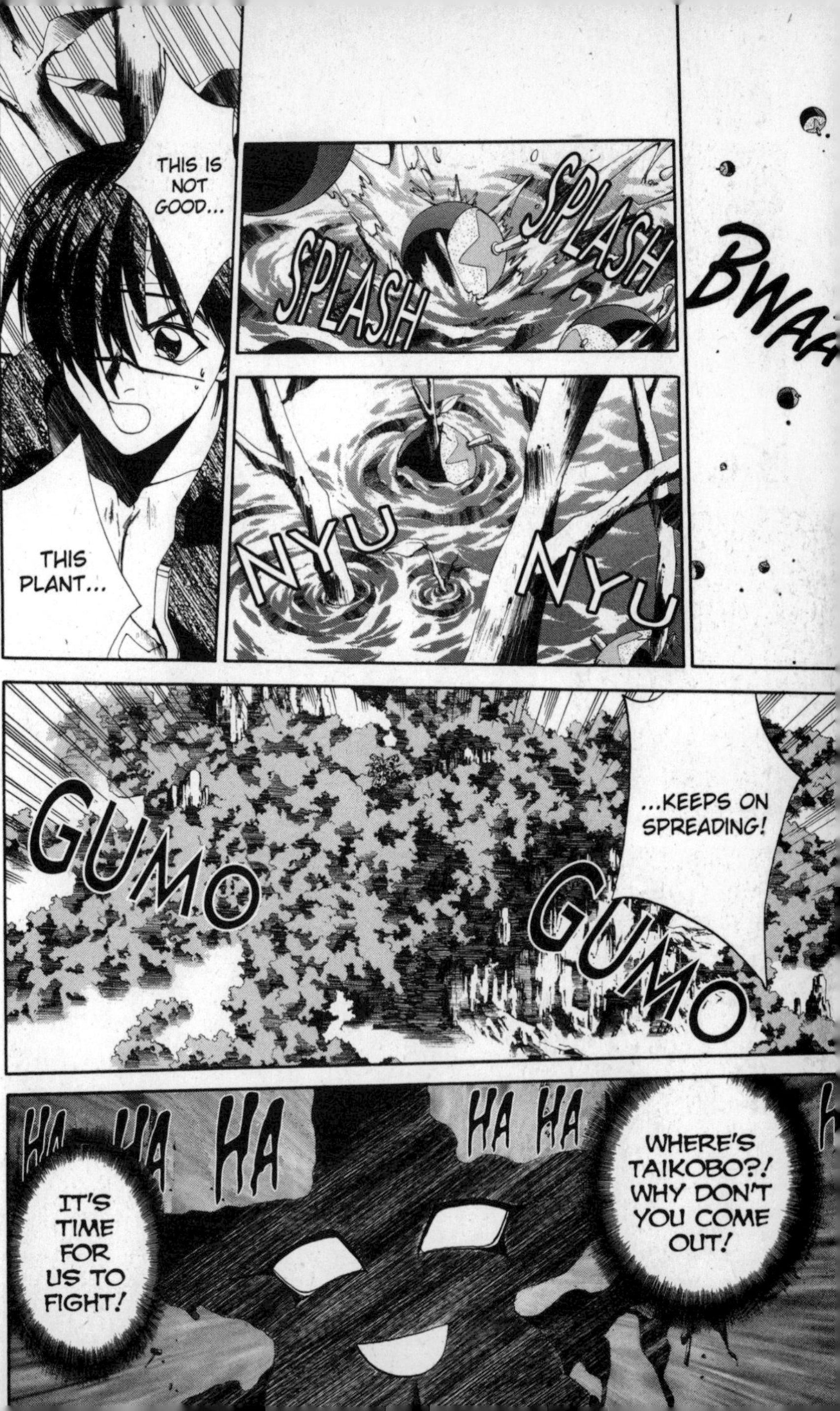
BWAA
SPLASH
SPLASH
NYU
NYU
THIS IS NOT GOOD...
THIS PLANT...
...KEEPS ON SPREADING!
GUMO
GUMO
HA HA
WHERE'S TAIKOBO?! WHY DON'T YOU COME OUT!
HA HA HA
IT'S TIME FOR US TO FIGHT!

READ THIS WAY

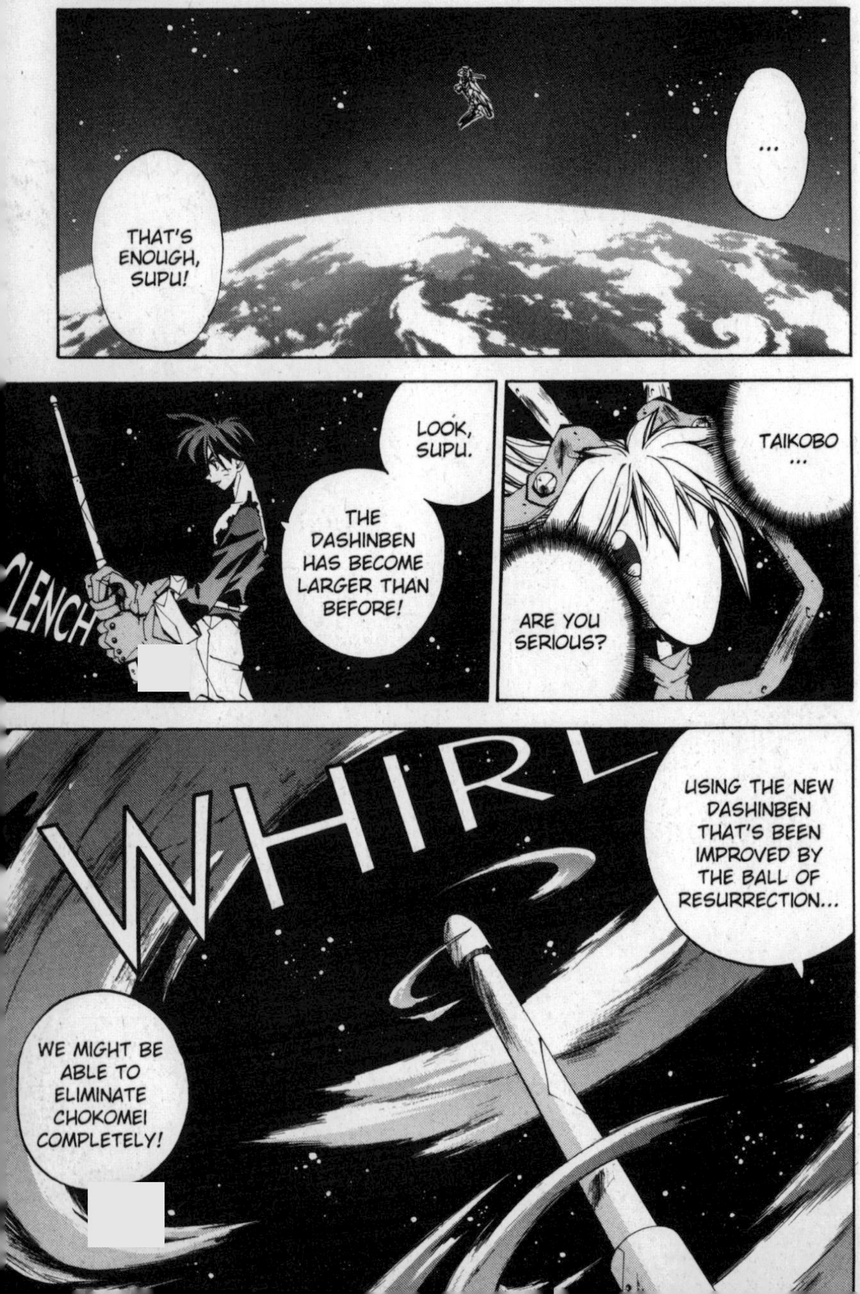
...
THAT'S ENOUGH, SUPU!
TAIKOBO ...
ARE YOU SERIOUS?
LOOK, SUPU.
THE DASHINBEN HAS BECOME LARGER THAN BEFORE!
CLENCH
USING THE NEW DASHINBEN THAT'S BEEN IMPROVED BY THE BALL OF RESURRECTION...
WHIRL
WE MIGHT BE ABLE TO ELIMINATE CHOKOMEI COMPLETELY!

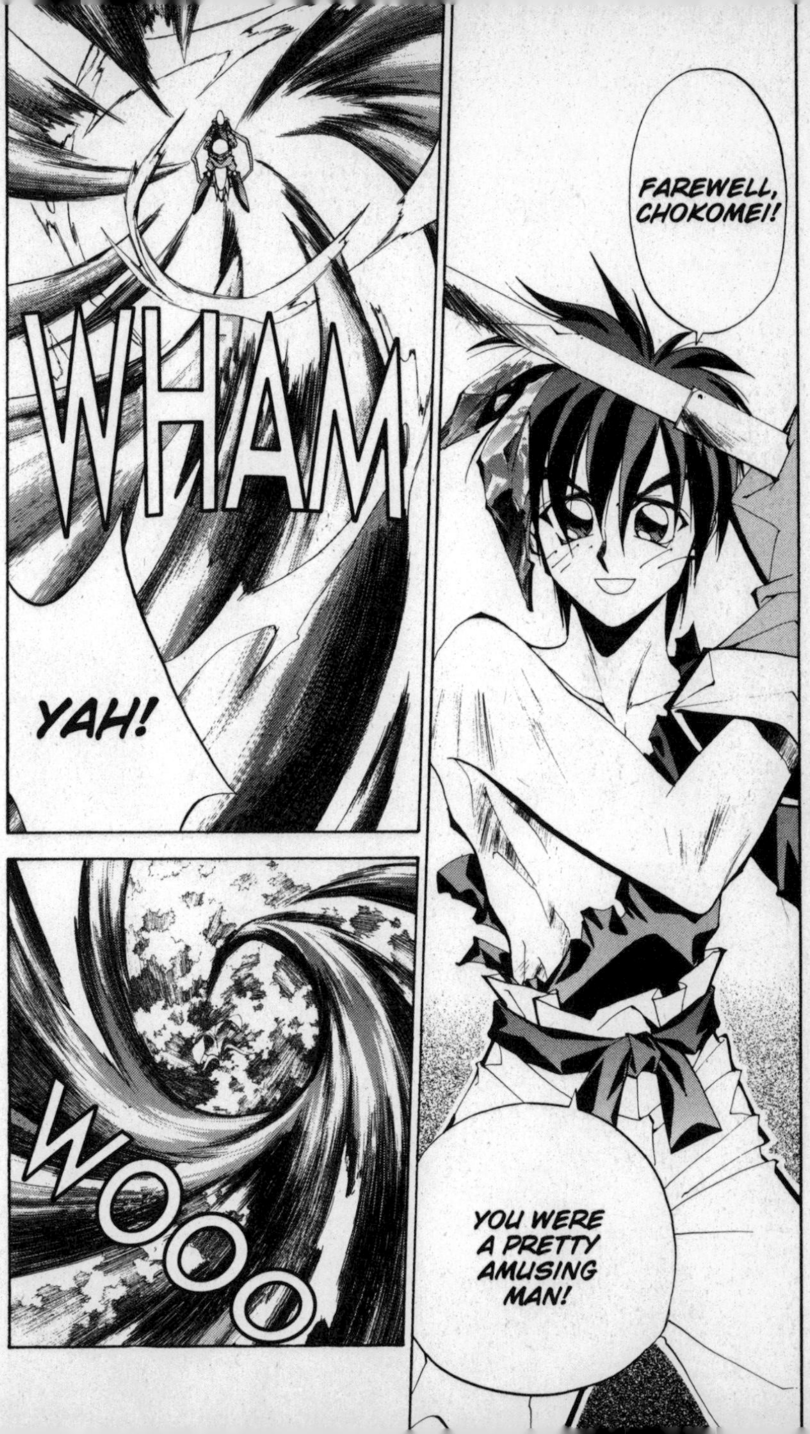
FAREWELL, CHOKOMEI!
YOU WERE A PRETTY AMUSING MAN!
WHAM
YAH!
WOOOO

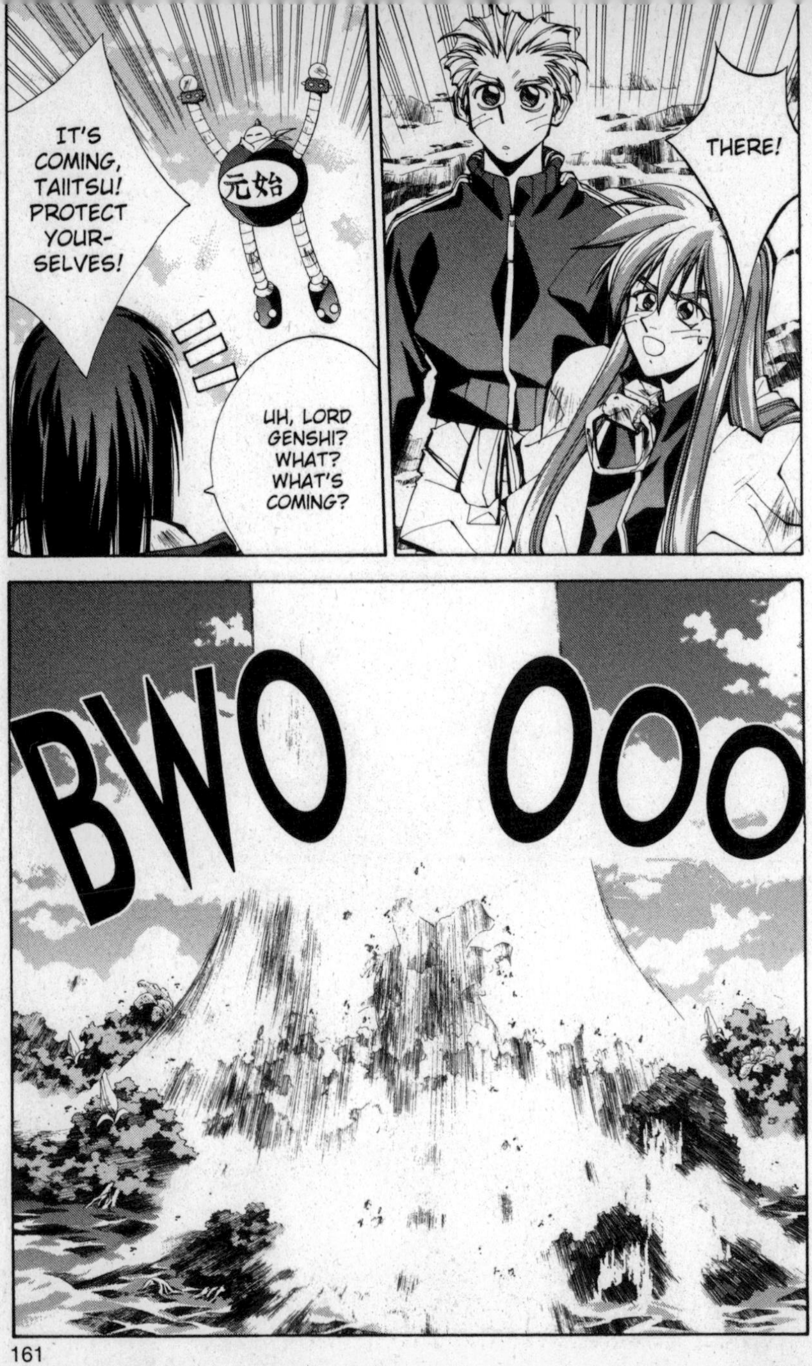
THERE!
IT'S COMING, TAIITSU! PROTECT YOUR-SELVES!
元始
UH, LORD GENSHI? WHAT? WHAT'S COMING?
BWO OOO

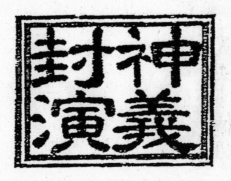

封神演義

CHAPTER 106:
MEDIUM-BOSS BATTLE, PART 8 - THE FALL OF THE ARISTOCRAT

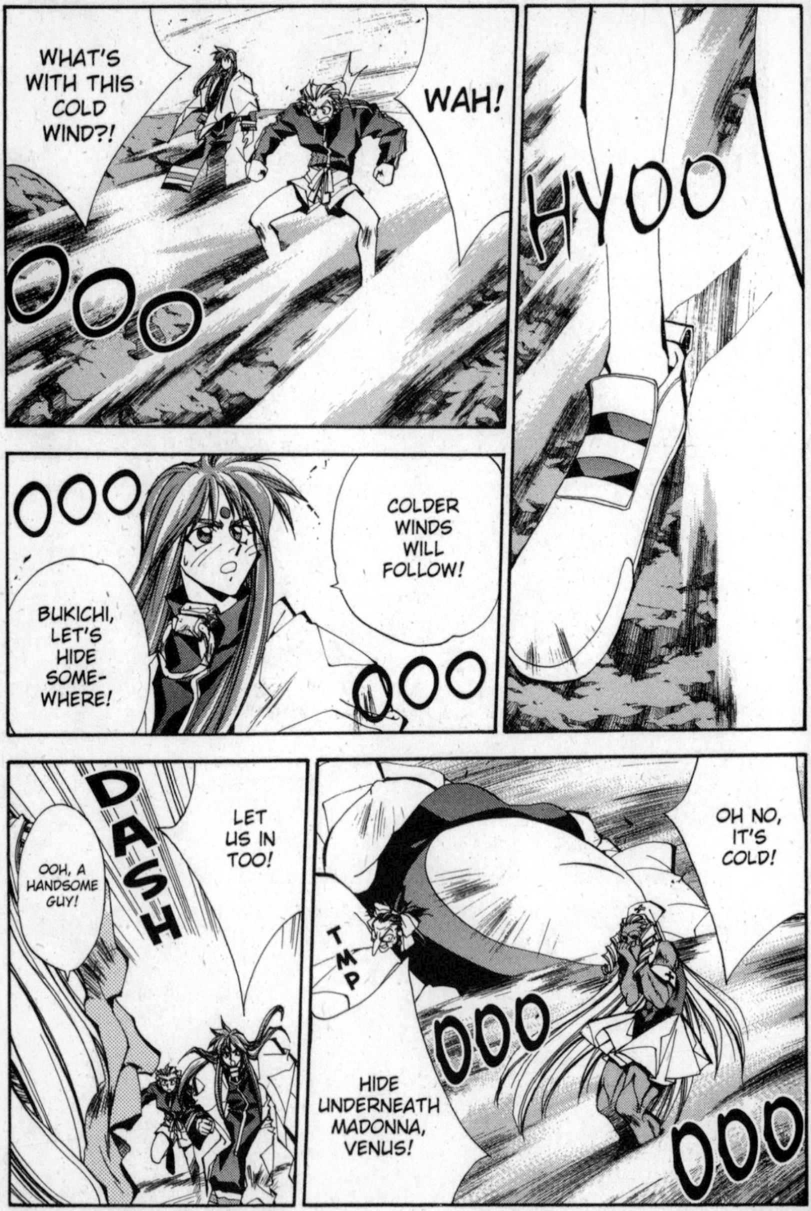
HYOO
WAH!
WHAT'S WITH THIS COLD WIND?!
OOO
COLDER WINDS WILL FOLLOW!
OOO
BUKICHI, LET'S HIDE SOME-WHERE!
OOO
OH NO, IT'S COLD!
TMP
OOO
HIDE UNDERNEATH MADONNA, VENUS!
OOO
LET US IN TOO!
DASH
OOH, A HANDSOME GUY!

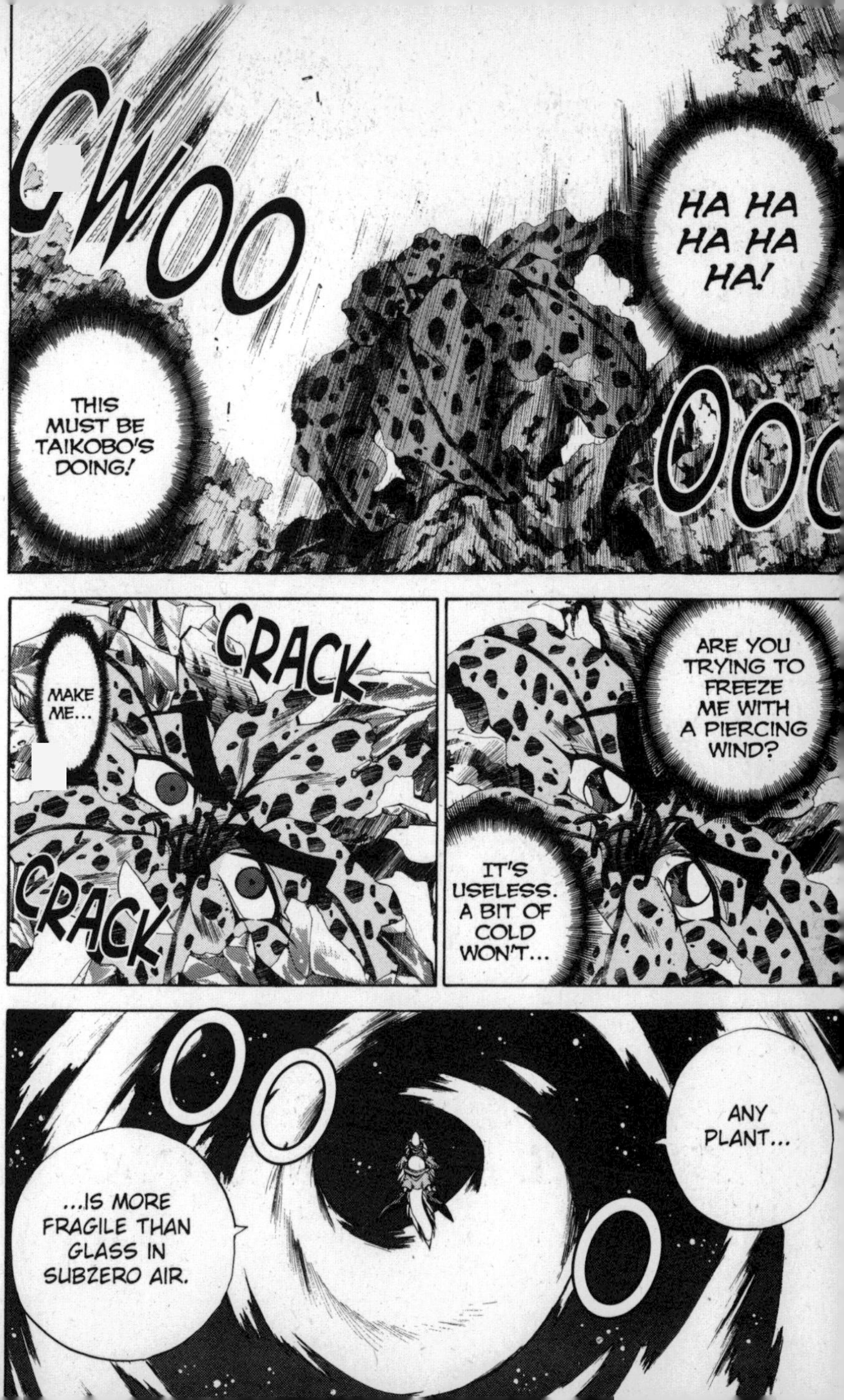
HA HA HA HA HA!
OOO
CWOO
THIS MUST BE TAIKOBO'S DOING!
ARE YOU TRYING TO FREEZE ME WITH A PIERCING WIND?
IT'S USELESS. A BIT OF COLD WON'T...
CRACK
MAKE ME...
CRACK
ANY PLANT...
...IS MORE FRAGILE THAN GLASS IN SUBZERO AIR.

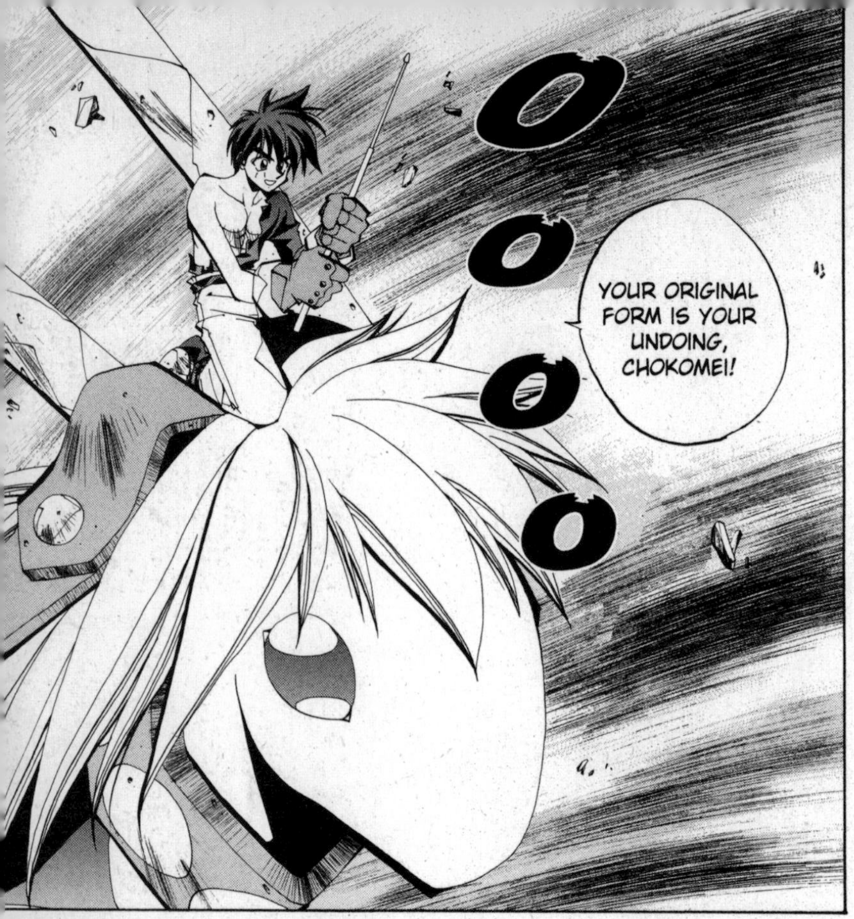
OOOO
YOUR ORIGINAL FORM IS YOUR UNDOING, CHOKOMEI!

Chapter 106

MEDIUM-BOSS BATTLE, PART 8
THE FALL OF THE ARISTOCRAT

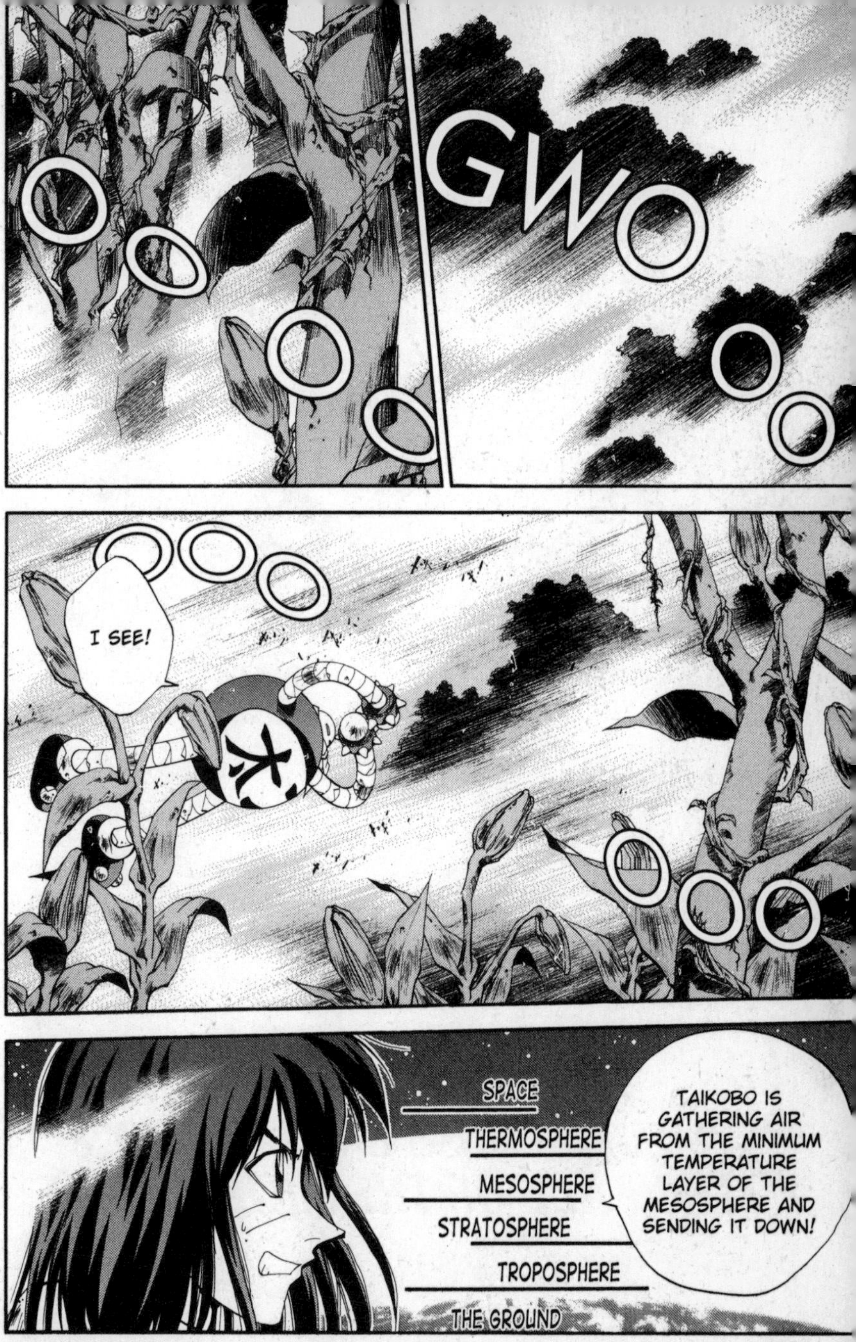
GWOOOO
OOOO
OOO
I SEE!
OOOO
TAIKOBO IS GATHERING AIR FROM THE MINIMUM TEMPERATURE LAYER OF THE MESOSPHERE AND SENDING IT DOWN!
SPACE
THERMOSPHERE
MESOSPHERE
STRATOSPHERE
TROPOSPHERE
THE GROUND

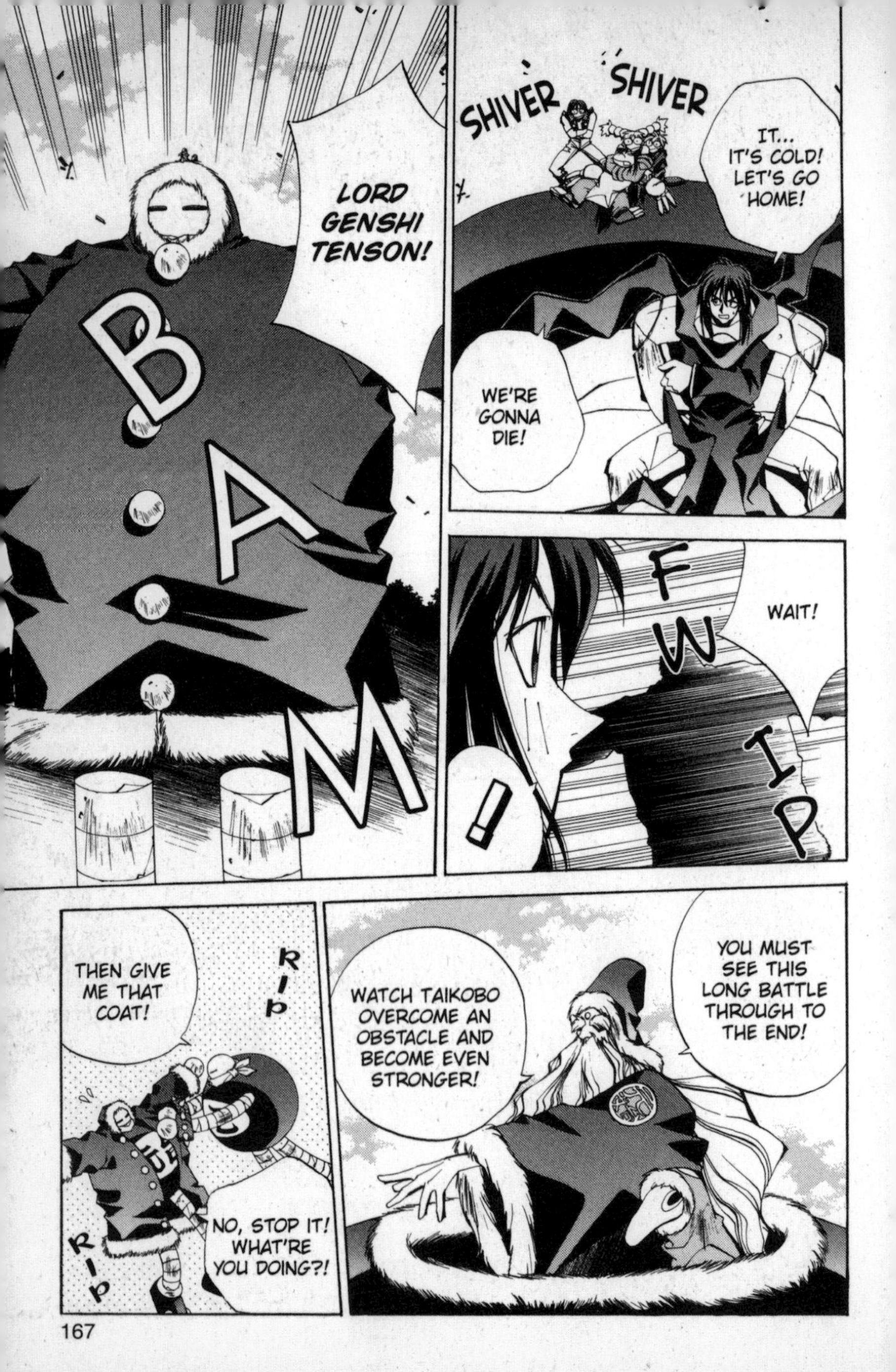
SHIVER
SHIVER
IT... IT'S COLD! LET'S GO HOME!
WE'RE GONNA DIE!
FWIP
WAIT!
!
LORD GENSHI TENSON!
BAM
YOU MUST SEE THIS LONG BATTLE THROUGH TO THE END!
WATCH TAIKOBO OVERCOME AN OBSTACLE AND BECOME EVEN STRONGER!
THEN GIVE ME THAT COAT!
RIP
NO, STOP IT! WHAT'RE YOU DOING?!
RIP

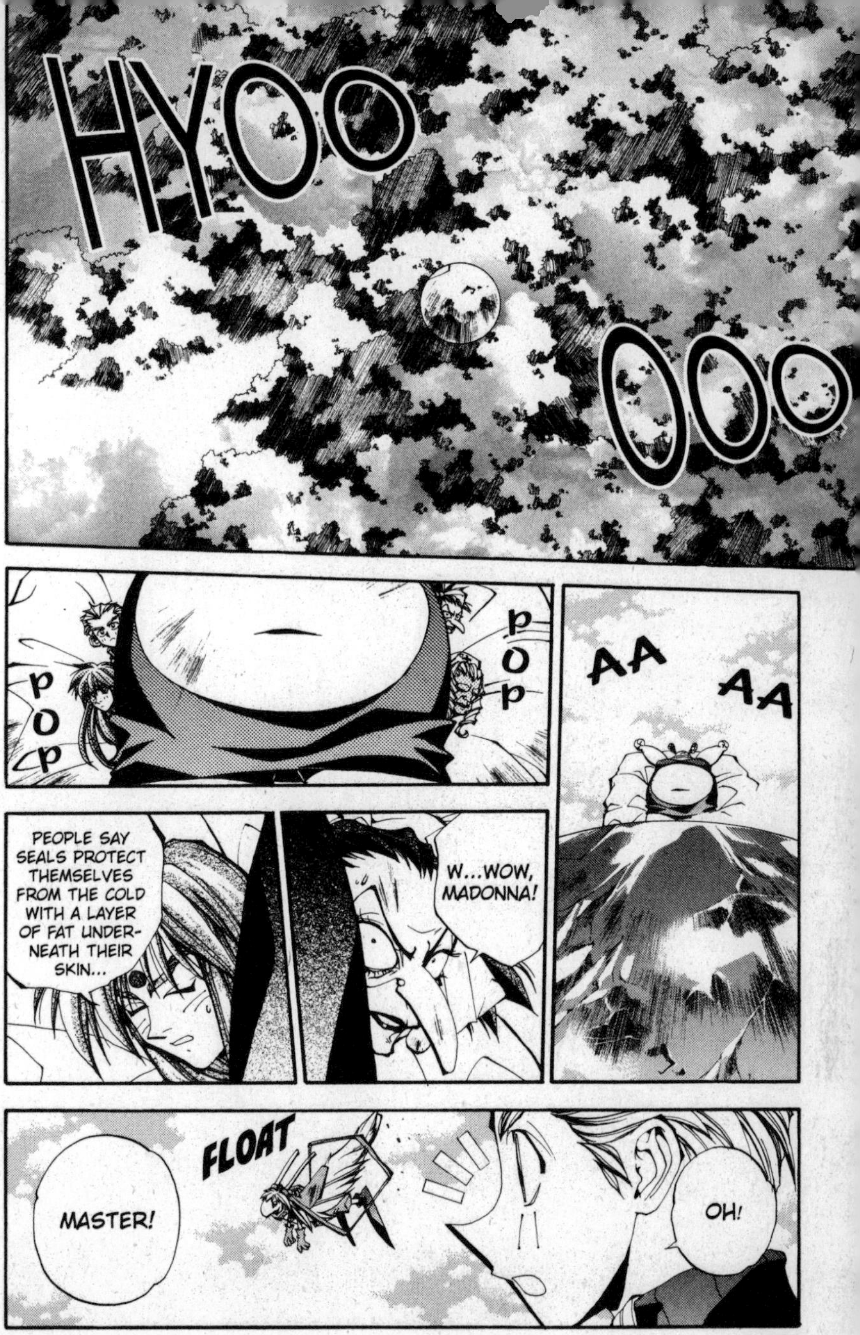
HYOO
OOO
AA
AA
pop
pop
W...WOW, MADONNA!
PEOPLE SAY SEALS PROTECT THEMSELVES FROM THE COLD WITH A LAYER OF FAT UNDER-NEATH THEIR SKIN...
OH!
FLOAT
MASTER!

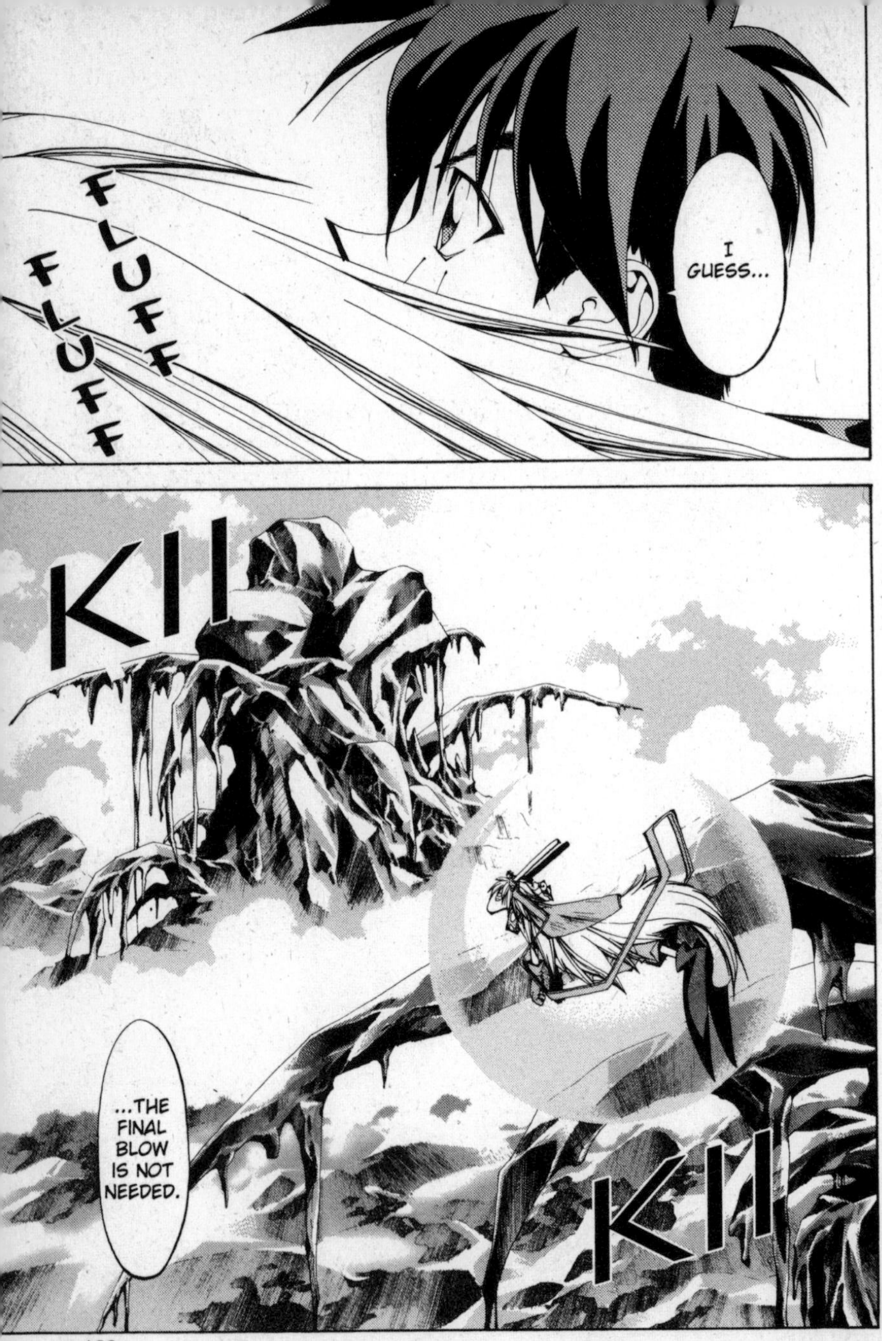
I GUESS...
FLUFF
FLUFF
FLUFF
FLUFF
KII
...THE FINAL BLOW IS NOT NEEDED.
KII

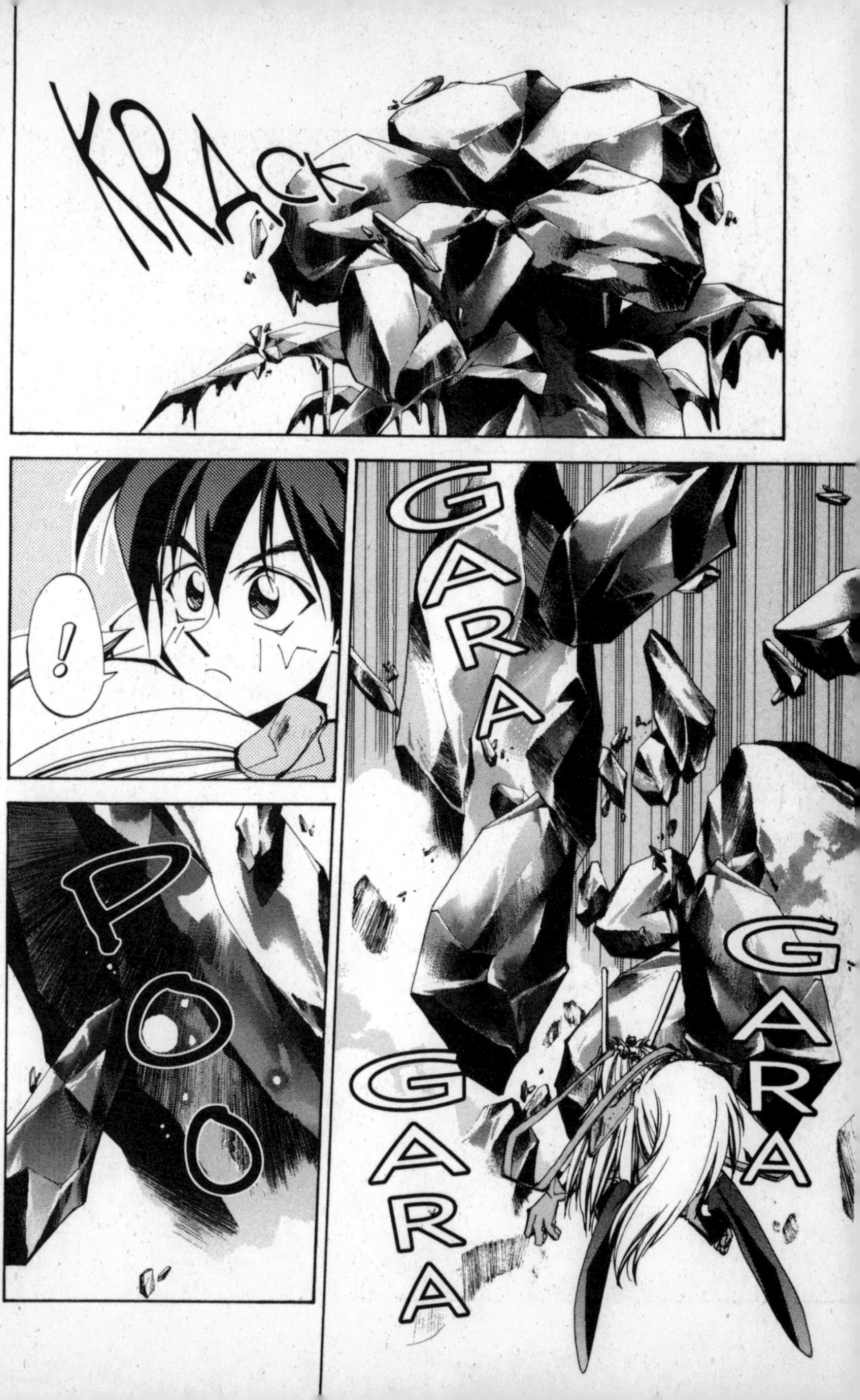
KRACK
GARA
GARA
GARA
GARA
!
POOO

READ THIS WAY

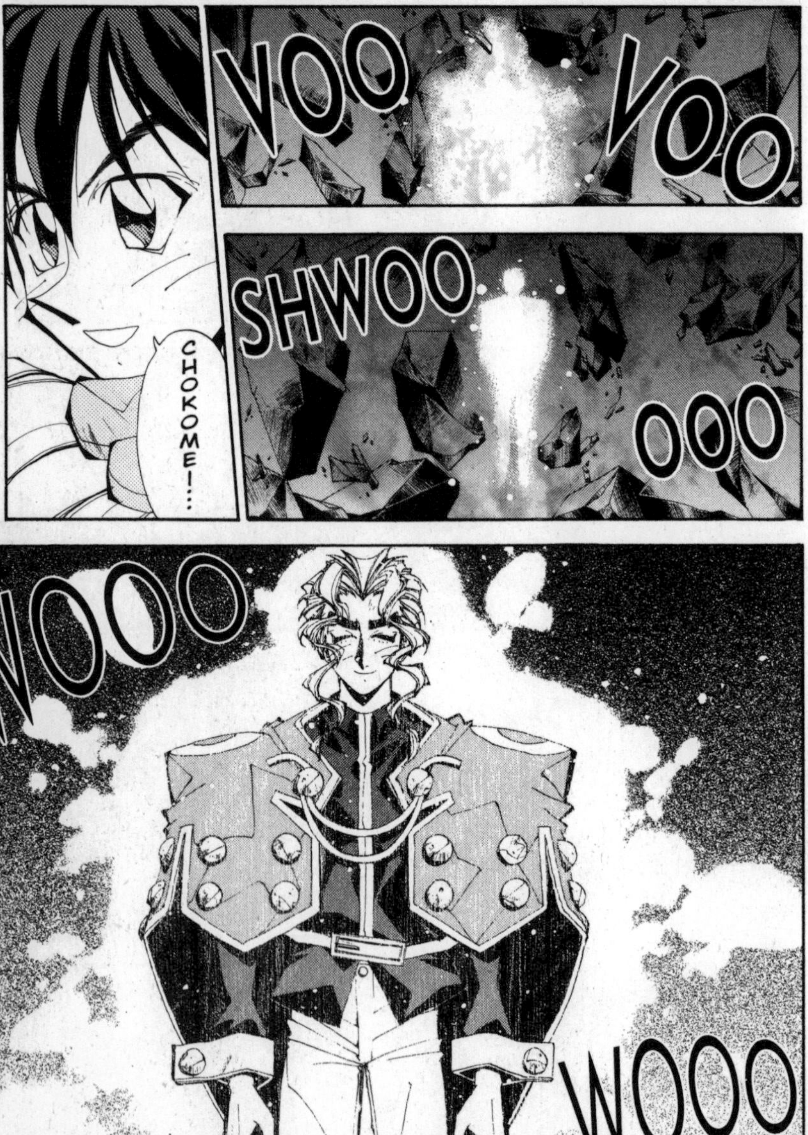

VOO VOO
SHWOO OOO
CHOKOME!...
WOOO WOOO

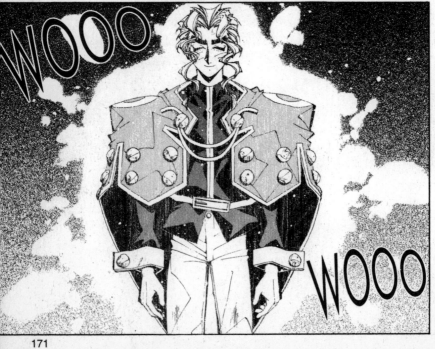

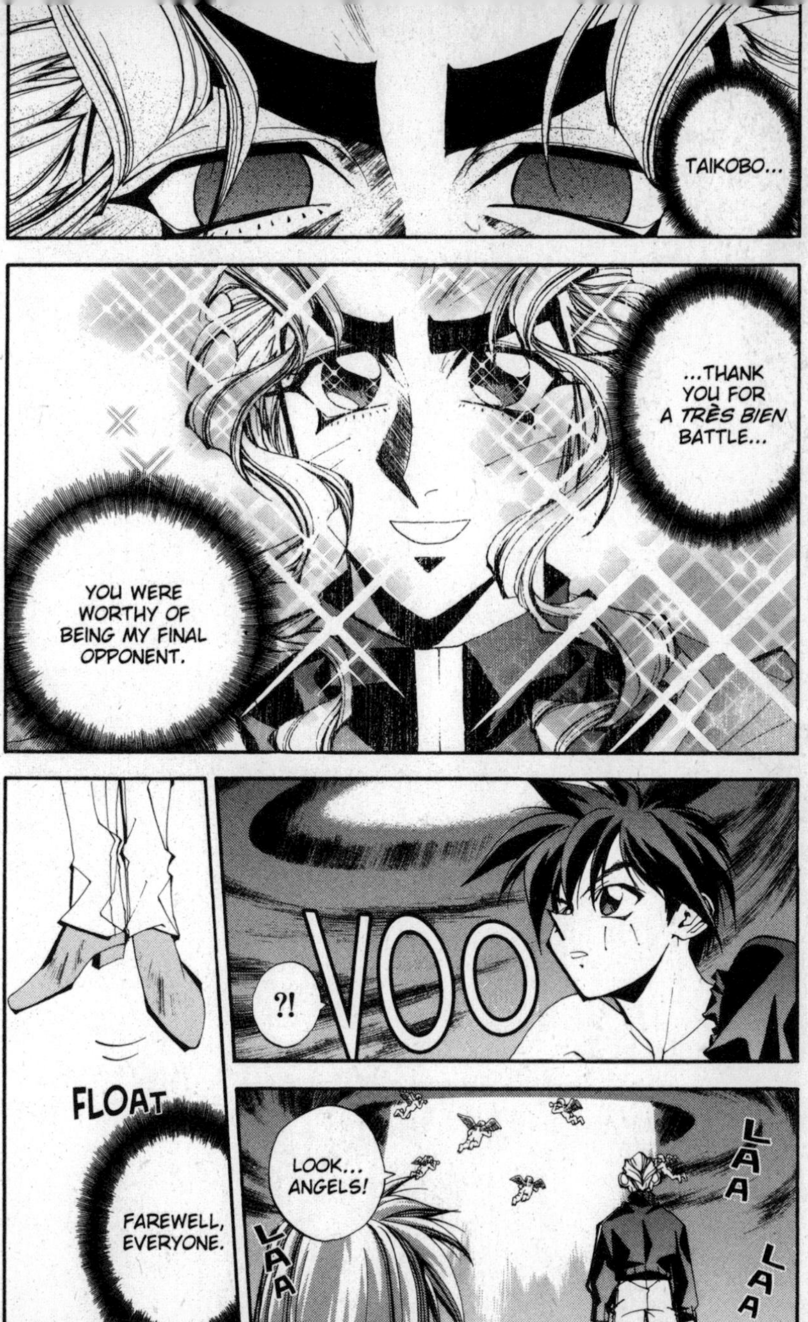
TAIKOBO...
...THANK YOU FOR A *TRÈS BIEN* BATTLE...
YOU WERE WORTHY OF BEING MY FINAL OPPONENT.
VOO
?!
LAA LAA
LAA LAA
LOOK... ANGELS!
LAA LAA
FLOAT
FAREWELL, EVERYONE.

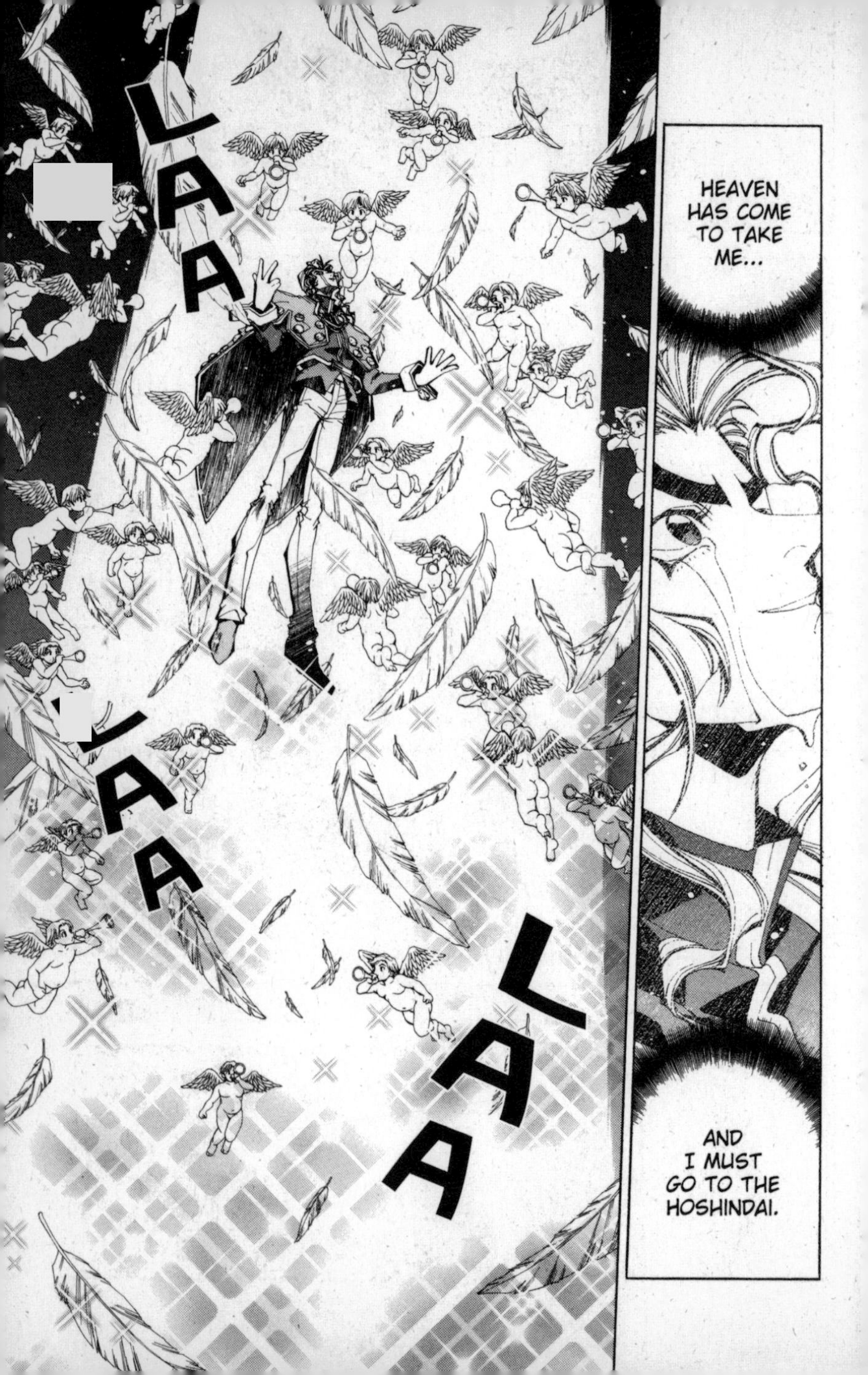
HEAVEN HAS COME TO TAKE ME...
AND I MUST GO TO THE HOSHINDAI.
LAA
LAA
LAA

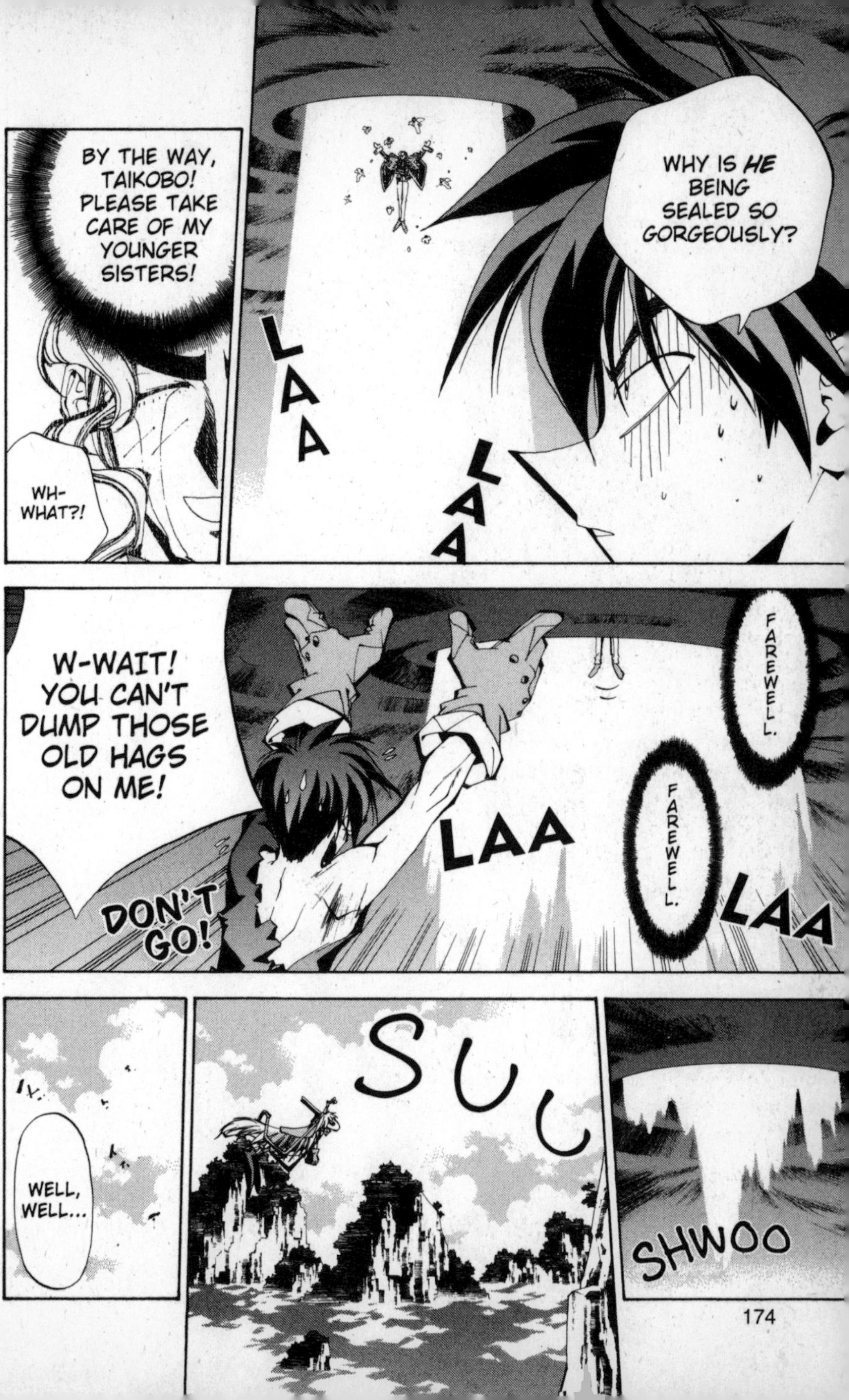
WHY IS HE BEING SEALED SO GORGEOUSLY?
LAA
LAA
BY THE WAY, TAIKOBO! PLEASE TAKE CARE OF MY YOUNGER SISTERS!
WH- WHAT?!
FAREWELL.
FAREWELL.
LAA
LAA
W-WAIT! YOU CAN'T DUMP THOSE OLD HAGS ON ME!
DON'T GO!
SHWOO
SUU
WELL, WELL...

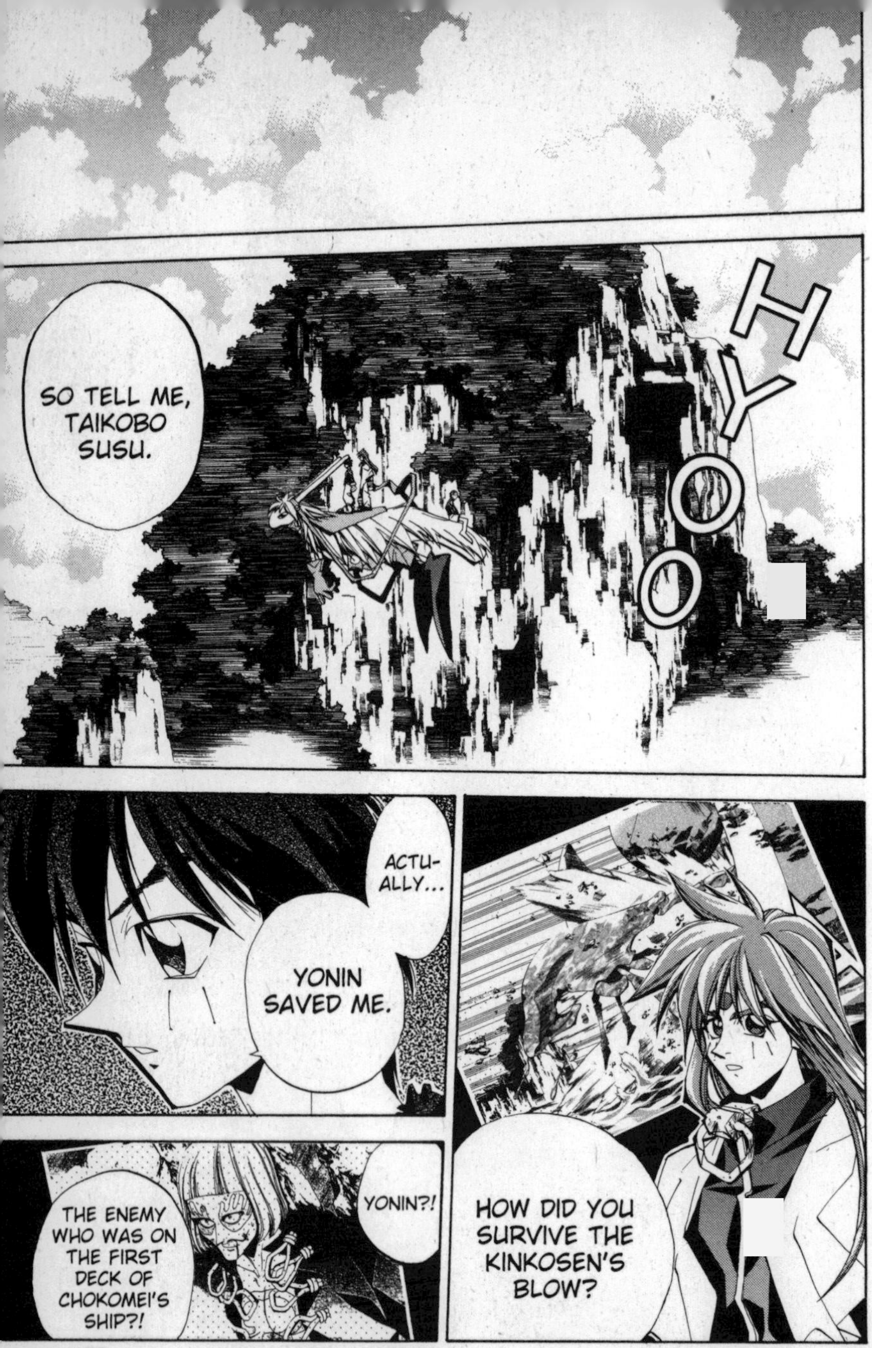
HYOOO
SO TELL ME, TAIKOBO SUSU.
HOW DID YOU SURVIVE THE KINKOSEN'S BLOW?
ACTU-ALLY...
YONIN SAVED ME.
YONIN?!
THE ENEMY WHO WAS ON THE FIRST DECK OF CHOKOMEI'S SHIP?!

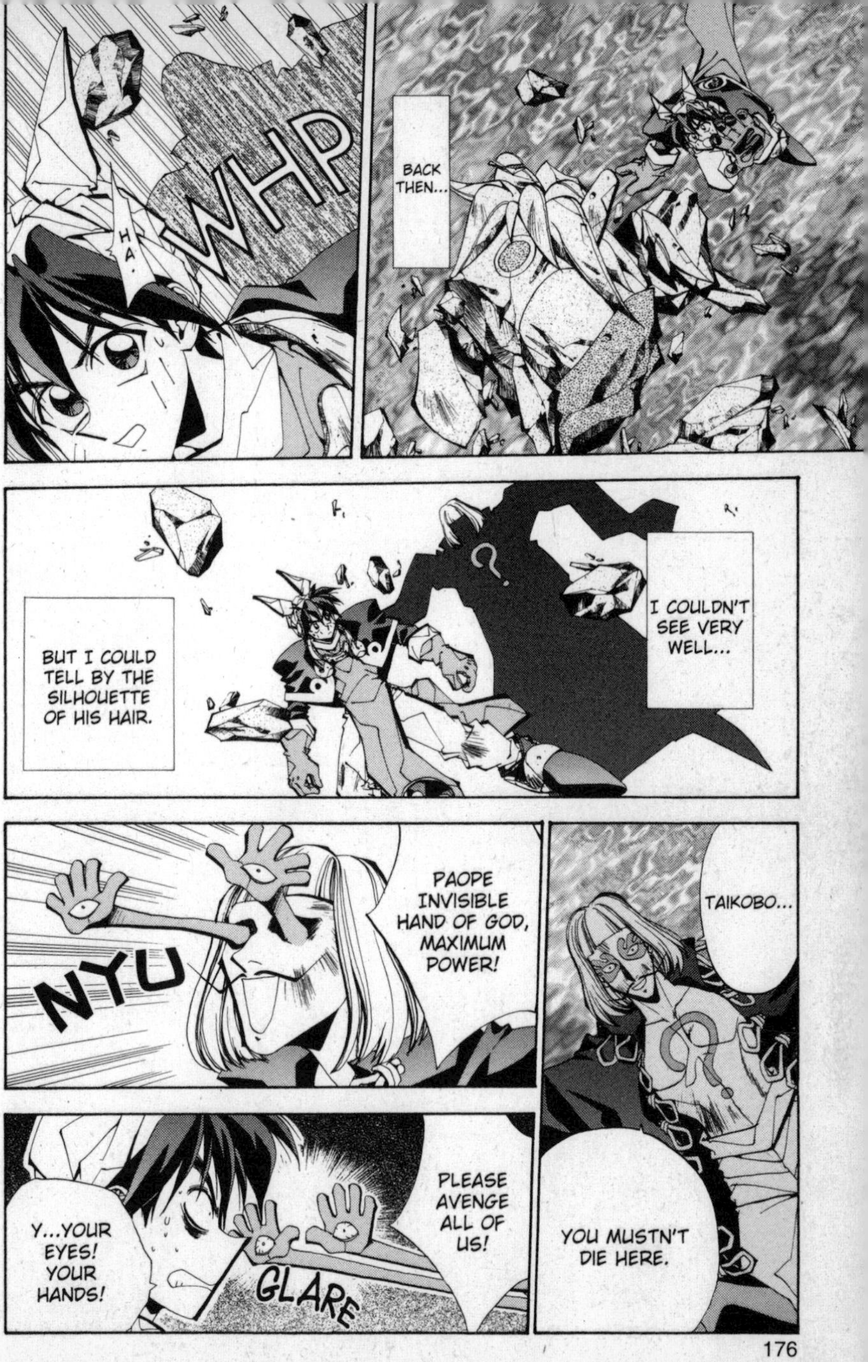
BACK THEN...
HA.
WHP
I COULDN'T SEE VERY WELL...
BUT I COULD TELL BY THE SILHOUETTE OF HIS HAIR.
TAIKOBO...
YOU MUSTN'T DIE HERE.
PAOPE INVISIBLE HAND OF GOD, MAXIMUM POWER!
NYU
PLEASE AVENGE ALL OF US!
Y...YOUR EYES! YOUR HANDS!
GLARE

READ THIS WAY

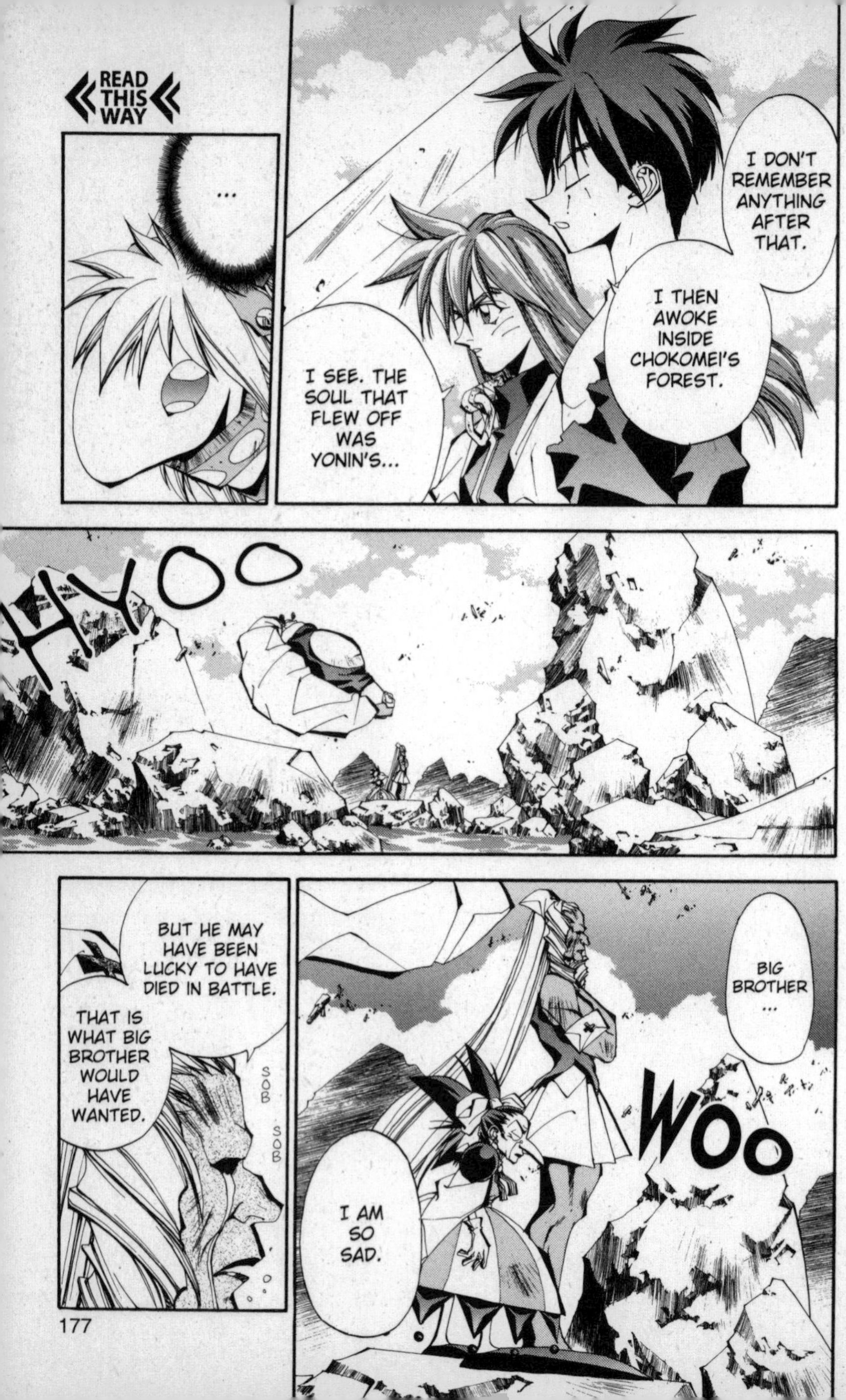

I DON'T REMEMBER ANYTHING AFTER THAT.
I THEN AWOKE INSIDE CHOKOMEI'S FOREST.
I SEE. THE SOUL THAT FLEW OFF WAS YONIN'S...
...
HYOO
BIG BROTHER ...
WOO
I AM SO SAD.
BUT HE MAY HAVE BEEN LUCKY TO HAVE DIED IN BATTLE.
THAT IS WHAT BIG BROTHER WOULD HAVE WANTED.
SOB SOB

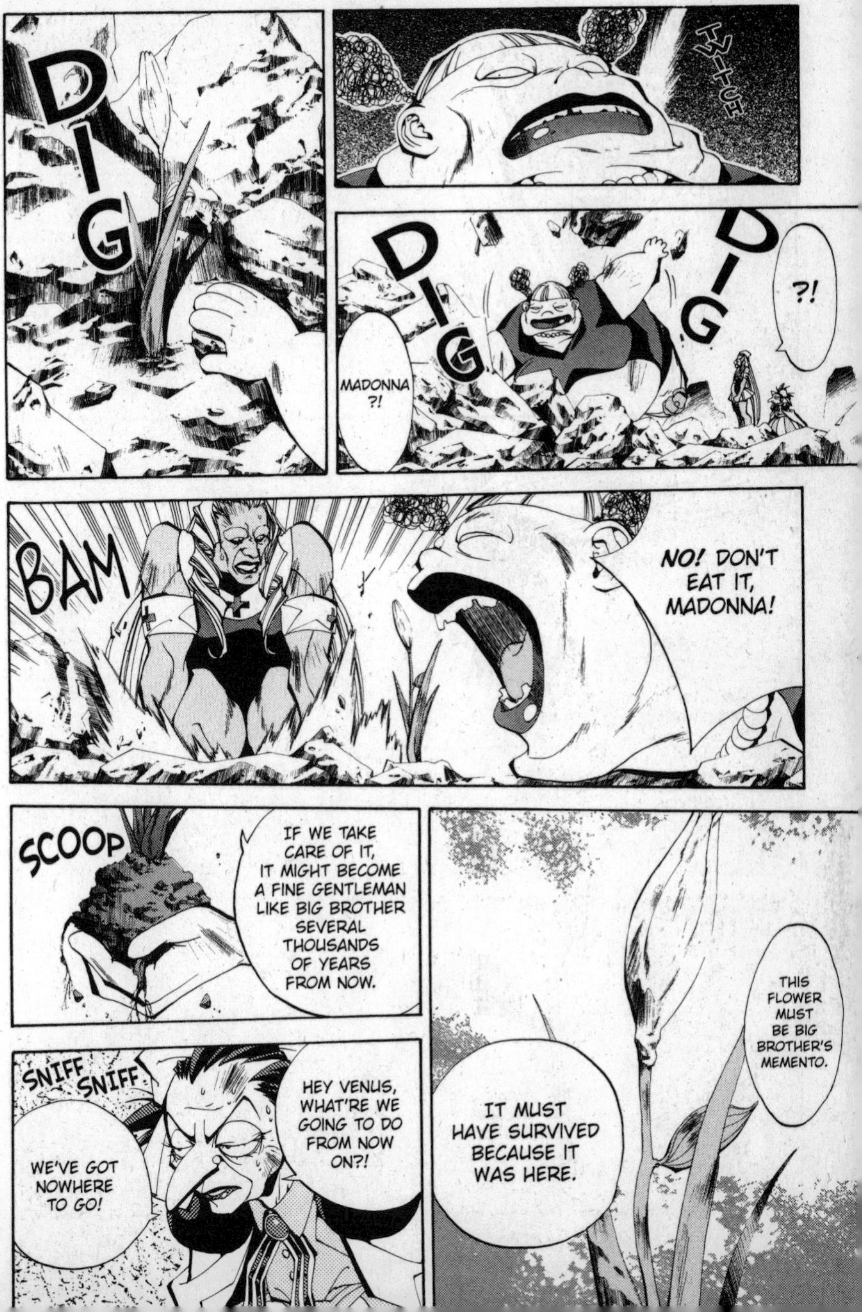
TWITCH
?!
DIG
DIG
MADONNA ?!
DIG
NO! DON'T EAT IT, MADONNA!
BAM
THIS FLOWER MUST BE BIG BROTHER'S MEMENTO.
IT MUST HAVE SURVIVED BECAUSE IT WAS HERE.
IF WE TAKE CARE OF IT, IT MIGHT BECOME A FINE GENTLEMAN LIKE BIG BROTHER SEVERAL THOUSANDS OF YEARS FROM NOW.
SCOOP
HEY VENUS, WHAT'RE WE GOING TO DO FROM NOW ON?!
WE'VE GOT NOWHERE TO GO!
SNIFF SNIFF

READ THIS WAY

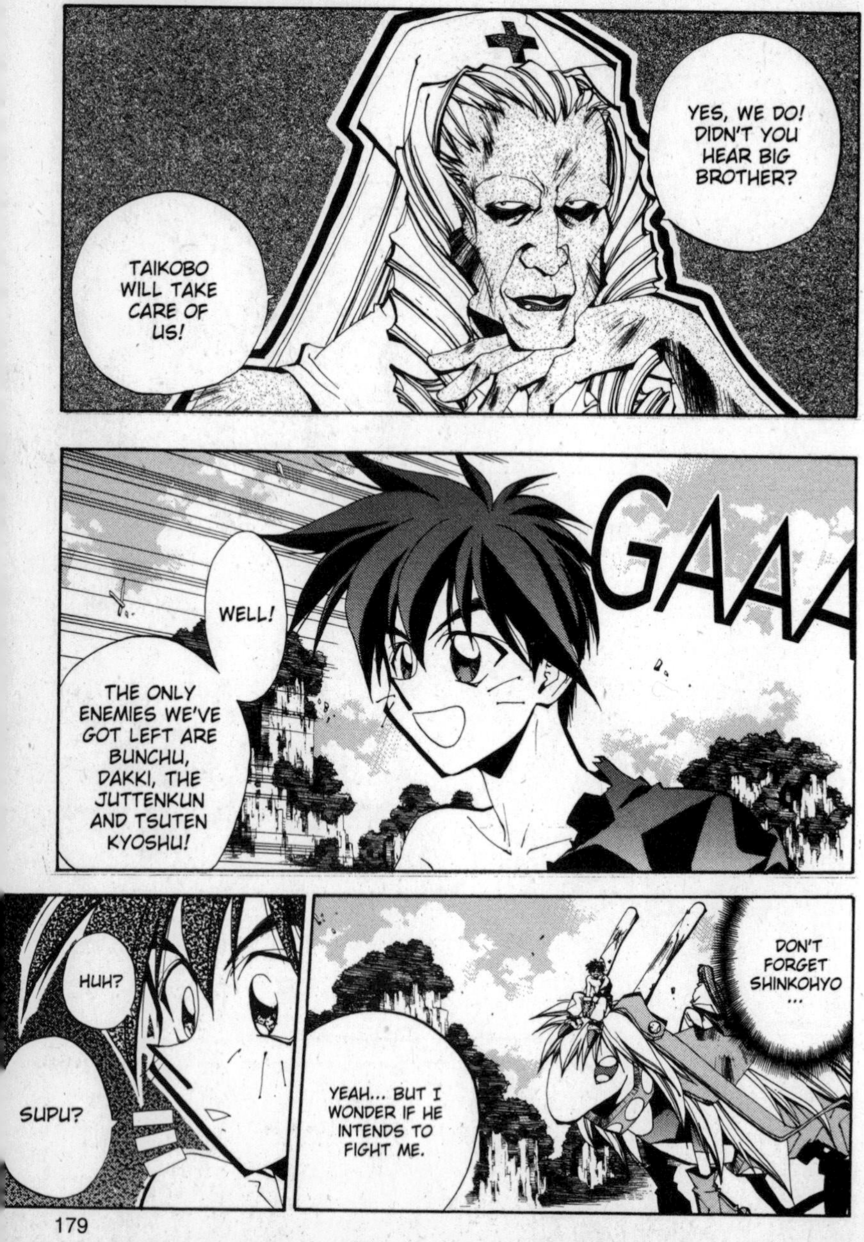

YES, WE DO! DIDN'T YOU HEAR BIG BROTHER?
TAIKOBO WILL TAKE CARE OF US!
GAAA
WELL!
THE ONLY ENEMIES WE'VE GOT LEFT ARE BUNCHU, DAKKI, THE JUTTENKUN AND TSUTEN KYOSHU!
DON'T FORGET SHINKOHYO...
YEAH... BUT I WONDER IF HE INTENDS TO FIGHT ME.
HUH?
SUPU?

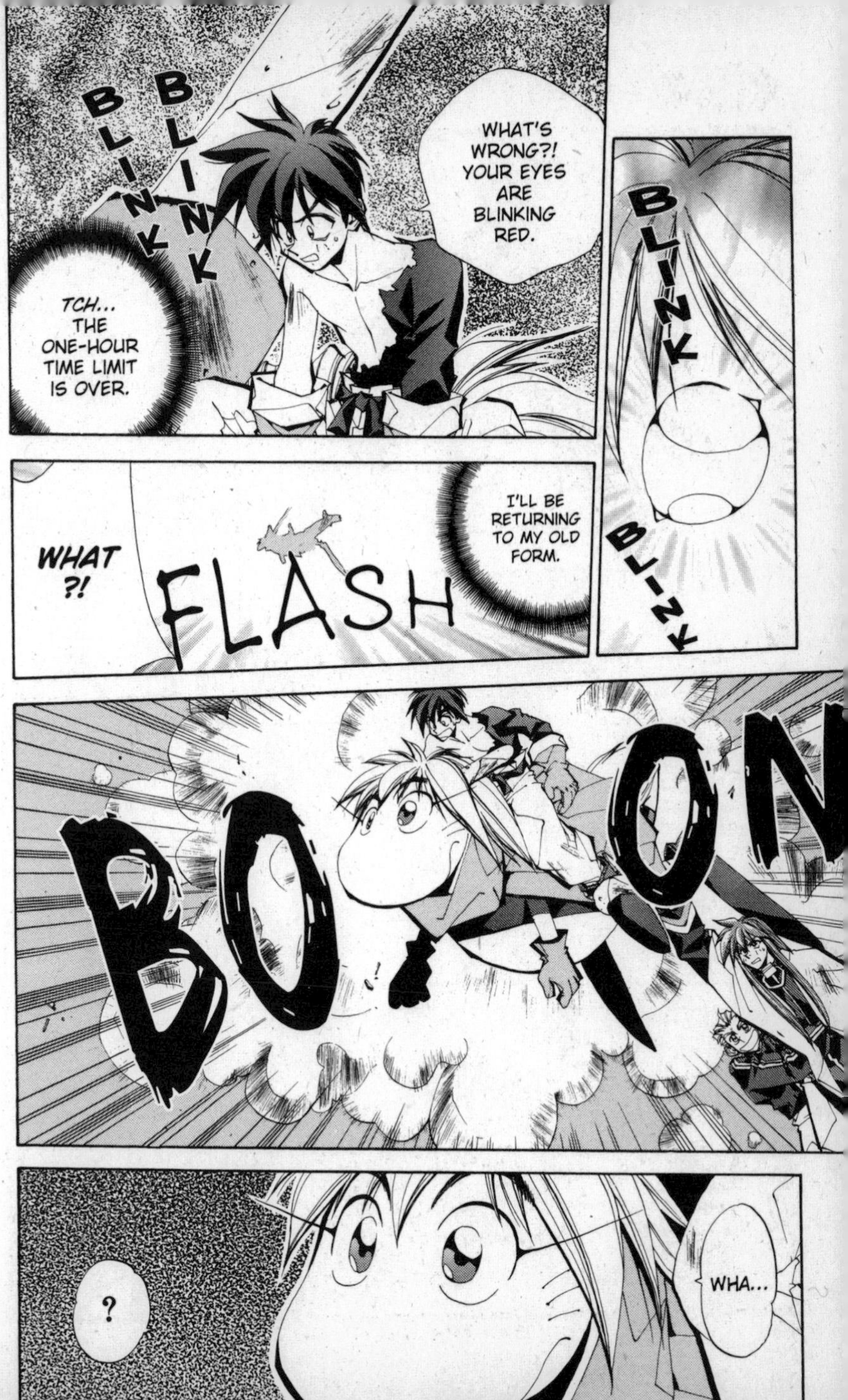
BLINK
BLINK
WHAT'S WRONG?! YOUR EYES ARE BLINKING RED.
BLINK BLINK
TCH... THE ONE-HOUR TIME LIMIT IS OVER.
I'LL BE RETURNING TO MY OLD FORM.
FLASH
WHAT ?!
BOON
WHA...
?

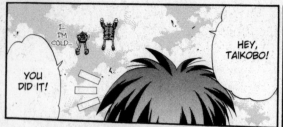

I... I'M COLD...

YOU DID IT!

HEY, TAIKOBO!

WHERE'S CHOKOMEI?

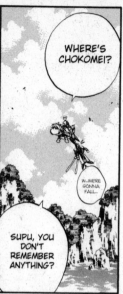

W...WE'RE GONNA FALL...

SUPU, YOU DON'T REMEMBER ANYTHING?

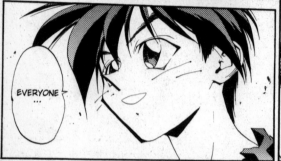

EVERYONE...

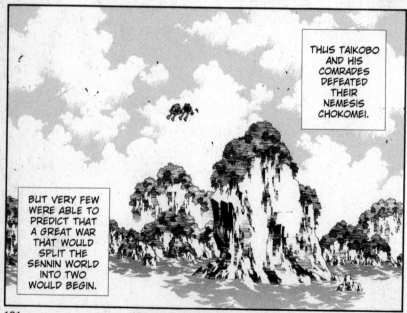

THUS TAIKOBO AND HIS COMRADES DEFEATED THEIR NEMESIS CHOKOMEI.

BUT VERY FEW WERE ABLE TO PREDICT THAT A GREAT WAR THAT WOULD SPLIT THE SENNIN WORLD INTO TWO WOULD BEGIN.

Based on the novel *Hoshin Engi*, translated by Tsutomu Ano, Published by Kodansha Bunko.

HOSHIN ENGI

RYU FUJISAKI

POPULARITY POLL!!!

No. 1 11,616 votes
SIGH
Taikobo
The hero was No. 1 by a wide margin just like the first time. The fans understand how strong he is!
No. 2 5,135 votes
Tenka Ko
His straightforward personality and his inborn fighting strength captured the fans' hearts!
Thank you so much!
No. 6 1,583 votes
Taiitsu Shinjin
He appeared even when he didn't have any business related to Nataku, such as making Taikobo's artificial arm. He's established his own standing!
No. 7 1,487 votes
Shinkohyo
He's observing things, as usual, but his presence may be No. 1.
No. 8 1,248 votes
Toh Sengyoku
Fans increasingly supported her because she transformed from a wacko into a woman who risks her life for love.
No. 9 1,199 votes
Tensho Ko
His monstrous strength as a Tennen Doshi at his age surpassed his father! He's playing an even more active part.
No. 10 1,172 votes
Hatsu Ki
He's usually undisciplined, but his speech when he declared war had the dignity of a king.

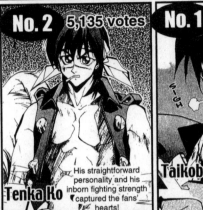

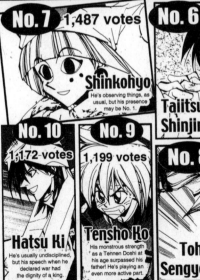

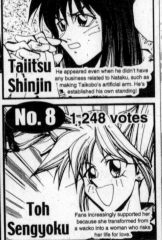

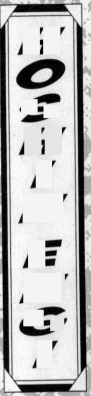

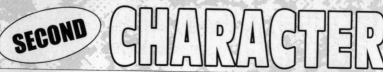

SECOND CHARACTER

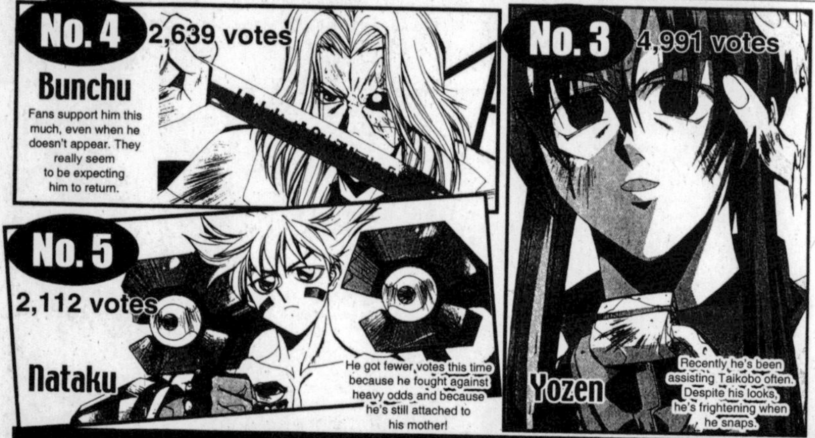
No. 3
4,991 votes
Yozen
Recently he's been assisting Taikobo often. Despite his looks, he's frightening when he snaps.
No. 4
2,639 votes
Bunchu
Fans support him this much, even when he doesn't appear. They really seem to be expecting him to return.
No. 5
2,112 votes
Nataku
He got fewer votes this time because he fought against heavy odds and because he's still attached to his mother!

A total of 42,646 votes!

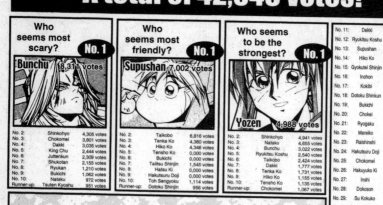

Who seems most scary? No. 1

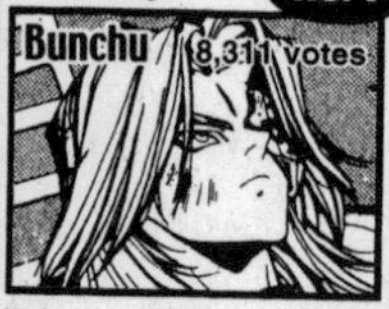
Bunchu
8,311 votes

No. 2:	Shinkohyo	4,305 votes
No. 3:	Chokomei	3,801 votes
No. 4:	Dakki	3,035 votes
No. 5:	King Chu	2,444 votes
No. 6:	Juttenkun	2,309 votes
No. 7:	Shukotan	2,155 votes
No. 8:	Ryukan	1,210 votes
No. 9:	Bukichi	1,062 votes
No. 10:	Nataku	972 votes
Runner-up:	Tsuten Kyoshu	951 votes

Who seems most friendly? No. 1

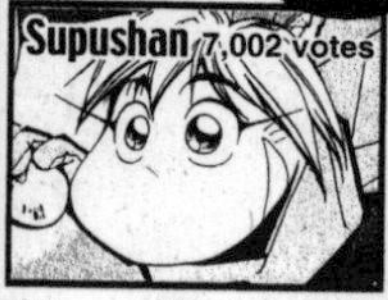
Supushan
7,002 votes

No. 2:	Taikobo	6,816 votes
No. 3:	Tenka Ko	4,360 votes
No. 4:	Hiko Ko	4,346 votes
No. 5:	Tensho Ko	0,000 votes
No. 6:	Bukichi	0,000 votes
No. 7:	Taiitsu Shinjin	1,545 votes
No. 8:	Hatsu Ki	0,000 votes
No. 9:	Hakutsuru Doji	0,000 votes
No. 10:	Toh Sengyoku	1,114 votes
Runner-up:	Dotoku Shinjin	956 votes

Who seems to be the strongest? No. 1

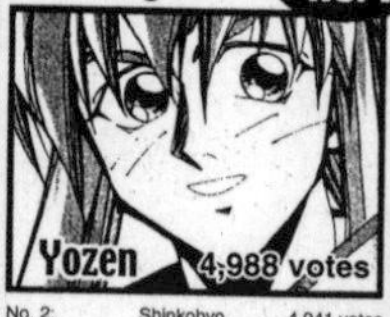
Yozen
4,988 votes

No. 2:	Shinkohyo	4,941 votes
No. 3:	Nataku	4,655 votes
No. 4:	Bunchu	3,022 votes
No. 5:	Ryukitsu Koshu	2,540 votes
No. 6:	Taikobo	2,424 votes
No. 7:	Dakki	1,777 votes
No. 8:	Tenka Ko	1,731 votes
No. 9:	Hiko Ko	1,155 votes
No. 10:	Tensho Ko	1,135 votes
Runner-up:	Chokomei	1,067 votes

No. 11:	Dakki	1,004 votes
No. 12:	Ryukitsu Koshu	956 votes
No. 13:	Supushan	768 votes
No. 14:	Hiko Ko	670 votes
No. 15:	Gyokutei Shinjin	670 votes
No. 16:	Inchon	625 votes
No. 17:	Kokibi	479 votes
No. 18:	Dotoku Shinkun	381 votes
No. 19:	Bukichi	333 votes
No. 20:	Chokei	237 votes
No. 21:	Ryogaku	202 votes
No. 22:	Mareiko	195 votes
No. 23:	Raishinshi	152 votes
No. 24:	Hakutsuru Doji	143 votes
No. 25:	Chokomei	127 votes
No. 26:	Hakuyuko Ki	102 votes
No. 27:	Inshi	94 votes
No. 28:	Dokoson	76 votes
No. 29:	Su Kokuko	61 votes
No. 30:	Genshi Tenson	52 votes

This article was published in Issue 36 of *Weekly Shonen Jump* in 1998.

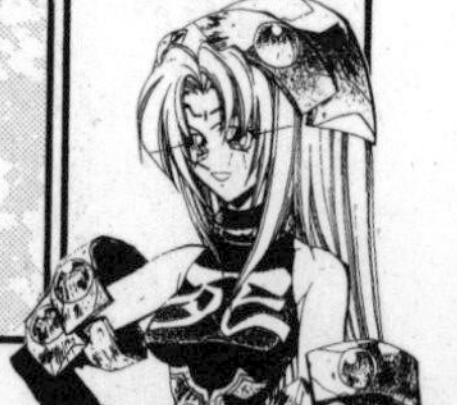

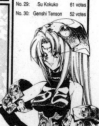

THE REAL CAUSES OF THE CONFLICT!

Hoshin Engi Secret

TER

The Yin-Zhou war is becoming more intense day by day! We thoroughly analyze why the main characters are fighting!

Taikobo is usually not too dependable, but he carries in his heart his thoughts for his lost clan.

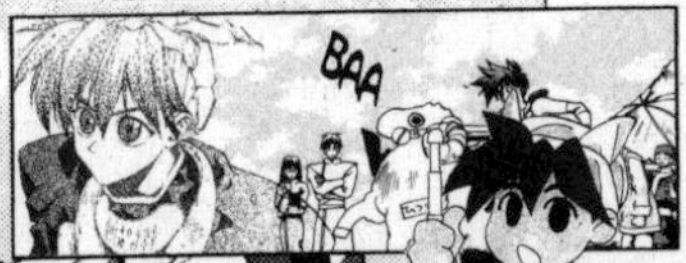

BAA

Taikobo

His ideal is a Human World without Sendo!

Taikobo was scouted by Genshi Tenson and then became a Doshi, but he's originally a member of the Qiang tribe. The village that he lived in was destroyed by Dakki's manhunt. Taikobo is trying to seal Yokai Sennin like Dakki into Shinkai and restore a peaceful Human World so that foolish Sendo don't make humans suffer like he did. When he fights Sendo, he fights as a Sendo himself. When he fights humans, he fights as a human!

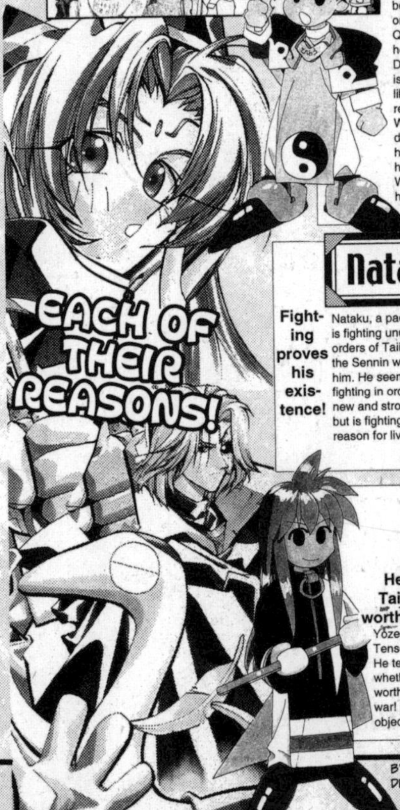

EACH OF THEIR REASONS!

The Reasons for War

The Zhou Army

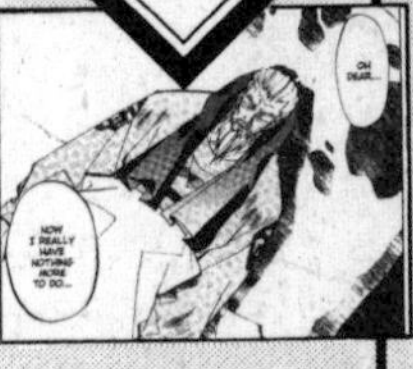

OH DEAR...
NOW I REALLY HAVE NOTHING MORE TO DO...

Sho Ki was supposed to become King of Zhou, but he passed away right before the war began. He conveyed his last wishes to his son Hatsu Ki and Taikobo.
Zhou used to be an aggregate of the western countries that was part of the 800 countries making up the Kingdom of Yin.
To save the people from Dakki's misrule, Taikobo made Hatsu Ki the King of Zhou, declared Zhou a state, and the war began!
The Yin Army has an overwhelming numerical advantage over the Zhou army, but the Zhou army is advancing towards Choka, the royal capital of Yin, with solidarity!

Nataku

Fighting proves his existence!

Nataku, a paope human, is fighting under the orders of Taiitsu Shinjin, the Sennin who created him. He seems to be fighting in order to receive new and strong paope, but is fighting his only reason for living?

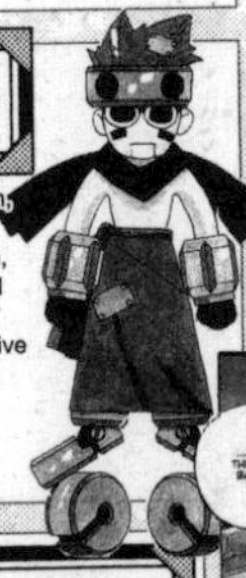

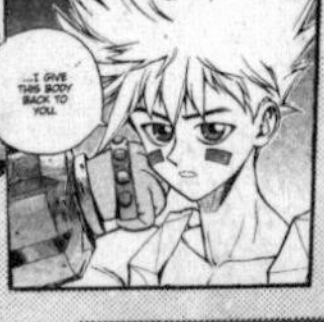

...I GIVE THIS BODY BACK TO YOU.

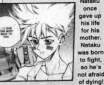

Nataku once gave up his life for his mother. Nataku was born to fight, so he's not afraid of dying!

Yozen

He recognizes that Taikobo is someone worthy of being a leader!

Yozen was ordered by Genshi Tenson to assist Taikobo. He tested Taikobo to see whether Taikobo was someone worth working for, then joined the war! He supported Taikobo's objectives from the beginning!

PEDIA

BY KISOSHA
DESIGN BY RYU FUJISAKI

CHARAC

THE TENSION MOUNTS IN
THE GREAT YIN-ZHOU WAR!

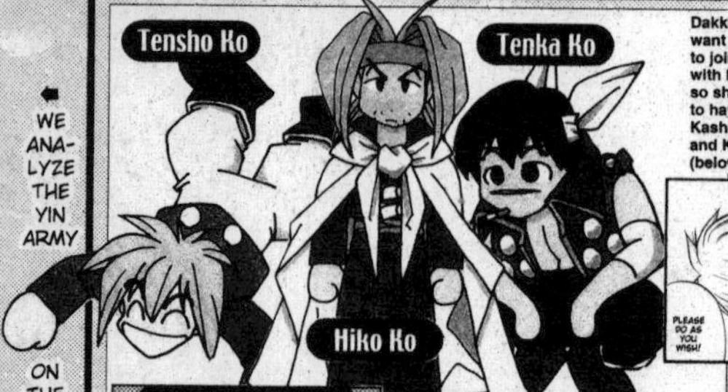

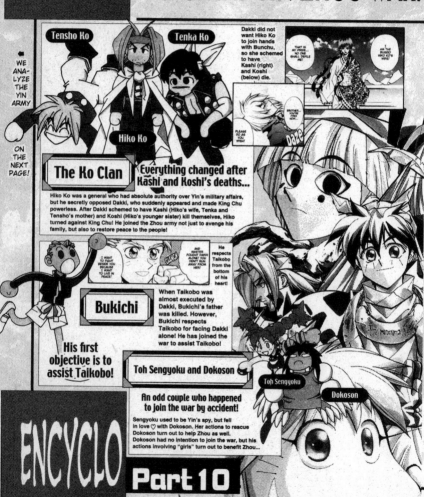

Tensho Ko
Tenka Ko
Hiko Ko

⬅ WE ANALYZE THE YIN ARMY ON THE NEXT PAGE!

Dakki did not want Hiko Ko to join hands with Bunchu, so she schemed to have Kashi (right) and Koshi (below) die.

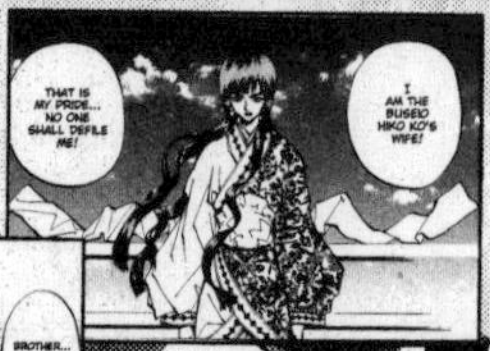

I AM THE BUSEIO HIKO KO'S WIFE!
THAT IS MY PRIDE... NO ONE SHALL DEFILE ME!

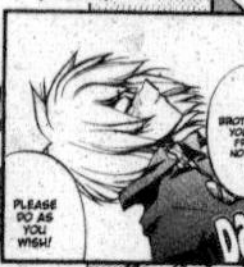

BROTHER... YOU'RE FREE NOW...
PLEASE DO AS YOU WISH!
DAZE

The Ko Clan

Everything changed after Kashi and Koshi's deaths...

Hiko Ko was a general who had absolute authority over Yin's military affairs, but he secretly opposed Dakki, who suddenly appeared and made King Chu powerless. After Dakki schemed to have Kashi (Hiko's wife, Tenka and Tensho's mother) and Koshi (Hiko's younger sister) kill themselves, Hiko turned against King Chu! He joined the Zhou army not just to avenge his family, but also to restore peace to the people!

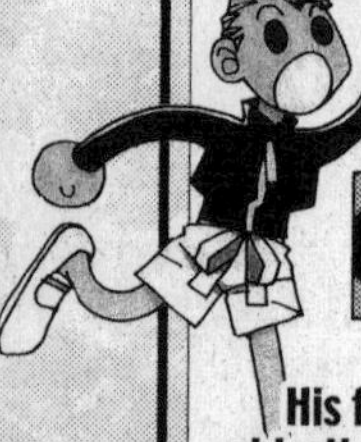

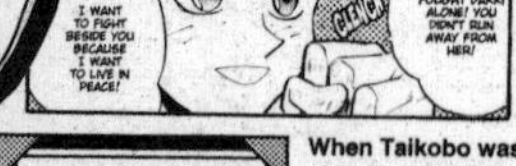

AND MASTER FOUGHT DAKKI ALONE! YOU DIDN'T RUN AWAY FROM HER!
CLENCH
I WANT TO FIGHT BESIDE YOU BECAUSE I WANT TO LIVE IN PEACE!

He respects Taikobo from the bottom of his heart!

Bukichi

When Taikobo was almost executed by Dakki, Bukichi's father was killed. However, Bukichi respects Taikobo for facing Dakki alone! He has joined the war to assist Taikobo!

His first objective is to assist Taikobo!

Toh Sengyoku and Dokoson

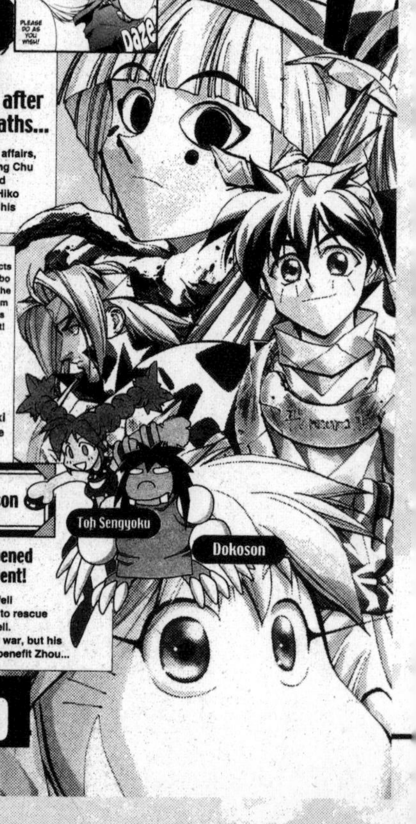

Toh Sengyoku
Dokoson

An odd couple who happened to join the war by accident!

Sengyoku used to be Yin's spy, but fell in love ♡ with Dokoson. Her actions to rescue Dokoson turn out to help Zhou as well. Dokoson had no intention to join the war, but his actions involving "girls" turn out to benefit Zhou...

ENCYCLO

Part 10

The Reasons for War

THE YIN ARMY

Dakki

Is she scheming to take advantage of the chaos?!

She caused the Yin-Zhou war. It looks as if her objective is not to win the war, but to make things even more chaotic by prolonging the war on purpose and dragging the Sennin World into it. What does she really have in mind?!

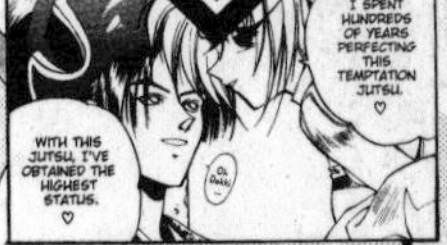
I SPENT HUNDREDS OF YEARS PERFECTING THIS TEMPTATION JUTSU. ♡
Oh, Dakki...
WITH THIS JUTSU, I'VE OBTAINED THE HIGHEST STATUS. ♡

Dakki is a peerless beauty. She took advantage of King Chu's sole weakness of "liking women," and took over control of Yin's politics.

Yin is China's oldest dynasty, and the then emperor, King Chu, was a master in the arts of pen and sword. But when the evil Sennyo Dakki became empress, she manipulated King Chu with her Temptation Jutsu. Evil Sendo ruled the royal palace, the people suffered in dire poverty, and the country fell into chaos. Taikobo and King Bu rose up against Yin and the war began!!

Shinkohyo

A cool observer of the great war!

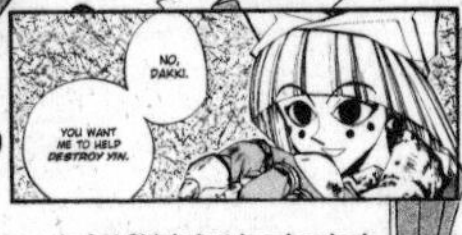
NO, DAKKI.
YOU WANT ME TO HELP DESTROY YIN.

It's even harder to figure out what Shinkohyo is scheming! He's a guest at Yin's royal palace, yet helps out Taikobo. Full of mysteries, he seems to be calmly observing the Yin-Zhou war and the Kongrong vs. Kingo war...but it looks as if he's investigating Dakki's true objectives!

Chokomei

There's no need for "reasons to fight"!

Chokomei's principle is to be "elegant." For him, fighting for something makes no sense! His objective is to fight elegantly!

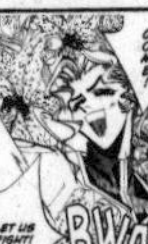
COME!
LET US FIGHT!
BWAA

For him, "elegance" is everything.

Bunchu and Chokei

Everything for restoring "Yin"!

Bunchu has been serving Yin for many years. For him, Yin is like his child. Bunchu intends to defeat Zhou, then fight Dakki and restore Yin. Chokei is Bunchu's right-hand man, and he's prepared to follow Bunchu until the very end!

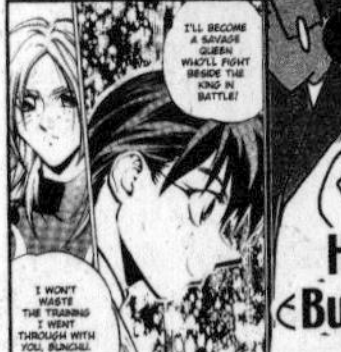
I'LL BECOME A SAVAGE QUEEN WHO'LL FIGHT BESIDE THE KING IN BATTLE!
I WON'T WASTE THE TRAINING I WENT THROUGH WITH YOU, BUNCHU.

Bunchu's former rival, Shushi. She became queen and then died, but her blood has been carried down to the Kings of Yin.

Chokei

Bunchu

He'll follow Bunchu all the way!

Chokomei's Elegant forecast of the war situation!

Hello, everyone. I will predict how the war will proceed! Please listen with your beautiful white ears that are like narcissus. Taikobo is the enemy, but he's wise. He understands that he cannot win against me by himself. He probably has called for reinforcements nearby. I expect he'll receive a new paope from his master...Genshi Tenson. But I won't lose against any enemies! I promise a victory with body, like first-class wine...

Inchon and Inchi

The tragedy of the brothers who couldn't protect their mother!

Inchon was once saved by Taikobo. He tried to settle his regret for having been too young to protect his mother by protecting Yin instead, and died in battle...

Inchon

Inchi

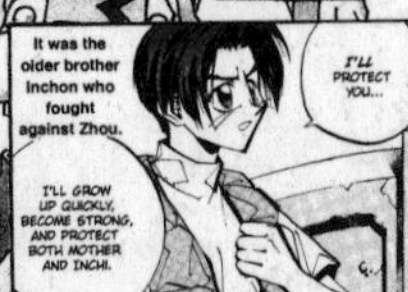
I'LL PROTECT YOU...
It was the older brother Inchon who fought against Zhou.
I'LL GROW UP QUICKLY, BECOME STRONG, AND PROTECT BOTH MOTHER AND INCHI.

This article was published in Issue 35 of *Weekly Shonen Jump* in 1998.

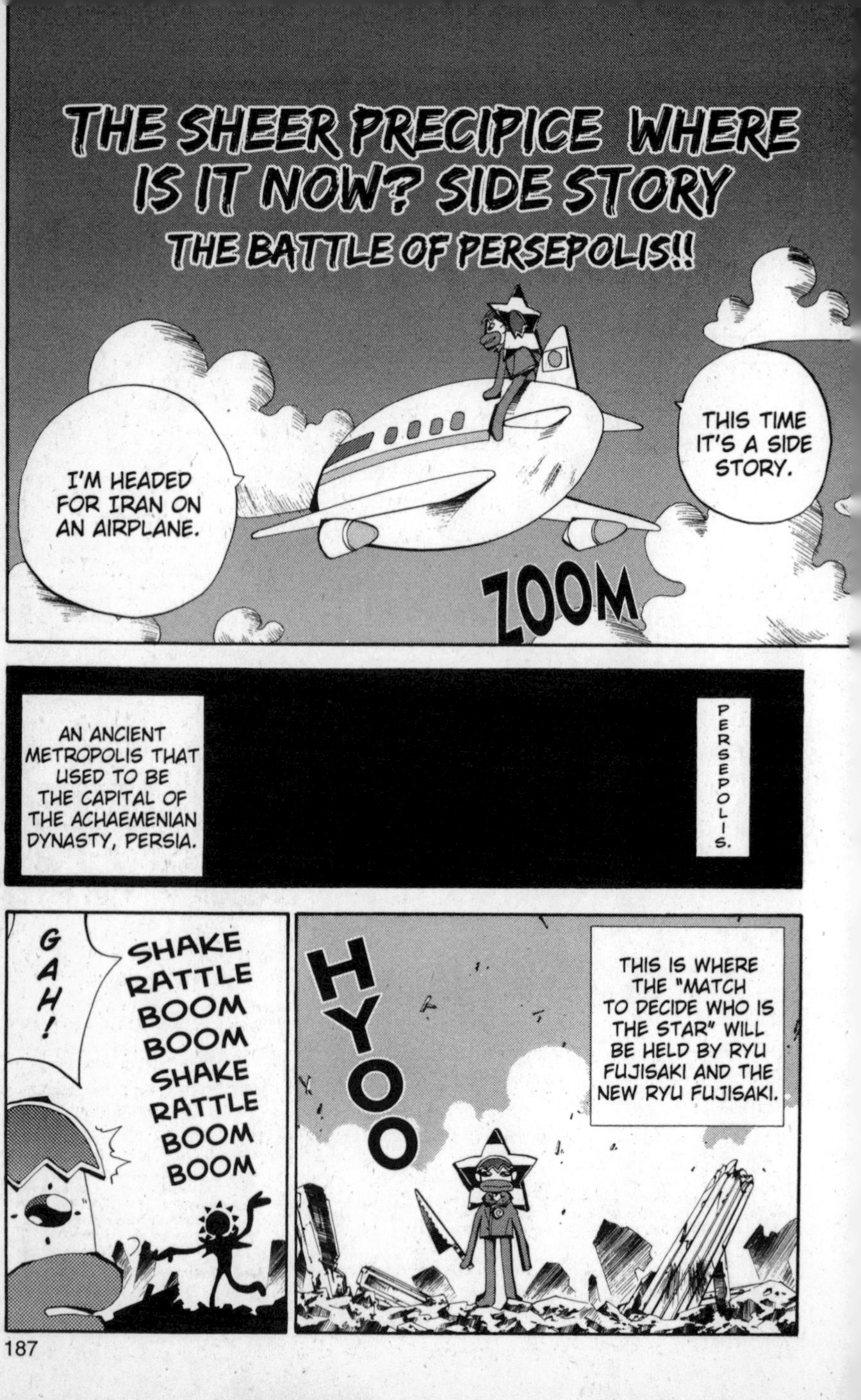
THE SHEER PRECIPICE WHERE IS IT NOW? SIDE STORY
THE BATTLE OF PERSEPOLIS!!
THIS TIME IT'S A SIDE STORY.
I'M HEADED FOR IRAN ON AN AIRPLANE.
ZOOM
PERSEPOLIS.
AN ANCIENT METROPOLIS THAT USED TO BE THE CAPITAL OF THE ACHAEMENIAN DYNASTY, PERSIA.
THIS IS WHERE THE "MATCH TO DECIDE WHO IS THE STAR" WILL BE HELD BY RYU FUJISAKI AND THE NEW RYU FUJISAKI.
HYOO
GAH!
SHAKE RATTLE BOOM BOOM SHAKE RATTLE BOOM BOOM

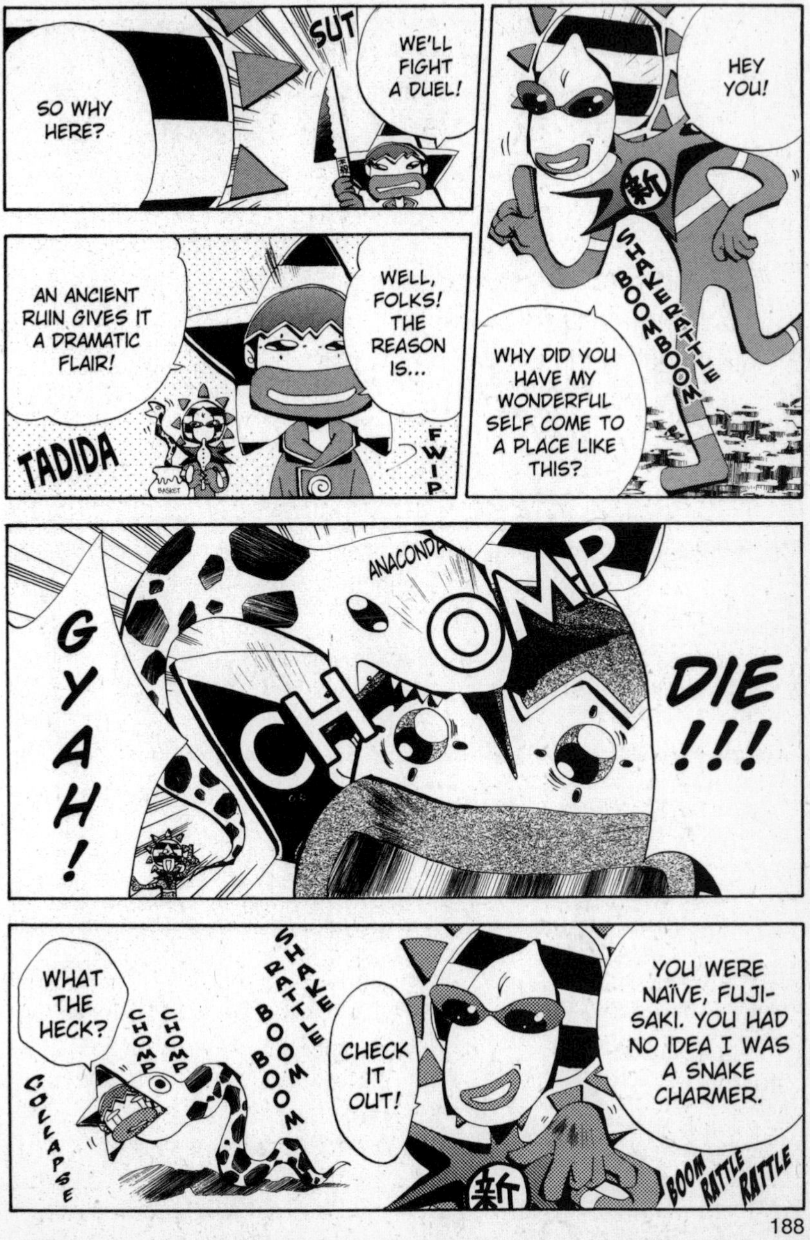
HEY YOU!
SHAKE RATTLE BOOMBOOM
WHY DID YOU HAVE MY WONDERFUL SELF COME TO A PLACE LIKE THIS?
SUT
WE'LL FIGHT A DUEL!
SO WHY HERE?
WELL, FOLKS! THE REASON IS...
FWIP
AN ANCIENT RUIN GIVES IT A DRAMATIC FLAIR!
TADIDA
BASKET
ANACONDA
CHOMP
DIE!!!
GYAH!
YOU WERE NAÏVE, FUJI-SAKI. YOU HAD NO IDEA I WAS A SNAKE CHARMER.
BOOM RATTLE RATTLE
CHECK IT OUT!
SHAKE RATTLE BOOM BOOM
CHOMP CHOMP
WHAT THE HECK?
COLLAPSE

YOU DON'T HAVE TO READ IT, BUT SINCE THERE'S AN EXTRA PAGE:

HACK WRITING X

△ THIS "HACK WRITING" HAS FINALLY REACHED THE TENTH INSTALLMENT.

△ THIS IS ALL THANKS TO EVERYONE.

△ THANK YOU SO MUCH.

△ NOW THAT I THINK ABOUT IT, THIS STRANGE PROSE FEATURE BEGAN WHEN I HAD TO FILL A PAGE IN VOLUME 1 BECUASE OF THE COLOR PAGES. HAVING A BLANK PAGE WOULD HAVE BEEN STRANGE. PUTTING AN ILLUSTRATION WOULD ALSO HAVE BEEN STRANGE, CONSIDERING THE FLOW OF THINGS. FUJISAKI IS AN ASPIRING NOVELIST, SO I THOUGHT I'D WRITE SOMETHING LIKE AN ESSAY WHILE PRACTICING HOW TO WRITE.

△ THAT'S THE SECRET STORY OF HOW THE "SIDE NOTES" WERE BORN. THIS WAS THE BASIS FOR THE HACK WRITING.

△ THE HACK WRITING STARTED IN VOLUME 2. DON'T YOU THINK THAT IT IS BECOMING EVEN MORE AND MORE STUPID?

△ SHOULD I HAVE REFRAINED FROM WRITING ABOUT TYPHOONS AND THE SMELLS OF THE ZOO, NOT TO MENTION WRITING ABOUT ***CHAMBER POTS?*** BUT A LOT OF ME IS DEFIANT, SAYING "IT'S ALL RIGHT."

△ DON'T MAKE FUN OF STUPID STORIES. THIS IS DIFFICULT IN MANY WAYS. I'M HAVING TROUBLE WITH "THE SHEER PRECIPICE, WHERE IS IT NOW" AS WELL. SOMETIMES ALL I THINK ABOUT IS "THE SHEER PRECIPICE" BECAUSE I HAVE NOTHING TO WRITE ABOUT. BUT WHEN ALL THESE HARDSHIPS PILE UP AND TAKE FORM, I AM PRETTY HAPPY.

△ I BELIEVE THE HACK WRITING WILL CONTINUE UNTIL THE END OF THIS SERIES. I PLAN TO CONTINUE WRITING "STUPID STORIES THAT YOU CAN READ OR NOT READ."

△ FUJISAKI RENEWS HIS RESOLUTION HERE.

END OF HACK WRITING

YOU DON'T HAVE TO READ IT, BUT SINCE THERE'S AN EXTRA PAGE:

HACK WRITING XI

△ I WILL DIE ONE DAY. AFTER I'M DEAD, A FUNERAL WILL PROBABLY BE HELD REGARDLESS OF MY WILL.

△ IF A FEW PEOPLE CRY AT MY FUNERAL, MY LIFE MIGHT HAVE BEEN A SUCCESS.

△ BUT WHAT SORT OF FUNERAL WILL BE HELD?

△ LET'S THINK ABOUT IT A LITTLE.

△ I DON'T WANT A NORMAL FUNERAL. IT'S DEPRESSING. BUT I DON'T WANT PEOPLE TO DANCE LIKE THEY WOULD AT A SAMBA CARNIVAL EITHER.

△ MY IDEAL IS A "SPACE FUNERAL."

△ I'LL BE PUT ON THE TIP OF A ROCKET, PASS THROUGH THE ATMOSPHERE, AND BE SHOT INTO SPACE WHILE WEARING SOMETHING COOL, SILVER AND FUTURISTIC.

△ I'LL BE POSING STRANGELY AND WANDER AROUND THE ASTRAL BELT FOR ETERNITY. IN THE FUTURE, I MIGHT BECOME A TOURIST ATTRACTION FOR SPACE TOURISTS. SINCE I'LL BE IN SPACE, I'LL BE PRESERVED JUST FINE.

△ WHEN I TALKED ABOUT THIS WITH MY ASSISTANTS, SOMEONE SAID, "MAYBE YOU'LL BE PICKED UP BY AN ALIEN WITH AN ADVANCED CIVILIZATION, AND YOU'LL BE RESTORED TO LIFE." BEING ABLE TO MEET ALIENS IS WONDERFUL, BUT I DON'T WANT TO BE RESTORED TO LIFE.

△ NOWADAYS, THERE'S SUPPOSED TO BE A SO-CALLED "HI-TECH FUNERAL."

△ I SAW IT ON TV, AND THE COFFIN WENT INTO A TUNNEL OF LASERS. THAT WOULD BE NICE TOO.

END OF HACK WRITING

Hoshin Engi: The Rank File!

You'll find as you read *Hoshin Engi* that there are titles and ranks that you are probably unfamiliar with. While it may seem confusing, there is an order to the madness that is pulled from ancient Chinese mythology, Japanese culture, other manga, and, of course, the incredible mind of *Hoshin Engi* creator Ryu Fujisaki.

Where we think it will help, we give you a hint in the margin on the page the name appears. But in addition, here's a quick primer on the titles you'll find in *Hoshin Engi* and what they mean:

Japanese	Title	Job Description
武成王	Buseio	Chief commanding officer
宰相	Saisho	Premier
太師	Taishi	The king's advisor/tutor
大金剛	Dai Kongo	Great vassals
軍師	Gunshi	Military tactician
大諸侯	Daishoko	Great feudal lord
東伯侯	Tohakuko	Lord of the east region
西伯侯	Seihakuko	Lord of the west region
北伯侯	Hokuhakuko	Lord of the north region
南伯侯	Nanhakuko	Lord of the south region

Hoshin Engi: The Immortal File

Also, you'll probably find the hierarchy of the Sennin, Sendo and Doshi somewhat complicated. Here, we spell it out the easiest way possible!

Japanese	Title	Description
道士	Doshi	Someone training to become Sennin
仙道	Sendo	Used to describe both Sennin and Doshi
仙人	Sennin	Those who have mastered the way. Once you "go Sennin" you are forever changed.
妖孽	Yogetsu	A Yosei who can transform into a human
妖怪仙人	Yokai Sennin	A Sennin whose original form is not human
妖精	Yosei	An animal or object exposed to moonlight and sunlight for more than 1,000 years

Hoshin Engi: The Magical File

Paope (宝貝) are powerful magical items used by Sennin and Doshi. Sometimes they look like regular objects, like a veil or hat. These are just a few of the magical items, both paope and otherwise, that you'll encounter in *Hoshin Engi!*

Japanese	Magic	Description
打神鞭	Dashinben	Known as the God-Striking Whip, Taikobo's paope manipulates the air and wind.
霊獣	Reiju	A magical flying beast that Sennin and Doshi use for transportation and support. Taikobo's reiju is his pal Supu.
五光石	Gokoseki	A rock that changes the face of whomever it strikes into a "weirdly erotic-looking" face.
莫邪宝剣	Bakuya no Hoken	Tenka's weapon, a light saber.
金蛟剪	Kinkosen	Two blades that transform into white and black dragons that chase the enemy forever until they devour it.
万里雲煙	Banri Kiun'en	A paope that shoots multiple flaming arrows.
火鴉壺	Kako	Lava that becomes a flaming bird and attacks the enemy.
霧露坤網	Muro Kenkonmo	A weapon that spreads water like a spider's web for defense. Can also shoot water like arrows.
紅珠液	Kojueki	A strong acidic liquid paope.
蜈蜂袋	Gohotai	A bag that manipulates bees using pheromones.
万刀車	Banjinsha	Flying cross-shaped blades that shoot at the enemy at high speed.
化血神刀	Kaketsu Blades	Blades steeped in poison protruding from a ball that moves irregularly when it attacks enemies.
飛来椅	Hirai-i	A vehicle paope like the Kokin Rikishi, but capable of warp travel.

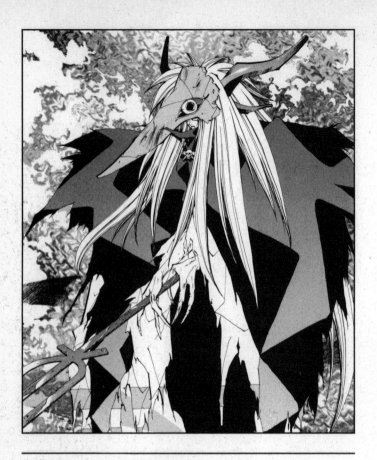

Coming Next Volume:
The Sennin World War

Taikobo and his allies confront an entirely new kind of threat:
a paope that acts as a virus. The strain is so virulent that it
has spread over both Kingo Island and Mount Kongrong,
infecting friend and foe alike!

AVAILABLE JUNE 2009!

Read Any Good Books Lately?

Hoshin Engi is based on *Fengshen Yanji* (*The Creation of the Gods*, written in the 1500s by Xu Zhonglin) one of China's four classical fantastical novels of adventure, magic and mystery. The other three are *Saiyuki* (*Journey to the West* by Cheng'en Wu, late 1500s), *Sangokushi Engi* (*Romance of the Three Kingdoms* by Guanzhong Luo), and *Shui Hu Zhuan* (*Outlaws of the Marsh*, by Shi Nai'an, mid-1500s).

Want to read these books? You can! They're all still in print, more than 500 years later!

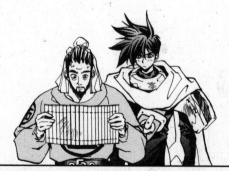

These books are North American in-print editions only.

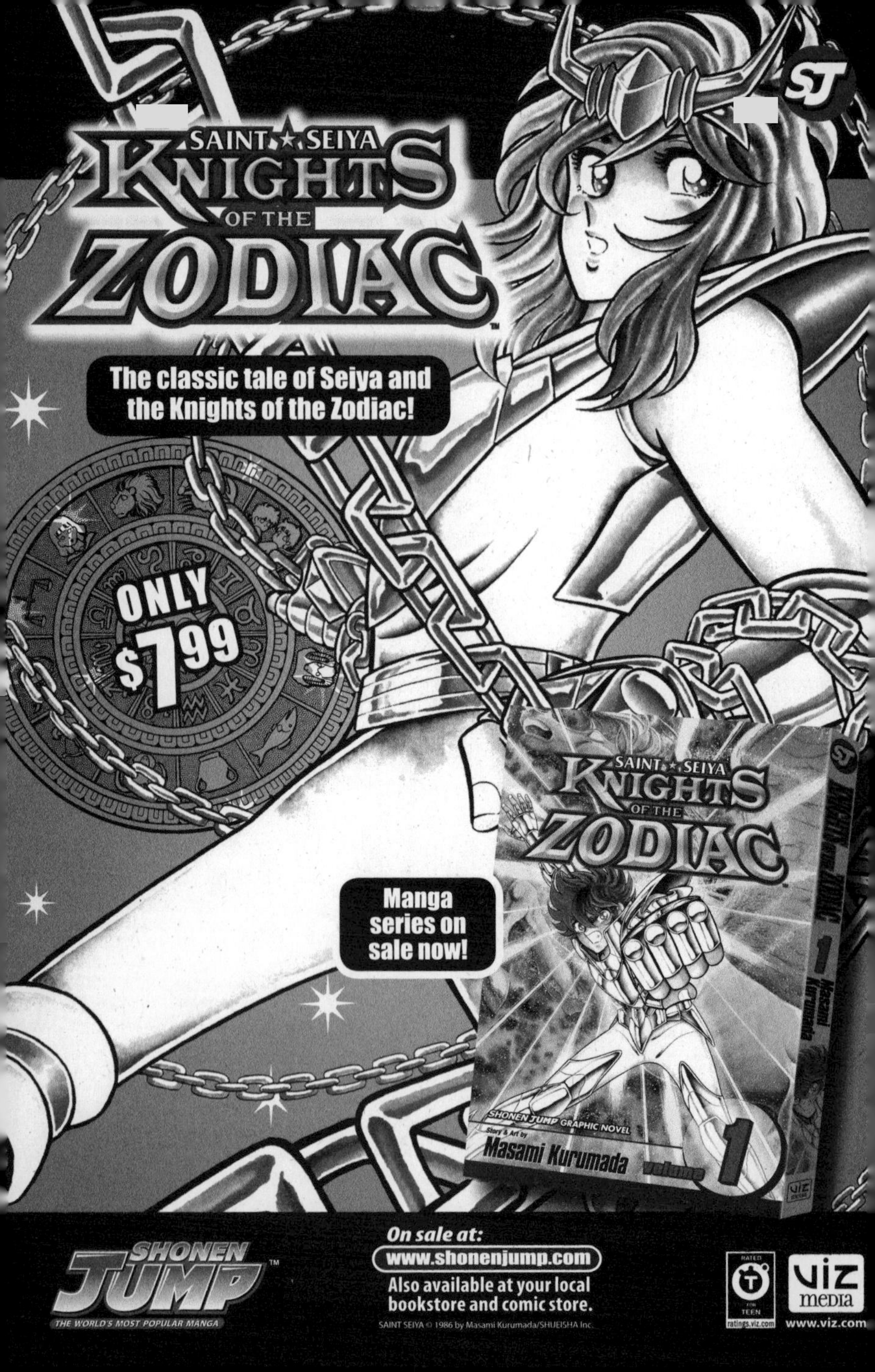
SJ
SAINT SEIYA
KNIGHTS OF THE ZODIAC™
The classic tale of Seiya and the Knights of the Zodiac!
ONLY $7.99
Manga series on sale now!
SAINT SEIYA
KNIGHTS OF THE ZODIAC
SHONEN JUMP GRAPHIC NOVEL
Story & Art by
Masami Kurumada
volume 1
SHONEN JUMP™
THE WORLD'S MOST POPULAR MANGA
On sale at:
www.shonenjump.com
Also available at your local bookstore and comic store.
SAINT SEIYA © 1986 by Masami Kurumada/SHUEISHA Inc.
RATED T FOR TEEN
ratings.viz.com
viz media
www.viz.com

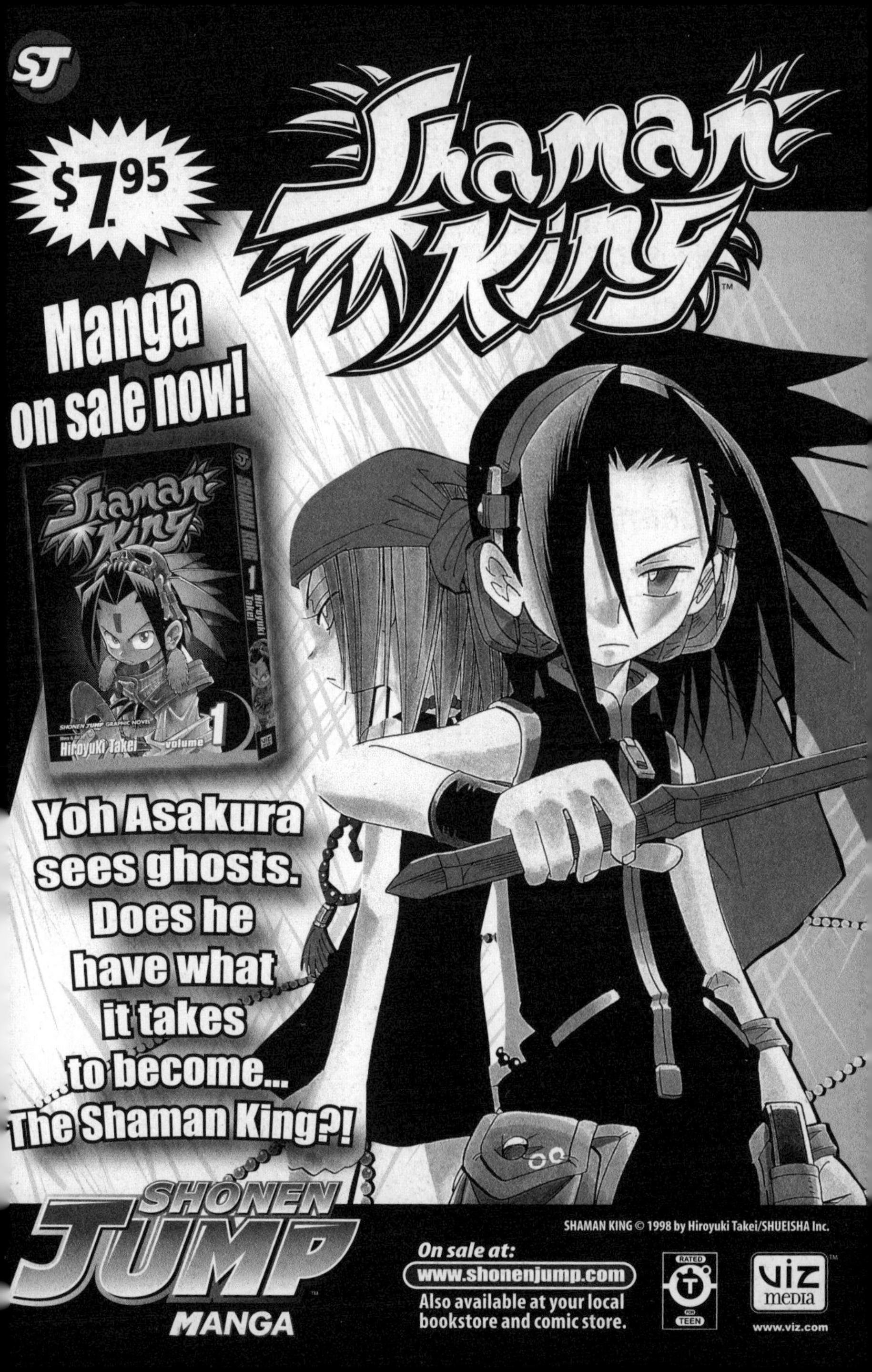
SJ
$7.95
Shaman King™
Manga on sale now!
SHAMAN KING
Shaman King
SHONEN JUMP GRAPHIC NOVEL
Hiroyuki Takei
volume 1
Yoh Asakura sees ghosts. Does he have what it takes to become... The Shaman King?!
SHONEN JUMP MANGA
SHAMAN KING © 1998 by Hiroyuki Takei/SHUEISHA Inc.
On sale at:
www.shonenjump.com
Also available at your local bookstore and comic store.
RATED T FOR TEEN
VIZ MEDIA
www.viz.com

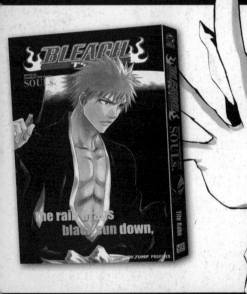
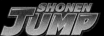

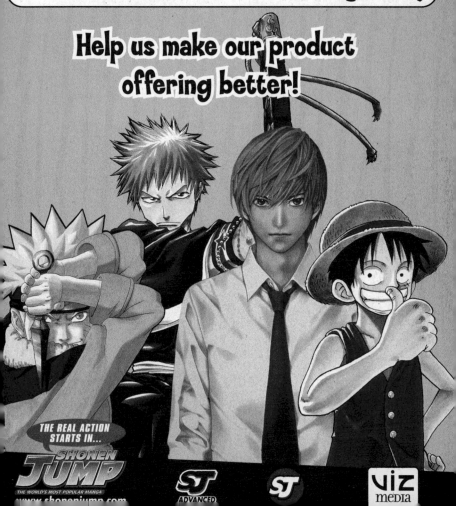

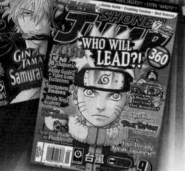
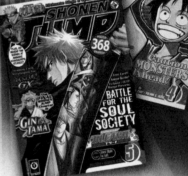

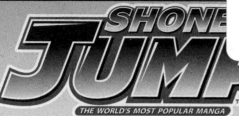
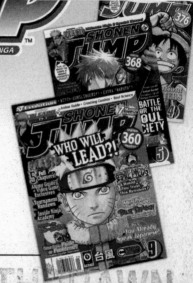
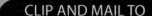